Elise C. Otté

Scandinavian History

Elise C. Otté
Scandinavian History
ISBN/EAN: 9783337397227

Printed in Europe, USA, Canada, Australia, Japan

Cover: Foto ©ninafisch / pixelio.de

More available books at **www.hansebooks.com**

SCANDINAVIAN HISTORY.

BY

E. C. OTTÉ.

WITH MAPS.

New York:
MACMILLAN AND CO.
AND LONDON.
1894.

CONTENTS.

Rulers of Denmark, Sweden, and Norway

CHAPTER I.

THE EARLY NORTH.

PART
  I. Hyperboreans
 II. Northmen in the South
III. Origin of the Northmen
IV. The Aryan Races

CHAPTER II.

THE DANES IN EARLY TIMES.

  I. The Northmen at Home
 II. Denmark
III. End of the Mythic Age

CHAPTER III.

THE NORTHMEN IN EARLY TIMES.

  I. Christianity in the North
 II. Denmark
III. Habits of the Northmen

CHAPTER IV.

DENMARK IN EARLY TIMES.

PART
I. First Queen of Denmark
II. Knud and his Sons

CHAPTER V.

I. Sweden and Norway
II. Northern Conquests
III. Norwegian Settlements .

CHAPTER VI.

I. Iceland
II. Sweden and Norway
III. Northern Discoveries

CHAPTER VII.

I. Svend Estridsen, the Father of Danish Kings
II. Svend Estridsen's Sons
III. Laws of Denmark
IV. Revenge of the Guild-brothers

CHAPTER VIII.

THE VALDEMARS

I. Troubles before the Valdemars
II. Death of Valdemar and Absalon

CHAPTER IX.

DENMARK FROM 1202 TO 1259.

PART		PAGE
I.	Denmark under Valdemar II. (Sejr) and his Sons	113
II.	Valdemar's Closing Years	117
III.	A Century of Troubles	122

CHAPTER X.

DENMARK FROM 1259 TO 1387.

I.	An Age of Troubles	128
II.	Decline of the Royal Power	130
III.	The Credit of Denmark revives	136

CHAPTER XI.

SWEDEN IN EARLY TIMES.

I.	First Christian Kings	143
II.	Troubled Times	147
III.	The Early Troubles of Norway	150

CHAPTER XII.

SWEDEN FROM 1250 TO 1400.

I.	The Folkungar Kings	151
II.	The Three Unfriendly Brothers	156
III.	Half a Century of Troubles	163
IV.	Sweden under Foreign Rule	165

CHAPTER XIII.

NORWAY FROM 1217 TO 1400.

PART	PAGE
I. Norway's Best Time	169
II. The Last of the Hakons	172
III. The Triple-Crowned Queen	175
IV. Sweden under a Queen	177

CHAPTER XIV.

DENMARK FROM 1412 TO 1448.

I. Erik loses Three Crowns	183
II. The Oldenburg Line begins	188
III. Sweden under Danish Rulers	192

CHAPTER XV.

DENMARK UNDER THE OLDENBURG LINE.

I. The Father of the Oldenburg Kings	198
II. Crown Bartered for Favours	203
III. The Brave Ditmarshers	205
IV. The Fall of the Stures	208

CHAPTER XVI.

DENMARK FROM 1500.

I. Christian's bringing up	212
II. The Swedish Crown lost	215
III. King Christian loses all	219
IV. Denmark accepts the Protestant Faith	224

CHAPTER XVII.

SWEDEN BETWEEN 1520 AND 1568.

PART	PAGE
I. Gustaf Vasa frees Sweden	227
II. Gustaf rules with a Strong Hand	232
III. Queen Elizabeth's Suitor	237

CHAPTER XVIII.

DENMARK FROM 1559 TO 1648.

I. War between Sweden and Denmark	244
II. The Greatest of the Oldenburg Princes	249
III. Denmark's Decline	254

CHAPTER XIX.

SWEDEN BETWEEN 1568 AND 1611.

I. The Sons of Gustaf Vasa	257
II. Religious Troubles in Sweden	263
III. The Rise of Swedish Power	267

CHAPTER XX.

SWEDEN FROM 1611 TO 1644.

I. The Hero-King of Sweden	272
II. The Death of the Swedish Hero	277
III. The Swedish Generals	285

CHAPTER XXI.

SWEDEN FROM 1644 TO 1697.

PART
I. The only Swedish Queen-Regnant .
II. Swedish Conquests
III. The King becomes Absolute .

CHAPTER XXII.

DENMARK FROM 1648 TO 1730.

I. Denmark Humbled
II. Absolute Power established .
III. The Origin of Titles
IV. "The Type-Quarrel" .

CHAPTER XXIII.

DENMARK FROM 1730 TO 1839.

I. A Period of Restraint .
II. Struensee's Rule
III. England humbles Denmark

CHAPTER XXIV.

SWEDEN FROM 1697 TO 1771.

I. The Swedish Conqueror
II. Charles in Turkey .
III. Sweden under a German Prince

CHAPTER XXV.

SWEDEN FROM 1771 TO 1872.

PART		PAGE
I. The Swedish Line of Kings	. . . . .	348
II. Troubles in Sweden	. . . . .	353
III. Great Changes in Sweden	. . . .	356
IV. A French Line of Kings	. . .	359

CHAPTER XXVI.

DENMARK SINCE 1839.

I. The Language Trouble	. . . .	363
II. Success of the Danes	. . . . .	369
III. The Reigning Dynasty	. . . . .	373

Index 377

LIST OF MAPS.

Denmark under King Gorm " Den Gamle " (9th Century) .	45
Settlements of the Northmen in the Western Ocean (9th and 10th Centuries)	65
Denmark under Waldemar Sejr (13th Century) . .	113
Sweden under the Vasas (in the 17th Century) .	263

RULERS OF DENMARK, SWEDEN, AND NORWAY.

DENMARK.	SWEDEN.	NORWAY.
GORM'S LINE.	*BJORN JERNSIDE'S LINE.*	*YNGLINGAR LINE.*
Gorm the Old, about . . . 860	Erik Sejrsæl . . 983	Harald Haarfager 890 ?
Harald Blaatand 936	Olaf the Lap King 993	Erik Blodöxe . 933
Svend Tveskæg . 985	Anund Jakob . 1024	Hakon I., Athelstan's fostre . 938
Harald 1014	Edmund the Old 1052	Harald Graafell. 963
Knud the Great . 1018		Hakon Jarl . . 977
Harthaknud . . 1035	*STENKIL'S LINE.*	Olaf Trygvassen 995
Magnus the Good, of Norway . . 1042	Stenkil 1055	Erik and Svend Jarl . . . 1000
	Inge I. 1066	Olaf (the Saint). 1015
THE ESTRIDSEN LINE.	Inge II. 1112	Svend . . . 1030
	Philip . . . . 1120 ?	Magnus the Good 1035
Svend Estridsen . 1047	*SVERKER'S LINE.*	Harald Hardraade . 1047
Harald Hejn . . 1076	Sverker I. . . 1130 ?	
Knud (the Saint). 1080	Erik IX. (the Saint) . . 1155	Olaf Kyrre . . 1066
Olaf-Hunger . . 1086		Magnus Barfod . 1093
Erik Ejegod . . 1095	Karl Sverkersson 1160	Olaf 1103
Niels 1103	Knud Eriksson . 1167	Ejsten . . . 1115
Erik Emun . . 1134	Sverker II. . . 1195	Sigurd Jorsalafar 1121
Erik the Lamb . 1137	Erik Knutsson . 1210	Magnus the Blind) 1130
Knud V. and Svend . . } 1147	Johan Sverkersson 1216	Harald Gille . }
Valdemar I. . . 1157	Erik Læspe . . 1222	Sigurd II. . . 1136
Knud VI. . . 1182	*THE FOLKUNGAR LINE.*	Ejsten . . . 1155
Valdemar II. . 1202		Inge 1157
Erik Plovpenning 1241	Valdemar . . . 1250	Hakon II. . . 1161
Abel 1250	Magnus Ladulaas 1279	Magnus Erlingsson . . . 1162
Christopher I. . 1252	Birger 1290	Sverre . . 1184
Erik Glipping . 1259	Magnus Smek . 1319	Hakon III. . 1202
Erik Menved . . 1286	Albrecht of Mecklenburg . . . 1363	Guttorm . . . } 1204
Christopher II. . 1319		Inge Bardsson . }

RULERS OF DENMARK, SWEDEN, AND NORWAY.

DENMARK.	SWEDEN.	NORWAY.
Interregnum . . 1332	Interregnum . . 1389	Hakon IV. . . 1217
Valdemar III. . 1340	Margaret . . . 1397	Magnus Laga-
Olaf 1375	Erik of Pomerania 1412	bæter . . . 1263
Margaret . . . 1387	Karl Knudsson,	Erik Præstehader 1280
	between	Hakon V. . . 1299
DENMARK AND NORWAY.	1448-57; 1467-70	Magnus Smek . 1319
	Sten Sture the	Hakon VI. . . 1355
Erik of Pomerania 1412	Elder . . . 1470	Olaf 1380
Christopher of	Svante Nielsson . 1503	Margaret. . . 1387
Bavaria . . . 1439	Sten Sture, the	
	Younger . . 1512	
THE OLDENBURG LINE.	THE VASA LINE.	
Christian I. . . 1448	Gustaf I. . . . 1523	
Hans 1481	Erik XIV. . . 1560	
Christian II. . . 1513	Johan III. . . 1568	
Frederick I. . . 1523	Sigismund . . 1592	
Christian III. . 1533	Charles IX. . . 1600	
Frederick II. . . 1559	Gustaf Adolf II. 1611	
Christian IV. . 1588	Christina . . . 1632	
Frederick III. . 1648	Charles X. . . 1654	
Christian V. . . 1670	Charles XI. . . 1660	
Frederick IV. . 1699	Charles XII. . 1697	
Christian VI. . 1730	Frederick of	
Frederick V. . . 1746	Hesse . . . 1718	
Christian VII. . 1766	Adolphus Frede-	
Frederick VI. . 1808	rick 1751	
	Gustavus III. . 1771	
DENMARK WITHOUT NORWAY.	Gustavus IV. . 1792	
	Charles XIII. . 1809	
Christian VIII. . 1839		
Frederick VII. . 1848	THE BERNADOTTE LINE.	
GLÜCKSBURG LINE.	SWEDEN AND NORWAY.	
Christian IX. . 1863	Charles John XIV. 1818	
	Oscar I. . . . 1844	
	Charles XV. . . 1859	
	Oscar II. . . . 1872	

SCANDINAVIAN HISTORY.

CHAPTER I.

THE EARLY NORTH.

Hyperboreans—Ignorance of Southerners in regard to Northmen—Pytheas; his travels; his voyage to Thule—The search for Thule—How the people lived 2,200 years ago—The Lung of the Sea, meaning of term—Pytheas a scientific traveller—Professor Nilsson—Phœnicians in the North; their religion—Superstitions of Northern people reflect the older faith—The Kimbri—Wulfstan and Ohthere—Alfred's history of Orosius—Northmen swarm southwards; the Romans defeat them—Ideas in regard to Scandinavia—Amber beads the cause of a better knowledge being gained—The Skalds—The Goths—The earlier inhabitants of the North—The days of the week; their names—The gods—Odin's faith; its precepts; his character; his favour given to the rich—The Norræna Mál—The Aryans—Our Aryan forefathers—Runes—The Væringjar—The Víkingar.

PART I.

HYPERBOREANS.

The Hyperboreans.—THE ancient Greeks and Romans had very false, and what seem to us, now that we know so much more about it than they did—very absurd ideas of the north of Europe; for they thought that it was all made up of ice, snow, mists, clouds and darkness, and that far, far away beyond the north wind, there lived a race of beings, whom they called *Hyperboreans*, or *Outside North-winders!*

These hyperboreans were fabled to be mortals living in perfect peace with their gods and among themselves, and dwelling in such a rich land, and under such bright sunny skies, that fruits and grains ripened there without needing the care of the husbandman. Plenty abounded everywhere. No one suffered pain or illness of any kind, and, therefore, as the old men and women in that blessed land did not die as elsewhere from disease or weakness, those who grew weary of living put a speedy end to their lives by throwing themselves headlong down some high cliff into the foaming depths of the sea, which opened to receive them, and then gently closed over their bodies.

By degrees, men began to doubt if mortals could find such charming abodes upon any part of this earth, even if they were lucky enough to get beyond the north wind; and so the belief in hyperboreans died out. But, for all that, the Northmen, as the natives of Scandinavia generally, or sometimes only the Danes, were called, had continued to swarm southward every year, from one century to another, before other nations learned to know from which direction they came, or what was the name of their country.

The most ancient account that we possess of the North was that by a native of Massilia, the present Marseilles, who lived more than 350 years before the birth of Christ. This traveller, whose name was Pytheas,[1] was either a trader, or an astronomer, sent by his Government to enquire into the position and nature of the northern lands from which the Phœnicians brought away tin and amber and other products, which they could not obtain nearer home. But, whether an astronomer or a trader, a Greek or a Phœnician, Pytheas must have been a bold man to have left the sunny skies of the South to embark upon a voyage which carried him over rough seas along the western shores of Europe to that far distant mysterious North, where even the learned men of his own, and much later times, believed there was nothing to be found beyond a dreary waste of mist

---

[1] We may reckon Pytheas as belonging to the same time as Alexander the Great, who was born in the year 356, and died in 323, B.C. Massilia or Massalia is believed to have been founded by the Phœnicians, who had there a temple to Baal, which in later times, when the Greeks became masters of the place, was used for the worship of Apollo. Ancient coins have been dug up at the spot, bearing on one side the image of the Sun-god, and on the other that of a wheel with four spikes, which was one of the chief emblems of Baal.

covered snow and ice. Pytheas, indeed, as a native of one of the greatest trading ports in the world, may have been better informed than the Latin and Greek authors, who, more than three hundred years after his time, criticised his writings and laughed at his accounts of what he had seen. Yet we can scarcely wonder that men like Strabo and others, who believed that no human beings were to be met with further north than the Elbe,—although they had some faith in the notion of a land *beyond* the north wind,—should have treated his narrative as nothing better than a mere traveller's tale. For us, however, who have to thank him for the earliest glimpse which we can obtain of the homes of the Northmen, his notices, scanty as they are, have special interest.

Pytheas in Thule.—The voyages of Pytheas brought him to our own shores, but, unfortunately, we know no more of his visit to Britain, which he calls "Albion," than the mere fact that he travelled over great part of the country. Although it is a matter of regret that no notice of his in regard to the inhabitants of Albion, more than two thousand two hundred years ago, has come down to us, we may form some idea of the condition of the inhabitants from what he relates of the people of the more northern countries which he visited, and which could not have been very far distant, as he tells us he reached them after sailing for six days away from the coasts of Albion. The most remarkable of the places described by him was an island which he calls *Thule*, and where, according to his report, amber was thrown up by the sea in such abundance that the people used it for fuel. The exact whereabouts of this spot is still undecided, and at one time its re-discovery was the object of much speculation and of many strange adventures, until, in the middle ages, the finding of the true *Thule* seemed to the minds of some persons nearly as important an exploit as the finding of the true sources of the Nile is to us in the present day. Some have thought that the Thule of Pytheas was the north of Jutland, but it would seem more probable, from what he tells us of the great length of the days there at midsummer,[1] that it was nearer the

---

[1] According to Strabo, Pytheas said that in Thule the nights at midsummer were only two or three hours long, and according to another authority, he was taken by the barbarians to see the place where the sun slept in winter.

north pole, perhaps one of the many islands which skirt the northern coasts of Sweden and Norway. At all events it must have been somewhere in Scandinavia, and on that account all that we read of Thule and the lands near it is of interest to us in regard to the early history of the condition of the ancient Northmen.

According to Pytheas, the natives of a land a little to the south of Thule thrashed the grain of which they made bread, in large roofed-in buildings, where it was carefully stored away under cover, "because the sun did not always shine there, and the rain and the snow often came and spoilt the crops in the open air." These people, moreover, enclosed gardens, in which were grown hardy plants and berries, which they used for food, while they kept bees, and made a pleasant drink out of the honey. They were very eager to trade with the foreigners who came to their shores for amber, but keen in making a bargain, and always ready and well able to fight, if they were offended, or thought themselves ill-used. This picture of the people of northern Europe about the time that Alexander the Great was making his conquests, or more than two thousand two hundred years ago, proves to us, therefore, that they were not mere savages, but had already learned many useful arts.

The Lung of the Sea.—There was one thing described by Pytheas, which, on first hearing of it, seems to have nothing in common with anything ever seen now-a-days. This extraordinary thing, which he called *pneumon thalassios*, "lung of the sea," was, according to Strabo's report of his description, neither earth, sea, nor sky, but a blending together of all three; a *something* in which land, water, and air seemed to float and mingle together, producing a heaving girdle round the shore, along which neither feet of men nor animals could make their way, nor boats be moved by oars or sails. For a long while this extraordinary thing excited the wonder of all who read or heard of Pytheas' account of it. But the wonder has ceased since it has been discovered that *lung of the sea* was a common name among the Greeks for the Jelly-fish or Medusa, numbers of which abound in the waters of the Mediterranean, and must have been well known to his countrymen of Massilia. Hence it has not unreasonably been conjectured that Pytheas, wishing to describe to his friends at home the appearance of ice floating on the waters of the ocean, which they had never seen, compared it to the shoals of Jelly-fish which fringed their shores in a living girdle of moving, white, half-transparent matter.

In spite of the ridicule of Strabo and others, Pytheas must have been what, in these days, we should call a scientific traveller, and the little that we know of his labours makes us feel that, whatever the ancients may have thought of him, he has given us the report of a careful and correct observer. We are, moreover, justified in putting confidence in him, as we know that he was one of the first who determined the position of the north pole in the heavens; and although he must have had very imperfect instruments, he also fixed the latitude, or true geographical position of places so correctly, that with all our better means of observing, we have only been able in the present day to detect an error of forty-two seconds in the latitude which he gives for Massilia, the present Marseilles.

Baal's worship in the North.—Of late years many learned writers of Scandinavia have made the history and travels of Pytheas a special object of their studies, and foremost amongst them stands Professor Nilsson of Stockholm, who has discovered many proofs of the presence of the Phœnicians in northern Europe in very ancient times. In a work which, although it is very learned, is also most charming, he has told us that there was a time when the people of Scandinavia worshipped the god Baal of the Phœnicians, and let their young children, as well as their cattle, and all that they held precious, be passed through the fire of Moloch. They set up images of the sun, which they represented under different forms, as circles, wheels, pillars, and similar figures, and they used great metal kettles in their sacrifices, remains of which have been dug up in different parts of northern Europe, and are exactly like those described in 1 Kings c. vii., as being made by Hiram, the Syrian, for Solomon's Temple. If any other proof were wanting that the ancient Phœnicians visited Scandinavia, and found people living there, so many ages ago, such proof is given us in the fact that the superstitions of the inhabitants of those countries still show traces of the old Phœnician worship of Baal. Remains of this faith may also be traced nearer our own homes; for, till very recent times, the country people in some parts of Ireland and Scotland, and even of England, had the custom of celebrating the return of midsummer-night on the 24th of June, by dancing together round a large fire lighted on some high hill, or running three times through the fire to secure the fulfilment of a wish. These midsummer-night dances, which were known in Britain as Beltanes, are nothing but the remains of an earlier form of Baal-worship, practised by the ancestors of the people, and followed long after their real meaning had been forgotten. In our word *yule* we have another vestige of the former worship of Baal, or the sun, amongst the races from whom we have derived our language, for yule once meant wheel, and the yule-tide of the ancient Northmen was the winter solstice in December, when the young men, with loud cries, rolled a large wheel downhill to celebrate the death of the old and the birth of the new year; a wheel being, in their eyes, an emblem of the year, or the sun. Long after Christmas-day had taken the place of the old yule-tide, and men had become Christians, they still continued their December wheel-runnings without knowing why, but simply because their forefathers had done it before them. Here, then, we have a very strong proof that in ancient times, before Christianity became the religion of the North, the people had learned the practices of the faith of Baal; for a superstition is nothing more than the shadow of a former belief that has passed away, which can no more have sprung up of itself than a shadow can be formed apart from the object which it represents.

According to Professor Nilsson, the worship of Baal extended over the whole of northern Europe at the time Pytheas was there, and the people who inhabited Scandinavia were of the same race as those men whom, in much later times, the Romans learnt to know under the name of Kimbri, Kelts, Vandals, Goths, &c.

PART II.

NORTHMEN IN THE SOUTH.

Northmen swarm Southward.—The little that the ancients have told us of what Pytheas had written of his travels, is all that was ever learnt from any traveller's report of northern Europe, until the time of our Alfred the Great. Then, exactly two thousand years ago,—for Alfred came to the throne in the year 871,—and twelve hundred years after the time of Pytheas, two travellers from Scandinavia, named Wulfstan and Ohthere, came to the court of the great English King, who loved learning and always welcomed learned men. Alfred took great pleasure in talking to them of what they had seen, and from their account of their travels, he composed a short history, which, together with a chart of northern Europe, he placed at the beginning of the translation which he had made of the Latin history of Orosius. The description given by King Alfred in this work of Scandinavia and northern Germany is, therefore, of extreme value, as it is the only one, on which we can rely, that has reached us from those early times.

During the twelve hundred years that separated the age of Pytheas from that of King Alfred, nothing was to be heard of the lives and habits of the people of Scandinavia in their own homes; although, from time to time, tribes of half savage, yellow-haired, blue-eyed, tall, strong Northmen poured southward, and became known to the Romans as Kimbri, Teutons, Germans and Goths. At first, the fierce mode of attack used by these men, the loud and guttural shouts with which they urged on their horses in battle, and their great strength and unflinching courage brought terror and defeat upon the Roman soldiers, who could not break through the long walls of shields chained together, which these unknown foes raised against them; but, after a time, the Romans, by their superior skill and discipline, overcame them. In the year 101 B.C. the Roman Consuls, Marius and Catulus, gave the Northmen battle and defeated them in the plains of northern Italy, near Verona, where a band of Kimbri, accompanied by their wives and children, were enjoying the charms of the sunny climate and the rich vegetation of that fruitful district. While the battle raged, the northern women remained in their camp, defended by the long line of their massive waggons, but, when they learned the defeat of their husbands, they rushed forth, and uttering loud cries of grief, slew themselves and their children, while the Romans carried away captive all the Northmen who had escaped death in the conflict.

After this great defeat at Verona, it was long before the Kimbri were heard of again so near Rome, but other northern tribes, scarcely less to be dreaded, kept up the memory of their valour, and disturbed the peace of the Roman frontiers. Yet in spite of their dread of these unwelcome strangers, the Romans took no pains to discover the precise part of the world from which they came; and Latin writers for a long time gave the name of "Scanzia," Scandinavia to the whole of northern Europe, which, according to their notions, was either one great island, or a group of many islands, lying in some unknown sea beyond the Northern Pillars of Heraklês, by which they meant to indicate the narrow channel between Sweden and Denmark known to us as "the Sound." Strangely enough, it was owing to a whim of the fashionable ladies of Rome, that more correct ideas of northern Europe first reached the South. By chance, some strings of amber beads had been brought to Rome, and soon these ornaments were so much admired that no grand lady in the city thought her dress complete unless she had a few rows of them, to wear round her neck or twist into the plaits of her hair. In those times it was the same in Rome as it is now in our great cities; as soon as anything was wanted for which rich people were willing to pay, there were always persons to be found who would brave toil and danger to procure it. Thus, then, when amber beads became the fashion at Rome, Roman traders set forth in search of them, and, month after month, tracked their way along the great rivers, and through the vast forests which then covered Eastern Europe till they reached the shores of those northern seas where, as they had been told, the waves threw up the precious product, which the Roman ladies coveted, but of whose nature they knew nothing.[1]

By degrees, the accounts given by these traders, on their return to Rome, of the countries they had visited, made the Romans better acquainted with the true position and nature of the lands from which those savage invaders had come, whose attacks had more than once threatened the safety of the city. The Northmen themselves also helped to dispel the ignorance of the southerners, for, wherever they went, they carried with them poets, or reciters, called *Skalds* in their own tongue, who sang of the glorious deeds of their forefathers, and told wonderful tales of the manner in which they feasted and sported, fought and vanquished, in their far-distant homes among the snow-clad mountains and ice-bound waters of the North. As these men showed much readiness in learning other languages, there is no doubt that, in the course of time, the tales, or *Sagas*, which they could recite, became known to the Romans and other foreigners amongst whom they lived; and thus a more correct knowledge of Scandinavia was, by degrees, spread among the people of southern Europe.

PART III.

ORIGIN OF THE NORTHMEN.

German Origin of Northmen.—When we go back to the oldest records of the Northmen, and hear what they have to say of themselves, and compare, and correct their accounts with what modern science and research have taught us, we learn that the Northmen were a German race. And we also find that, like all the nations who now people Europe, they

[1] According to one ancient myth, or fable, amber was formed from the tears shed by the sisters of Phaethon when they heard of his death. Before it was known that amber is a resin, not unlike coal in its nature, the people in the Baltic lands, where it was found from very ancient times, called it *meerschaum*, sea-foam, from the idea that it was the hardened scum of the waves. The true *meerschaum*, used for pipes, is a naturally soft, soapy kind of earth or mineral, found near the Caspian, and in several parts of Russia and Turkey.

had come from Asia, and made their way along the eastern limits of our continent, till they turned aside to follow the line of route that each tribe chose for itself.

The special German nation to whom the natives of Scandinavia belong, was early known as that of the Goths. These people, in very remote times—before they had any written history to fix the date, had pushed their way northward and westward from their older homes in the East, till they reached the shores of the Baltic and the German Ocean, where they settled themselves upon the islands and coast lands of those seas, driving out the inhabitants. Whenever they found themselves strong enough to subdue the natives of the country, they made slaves of them, but if they could not do that, they generally ended by forming friendly compacts with them.

It seems to be certain that, when the Goths came to the Baltic, they found the lands peopled by older tribes of Kelts, Kimri and others, who, in their turn—but long before—had also come from beyond the shores of the Black Sea. These people were now for the most part driven by the new-comers into the more barren and colder districts, where we still find their descendants under the names of Finns and Lapps.

Some of the old Finnish tribes were much braver than their neighbours, the Lapps, and could not be so easily pushed aside by the Goths, who, therefore, were forced to try to make friends of them, and to pay respect to their gods and goddesses. In the course of time the most dreaded of these imaginary beings were placed among their deities, and worshipped as much as their chief god Odin himself. Other Finnish or Lapp tribes were held in fear by the Goths, more perhaps on account of their craft and cunning than their bravery, for we find that in the Scandinavian myths or sagas, these people are made to appear, sometimes as giants of evil repute, and sometimes as artful, hideous dwarfs.

As we have already seen, the religion of Scandinavia was, in ancient times, a form of the worship of Baal, in which the sun and fire were objects of great veneration as the sources of light and heat. But, after the Goths had settled in northern Germany and Scandinavia, this older religion only lingered in the form of superstitions, for the new-comers established their own faith, which was that of Woden, or, as he is called by the Northmen, Odin.

We English retain in the days of the week the remembrance of this religion, which was brought to our shores more than 1400 years ago by the Angles and Saxons, who came from northern Germany and western Denmark to give us a new name and a new fate in the world. The Angles and Jutes and Saxons who landed in Kent and Sussex, first taught the people of Britain to divide the week into their *Sun*-day, *Moon*-day, *Tys*-day (Ty being their god of War answering to the Mars of the Romans), *Woden's*-day, *Thor's*-day and *Freia's*-day.

Thor, to whom they dedicated the fifth day of the week, was the strong and brave son of Odin, or Woden, and a special favourite among the northern gods, while Freia is believed, by some, to have been a Finnish goddess adopted by the Northmen as their goddess of Beauty.[1]

Here we may see, therefore, that we not only retain the memory of the Teutonic, or German gods of our Saxon forefathers in the names of some of the days of the week, but that we have still amongst us, in the word "Friday," something to remind us of that earlier form of Finnish worship, which the common ancestors of the Saxons and Angles had found in northern Europe when they first settled there, and which we know to have been a Phœnician form of religion. Some persons believe that Thor, from whom we have taken our Thursday, was as much an early northern divinity as Freia, and that he had been worshipped as the god of thunder, strength, and all the powers of nature, before the Gothic settlers taught the faith of Odin to Scandinavia. Thor was the favourite god of the people of Norway, and even in Sweden, in the temple of Odin at Uppsala, his statue was honoured with as high a place as that of Odin himself, but in Denmark he was never so much regarded.

The Northern Gods.—Nothing certain is known in regard

---

[1] The name of Saturday the Britons owed to the Roman god Saturn, but the last day of the week was known among the early Northmen as washing-day. It is possible that our Anglo-Saxon forefathers may have wished to change this name when, in later times, they had ceased to have only *one* washing-day out of the seven like their northern ancestors.

to the precise time when the Goths first came to the north of
Europe, or when they began to follow the religion of Odin.
Some persons have thought that under the name of Odin, or
Woden, men worshipped the powers of nature; others, that the
fables invented in regard to him and the other northern gods,
who were called *Æsir*, and were said to have dwelt in a home
known as *Asgaard*, were all founded upon events that had
happened to the people before they left their distant homes
in the far East. Perhaps both these sources, and others besides,
helped to make up the mythology of the Northmen. On the
whole, the true worshippers of Odin held a moral faith. They
believed that the first duty of mortals was to fear and love the
All-father, or Creator, and that the next was to love and cherish
their kindred and the friends to whom they had sworn to be
faithful. But they did not see any virtue in forgiving the guilty
or sparing the innocent, if they had any wrongs to avenge.
When a man was slain in combat with a private foe, his kindred
felt bound to take vengeance on the slayer, and to kill him and
as many of his relations as they could; and if they were unable
to do it in any other way, they thought it quite fair to attack
them by night, and either slay them or burn them alive in their
houses. This act, which they called *nema hús á cinn*: "to take
a house from one," was not to be performed, however, until all
the women, children, old people and slaves had been allowed
to make their escape. So, even in their worst deeds, they
showed some mercy to the feeble, and proved that they were
not without a natural sense of justice.

Odin-Al-fadir.—In Odin, the Northmen worshipped the Alfadir,
or Father of all men and all things—the Creator. They believed
that he knew all things, and, in his character of All-father, would
survive, when this earth and all the lesser gods, or Æsir, had
been swallowed up by time, to be regenerated according to the
good or the evil that was in their nature; for the religion of
Odin taught that the good would dwell in *Gimli*, or the golden,
and the evil be doomed with cowards, liars, and deceivers,
to remain in *Nastroend*, the low strand, in a dwelling made
of serpents' bones. Before this final judgment, Odin was
believed to look down on earth from his seat in Valaskjálf,
learning all that happens there and in heaven from his ravens,

who sit one on either side of his head and whisper into his ear. In the hall, Valhal, with its five hundred and forty gates, each wide enough to admit eight hundred men abreast, he received all brave and good men after their death, and there the slain warriors pursued the life they had loved best on earth, fought their battles over again, listened to the songs of past victories, and feasted together without sorrow or pain to disturb them. Odin was supposed to award his special favours to those warriors who brought gold, or other precious substances, with them to Valhal, and who had led an active life and wandered far and wide; hence the Northmen very early showed the greatest eagerness to gather together riches on their distant voyages. This was not so much for the sake of spending their wealth, as in the hope of securing a welcome from the god whenever they might have to appear in his presence. They often ordered their children, or followers, on pain of severe punishment after death if they disobeyed them, to bury their riches with them; or they hid them away in places, known only to themselves, under the idea that Odin, who saw everything that passed on earth, would approve of their deed and reward them accordingly.

PART IV.

THE ARYAN RACES.

Northern Tongue.—The Gothic tribes who settled in Scandinavia brought their own language, as well as their own religion, with them. In the course of time this came to be known—first, as *Norræna Mál*, or Northern speech, and next as *Dönsk tunga*, or Danish tongue—which shows that at one period the Danes were the chief people among the Scandinavian nations, or they would hardly have given their name to the common language of all the Northmen.

But before the Germans and Goths parted from the many other tribes who, like themselves, had come into Europe from one common home in Asia, they had also had one common language, for they were all of one race, which we call Aryan, from Arya or Iran, the old name of Persia, and sometimes Indo-European, to distinguish it from the other great branch of nations, known as the Semitic, to which the Hebrews, Egyptians, and many other ancient peoples belong. Our own and nearly all the present nations of Europe and some of the people of Asia are descended from the Aryan stock, and, in times so long past that there is no certain record of their date, our common forefathers lived together in their Asiatic valley-homes beyond the Black Sea, and spoke a language which was perhaps more like the present Indian written language, Sanskrit, than any other that we know of. But when these Aryan races began to wander westward in search of new homes and came into Europe, they separated into different nations, and by degrees came to speak different dialects, until at last distinct languages were formed among them, which varied so much from one another, that it requires great learning to be able to trace them back to one common tongue.

Perhaps climate had something to do with the changes which crept into the speech of the Aryan nations as they advanced into different parts of Europe; for, as we know, all southern nations speak much more softly than do people in northern countries. We cannot now decide whether our Aryan forefathers brought with them from the East the guttural sounds of the northern tongue, or caught them up after they had reached Scandinavia, and become affected by its climate. All that we can now say decidedly in regard to the *Norræna Mál* is, that we know how it was spoken by the Northmen, one thousand years ago, for then a number of Norwegians went to Iceland, where they made new homes for themselves, keeping, however, to their old religion and their mother-tongue. Since that time the Scandinavians at home have altered their modes of speech so much, that a Swede, a Norwegian, or a Dane, can no longer understand the language still spoken by the Icelanders, which has remained unchanged for a thousand years.

Runes.—The letters used by the Northmen were called runes, from *rún*, a secret. There were sixteen of these runes, of which each was the sign for several sounds as well as words. They were either carved on wooden staves, or cut into stone, and were much used by persons pretending to deal in magic. As they were alike difficult to form and to read when formed, it was only the learned who were able to employ them to convey messages; but as the same runes were used by all the early Scandinavian people, they formed a means of maintaining intercourse between the various branches of the great northern stock. Thus we are told that, during the eighth and ninth centuries, when the Northmen had extended their power over so many parts of Europe, letters written in runes were frequently sent from one prince to another, and could be equally well read at Anglo-Saxon, Frankish, Gothic, Russian, and Scandinavian courts. Even in the East, at Constantinople, there were many men in the imperial palace, well versed in runes, and eager to welcome the northern skalds, who were able to recite to them the sagas of Scandinavia. This was owing to the fact that the body-guards of the Emperors, known as *Væringjar*, or wanderers, were Northmen, who, although often of noble birth, had been tempted by their love of roaming and the prospect of gain to take service in ancient Byzantium, where for centuries they formed the only trustworthy defenders of the lives and freedom of the inmates of the imperial palace. In Russia, too, the Northmen had formed important settlements in the ninth century, and had made themselves princes in the land; and by the intermarriage of these conquerors with the Slavi, or original inhabitants, a race sprang up, from which have descended the Czars of Russia and many of the leading families of the Russian empire.

Vikingar.—The Northmen were such a wandering, restless race of people, that from the latter times of the Roman Republic till very nearly the days of our William the Conqueror, who was himself of direct Scandinavian descent, they were always swarming southward from their northern hives, like so many hungry bees, ever eager to settle on the first pleasant spot that seemed to offer them the food and shelter which they sought; and ready, like those busy insects, to throw off fresh broods whenever the new hives grew too crowded for them. Tribe after tribe appeared every year with the return of warm weather; and when the Roman empire had ceased to exist, and Charlemagne had formed a new empire in Europe, these ancient foes of Rome, under other names perhaps, but with the same spirit as of old, hung upon every frontier, and attempted to penetrate into the interior through every stream and river that opened a way to pillage. In the later times of their wanderings, the leaders among the Northmen were known as *Vikingar*, a name derived from *vik*, a bay, from the habit which these men had of lying under covert in some little bay, or vik, and darting out in their barks to waylay and plunder any vessel passing by. The art of coming unawares upon others, whether singly or with a large fleet, was for this reason known as a "*viking*." After a time these vikingar joined themselves into bands, and went forth in well-manned flotillas of small vessels, or rowing-boats, to attack foreign shores. After roaming over the seas from spring to autumn, they returned to their northern homes before the frost closed the harbours, and spent their winters in feasting and in athletic sports, or in preparing their shattered barks for future *viking* cruises But faithful to the precepts of their religion, they never failed to offer sacrifices and gifts to Odin, and their favourite gods, in gratitude for past favours, and in the earnest hope of securing, by these acts of devotion, a rich harvest of spoil for their next voyage.

CHAPTER II.

THE DANES IN EARLY TIMES.

The homes of the Northmen, who first came to Britain—The names of the Danish provinces—Saxo Grammaticus, the writer on old Danish history—King Dan, the so-called founder of the Danish monarchy; what was done to his body after death—King Frode, his golden bracelets, which served as his money-bank—Stœrkodder, and who alone could kill him—Rolf Krake, the slim and handsome; his Berserkers, and why they were so called—The battle of Bravalla—Odin's last appearance on earth—How the god gave the victory to the Swedish king, and killed the Danish monarch Harald with his own battle-axe—Regner Lodbrog, why he wore leather leggings, how he died, and what vengeance his sons took on his slayer—King Ælla of Northumbria—The torture of the "Spread Eagle"—The victories of King Alfred the Great—The Northern sea-rovers driven out of England—The little we know of the Danes in their own country a thousand years ago.

PART I.

THE NORTHMEN AT HOME.

Our Interest in the Northmen.—IN the former chapter we have seen that the north of Europe was left almost unvisited and certainly undescribed by foreigners, as far as we know, from the age of Alexander the Great of Macedon—more than 300 years B.C.—to that of Alfred the Great of England, nearly 900 years after the birth of Christ. In the present chapter we shall have to see by what means the people of our own and other lands became acquainted with the Northmen; and beginning with the Danes as the nation best known to ourselves, we will take a glance at their country, and pass on to the accounts given of them in early times by their own historians. The Northmen who had carried on wars in Southern Europe against the Roman empire, and on its decline had formed kingdoms for themselves, either as Goths, Vandals, or others, regarded themselves as one nation descended from the same common stock, and were governed by the same laws and customs. In later Christian times, too, when northern invaders poured like a devastating flood over middle and southern Europe; although they bore the names of Danes, Swedes, Norwegians, Jutes, Saxons, and Angles, they all traced their origin back to the same sources, and followed very nearly the same laws and religion. This identity of origin and habits among the Northmen of old makes it thus all the more interesting and necessary for us to acquaint ourselves with the home-lives of the Scandinavians, since we retain to the present day deep traces in our laws, usages, and perhaps even in our character, of the influence of our Anglo-Saxon forefathers, whose arrival in Britain more than 1,400 years ago was the true beginning of our national life. When we bear in mind the love of roaming shown from the earliest times by the Northmen, and their bold habit of pushing off to sea on the return of each spring, to seek out some richer lands than their own, we need not wonder that they should have found their way to Britain. We know, too, that after the Romans left our island, in the year 401, the Britons were so timid and weak that they could not defend themselves against the Picts and Scots. They were not likely, therefore, to make any very strong defence against the fierce Northmen. But according to the accounts written down long afterwards by the monk Gildas and others, the Northmen came to Britain, not only because they loved roaming about and robbing their richer fellow-men, but because some of the British princes, or chiefs, had sent to them to beg that they would come and protect them against their Scottish and Pictish neighbours. This is said to have happened about the middle of the fifth century, and if it was really the reason why the Northmen came to Britain, the Britons must soon have regretted what they had done; for before many years had passed, the Angles, Jutes, and Saxons had poured into Britain in such large numbers that they had found themselves strong enough to drive the natives back into the mountains and waste parts, and to set themselves up as masters and rulers in almost every part of the island.

The Jutes founded a kingdom in Kent as early as 449, but they did not go on spreading themselves over Britain as fast as the Angles and Saxons. The last-named of these tribes appear to have been the first to settle in England, but they were soon followed by the Angles, who came in such numbers, that their own country, Angeln, was left almost without inhabitants. This small district, from which we Englishmen have taken our name, was a fruitful strip of land, stretching from the site of the present town of Flensborg in Slesvig to the fjord, or inlet of the Slie, and lying to the south of the land of the Jutes, since known as Jutland.

Chersonesus Cimbrica.—The Romans gave the name *Chersonesus Cimbrica* to the whole of that north-western extremity of Germany which lies north of the Elbe, and which included the ancient homes of the Jutes and Angles, but the Northmen themselves called it *Reid-Gotaland*, or the Firm (Continental) Goth's land, while they gave the name *Ey-Gotaland*, "Insular Goth's land," to all the Danish islands between the old Cimbric Chersonesus and the coasts of Sweden. These names confirm to us the fact of which we have already spoken, that the Danes, like all the other northern people, belonged to those Teuton or German tribes who were known as "Goths." The Saxons lived near the Angles, but mostly on the south side of the Elbe, and along the neighbouring German sea-coast; and these two nations, with the Jutes, spoke one and the same northern tongue, when they came into Britain, although perhaps with certain unimportant differences.

When the land of Angeln was left after the great immigration of the people into Britain, Jutes from the North, and Goths from the Danish islands, flocked into the deserted country and made themselves masters of it. Considering the few men left in it, this was no great feat, but, being fond of boasting, the new-comers called themselves the Conquerors of the land, while their skalds composed, in honour of this pretended conquest, songs and sagas, which were handed down from one generation to another. In the course of time these boastful tales came to be believed in as if they gave only the true account of the manner in which the Jutes and the men of the islands had made themselves masters of the whole country, from the extreme north of Reid-Gotaland down to the lands of the Saxons.

These Jutes and Danish Goths soon formed a number of small states or kingdoms, ruled over by chiefs who were very aptly called "*Smaa-kongar*," or small kings, as they had often no larger realm to boast of than the ground on which they and their few followers lay encamped, or the strand on which their boats were moored. The northern name for king, *konüngr*, was made up of the two words, *konr*, kind or family, and *ungr*, youth, and in its earliest sense meant simply a young chief of good birth; and we must, therefore, regard the many Danish kings of whom we hear in early English and Frankish history, as only leaders of small bands of Vikingar, or sea-rovers. By degrees all Scandinavia was split up into these small states, with Smaa-kongar at their head, who ruled without any regard to each other. Petty wars and changes of rule must have been very common in this state of things; but as the different branches of the Danes themselves hardly knew anything of each other in those ages, it is quite impossible, at this distance of time, for us to learn very much of the history of the people. During the fifth and sixth centuries, Danes from the larger islands, and Frisians from the smaller islands of the northern seas, often pillaged the coasts of the Frankish lands, advancing boldly into the interior by means of the rivers, and carrying away with them as many captives and as much booty as their barks would hold. The chroniclers speak of these invaders as the scourge and torment of the poor inhabitants, but they cannot tell us more of the country whence they came than that it was somewhere to the north of their own. It was not till the eighth century that the Frankish writers of annals knew that there were lands north of the Elbe; and long after the victories of Charlemagne in Northern Germany had made known the name of the Danes, the Franks remained in ignorance of the fact that there were any people of the race except those living in the lands of Slesvig and in Jutland.

Before Charlemagne was crowned Emperor of the West, and when he was only plain King Charles of the Frankish territories, he had carried on a war against the Saxons, which lasted thirty years, and ended in the year 777, after much hard fighting, in making the Saxon tribes submit to him and receive baptism. But Wittekind, their chief, although he knew that his people had been beaten, and could never hope to regain their old freedom, would not declare himself a Christian; and, fleeing in all haste, he took refuge with his friend, Siegfred, a king in Jutland, who like himself was a heathen, and worshipped Odin, or Woden. With him Wittekind remained safe for many years, only coming forth from his place of retreat to attack the Frankish troops, until at length, wearied-out with the hopeless struggle, he allowed himself to be signed with the cross in the year 785, and renounced paganism.

The Danes of Jutland and the Isles.—To these events we owe the first notice of the continental Danes by the Frankish writers of those times, who felt no little surprise that there should be heathen kings near their own frontiers, strong enough to shield the foes of their great ruler, and defy the power of the Christians. But while the Franks thus learnt to know the Danes of Jutland, the people of England were also beginning to be harassed by Danish vikingar, whom they called *Ostmanni*, or East-men, from the direction whence they had come. The Anglo-Saxon race that had sprung up in Britain, while they retained northern customs and followed northern laws and usages, keeping up through their superstitions the memory of the old worship of Odin even after their conversion to Christianity, seem to have ceased to care for the ancient homes of their forefathers, and to have lost all knowledge of the Reid-Gotaland, from which they had taken their origin, and to which many of the later Danish invaders of England must have belonged. Thus, while the Franks thought all Danes came from North-Elbian lands, the Anglo-Saxons believed they were all islanders.

These two branches of the Danish stock appear for a long time to have been nearly as ignorant as foreigners in regard to their respective histories. Each regarded themselves as the chief people of the country, and each cherished a rich store of national tales, setting forth the power and glory of their kings, and claiming for them direct descent from Odin. Lejre, or Ledra, in the island of Sjælland, was the chief seat of the power of the eastern Danes, and the kings who ruled there were certainly among the most renowned of the ancient royal heroes of Denmark; but, at the same time, there must have been kings of some importance among the western Danes, as their sagas were equally full of the exploits of kings ruling over the Jutlanders. It is probable that these two Danish branches, before they were united into one nation and brought under one ruler, were entirely independent of each other, and lived under Smaa-kongar, who were perhaps, in some way, tributary to a few greater rulers, of whom the King of Lejre was the chief in the islands; but we do not know where the head-kings in Jutland kept their court.[1]

PART II.

DENMARK.

Position of Denmark.—Before we begin to discuss the history of Denmark, we must turn to the map of Europe and note the position of the lands occupied by the insular and the continental Danes, which, at a later period, were joined into one kingdom. The *Reid-Gotaland* of the Northmen—that is, the territories of the western or continental Danes, were included in the long, narrow strip of land which runs almost due north from the mouths of the Elbe to about 57° 45' N. lat., where it terminates, at the extremity of Jutland, in a sharp point of land known as the Skage. This horn-like projection of the German continent, which separates the German Ocean from the Cattegat and the smaller channels of the Baltic, was the Chersonesus Cimbrica of the Romans, and now includes Holstein, Slesvig, and Jutland. The *Ey-Gotaland* of the Northmen, which was

---

[1] The Danes have retained very few of the traditions of Jutland, and their skalds have, in general, chosen the subjects of their songs from the tales and sagas of the islands. It is believed that the story of Amlet, immortalized by Shakespeare under the name of Hamlet, is founded upon some saga referring to a Jutish prince, although, as we know, the scene is laid at Elsinore, in Sjelland. There is no trace of such a story in connection with any prince of the Eastern Danes.

occupied by the eastern or insular Danes of later times, is composed of that group of islands between Sweden and continental Denmark which we know under the names of Sjælland, Funen or Fyen, Laaland, Falster, Langeland, &c. In early times the provinces of Skaania and Bleking, on the eastern or Swedish side of the Sound, formed part of the Danish monarchy; and for many ages after the introduction of Christianity, Lund, the chief town of Skaania, was the see of the primate of Denmark.

The names of almost every island or province of Denmark told the character of the country. Thus, the name of *Denmark* meaning the darkly-wooded land, reveals the fact that once the land was densely covered with sombre firs. Skaania took its name from its numerous moors and morasses, *skaun* being a moor, in old Northern; Blecking, which lies along the sea, from *blek*, a smooth beach; Laaland, from *lav*, low; Sjælland, from *sjæ* or *soe*, the sea; Langeland, from *lange*, long—all these names thus showing either the nature or position of the land.

Although the north of Europe remained for so many ages wrapped in darkness as far as the rest of the world was concerned, the people of Scandinavia were early in possession of an immense number of tales, or sagas, as they were called, which pretended to give true accounts of their great kings, vikingar, and heroes from the first settlement of their forefathers in the north. The sagas handed down by Danish skalds from one generation to another, in very early times, have reached us in a more genuine form, perhaps, than those of the Swedes and Norwegians, because all the popular tales that could be collected in Denmark in the twelfth century were then carefully written down, and have since been preserved and put into modern Danish. Denmark owes the preservation of these curious tales of old to a pious monk, Saxo, surnamed *Grammaticus*, from his being well versed in the knowledge of the Latin language or grammar. Saxo and his friend, Svend Aagesen, were encouraged by their patron, Absalon, primate of Denmark under the Valdemars, to complete a history of their native country, and to collect and write out for that purpose all the songs and tales that were still remembered by the older people. They lived for many years in the monastery of Sorö, near the present city of Copenhagen, and when Saxo died, in 1204, that is, about five years after our King John had succeeded his brother Richard I. on the throne of England, he left a complete history of Denmark, carried down to his own times, and professing to relate the origin of the kingdom, and to give an account of all the kings who had ruled over the Danes. As, however, we find long lists of the names of princes said to have been great and powerful for ages before the birth of Christ, we cannot put much trust in these records of ancient Danish rulers. Saxo's history is written in Latin and composed of sixteen parts, or books, the first nine of which contain little more than popular traditions. These, however, are so far interesting that they give us a record of what the Danes themselves accepted as their earlier history in the days when Saxo wrote, and on that account, as well as because many of the heroes or demigods, of whom the old monk of Sorö had such wonderful things to tell us, are constantly referred to in Danish literature, we must not pass them wholly by without notice.

Dan the Famous.—According to Saxo, Denmark takes its name from Dan Mykillati, or the Famous, who taught the people many useful arts, and made all the small kings around tributary to him. His last directions were that, after death, his remains should not be burnt, as had always been done in olden times. Accordingly, when he died, his people built a great stone chamber, in which they laid his body together with his most costly arms, and after killing his favourite horse and placing it fully harnessed by his side, they closed the opening and raised a high mound over the whole. This Dan, we are told, was followed by a long line of descendants, until, after many ages, there ruled a king, known as Frode, " the Peaceful," because in his time peace and plenty prevailed in the north. This golden age was owing to the birth of the Saviour, which, according to the legend, took place during the time of Frode, in whose reign there was neither wrong nor want, nor were there thieves or beggars, so that the good King Frode could leave his golden armlets on the wayside, as he journeyed through his kingdom to hear and make right all causes of dispute among his people, and no man would steal or injure his property. As these armlets were to the wearer a kind of bank, or treasury, men must have been very honest not to have taken them; for, since they could be broken up, or divided into links and rings to be used instead of money, it would not have been easy to detect the thief. In those days there was very little money in the shape of coins, and so men were obliged to carry their gold and silver about with them in the form of rings or bands for the head, arms, or legs, and twist, or break off bit by bit, as they wanted to pay, or give away any of the precious metals.

Stærkodder.—King Frode, in spite of his name of Peaceful, is said to have subdued two hundred and twenty foreign kings, and ruled over all the lands between Russia and the Rhine. But great as he was, according to Saxo's account of him, which fills one book of the Danish history, his fame is far exceeded by that of the great northern Hêraklês, Stœrkodder, who had giant forefathers, and was so hugely big and brave and strong, that it was almost impossible for any one to contend with him. Indeed, according to the legend, he never would have been overcome even after old age had lessened his strength, had he not in early life slain his friend and brother-in-arms, the brave Hother, by treachery. The remembrance of this act weakened his arm when, in later years, the son of the murdered man attacked him, and, being unable to defend himself, he soon fell beneath the blows of his foeman. This hero is rather a demigod than a mortal, for he is heard of again and again in northern history, for nearly three hundred years, and he only disappears after the battle of Bravalla, in which, as we shall presently see, Odin revealed himself for the last time to the eyes of mortals.

While Stœrkodder may be regarded as the Hêraklês of the North, Rolf Krake ranks as a model of all the kingly virtues esteemed in ancient times, and as a pattern of royal generosity and dignity. This king is believed to have been killed about the year 600, or very nearly at the time when Christianity was being first preached in England by Saint Augustine. His valour, goodness, and justice attracted the most renowned vikingar, skalds and strangers to his court at Lejre, and he was so much beloved by his own men that, after he was treacherously slain by Hjartvar, one of the Smaa-kongar, who paid him tribute and who had married his sister Skulda, all his faithful attendants, excepting one, followed him in death. This one, called Vögg, only waited till he could avenge Rolf, and when the traitor Hjartvar held out his sword to receive his oath of fidelity, he caught hold of the weapon, and after thrusting it into the heart of the king, met his death at the hands of the men of Oeland without uttering a cry or flinching a step. Rolf Krake, who received his name from the word *Kraki*, meaning the straight stem of a tree, on account of his slim and graceful figure, was the grandson of the Danish king Helge, who was esteemed one of the bravest vikingar of his times. Rolf was, in general, attended by his twelve Berserker when he went forth in search of adventures, and these were the men who fell with him at Lejre, when his brother-in-law surprised and slew him in the night, after they had shared in a great yule-tide feast. The name Berserker has a strange meaning, for it signifies *men in bare shirts* or *sarks*, that is *bare-sarkers*. The reason why this name had been taken by many of the vikingar was, that at one time there was a fashion, among the bravest of their number, of working themselves up into a frenzy before they went into battle. This they did by rushing and striking at everything in their way, until they grew so excited that they did not seem to feel pain, cold, or heat, and as they generally stripped themselves to their shirts on these occasions, this state of wild fury was called a berserker-gang, and those who took part in it were known as Berserkers.

PART III.

END OF THE MYTHIC AGE.

Northern plains of Troy.—The Northmen like the Greeks of old had a battle-plain on which, according to their best-loved myths, their gods and goddesses shared in the struggles, defeats, and victories of mortal warriors. This Trojan plain of Scandinavia was in East Götland, where, at a spot called Bravalla, near the river Braa, and within sight of the hostile fleets that lay moored in the Baltic, gods and men were fabled to have met in a fight as fierce as that described by poets as having been fought before the walls of Troy. The battle of Bravalla seems from the first to have been a very favourite subject with the skalds of Sweden as well as Denmark, and was fought between the Danish king, Harald Hildetand,[1] and his young Swedish kinsman, Sigurd Ring. The sagas tell us that immense preparations for the fight were made on both sides, and that while Harald's fleet stretched from Sjœlland across the Sound far up the coast of Sweden, young Sigurd sailed out of the harbour of Stocksund at the head of two thousand five hundred ships.[2]

The skalds relate that Odin, seeing all this vast array, and hearing from his ravens that Frisians, Wends, Finns, Lapps, Danes, Saxons, Jutes, Goths, and Swedes, were flocking towards the field of Bravalla to take part in this great battle for the mastery of the North, resolved to appear in the mêlée. Springing on the chariot of the aged and blind Harald, the god carried him into the midst of the fight and slew him with his own battle-axe. Harald, who had recognized the hand which guided his chariot so firmly through the ranks of the foe, had implored the god not to forsake his faithful Danes in this hour of their peril, but Odin's reply had been, that he himself had taught the secret of victory to the young Sigurd Ring. Then the aged Danish king felt that all was over; for till that moment he alone of all living men had known the art of ranging his army in the wedge-shaped form which he had learned in early youth from Odin, and which, as he had often proved, always brought victory with it. The dead lay heaped in huge piles when that day's fight was done, and as the chariots of the victors passed from the field, the bodies of the slain which fringed the narrow road reached to the axle of the wheels. As usual in great northern battles, only nobles were counted among the dead, but of these there were twelve thousand of Ring's army and thirty thousand Danes.

This, the skalds say, was the last time Odin appeared on earth; in other words, men were beginning to disbelieve in the

---

[1] Harald "*Hildetand,*" Glistening Tooth, was grandson of the great Swedish or Skaanian king, Ivar Vidfadme, or the Far Stretching, so called from his great conquests. Harald's father was Helge, who, with his brother Rerik, reigned at Lejre in the seventh century.

[2] Sigurd Ring was grandson of Harald Hildetand's mother Audur by her second husband, King Radbard of Gardarike, Russia.

presence of gods and goddesses, and hence we hear no more of them after the battle of Bravalla. The account of this great fight ends with the relation of the manner in which young Sigurd Ring honoured the memory of his foe, by causing the remains of the Danish king to be burnt with great pomp and ceremony in the presence of all the armies, while he himself fed the burning pile by throwing into the flames his weapons and many golden and silver ornaments, which he had gathered together in the course of his viking expeditions.

Regner Lodbrog and his Sons.—The battle of Bravalla is supposed to have been fought some time in the eighth century, and it probably gave Denmark to the successful young king of the Swedes, Sigurd Ring, whose son, Regner Lodbrog, is a great favourite among all the early writers of Scandinavia. The number of dangers and adventures that this hero met with in the course of his life, more especially when he went forth in search of a wife, which he did more than once, surpass the powers of any mortal man. But the greatest difficulty in regard to the history of this hero is that, while the Danes speak of him as living in one century, the Anglo-Saxons, among whom he often appeared, give a different date for the same events as the Danish writers describe. His nickname of Lodbrog, or Leather Leggings, he owed to the fact of his having adopted the fashion of wearing these leg-protectors when he was making court to the Gothic Princess, Thyra, a young lady who lived in a bower defended by a venomous serpent, which had the very inconvenient practice of biting at the legs of all her suitors.

After a long course of viking, Regner of the leather leggings met his death at the hands of Ælla, King of Northumbria, who, having seized him in the act of invading his country, caused him to be thrown into a pit filled with adders, as he would not declare his name and the cause of his appearance on the Northumbrian coast. Regner bore the torments of his slow death without complaint, simply remarking that "the young pigs at home would grunt aloud when they found out what had become of the old boar, their father !" According to the old sagas, his sons certainly did cry aloud when they heard of the death he had suffered, and never rested till they had taken a still more cruel revenge on Ælla. We are told that these sea-rovers landed in Northumbria, some years afterwards, with a large fleet and a great number of other vikingar, and over-ran and pillaged the country; and that they took the king captive and killed him by cutting open his back, tearing out his heart, and after thus torturing their victim, ended by carving the figure of an outspread eagle on his back, shoulders and loins. After thus satisfying their vengeance, the sons of Regner are said to have divided Ælla's territories and cast lots for their father's many lands, Ivar Benlos taking Northumbria, Hvitsek Jutland, Björn Sweden, and Sigurd Skaania and the Danish islands. Anglo-Saxon writers record an invasion a century later by Danish vikingar, or Sea-Kings, as they were often called, amongst whom we meet with the same names; but they do not seem to know that the coming of their unwelcome guests had any other motive than the usual one of pillage, and here, as in many other instances, it is altogether impossible to reconcile the accounts given by Northern and English authorities in regard to the same persons and events. Truth and falsehood seem to be so closely mixed together in the early history of the Danes, and time so thoroughly set at defiance, that it is hopeless to attempt to make the narrative agree with what foreigners have to tell us from their own acquaintance with Danish heroes.

The dreaded Vikingar.—It would seem that after the time of these vikingar, who were either the sons or grandsons of Regner Lodbrog, the whole of Scandinavia was split up into a great number of small free states, some of whose more distinguished rulers may have helped to swell the long lists of royal names given by Saxo. In the eighth and ninth centuries the Danish vikingar first became formidable to the English, and from about the year 830, they came spring after spring to plunder the unhappy land of England, roaming over the country like pirates at sea, robbing, killing, and destroying as they went on their way, till their course might be everywhere tracked by the misery and desolation they left behind them. This state of things continued with little change till the time of our King Alfred, who, before his death, in the year 901, had, however, so completely overmastered these terrible invaders, that all who were unwilling to settle peacefully in the land, and accept Christianity for their religion, were forced to leave the kingdom.

When they could no longer carry on the course of pillage in which they took such delight, the Northmen did not care very much about coming to England; and we find that, about the time when they ceased to torment the Anglo-Saxons, they began to appear in great numbers on the Continent. The Franks and Germans now learnt to fear their name as much as the English had once done, for in the lands where Charlemagne had reigned there was no prince strong enough to drive them out of his territories, and secure peace from their attacks as Alfred had done for his subjects.

We have said nothing of the Danish wars in England, because they are fully described in the Old English History,[1] but we shall now have to notice more at length what the Danes did in Gaul and Germany after they had ceased to plague England. It happens strangely enough that we know the least of the state of Denmark, and of what the Danes were doing in their own homes, at the very time that they were making their name the most feared and hated all over Christendom. The reason of this is that one thousand years ago—in 871—when Alfred the Great became King of England, and his subjects were in terror lest the Danes would deprive them of their pleasant English homes, Denmark itself was left quite unprotected, and was so deserted by the Danish people, that it may be said to have had no history of its own.

We may compare this period to the darkest hour of the night, just before the dawn of day is breaking in the sky and letting in the first faint streak of light, which is by and by to burst into full day. In the middle of the ninth century the darkness of paganism was the deepest in the North, and all objects around seemed buried in night, but at the beginning of the tenth century the course of events in Scandinavia begins to grow bright and clear. Before the death of our Alfred, in 901, Denmark, Sweden, and Norway can scarcely be said to have had any *true* history, but after that period—in Denmark at any rate—we begin to see our way through a regular succession of reigns, and we are able to form some idea of the manner in which the people lived, and the northern kingdoms were ruled.

[1] See more especially Chapters VIII. and IX. "Old English History." E. A. Freeman, D.C.L. Macmillan and Co. 1871.

CHAPTER III.

THE NORTHMEN IN EARLY TIMES.

How the Gospel came to be first preached to the Northmen—The wish of the Emperor Louis I to convert the heathen—Ebbo's mission to Jutland—King Harald Klak baptized, his sponsors, the oath he took—His presents, which required many barks to carry them to Denmark—Louis looks out for a missionary—Anscarius is sent forth to convert the Northmen; his bad success; his return to the Emperor's court; his second voyage to the North, and his labours in Sweden; he is made Archbishop of Hamburgh; what happens to him there; his death—The fate of Christianity in the North—Gorm the Old, first king of all Denmark; his birth and descent; his mode of being brought up; his adventures at Ashloo—Charles the Fat, Emperor of Germany; his foolish conduct and cowardice; his laws in favour of the Northmen—The siege of Paris—The Germans grow tired of their Emperor, and choose a very different ruler, who beats the Danes at Louvaine—Gorm's return to Denmark.

PART I.

CHRISTIANITY IN THE NORTH.

First efforts to Convert the Northmen.—BEFORE we enter upon the history of the reign of Gorm the Old, first king of all Denmark, we must go back nearly fifty years, in order to relate the manner in which Christianity was first introduced among the Northmen, and Christian monks were led to penetrate into the unknown lands of those dreaded pagans. In the time of our Ecgbert, the grandfather of Alfred the Great, foreign nations, as we have seen, knew little or nothing of the homes of the Northmen, and the people themselves were too much absorbed in viking abroad to care much for what was going on in their own countries. An event did, however, happen in Denmark about fourteen years before King Egbert's death, which the Frankish chroniclers felt to be so important that they were at great pains to record all they knew about it. This event was the preaching of the Gospel in the North, in 823, by Frankish monks, who entered upon their dangerous mission in compliance with the earnest wishes of their pious Emperor, Louis le Débonnaire, but not in obedience to any command of his, for he had declared that "in so holy a work the labourers must go willingly and not by constraint."

This Louis was the son and successor of Charlemagne, the great emperor of the West, but so unlike his father in everything but his respect for the Church, that under him the newly formed empire fell rapidly into decay, and the prelates and nobles were able to make themselves independent of the crown. The vast empire, which it had cost the father so many years of anxious toil to complete, was broken up under the son into numerous states, which were free except in name; for although their rulers still did homage to the emperor for the lands which they held under him, the power of the crown seemed at an end. In this state of things, while the princes of the land did as they liked within their own domains, and cared nothing for the general welfare of the State, and the emperor spent his time with priests and monks, the boundaries of the empire were left unprotected; and very soon the poor Franks found themselves exposed to the attacks of pagan invaders, who poured in upon them from every direction. The emperor made no effort to protect his subjects, but he bent his mind to the task of finding means to convert the pagans. To lead heathens to the font and sign them with the cross, seemed to him far nobler than to subdue them by the sword. As soon, therefore, as he came to the throne, he took counsel with his friend Ebbo, archbishop of Rheims, how best to carry out the work of conversion, and at his desire the primate, who shared in his wishes, hastened to Rome to demand the Pope's permission to send monks into Sleswig and Jutland to convert the inhabitants, of whose pagan practices fearful accounts had been brought to Germany.

Ebbo himself undertook the conduct of this first mission into the northern lands, but after a short stay in Slesvig he was forced by the savage state of the country to return to Germany. The only apparent result of the undertaking was the conversion of a prince, called Harald Klak, who accompanied the primate to the imperial court, and together with his family and followers received baptism at the font of the church of St. Alban's at Mayence, when the emperor and his empress, Judith, stood sponsors for them all. The Danes on this occasion took an oath abjuring paganism; and to the question, "Forsachista Diabolac?" (Dost thou forsake the devil?), each one answered, "Ec forsacho Diabolæ" (I forsake the devil); and when Ebbo put the question, "Allum Diaboles Wercum?" (All the works of the devil?), the pagans replied, "End allum Diaboles Wercum end Wordum, Thuncer end Woden, end allum them unholdum, the hira Genotas sint" (And all the works and words of the devil, Thor and Woden and all the ungodly ones, who are their helpers).

After this great event Harald returned to Jutland, laden with the many rich giftst hat Louis and the empress Judith had given him and his family; and the emperor called together all his chief bishops and nobles, and begged them to take counsel with him and decide how he could best go on with the good work of converting the pagan Northmen. But for a long time nothing could be done, for no one could be found bold enough to go among such fierce heathens. At last the emperor's cousin Walo, Abbot of Corvey in Picardy, announced that he knew a young monk, willing and able to endure all hardships in the cause of Christ, who had long been blessed by happy, holy dreams, and whose heart was set on the hope of earning for himself a martyr's crown of glory.

"Send for this holy brother with all speed, good Cousin." said Louis, when he heard his report. Accordingly this young monk, who since his infancy had dwelt in the monastery of Corvey, was sent for and brought before the emperor. Louis, on hearing his willingness to seek the heathens of Denmark, gave him a present of a bible, and caused him to be provided with tents and all things needed for his dangerous journey, together with the sacred vessels and white robes required to

D

perform the services of the Church and to baptize the converts that he might make.

Anscarius, the Apostle of the North.—This monk, who is looked upon as the true apostle of the North, was named Anscarius, or Anskar. Although a man of noble origin, he was so humble-minded that he scrupled not to labour with his hands to gain his living, and never asked the monks placed under him to perform any menial kind of work in which he did not take his share. He and his friend, the monk Autbert, set sail in 827 for Slesvig, and, after undergoing all kinds of hardships in the company of the rude and half-savage Danes, with whom they made the long voyage, they landed at Hedeby (the present Slesvig), and at once began the work of conversion by buying young slaves and baptizing them.

Louis was full of hope and joy at the prospect of bringing the whole of Denmark, as he believed, to the faith of Christ. But, to his great sorrow, he soon learnt that the poor missionaries had been obliged to flee for their lives. Instead of being received at the royal court of Denmark, as they had expected, when they reached Hedeby, and being helped by a powerful king, they had found that Harald Klak, if he ever had been a king, certainly no longer had a kingdom or subjects. Instead of helping them, he had been obliged, like themselves, to leave the country in all haste and return to the court of the emperor. This was a sad blow to the hopes of the good and pious Louis le Débonnaire, who, as usual with him, had no money to spare to send the ships and men which Harald declared were needed to protect the Christian preachers, and therefore Anscarius and Autbert were forced for a time to give up the work they had so much at heart.

A few years later, a Swedish king, Björn,[1] sent a letter written in runic characters to Louis, begging him to let Christian monks come to his country that he and his people might learn the religion of Christ. On this the emperor again sent for Anscarius, who willingly undertook the task, and with a few monks

---

[1] This Björn was a king of the Svea, or Upper Swedes, and had his chief town at Uppsala near the great temple of Odin. The first visit of Anscarius to his court took place in 829; and in 853 he again ventured amongst the pagans of Sweden.

and servants entered upon the long and perilous journey to Sweden. In the course of their voyage across the Baltic they were seized on by pirates, robbed of their greatest treasures—the forty manuscript books which the emperor had given them— and after enduring many hardships, were put on shore sick, hungry, and nearly naked. In this wretched plight, and not knowing a word of the language, they made their way across lakes that seemed to them like vast seas, through forests infested with bears and wolves, and over snow-covered mountains, till they reached the port of Birka, where they were well received by King Björn and his people, and allowed to preach and to baptize all who wished to become Christians. A rich Swedish noble even built a church for the converts, and Anscarius remained amongst the Svea for many months converting and baptising a great number of persons. As soon, however, as he went away, the new religion fell into neglect, and when, twenty years later, he returned to Sweden, although he was allowed for a short time by the Diet of the Goths, known as the "Ting allra Göta," to preach the new faith, the people were so afraid of bringing down the wrath of their gods upon their own heads if they listened to the preachers, that they threatened to kill them unless they left the country without further delay; and thus Anscarius and his monks were forced to depart and leave their work incomplete.

Anscarius, on his return to Germany from his first mission to Sweden, was rewarded by the emperor for his many and great labours by receiving the archbishopric of Hamburgh, which had at the special request of Louis le Débonnaire been created on purpose for him, and was to include all the north of Europe, both the lands which were known and such as might be yet discovered. This seemed a brilliant recompense for the labours he had undergone, but the poor archbishop soon found that there were only very few, if any Christians, in his see, and as he had no revenues, and Hamburgh was at the time little more than a fishing hamlet, he was forced, like his few followers, to earn his scanty means of living by making nets and sails, while a hut served for his palace, and a shed for his cathedral. Here he laboured for some years, until an invasion of Northmen, during which Hamburgh was reduced to ashes, forced him to seek safety elsewhere, after he and his converts had been robbed by the pirates of everything they owned. The closing years of this good man, who gave his whole thoughts to the labours of converting the heathen, were spent in comparative quiet and safety at Bremen, which had been joined with his own see, and which was not exposed like Hamburgh to attacks from the pagan Danes; and here, after forty years of dangers and labours at home and abroad, he died peacefully in the year 865. After his death, his grateful monks and converts fancied that miracles were done and cures wrought at his grave. No wonder that in those ignorant times the people should think that so good, and brave and pious a Christian as Anscarius, would receive more than common favour from God, and be allowed to do what no common mortals could ever hope to do!

And thus, more than a thousand years ago, when our King Alfred was still a youth, the Christian faith was carried into the far-distant savage North; but after the death of Anscarius the good seed of truth seemed to be stifled. The Pagans raged and roamed over the lands in which he had first preached the Gospel, and nearly two hundred years passed away before Christianity was received as the faith of all Denmark, and a still longer time before it quite thrust out Paganism from Norway and Sweden. Having thus seen how Christianity was planted in the North, and how rapidly it died out again there, we will now turn to the story of Gorm, one of the greatest foes of the Christian faith in that age.

PART II.

DENMARK.

Gorm the Old.—The first King of all Denmark, called by the Danes, *Gorm den Gamle*, or *The Old*, lived between 860 and 936. He is said to have been the son of a Norwegian chief of royal descent, Hardegon, or, *Hardeknud*,[1] as some give his name, a fierce Pagan warrior, who, wishing to better his

[1] Hardegon was a grandson of Regner Lodbrog.

fortune, had looked about him to see where there was a small kingdom to be gained by fighting. Luckily for himself he made choice of Lejre, also called Ledra, in the fruitful Danish island of Sjœlland. Here the country was in a worse state than usual, which is saying very much, and Hardegon did not find it a very hard task to make himself master of Lejre, and turn out the rightful king, young Siegric, who had only just got back his throne from two usurpers, called Ehnob and Gurd, the sons of a Swedish chief, Olaf. This Olaf had come some years before from Sweden to seek his fortune, just as Hardegon came from Norway with the same purpose, and having defeated and killed the king of that time, who belonged like young Siegric to the royal race of Regner Lodbrog, he and his sons had reigned, as a matter of course, till their turn came to be put away from the throne.

The people seem to have been content with Hardegon, who was able when he died to leave the throne to his son Gorm, and that young prince was received by the men of Lejre as their king. If Lejre had been only a small kingdom, like the many other states belonging to the "*Smaa-kongar*" of the Danish isles, Gorm might never perhaps have been heard of in history, and certainly would not have found it so easy to make himself King of all Denmark. Lejre was, however, looked upon as one of the most sacred spots in the North, for it was there that the great sacrifices of Odin, the chief god of the Northmen, were held. It was at yule-tide, or, as some writers say, in early spring, that the worshippers of Odin came from every part of the north of Europe to share in these sacrifices and to offer gifts of silver and gold, precious stones, and costly stuffs to the twelve high priests of whom the King of Lejre was always the chief. Such offerings as these could of course only be made by the very richest men; that is, by those chiefs who had had the best luck in pillaging the wealthier people of Gaul, Germany and Italy on some great viking-cruise. But all persons—whether poor or rich—were expected to bring to Odin's temple a horse, or a dog, or a cock, for these animals were counted sacred to him, and were killed in large numbers to do him honour at his yearly sacrifices.

Odin's Victims.—Every ninth year the people flocked in great

crowds to Lejre, for then the most solemn services of Odin
were celebrated amid more than ordinary feasting, and with
games of all kinds. It is believed that at these ninth-year
festivals human victims were offered to the god, together with
the usual sacrifices of horses, dogs, and cocks, and for this
purpose the great vikingar spared the lives of some of the
captives whom they had taken in viking or in battle, under the
idea that Odin was best pleased with offerings that had been
won in war. The King of Lejre, as the chief pontiff of these
sacrifices, acquired great wealth as well as power, for the Northmen always accompanied their offerings to the god with rich
gifts to his priests, and thus young Gorm, who seems to have
been a brave, clever, and ambitious prince, was soon able to
increase his dominions, and to raise himself to a much higher
rank than his father. Before the close of his reign he had
become King of all Denmark; not only the ruler of a small
kingdom, but the one monarch of Jutland, Slesvig, part of
Holstein, Sjœlland, Fyen, Falster, Laaland, and all the many
other islands occupied by the Danes between Germany and
Sweden. Besides these lands he owned some portions of
Norway, and the Swedish provinces of Bleking and Skaania,
which continued for several hundred years after his time to be
a part of Denmark. How he changed his small state into a
great kingdom no one knows. The writers of Danish history
say that he did it by buying one bit of land, bartering for
another, seizing upon one district and getting another given to
him, and so on, but this does not make his success very clear
to us. This is, however, all that they have to say about his good
fortune, and therefore we know only this much, that Gorm the
Old, who began life as the landless son of a poor, although
nobly born Norwegian sea-rover, ended his days as King of
Denmark, which was larger in that age than the Denmark of
our own times.

PART III.

HABITS OF THE NORTHMEN.

Northern Life.—Before we enter upon the little that is known of the events which happened in the latter part of King Gorm's reign, we must see what kind of life the Northmen of noble birth led in the times of which we are speaking, and the adventures in which they took part. In the first place we must bear in mind that the sons of a northern chief learnt from their earliest years how to endure hunger and cold without complaining, and to practise all kinds of exercises by which their bodies could be strengthened and hardened. They were taught to trap and kill wild animals in the water and the air, and on the dry land; to throw stones, darts and javelins; wield heavy axes and clubs; to use oars, steer boats, and to keep their barks in good trim for all weathers and seasons. They could ride and swim, and scud along upon snow-shoes, or skate long distances over the ice. They wrestled and fought together, and played at being vikingar in such good earnest when they were small boys, that they hardly had patience to wait till they were men before they clamoured to share in all the dangers of their fierce fathers, who, after having had the same training as themselves, had rushed out into the world to seek adventures. The love which for a long time the early Northmen bore to their homes, and to the religious customs and social habits of their country, brought them back to the North at the end of every summer's short cruise. They spent the winter-months in repairing their shattered barks, collecting fresh crews, planning new expeditions, and feasting among their kindred upon the rich plunder they had made on their latest voyage. Sometimes the great vikingar stayed away in strange lands for many years, but when they had been so long absent they must have had all the more to tell of the strange sights they had seen, and the great deeds they had done. Thus the boys and youths who heard their wonderful tales, soon began to think that there was nothing on earth so noble and charming as to become a sea-rover, and go forth like their elders to win renown, wealth, and glory—perhaps even a small kingdom all to themselves.

Northern Rovers.—Gorm, who had been brought up like other nobles of the North, went early on a cruise along the coasts of the Baltic, and even joined some of his countrymen in a hostile incursion into Garderike or Russia, where they had made their way to Smolensko and Kief, pillaging and conquering as they went. Next we hear of him in the year 882 in Germany, where he was one of the chief captains of a band of daring Northmen, who had entrenched themselves at a place called Aschloo on the river Maas, whence they sallied forth and laid waste everything far and near, setting fire to Maestricht, Louvaine, and Tongern, from whose ruins their course might be tracked by the barren fields and burnt homesteads on the roads to Juliers and Aix-la-Chapelle. At the latter place they stalled their horses in the beautiful chapel where the great Charlemagne lay buried, and stripped off the gilded and silvered railings that enclosed his tomb. Nor would a fragment of gold or silver, a single precious stone, or a shred of costly silken or linen-fabric have escaped, had not the terrified monks shown themselves very quick and skilful in hiding away every bit of plate, every ornamental hand-written book, and every vestment that they owned.

When they had got all they could lay their hands on at Aix-la-Chapelle, they pillaged and burnt the monasteries of Prün, Stablo and Malmedy, killed or made captive some of the monks, and boldly bade defiance to the army which advanced towards Ashloo to destroy their entrenchments. The emperor, Charles the Fat, had brought such an enormous array of Frankish, Bavarian, Swabian and Saxon troops against them, that one would have thought the Northmen must all have been cut to pieces. But instead of that, the Danes were clever enough to persuade the emperor not to strike a blow against them, and to pay them as much as 2,000 pounds of silver and gold, on their promising that they would be baptized. Then when they found how easy it was to get money from the emperor, they asked for more, and stayed in their safe quarters till they had secured such a large booty, that it required two hundred ships to carry away their plunder. When the great vikingar Siegfred and Gorm, with the other small kings, who had fought with them at Aschloo, returned to Denmark and showed their treasures to their Danish friends, the Danes became more eager than ever to join in the next viking expedition against the unhappy subjects of Charles the Fat.

This monarch, instead of fighting bravely to drive away the fierce pagan Danes, passed a law that anyone who killed a Northman should have his eyes put out, and even in some cases lose his life. The Danes when they heard of this strange law could not at first believe the good news, but when they came back into Charles' empire, and found that such a law really had been passed, they were filled with joy, and becoming more insolent than ever, they demanded 12,000 pounds of silver as the price of peace. It would take too long to relate how often they deceived the poor Franks and how many times they forced the emperor to buy them off. But before we leave the story of the doings of the Northmen in France we must glance at the great Siege of Paris, which began about the yule-tide of the year 885, and did not end until the spring of 887.

The first Siege of Paris.—We do not know what Gorm had been doing after the breaking up of the camp at Aschloo, but in the autumn of 885 he seems to have joined his old friend, Siegfred, who not content with the little kingdom which he had taken at Louvaine, now and then went off with all his best men to burn and pillage some other district. It was on Siegfred's return from a tour of this kind, when he had burnt down the rich town of Pontoise, that one stormy day in December of the year 885, this old warrior, at the head of 40,000 pagan Danes appeared before the gates of Paris and demanded a free passage up the river Seine for himself and all his men, with the 700 barks that they carried with them. At that time Paris was a very small and poor place compared to what it now is, and the whole of the town was built upon the little island, known as *l'Ile de la Cité*, from which two bridges, flanked by strong towers, joined the city to its faubourgs on the mainland.

"Give us a free passage up your river," cried Siegfred to Gozelin, Bishop of Paris, who had appeared at the gates to demand what the pagans wanted; "if you do not hinder me and my men, we will not harm you and your townsmen." "And what pledge will you give me," asked the bishop in reply, "that you will keep good faith with us?" "I will pledge you my head, my sword, and the honour of my grey hairs," answered the pagan; adding, "but if you will not grant the free passage that I ask at your hands, arrows, stones and darts shall be showered on you, year in and year out, and famine and war be your portion!"

These words proved no idle threat, for the next morning when Siegfred saw that the Parisians would not open their gates, he and Gorm and other chiefs led forward their men, and without further delay began a fierce assault on the north tower near the church of St. Germain's, known to us as *St. Germain l'Auxerrois.* From that hour for fifteen months the citizens had little rest from attacks either by night or by day, for the river and the banks on both sides swarmed with fierce Northmen and sea-rovers from every part of Scandinavia, who had flocked to the spot in great numbers, as soon as they heard of the siege of this greatest and richest city north of Rome. The men-at-arms tried to force an entrance by undermining and setting fire to the walls. The horsemen dashed forward, armed with slings, bows and spears, ready to hurl stones, arrows and darts at the towers, while the men in the boats aided their friends to do all the mischief they could, and helped them very much by keeping them well provided with food, which they often took by force from the Frankish vessels bringing provisions to the city.

The poor Parisians did their best to beat off the enemy by throwing hot pitch, oil and boiling water on the heads of the Northmen and injuring them as much as they could; and it was well they helped themselves, for they did not get much help from others. The emperor left them nearly a year without aiding them in any way, although the bishop as well as the governor of Paris, Count Odo or Eudes, had often sent letters and messengers to him, praying him to make haste and bring an army to succour them, and the Pope had ordered him and all other Christians to hasten to the relief of the unhappy city. Charles the Fat did not much like meeting the Northmen in the open field, and instead of coming in person he sent his margrave, Henry of Neustria, with an army to Paris. When this prince came within sight of the Danes, he found them encamped on either side of the high road leading to Soissons, and thinking that their numbers looked very small and that he could surprise, them he dashed forward, followed by many troops, but before he could reach their camp, he and all his men and horses found themselves sinking into pits and pools, which the enemy had dug before their tents and then covered over with loose branches and pieces of sod. The margrave was cut down, and all of his men who could, ran away as fast as they were able, and the Danes under Gorm and another king, Sinrik, chased them into the town of Soissons, where they seized as many captives as they wanted, and made a great booty.

The Emperor came at last. — In October, 886, Charles the Fat came with a great army, and made his camp at Montmartre, but he never struck a blow, and instead of fighting he made peace with the Danes, gave them the province of Burgundy to keep for their winter-quarters, and promised that he would pay them in the month of March 700 lbs. of silver. How the Danes must have rejoiced at this good fortune, and despised the weak emperor who had been too great a coward to bring his huge army against them!

The people of Paris, enraged at the emperor's cowardice, refused to let the Northmen go up the Seine, on which the Danes, who were tired of fighting, harnessed their captives to their boats—twenty men to every boat—and dragged them some distance by land till they could launch them on the river. After spending the winter at Sens they returned to Paris in the spring to demand the 700 lbs. of silver promised them, and after receiving the money they withdrew a day's march from the city, and made themselves very happy under the idea that they could procure more whenever they liked to ask for it. But by that time the Franks and Germans had grown weary of their feeble rulers, and while the former made Count Eudes their king, the latter chose a brave prince, called Arnulf, to reign over them.

With these new rulers a new state of things began, and before many years had passed the Northmen were forced to leave Germany and Gaul. Gorm of Denmark returned to his own country, after having taken part in the battle of Louvaine, in 891, when the Northmen were so thoroughly beaten by King

Arnulf, that sixteen of their royal standards were taken by the victor, while their great vikingar Siegfred and Gotfred were left on the field, and only a remnant of the Northern forces were fortunate enough to escape alive. The German chroniclers try to give still greater importance to this glorious victory by declaring, that while the waters of the little river Dyle were red with the blood of hundreds of thousands of slain Northmen, only one man was missing from the German ranks, when King Arnulf, with beat of drum, called together his troops after the fight, to hear the priests chant the *Te Deum* in honour of their success.

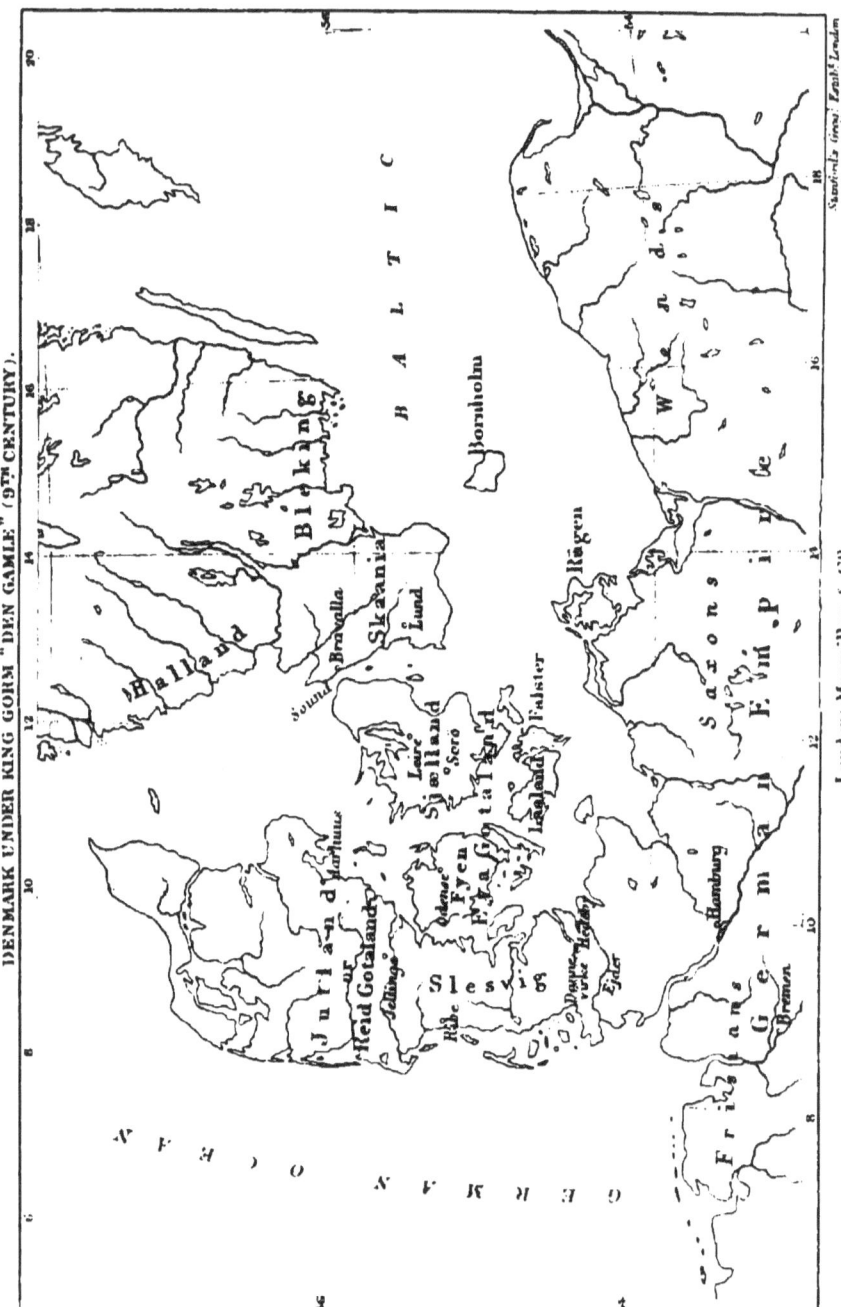

CHAPTER IV.

DENMARK IN EARLY TIMES.

Queen Thyra rules in Gorm's absence—Her memory much respected—She and her eldest son Harald favour the Christians—Knud her second son follows his father, King Gorm's religion—Gorm known as *Worm*, and why—His war with, and defeat by Henry the Fowler of Germany— Christians tolerated—How Queen Thyra built up ramparts in Gorm's absence; the way in which she told Gorm of his son Knud's death— Gorm dies of grief—H's and Thyra's grave-mounds—Harald's son Svend; his bringing up under Palnatoke—The story of Palnatoke's famous archery—Harald's death—Svend's invasion of England, his death—Knud's reign; his conduct; his murder of his brother-in-law Jarl Ulf; his remorse; his blood fine—Knud's sister Estrid; her husband, Robert le Diable—Knud's death—His sons—Their reigns and early deaths—Magnus the Good of Norway becomes King of Denmark —His kindness to Svend—The death of Magnus—His generous conduct in forgiving Svend on his death-bed, and bestowing on him the kingdom of Denmark.

PART I.

FIRST QUEEN OF DENMARK.

Queen Thyra.—It would seem that, when Gorm was absent on a sea-roving voyage, his queen, Thyra, who is spoken of in the northern sagas by the name of *Danebod*, or the "Danes'-hope," ruled the land very wisely for him. This princess, whose name is still honoured by the Danes, is said by some writers to have been the daughter of an Anglo-Saxon prince, while others believe her father to have been a Holstein chief, and assert that her grandfather went in the year 826 with Harald Klak to the court of the German Emperor, Louis le Débonnaire, where he was baptized. Queen Thyra herself early showed favour to the Christians, and she caused some of her children to be signed with the cross.

King Gorm, on the other hand, was a fierce pagan, and on account of his cruel treatment of his Christian subjects, he gained from them the nickname of the "Church's worm," because, like a worm, he was always gnawing at its supports. It is not to be supposed that Gorm cared very much about the bad names that the poor Christians might give him, but he found there was some cause for trouble when he learnt that his conduct had roused the anger of the great German Emperor, Henry I. the Fowler. At first he hoped that the affair would end in threats, but he soon learnt his mistake, for when Henry found that his messages to the Danish king were not heeded, he marched in haste to the banks of the Eyder, at the head of a large army, and there made Gorm clearly see that unless he ceased from troubling the Christians, as the emperor commanded, Slesvig and Jutland would be over-run and taken from him, and the rest of his kingdom, perhaps, also invaded by the great armies of the empire. Some writers have stated that Henry the Fowler called upon the Danish monarch to pay him tribute, in proof of his being a vassal of the German emperors, and that Gorm accepted peace on those terms. It is not certain that this really took place, but we know that the Danish king soon afterwards allowed Unni, Archbishop of Bremen, to preach the gospel in his kingdom, and to restore the churches which had been burnt or pulled down by the pagans, and sign with the cross his younger son, Harald, who like Queen Thyra had long favoured the Christians. Gorm himself never forsook the faith of his forefathers, and his eldest son Knud, called "Dan-Ast," or the "Danes'-joy," was also a pagan. This prince was like his father in many things, and while Gorm and he went forth for years together, following the life of the vikingar. Harald in his youth seldom left the northern seas, although in his later days he more than once headed large fleets in invasions of Britain and Normandy.

When the king and his sons were absent, Queen Thyra did

the best she could to rule the country in peace and quiet, and a hard task she must have had, because the Germans were always making inroads into Slesvig and Jutland, and turning the border-lands on the Eyder into a desert. Once when Gorm stayed away longer than usual she formed a plan for saving the unhappy people from this constant source of trouble. Having landed at Hedeby, in Slesvig, after leaving her pleasant home in Sjœlland, she sent forth letters to all the provinces of Denmark, requiring them to provide able-bodied workmen to help in building a long line of ramparts on the Danish side of the German frontier.

The Dannevirke.—In obedience to Queen Thyra's summons a great number of men came to the spot, and then the Queen caused a wall of defence to be built, from forty-five to seventy-five feet high, over a space of eight miles, stretching from the Selker Noer on the Slie, to Hollingsted on the Treene, and lying somewhat to the north of an old earthwork, known as Gotfred's Wall. Thyra's ramparts, of which remains can still be traced and which have formed the groundwork of all later Dannevirke or Danish outworks, took three years to finish and were very complete of their kind. They had strong watch-towers at equal distances, and only one well-protected gate, before which stretched a broad and deep ditch, which it was not easy to cross when the bridge over it had been taken away. The Danes were very grateful to Queen Thyra for her Dannevirke, and they sang her praises in their national rhymes for many ages, and told wonderful tales of her clever way of ruling the land, and keeping off foes when her husband was busy in viking far away from Denmark.

In the old sagas which the Northmen carried to Iceland, much praise is given her for the artful manner in which she more than once turned away Gorm's anger from his people, and even from his own children. One of these sagas relates that her two young sons, the princes Knud and Harald, did not bear each other as much brotherly love as they ought. Gorm, who knew of this, had sworn an oath that he would put to death anyone who should attempt the life of his first-born son, or tell him that he had died. When, therefore, tidings were brought to Queen Thyra that Knud Dan-Ast had been drowned while bathing on the coast of England. and that the immediate cause of his death was a wound which he had received from an arrow aimed at him from one of his own ships while he was in the water, she determined to inform Gorm in a figure of speech of the fate of their son. Accordingly she put herself and all her attendants in deep mourning and caused the chief hall of her house to be hung with the ashy-gray coloured hangings used at the grave feasts of Northmen of noble birth. Then, seating herself with her women at the entrance door, she awaited Gorm's approach. The King noticing these signs of mourning and struck by the silence and dejection of the Queen at once guessed the truth, and pausing at the threshold, exclaimed, "My son, Knud, is dead!" "Thou hast said it, and not I, King Gorm," answered Thyra, and thus the news of Knud's death was conveyed to his father without being followed by the vengeance which had been threatened to those who informed him of it.

Harald, 936—985.—Gorm died soon afterwards, of grief it was said, and was succeeded by his son Harald, Blaatand, or Blue Tooth,[1] who was believed by the people to have been the murderer of his brother. He was a man of a cruel and crafty nature, and when his nephew Guld, or Gold-Harald, demanded part of the kingdom in right of his father Knud, Harald put him off by promising him help to conquer Norway, and having enticed the Norwegian king, Harald Graafell, to his court, on pretence of wishing to send cattle and corn into Norway, where there was a famine at the time, he induced Guld-Harald to slay Harald Graafell. Then, instead of fulfilling his promises to his nephew, he sent for the Norwegian traitor, Hakon Jarl, with whom he had formed a secret compact, and helped him to obtain Norway on condition that he should rule as his vassal. The Jarl at first paid the required taxes to Denmark and acknowledged Harald as head king in Norway, but when

---

[1] Harald caused two grave mounds, one of 100 feet, and the other of 50 feet in height, to be erected at Jellinge, in the district of Ribe in Jutland, in honour of his father Gorm and his mother Thyra. This is recorded in runic letters upon a large stone that once stood on the lower mound, which is supposed to have enclosed the remains of the queen. These high mounds, which still exist, have been found to contain rooms, in which were stored away small silver and gilt cups and other things that might have been used by the king and queen in their every-day life.

the Danish King, with his habitual treachery refused to give him, in accordance with his former promises, any of the treasures of Guld-Harald, who had been murdered by his uncle's orders, Hakon quarrelled with him and made himself independent of him.

Harald Blaatand professed to be a Christian during the latter years of his life, and allowed himself, together with his queen and his son Svend, to be publicly baptized by the German monk Poppa. This man according to the legend had performed miracles, and had led many Danes to renounce paganism by taking up in their presence red-hot bars of iron, and letting a waxen covering be consumed upon his body while he was reciting psalms. When the people saw these wonderful things they admitted that his God was more powerful than theirs, and allowed themselves to be signed with the cross. Bishoprics were soon afterwards established at Aaarhus, Ribe and Slesvig; but when the Emperor Otho I. assumed the right of granting charters to the prelates of those sees, freeing them from the payment of all taxes and services to the Danish crown, King Harald tried by force of arms to seize upon their lands. Then the Emperor came in 975 with a large army into Holstein, and by the treachery of Hakon Jarl, who had been called upon to help the king, the Dannevirke were burnt and the German troops enabled to overrun all Slesvig and Jutland, on which Harald was forced to submit, and peace was restored on condition of his leaving the bishops unmolested.

The only one of Harald's many sons who outlived him was called Svend. This youth, although he had been baptized with his parents, hated the Christians and tried to follow in his grandfather King Gorm's steps, and do as much harm to them and their religion as he could. Like many other princes in those times, he had been sent away from home when a boy to learn the use of arms from some brave warrior. It happened that the chief in whose house he was trained was a very great pagan, named Palnatoke, and from him he learnt to despise the faith which his old father King Harald had accepted. When the King found that Palnatoke was teaching Svend to hate all Christians, he wished to withdraw him from his care; but the youth would not leave his friend, and then Harald in his artful way tried to ruin and destroy Palnatoke ; and one of the means which he took to do this was the same as the device by which it is said the Austrian governor Gessler, more than four hundred years later, strove to injure the brave Swiss peasant William Tell.

The Danish writer of history, Saxo Grammaticus, who lived in the time of our kings Richard I. and John, tells us that one day, when Palnatoke was boasting before the King of his skill in archery, Harald told him that, for all his boasting, he knew there was one shot which he would not venture to try. The latter replied, that there was no shot which he would not venture to try, and on that the King ordered him to shoot an apple off the head of his eldest son, Aage. Palnatoke obeyed. The arrow entered the apple, and the boy escaped unhurt, but his father, enraged at this and other proofs of Harald's cruel hatred of him, became his sworn foe, and soon after withdrew to the little island of Wollin, in Pomerania. There he gathered round him a band of fierce pagan vikingar, and founded the brotherhood of Jomsborg, which for many years proved a frightful scourge to all the Christian lands on, and near the Baltic Sea. Harald, after a long reign, during which he more than once carried ships and men to Normandy to aid the young Duke Richard against the French king, died in 985 from the effects of a wound, which he received in a battle fought by him against his pagan son, Svend, and Palnatoke. It is said Svend himself slew his father on the battle-field, while Palnatoke stood by, but the old King's death, instead of bringing these men the good they had hoped from it, roused strife between them, and to the end of his days Svend, called Tveskæg or "Cleft beard," had no worse foes than Palnatoke and the men of Jomsborg.[1]

Svend Tveskæg, 985-1014.—This Svend Tveskæg, was the "Sweyn" who invaded England in the time of Ethelred the Unready, and who, after having driven Ethelred out of the country and made himself master of great part of England,

---

[1] Under Palnatoke's successor, Sigvald, the pagan republic of Jomsborg began to decay, and after a great battle fought with the Norwegians under Hakon Jarl in 994, this much-dreaded confraternity was subdued and broken up.

died suddenly at Gainsborough, in the year 1014, leaving his son Knud, then a boy of fourteen, but afterwards known to Englishmen as Canute the Great, to complete the conquest of the English throne and impose upon the nation a short-lived line of Danish rulers.

PART II.

KNUD AND HIS SONS.

Knud the Great, 1018-35.—The reign of Knud the Great belongs more to the history of England than to that of Denmark; and as all that refers to these times is fully described in the " Old English History," we need not here attempt to follow the progress of the Danes in England under Knud and his sons. When the Danish king Svend, or Sweyn, died at Gainsborough in the year 1014, he left another son, Harald, who was younger than Knud, and was chosen to be king by the Danes as soon as they heard of Svend's death. Knud wanted his brother to give him some share in the government of the kingdom of Denmark; but Harald refused, telling him if he wished to be a king he must go back and gain England for himself, in which case, he should have a few ships and men to help him; and as we all know he returned to England and became a much greater king than his brother.

Harald died in 1018, and then the Danes chose Knud for their king, which proved of great importance to Denmark; for, as he was a Christian, he caused the Christian religion to be made the faith of the nation, and the worship of Odin to be put down in all the Danish provinces. Knud was more partial to England than to any of his other dominions, and only stayed in Denmark long enough to settle the affairs of the Church by putting Englishmen as bishops over the Danish clergy, and to improve the state of the country by getting workmen in every trade from England to teach the Danes, and make them more like the people of Christian civilized countries. It thus happened that, although the English had been beaten by the

Danes, Denmark was made by its own king, Knud, to feel that England was superior to it in all great and useful arts.

Knud was a very devout Churchman, but he often let his passion get the better of him, and at such times he spared his friends as little as his foes, and would listen to no counsel, even from the clergy, to whom he in general paid great respect. As soon, however, as his anger had died out, he tried to make all the amends he could to the kindred of his victims, and showed himself ready to submit to any penance laid upon him by the Church. Thus, when he had killed one of his house-churls, or servants, for some slight offence, he made public confession of his crime, and afterwards paid the same blood-fine that would have been claimed from a man of lower rank. There was one act that caused Knud more remorse and grief than anything else he had ever done, and that was the murder of his old friend and brother-in-law Ulf Jarl, towards whom he had long borne ill will on account of his having proclaimed his son, the young prince Harthaknud, king of Denmark, while Knud himself was in England, and knew nothing of what was going on in his Danish states. At that time Ulf was ruling over Denmark for King Knud, and he had made himself so much beloved by the Danish people that they were ready to do anything he wished. This was well known to Queen Emma, and when she found that she could not persuade her husband, King Knud, to set their little son Harthaknud on the throne of Denmark, she made up her mind to get the crown for him without Knud's knowledge.[1] She therefore sent messengers with letters to Ulf, telling him that the King desired to see the young prince on the throne, but was anxious not to do anything the people might not like. Ulf, believing her story, had young Harthaknud crowned king, but when he learned the deceit that Queen Emma had been guilty of, he much feared the effect of Knud's anger, although the latter for a time treated him with the same

---

[1] Queen Emma was the widow of Æthelred the Unready, the last Anglo-Saxon king of England, and daughter of Robert, the Fearless, Duke of Normandy. King Knud was only twenty-two years of age when he married her in 1017, but she must have been very much older, and her marriage with the man who had dethroned her former husband and driven her sons from their country and heritage does not give us a very high idea of her character.

favour as of old. The Danish king was at war with Sweden when these events took place, and had often had great help from the Jarl, who once saved him from certain defeat by coming to his rescue just as the royal fleet was nearly swamped by the sudden opening of the sluices, which kept back the swift waters of the Helge-aae. Ulf, at that time, had taken Knud on board his own ship and brought him safe back to Sjœlland, while he left his men to help the Danish seamen in their escape from the pursuit of the Swedes. But the King, instead of feeling grateful for the services of Ulf, thought how he could get rid of the man who had helped him. He, however, begged the Jarl to come with him to his palace of Roeskilde, and on the evening of their arrival offered to play chess with him as if they were still good friends. In the course of the game Knud made a false move by which Ulf was able to take one of his knights, and when the King refused to let this move count, and wanted to have back his own man, the Jarl jumped up and declared he would not go on with the game. The King, seeing this, cried out, "The coward Norwegian Ulf Jarl is running away!"

"You and your coward Danes would have run away still faster at the Helge-aae," answered Ulf, "if I and my Norwegians had not saved you from the Swedes, who were making ready to beat you all like a pack of craven hounds!"

These hasty words cost the Jarl his life. Knud brooded that night on the insult he had received, and early the next morning went forth from his bed-chamber, and called to him one of his body-guard who was at the door. "Go and kill Ulf Jarl," he cried, in angry haste. "My Lord-King, I dare not!" answered the man; "Ulf Jarl is even now at prayers before the altar of the church of St. Lucius!" Knud paused a moment and then, seeing a young Norwegian man-at-arms who had been in his service since his boyhood, he turned towards him, saying, "I command thee, Olaf, to go to the church and to thrust thy sword through the Jarl's body!" The youth obeyed, and the Jarl was slain before the altar-rails of the church of St. Lucius. Then, as usual with King Knud, he began to lament his crime, and to show signs of the deepest remorse; in proof of which he paid over to his sister Estrid, the widow of Ulf, as a blood-fine a large sum of money, and gave her two villages which she left at her death to the church in which her husband had been killed. Knud, moreover, took his nephew Svend, Ulf's eldest son, under his special care and caused him to be brought up as one of his own children. After a time the widowed Estrid married Robert, Duke of Normandy, the brother of Queen Emma; but this prince, who was long known as "Robert le Diable," on account of the many evil deeds ascribed to him, did not like the new wife whom his brother-in-law King Knud had given him, and without much regard to her feelings, he sent her back to the English court very soon after their marriage. This Duke Robert was the father of William of Normandy, who in 1066 came over to England and conquered the land.

Knud's Death.—When King Knud died, in 1035, the master of six so-called kingdoms—namely, England, Denmark, Sweden, Norway, Scotland, and Cumberland—he was not more than thirty-six, which was about the age of William the Conqueror when he won the crown of England by his victory at the battle of Hastings. This was an early age at which to have made so many conquests, for Denmark was the only one of his states that he had not gained for himself by force of arms; and when we read of all that he did to improve the condition of his subjects, and of the quiet and order which reigned in England under him, we cannot wonder at the praise given to him by the writers of his time. Nor can we help sharing in the surprise which they express that a prince, who like Knud had been born a pagan and had grown to manhood without receiving any instruction, should in so short a time have become so learned, that when he went to Rome to receive the Pope's blessing, his knowledge and wisdom were the admiration of all who saw him and spoke with him. None of his sons had his talents, and none of them lived long enough to enjoy their great heritage beyond a few years. When Knud conquered Norway, in 1030, he had placed his son Svend on the throne; but the misconduct of this youth, who was only fifteen years old at the time his father raised him to this great dignity, had roused the angry spirit of the people, who drove him out of the country and obliged him to hasten to England to ask for help from his father. Before he landed, in 1035, Knud was dead, and young Svend met with no welcome from his stepmother, Queen Emma, who was in great anxiety about her own son, his half-brother Harthaknud, then absent in Denmark; for although she had sent to inform him of his father's death, and urged him to return with all speed to England and secure the crown for himself, he lingered in the North and paid no respect to her wishes and warnings.

Knud's Sons, 1035-1042.—But while Harthaknud loitered away his time in Denmark, his half-brother Harald, known to us in English history as Harold Harefoot, was crowned king of England, only, however, to enjoy a short reign of four years, for he died in 1039, and then both the Saxons and Danes in England were eager to have Harthaknud for their king.

Harthaknud, 1039-1042.—Harthaknud had excited greater hopes than he fulfilled, and during his short reign he and his mother Queen Emma seemed to think more of securing vengeance on their own private foes than in doing much for the good of the people. One of his first cares had been to reward the seamen of the ships which had conducted him from Holland to England at the time of his brother Harald's death, and he gave great displeasure to the Anglo-Saxons by demanding a sum of thirty-two thousand pounds of silver for the fleet and army. Danish soldiers were sent through the country to collect this tax, and the insolence with which these men performed their duty led to constant disturbances. The King favoured them so greatly that Anglo-Saxons had to submit to insults of every kind at their hands; and if a number of Saxons saw one Dane coming they had to wait till he had passed, as the slightest assertion of independence on their part was sure to be visited upon them in some unpleasant way or other. The liberality which the King and his mother showed to the clergy, by bestowing numerous valuable estates on churches and monasteries to found masses for the soul of King Knud, secured them from ecclesiastical reproof, and gained over to their cause some of the highest prelates in the kingdom, who did not disdain to take part in the most undignified acts at the command of the sovereign. Thus, when Harthaknud immediately after his coronation determined, by his mother's advice, to give a public proof of his hatred for his half-brother King Harold Harefoot, he entrusted to Ælfric, Archbishop of York, the unworthy office of going with the executioner Thrond and others to disinter the body of Harold, and see the head cut off and cast into the Thames.

This act gave great offence to the people of London, and in order to try to regain the good will of the Anglo-Saxons, the young King began to show much favour to those who were known to have been the friends of the former princes. He even threatened to punish all who could be proved to have taken part in the murder of the Ætheling Ælfred, his mother Queen Emma's son by her first husband, King Æthelred the Unready. It was well known that this young prince had been put to death by the orders of Earl Godwine; and this rich and powerful noble, fearing that the young King, on pretence of avenging his half-brother, would have him killed for the sake of seizing upon his great wealth, came forward of his own accord to swear upon his oath that, in all he had done against the Ætheling, he had only obeyed the orders of the King's father, his master Knud. At the same time he begged Harthaknud to accept, as a token of his love and duty, a small gift that he had caused to be made ready for him. When Harthaknud saw this "small gift," he said no more of punishing his half-brother's murderers, but showed greater favour than ever to Earl Godwine. The present that had worked this change in the King's feelings was indeed worthy of some handsome reward, and must have cost the wealthy giver a large sum of money, for it was the most splendid ship that could be made in those times, and besides being richly gilt and fitted up with finely-carved seats for the rowers, had brightly-painted sails and a gold-headed beak or prow. It was manned by eighty strong and well-grown soldiers, each one of whom bore on either arm a golden bracelet of sixteen ounces in weight, and on his head a gilt helmet. They had also gilded swords and Danish battle-axes inlaid and bound with bands and bosses of pure gold. This was indeed a most costly gift, but one which needed a rich man to be the receiver as well as the giver.

Denmark bartered.—Harthaknud's sudden death in 1042 put an end to the short rule of the descendants of King Knud in England, and at once split up the great empire which he had founded. Before the Danes could take measures to decide whom they should choose to fill the vacant throne, they learnt, that by a compact, entered into between the late King Harthaknud and Magnus the Good of Norway, the territories of either prince were to fall to the survivor. Thus, in case Magnus had died first, the crown of Norway was to have gone to the king of England and Denmark, but now that he survived Harthaknud, he had the right to come forward and take the Danish throne. As soon, therefore, as the news of Harthaknud's death reached Norway, Magnus collected a fleet and sailed over to Denmark to advance his claims. The people, who knew him to be a just, although a severe ruler, and who had no prince among them to whom they cared to give the Danish crown, were content to accept him in spite of the strange way in which he had been thrust upon them; and thus it came to pass that for five years, from 1042 to 1047, Denmark was joined with Norway under one king.

Magnus was much beloved by the Norwegians, to whom he gave the first book of written laws that they had had. He proved, also, a very kind friend to young Svend the nephew of Knud, but he did not meet with the return he deserved; for after he had made Svend Jarl of Denmark and trusted him to rule in his name, that prince joined the enemies of Magnus, among whom was the King's own uncle, Harald, and made war upon him. More than once King Magnus forgave Svend, but that did not make him more faithful; and after having stirred-up revolts from time to time, he again raised an army against his friend and gave the royal troops battle. Svend was beaten, and when he saw his best men scattered and routed, he took to flight, on which the King went in pursuit of him; but as Magnus was riding off the field of battle a hare crossed the path and startled his horse, by which he was thrown to the ground, and so much injured by the fall, that he died in a few hours. Before his death he caused Svend to be brought before him, and raising himself up, he bade all present to bear witness that he gave back to him all the rights to the crown of Denmark which he had received from the late King Harthaknud, and that he chose his uncle Harald to rule over Norway after him. Magnus was much beloved by his subjects, and both the Danes and Norwegians showed themselves willing to comply with his wishes; and thus, while Harald had to content himself with Norway, Svend Estridsen, the nephew of Knud, became king of Denmark in 1047.

CHAPTER V.

SCANDINAVIA IN EARLY TIMES

Little known of Sweden and Norway before the introduction of Christianity—The Danes the best known—The reason of this—How the Goths were first led to settle in Sweden—Odin's arrival—His conflict with the King of the Goths—The worship of two Odins—The Ynglingar—Their descent from Odin—How they lose Sweden—Ingjald—The Uppsala burning of six Small Kings—The Braga-cup oath—Ingjald kills himself—Olaf the "Tree Hewer" clears the border lands—His successors found the kingdom of Norway—The Ynglinga saga—Religion of Swedes and Norwegians—King-pontiffs—Skaania—Ivar Vidfadme the great conqueror—Danes and Swedes claim the same great men—Reason why we know so little of Sweden in early times—Founders of Russia came from Sweden—Rurik—Daring of Norwegian sea-men—Their discoveries, and what led to them—Stern rule of Harald Haarfager—Struggles in Norway—"Strand-hug"—Gaungo Hrolfr, or Rollo "the Walker"—Settlement of Normandy—Danish settlements in Scotland and Ireland—The men of Lochlin—Harald's death—Hakon Æthelstane-fostre—Hakon placed on the knees of King Æthelstan—Splendid gift of golden-beaked ship—Hakon's good training in England.

PART I.

SWEDEN AND NORWAY.

State of Sweden and Norway.—BEFORE we enter upon the reign of Knud's nephew and successor, Svend Estridsen, whose descendants have ruled over Denmark from that early time (1047) till the present day, we must learn something of Sweden and Norway, which were very little known to the rest of the world before the beginning of the eleventh century.

This may have been owing to their greater distance from Christian civilized lands, or to the rigour of the climate, which closed their harbours for many months in the year, and made those rugged parts of Scandinavia unattractive to strangers. The Danes were, in fact, for many ages the only one of the Northern nations known to the Christians of Europe, and although it is very probable that Swedes, and after a time Norwegians also, took part in the great Danish invasions of England and of the Frankish empire, they were all included by the people of those countries under the common name of Northmen, or Danes. And, as all the three northern nations continued to speak the " Dönsk tunga " (Danish tongue), to follow the same forms of religion, and to show the same spirit of fierceness, courage and daring long after they had separated and formed distinct kingdoms, it was no wonder foreigners should have supposed them to be only one people. This idea was, moreover, quite correct, for we now know that, in spite of their divisions into Danes, Swedes and Norwegians, the Northmen were only one people, tracing their descent from the same common Gothic forefathers who had come from the far East, and spread themselves over the islands and the most fruitful coastlands of the Baltic.

The Goths probably stayed in those more genial parts of Scandinavia as long as their leaders found space enough for themselves and their followers, but when their numbers increased, and "the Small Kings" began fighting among themselves and interfering with each other, the younger chiefs with the restlessness of their race set forth in search of new homes. Some such causes, it is believed, led to the settlement of the southern parts of Sweden by the Goths from Ey-gotaland, or the Danish Islands.

In the old Swedish legends it is related that Odin founded the empire of the Svea, and built a great temple at a spot called Sigtuna, near Lake Maelar, in the present province of Upland, which was known by the Northmen under the name of the " lesser Svithjód " to distinguish it from that " greater Svithjód," or Scythia, from which they believed that he had led his followers. When Odin arrived with his twelve pontiffs, or chief priests, he is said to have found that great part of the land was occupied by a people who, like himself, had come from Svithjód, but in such long past ages that according to their own account no one could fix the time. These people, who called themselves "Göta," or "Gauta," Goths, and boasted that they had driven all the dwarfs, giants and "Fenni"[1] of the country back into the mountains and dreary wastes, were so strong that Odin was forced to make a compact with their king Gylfe, before he could settle in the land. But after these two great chiefs had proved each other's strength in a trial of magic, they lived together on friendly terms, and Sweden was thenceforth divided into the two free nations of the "Svea," Swedes, and the "Göta," Goths. The Svea were governed after Odin's death by his pontiffs, who had charge of his temple at Sigtuna; and this tribe by degrees grew so much more powerful than the Göta, that they were allowed to take the lead in all public matters, and their rulers were looked up to as *chief kings* by all the "Smaa-kongar" of the Goths as well as Swedes. In these and other legends of the same kind it is not easy to discover whether the old Swedes honoured Odin as a god, or as a mere human chief of their race; but it has been supposed by some writers that long after the first Gothic invaders brought his worship into Sweden, a second band of the same tribe may have come, under a leader called by his name, who set up a newer form of faith, which gained such hold over the minds of the people that in time they came to worship the two Odins under one common faith.

The Ynglingar. — Like the Danes the Swedes traced the descent of their early kings back to Odin, through his successor in Sweden, the pontiff Njord, whose son Frey-Yngve was the founder of the royal race of the Ynglingar. We are told that this prince, who built a great temple to Odin on the ruins of the more ancient one of Sigtuna, and called it Upp-Sala (or the High Halls), was so much beloved by his subjects, that when he died his family did not venture to proclaim his death lest trouble should arise among the Svea, but laid his body within a carefully-built stone mound, to which they continued for three years to carry all the gifts and annual offerings of the people. They did not burn the body according to their ancient custom, because it had been foretold that as long as Frey Yngve stayed in Lesser Svithjöd all would go well with the land; but when they found, at the end of three years, that the seasons continued

[1] The Finns and Lapps.

to be good, they ventured to make known his death, and the people, in gratitude for all he had done for them on earth, placed him among their gods and prayed to him for peace and plenty.

This king, Frey-Yngve, was counted as the last of the gods, but his descendants continued to rule over the Svea for several generations till enmity sprang up among the different members of the royal house. Then the Ynglingar lost all power over the Small Kings of Sweden through the evil deeds of one of the race, called Ingjald and surnamed "Ill-raada," the Bad Ruler. This prince, who was a cruel and crafty man, drew upon himself the anger of the people by burning alive six Small Kings on pretence of doing honour to his father, the good King Anund. His treachery on this occasion was equal to his cruelty for, in order to get as many kings into his power as possible, he had sent messengers to all those of his kinsmen who were "Smaa-kongar," and begged that they would show their respect for the late King by attending his grave-feast.

Six of the Small Kings obeyed the summons, and were according to ancient usage invited to take their places on the high-seat at the end of the hall, which in the dwellings of the Northmen was always reserved for the master of the house and his most honoured guests. Ingjald, as the giver of the feast, sat on a low stool at their feet, since it was not considered right for the heir to take his father's seat till the grave-feast was over and the last toast had been drunk to the memory of the dead. When his turn came to drink from the "Braga," or "Good-health" horn, he arose to his feet, and said he claimed the right of making a sacred vow before he drained the cup. Such vows made in the act of drinking the last "Braga" or toast to the dead, were held to be more binding than any others. And when the feast was over, he caused the six kings to be seized and burnt alive, on the plea that the gods had constrained him to swear that he would sacrifice them all in memory of his father. This grave feast, known as the "Uppsala Burning," was soon followed by another burning even worse than the former, if the numbers of the victims be considered. In this second burning, the King and his wicked daughter, Aasa, perished in the flames which they had them selves kindled to escape from the vengeance of their enemies. For having been warned that young Ivar of Skaania was drawing near to avenge the death of his father, Halfdan, who was one of the six kings burnt at Uppsala, Ingjald and his daughter set fire to their palace, and after having drugged the mead of the servants in order to prevent an alarm being given and closed the doors while the men were buried in sleep, they and all who were in the building were consumed to ashes.

After these events, the Svea would have no more of the Ynglingar for their kings, and Ingjald's children were driven out of the country. His eldest son Olaf, fearing the anger of the people, fled with a few companions beyond the mountains to the dense forests, which then covered the border-land between the present Sweden and Norway, and began to clear the ground by burning the trees, in order to make it fit for human habitation. This Olaf was known as "*Trætelje*," or the Tree-hewer, and the land which he cleared was thenceforth called Vermland, in memory of his having warmed it by setting fire to the great forests. Like his father Ingjald, this prince also met his death by burning; for when some years afterwards his people suffered from famine, they laid the blame on Olaf and forced him to submit to be burnt at the great Sacrifice to Odin, in order that the god, in return for a royal victim, might avert the evil that had come upon them. Odin was believed to have accepted the offering made to him, as fruitful years followed the sacrifice of Olaf, whose descendants passed over from Vermland into Norway, and became the founders of that kingdom.

Ynglinga Saga.—Such are the accounts given of the rise of the Swedish and Norwegian monarchies in the legend, known as the Ynglinga Saga, which was written down by scribes in Iceland from the old songs brought over to that country by the early settlers and handed down by them to their children, and through them to later generations. This and other sagas, which related to the rise of the royal races of Sweden and Norway, were no doubt based on real events, which in the course of time were mixed up with many fables. We owe our knowledge of them to King Harald Haarfager, for they were collected and recited aloud by famous skalds at the court of this King, who reigned over Norway between 863 and

933, and boasted of being an Ynglingar through his descent from Olaf Trætelje, the Tree-hewer.

Thus all three of the royal houses of Scandinavia claimed Odin as their founder; for although Göta-land, or the land of the Goths, was not reckoned as part of the monarchy of the Svea, it was admitted to have been first settled by "Got" or "Gaut," from whom it had derived its name and by whom it had been raised into a free state. And as Got and Gaut were only other names of Odin, the Goths of Sweden thought they had as good a right as their neighbours, the Svea, to count the chief god of their religion as the founder of their nation.

The Swedes—under which name are included both the Göta and Svea—and the Norwegians retained their old faith much longer than the Danes, and the few glimpses which we catch from the sagas of their character and conduct in those early times show us how little regard they paid to life. In Denmark human sacrifices were only very rarely practised, but in Sweden, where they are said to have been enjoined as a religious duty by Frey-Yngve, the first of the Ynglingar race, they appear to have been very frequent. We even read of one Swedish King called Ane, who tried to gain from Odin length of life from year to year by offering up one of his sons at each annual sacrifice to the god. According to this saga, when nine of his children had thus been slain, the Svea, in spite of their dread of Odin and of the King who was his high priest, rose in anger against Ane, and saved the tenth and last of his sons from sharing the fate of his brothers.

Pontiff-Kings.—Throughout all the North every king was the pontiff or high priest of his people, and one of the most important and sacred of his duties was to offer annual sacrifices within the temples of his kingdom, and this gave some of the northern kings greater power than others. Thus in Denmark, as we have seen, where the chief temple to Odin was at Lejre or Ledra in Sjœlland, Gorm as the pontiff-king of that district was looked up to by the neighbouring small kings and enabled to secure a strong influence over them, which helped him greatly in his efforts to make himself king of all Denmark It was the same in Sweden, where the Ynglingar who had charge of Odin's chief temple at Uppsala were, from the first, head kings of the country, just as the kings of Lund, in whose territories there was another great temple, early made themselves head kings in Skaania. The province of Skaania in South Sweden, which took its name from the old northern word "Skaun," a swampy land, was before Christian times one of the best known of the northern states; for not far from its capital, Lund, which was enclosed with high sharply-spiked walls, a large trading port had sprung up near the temple to Odin. The position of this ancient pagan stronghold on the eastern shore of the Sound, leading into the Baltic, made it a very important and convenient harbour for the trading or plundering fleets, which every summer passed to and from the lands of Scandinavia and the rich states of southern Europe. Here many of the northern vikingar kept the wares and gold and silver, which they had collected on their viking expeditions, paying toll to the king of the district for leave to put into the harbour, and wait there with their treasures till the season came round for darting forth again in search of fresh booty. Long before the ninth century, when King Gorm of Denmark took possession of this rich province and joined it to his other Danish lands, Skaania had been a free state, ruled over by kings of its own, a few of whom gained for themselves great renown. Amongst these there was none more celebrated than "Ivar Vidfadme" or the "Far-stretching," who was made chief King over the Svea, as well as the Göta, after the death of Ingjald "Ill-raade," the last of the Ynglingar in Sweden.

This Ivar, who is believed to have lived in the seventh century, plays a great part in the sagas of the Icelanders, for he is there said to have conquered Sweden and Denmark, a large portion of the lands of the Saxons and one-fifth of all England.[1] But on the other hand Saxo-Grammaticus, the Danish historian, does not even mention his name among the rulers of Denmark, nor do Anglo-Saxon records make any reference to him. The Danes, however, speak of him as the grandfather of their King Harald Hildetand, of whose defeat in his old age by the young Swedish king, Sigurd Ring, at the battle of Bravalla, we have read in a former chapter.

[1] Ivar's daughter, Aulfur, was married to Rerik, a King of Lejre, and their son Harald, surnamed Hildetand, became in time King of Denmark and Sweden.

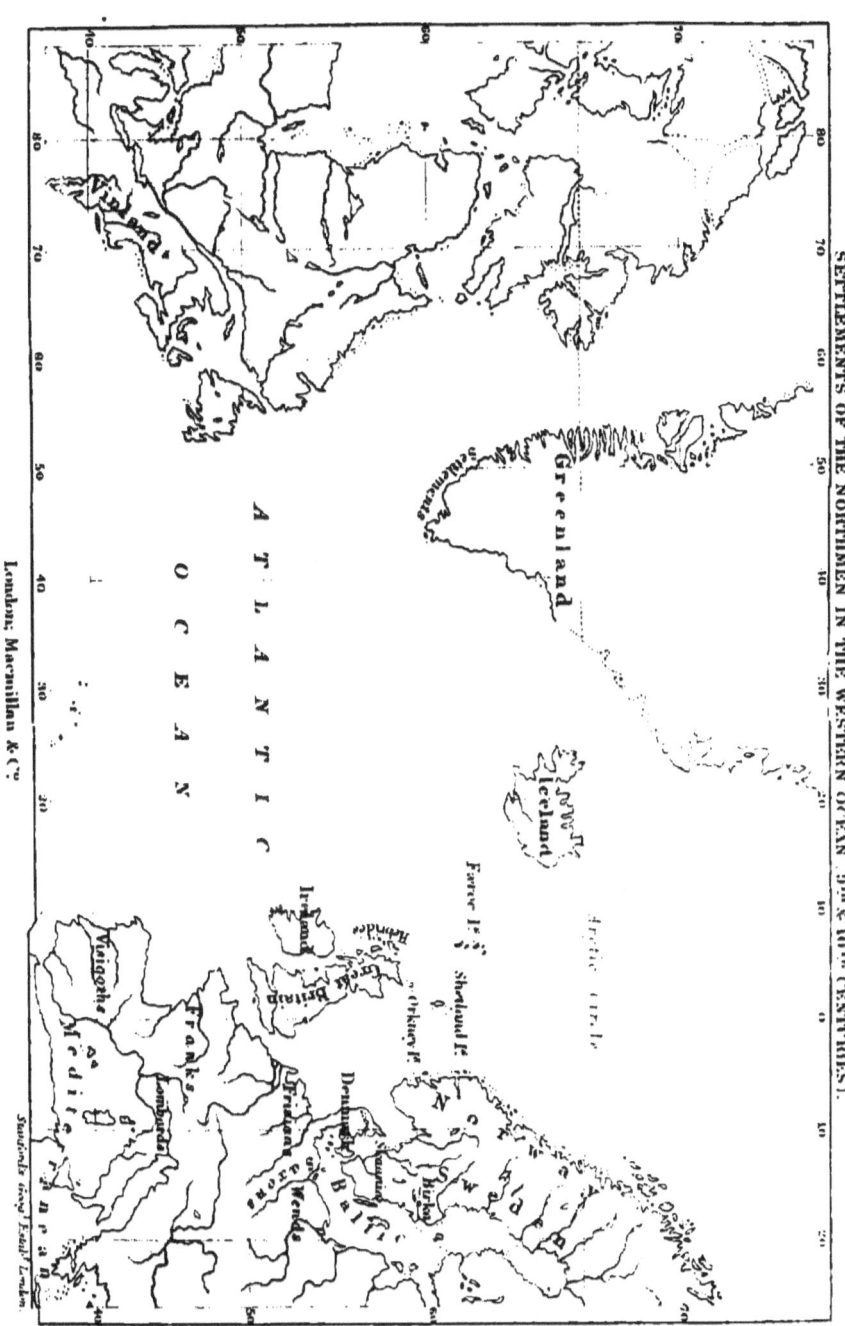

In this, as in other periods of Northern history, the kings and heroes of Denmark and Sweden are so intermingled that it is often impossible to decide to which nation we must refer any one of them. The Danish and Icelandic sagas generally agree in making all great northern chiefs Danes or Norwegians, whilst the Swedes as often claim them for their own country. This is especially the case in regard to the favourite demi-god Stærkodder, and to Ragnar, called "Lodbrog" of the Leather Leggings, whose numerous sons or grandsons ranked amongst the most daring and fiercest of the vikingar of the ninth century.[1] The history of Sweden is, moreover, so confused and so shrouded in fable before the time of Olaf, "the Lap-king," who reigned from 993 to 1024, and was the first Christian king of the Swedes and Goths, that it would be quite useless to try to give a continuous account of what happened in that kingdom before the establishment of Christianity. Another cause of our great ignorance of Swedish history in those early times was, no doubt, that the Swedes, instead of fitting out great fleets of rowing and sailing boats year after year, like the other Scandinavian nations, to attack the Southern lands of Europe, turned their arms against the Finns, Quens, Lapps and Wends, who lived north and east of them, and whom they could reach by crossing the mountains and frozen gulfs which separated them from those remote tribes. In this manner they were kept out of contact with the more civilized nations of Europe, who hardly knew of their existence till the middle ages.

PART II.

NORTHERN CONQUESTS.

Russia Peopled.—The people of Sweden early gave the name of "Vanen," or Wends, to all nations living to the east of them, and they also called the Finnish tribes "Jötunar," which was the same word that they applied to the giants of their mythology. The Finns on the other hand have continued from

---

[1] His name is spelt *Regner* by the Danes; see chap. ii.

ancient times till the present day to call the Russians "*Wänälaiset*" (Wends), and the Swedes "*Ruotsalaiset*" (Russians) from Roden or Rosen, the ancient name for the part of Sweden nearest southern Finland. This mixing up of different names for the same people renders it very difficult to follow the accounts of the wars and conquests which the Swedes are said to have made in early times amongst the Finns, Wends, and Russians. We know, however, that the greater number of the Varingjar, or Northern rovers, who passed through Garderike, the present Russia, on their way to Miklagaard (Constantinople), were Swedes, while it was from the name Ruotsalaiset or Russians, which the older inhabitants gave them, that the country became known in after times as Russia.

According to Russian chroniclers, it was in the year 859 that a band of the Varingjar, who had come over the sea and were under a leader called Rurik, first appeared in Garderike, where they subdued all the Slaves and Finns whom they met on their march. After a time, however, these older inhabitants of Garderike took courage to attack the small number of strangers who were making themselves masters of their country, and drove them out. Then Rurik and his men made haste to follow their companions who had pushed straight on towards Greece, and for the next two years Garderike was left clear of the Northmen. But at the end of that time the Slaves and Finns having found that they were worse treated by their own chiefs than they had been by the strangers, sent messengers into Greece to the Varingjar, whom they knew both under the names of "Rhos" and "Ruses." "Our land is large," they said, "and blessed with everything good for man; all we need is order; come then, be our princes, and rule over us." On receiving this message the Varingjar took counsel together, and it was decided that those amongst their number who wished to return to Garderike, should cast lots to see whom Odin would choose to be leaders over the rest.

The lot fell upon Rurick and his two brothers, Sineus and Truvor, and these men with their families and a numerous band of followers left Miklagaard and returned into the land of the Slaves. Rurik chose the district now known to us as Novogorod—or New Town—where he built a city which was thenceforth filled by the people of Varingjar origin, while the old land of the Slaves received the name of Russia from the strangers who had become masters of it. Such is the account which the Russians have given us of the manner in which their empire in early times ceased to be wholly Slavonic, and passed under the rule of Scandinavian vikingar whose descendants have since then composed the upper classes among the people.

Ocean Discoveries.—In the same age in which the Danes were hovering on the coasts of England, penetrating into the interior of Gaul and Germany, and the Swedes were making conquests in Eastern Europe, the Norwegians with an inborn love of adventure were striking boldly out into seas where no European—and probably no human being—had ever yet dipped his oar. After they had once begun their daring course of ocean-voyages, they never rested till they had moored their barks on every island in the Northern Seas, and pushed their way beyond the north-western limits of Europe to that new world which we have since called America. Before the close of the ninth century, and while Alfred the Great was still ruling in England, the Pagan Norwegians of whose country he had learnt something through the narrative of the travellers, Ohther and Wulfstan, had made settlements on every side of his kingdom, in Scotland, Ireland, the Isle of Man, the Orkneys, Hebrides and Shetland. They had also discovered and peopled Iceland and the Farö Islands, while before Alfred died in 901 the north-east of the present France had been seized on by their countryman, Rollo, whose descendants in the next century brought back to England the power of the Northmen from which he hoped he had for ever freed his kingdom. The desire of the Norwegians to make new settlements for themselves in foreign lands during the latter half of the ninth century was much stimulated by the state of public affairs in their own country. In Norway, as in the other Scandinavian lands, the country had from the earliest times been divided into a great number of districts, ruled over by Small Kings, and having each a separate "Thing," or Public Assembly, and a certain number of barks and men-at-arms, with which to fight or to defend its own frontiers. Halfden Svarte, a descendant of Olaf *Trætelje*, the "Tree Hewer," who lived in the middle of the ninth century, had conquered several of these little kingdoms and joined them with his own state of Vestfold. At his death in the year 863, his son Harald, known in history as *Haarfager*, " the beautiful-haired," succeeded to these states, but, not content with his heritage, he resolved never to rest till he had made himself sole King of Norway. In proof of his being thoroughly in earnest, he took a solemn oath that he would neither cut nor comb his long yellow locks till he had subdued all the Small Kings in the land. This oath Harald redeemed by making himself master of all Norway from the extreme north of Finnmark to the Næs, or the most southerly cape on the Skagerage. According to the old sagas he was urged on to attempt these conquests by his love for the beautiful Gyda, who refused to marry him as long as there was any other king in the land.

The fate of Norway was decided in a great sea-battle fought in Hafurstjord, near the present Stavanger, where Harald in 872 scattered the fleet which some of the Norwegian chiefs had collected in the hope of defeating him, and forced them either to submit to his power, or leave their native land as outlaws. Harald followed up his victory by imposing a heavy tax upon every district in Norway, and setting his own friends over the different small kingdoms with the title of Jarls. The severity with which the king and his officers caused the laws to be carried out against the rich as well as the poor enraged the old chiefs, and many of them declared that " rather than submit, like low-born churls to rule and order, they would leave their country." Then it was that some of the noblest Norwegians, taking their families and servants with them, embarked on board their ships, and after making solemn offerings to the gods of their fathers and calling down divine vengeance on the head of King Harald, left their native land for ever and set sail in search of new homes.

PART III.

NORWEGIAN SETTLEMENTS.

Rollo the Norman.—One of the most noted of the Norwegian families who were driven from their native land at this period was that of Rögnvald, Jarl of Mære, who like King Harald claimed to be descended from the famous Sigurd Ring, conqueror of Denmark. When King Harald found that the Jarl had not carried out against his own son Hrolf, or Rollo, the orders which he had received to punish piracy by death, he sent the Princes Gudröd and Halfdan to invade Rögnvald's lands and drive his family from their home. The Jarl Rögnvald was slain in battle, and his eldest son Ejnar driven into exile, while the younger son Rollo, who had been the cause of the feud between the king and his family, was still absent from Norway on a viking cruise. This youth, who on account of his great stature, which prevented any horse from carrying him, was known as *Gaungo Hrolf,* or "the walking Rollo," was one of the most famous vikingar of his age, and noted for the success with which he followed the old northern practice of "*Strand-Hug,*" or seizing by force from off the sea-coast lands upon anything which he or his crews might want, and then going off to sea again with the booty. This way of taking what did not belong to a man King Harald called by the plain name of "stealing," and was resolved to punish whenever he could; accordingly when Rollo, who did not know of the death of his father and the disgrace of his family, landed on the island Vigen and began his old habit of using Strand-Hug, he was seized by orders of the king, who caused him to be brought before the Thing, and to be condemned as an outlaw. Rollo's mother and friends offered large sums of money to appease his anger, but to no purpose, and the young man, seeing that Harald would not pardon him or allow him to remain in Norway, set forth in search of a home elsewhere. The Icelandic sagas tell us that, having crossed the sea, he went in 876 to Walland (Gaul), where he carried on war against the king, and at last gained for himself a great

Jarldom, which he filled with Northmen, and which on that account was called "Nordmandiet," or Normandy. "From this stock came the Jarls of Normandy, and, in course of time, also the Kings of England, for Rollo's son William was the father of Richard, and this Richard had a son of his own name, whose son Rollo, or Robert, was the father of William the Conqueror of England." Such is the old northern account of the settlement of Normandy and of the line of descent which the Norwegians give of the first of our Norman kings.

According to northern traditions the Danes had as early as the fifth century made settlements in Scotland, but the Norwegians did not attack the country in any large numbers till the reign of Harald. In Ireland the northern vikingar were known under the name of "Lochlanach," and the lands from which they came under that of "Lochlin." The Irish annals record the arrival in 852 of an "Olauf, King of Lochlin," to whom all the Northern Gât, or Strangers, submitted. He reigned in Dublin, whilst two other northern chiefs, Ivar and Sigtrygg, made small kingdoms for themselves in Waterford and Limerick. The descendants of the vikingar continued to rule over those parts of Ireland till the time of our Henry II., when the island was invaded by the English in 1172. But long after that time the former presence of the Northmen, or "Eastmen," as they were then called, could be traced in the laws and usages and even in the appearance of the people of those districts.

The close of Harald Haarfager's reign was troubled by quarrels amongst his many sons, and at last to escape from these family troubles he retired to a little island near Stavanger, leaving his ungrateful children to govern the state as they liked, and died at a great age in 936, after having spent three years in this retreat. A short time before his death Harald sent his youngest son Hakon to his friend the English King Æthelstan, in order that the boy might be brought up at his court and kept safe from the hands of his wicked half-brother Erik. This little prince, who to the end of his life was known as Hakon, "Æthelstan's fostre," or Æthelstan's foster-child, is said in accordance with an old northern custom to have been brought by his attendants to the English prince, and placed on the knees of Æthelstan while he sate on his throne holding a court of his nobles. This act of placing a child in the lap of another person was considered to make the latter the foster-parent or guardian of the child, and according to some writers it was looked upon as an insult, since whoever became the foster-father of another man's child was counted as his inferior.

In the case of Hakon, however, no insult can have been intended, for his uncle, the Jarl Sigurd who brought him to the English court, was the bearer of many costly gifts from King Harald to King Æthelstan, amongst which we read of a ship with a golden beak and purple sails which had gilded shields to shelter the oarsmen on their benches. Æthelstan treated the young prince with kindness, and after having had him trained in all respects like one of his own children and instructed in the Christian faith, he sent him after several years' stay in England back to Norway, loaded with gifts of many kinds.[1]

[1] See "Old English History," chap. ix. p. 159.

CHAPTER VI.

NORWAY IN EARLY TIMES.

Norwegians under Harald Haarfager go in search of new lands—Discovery of Iceland doubly important as leading to those of Greenland and America—Iceland first visited between 861 and 868; reported to be a land of mountain giants—Norwegians venture to revisit the island—Its settlement by Ingolf—He throws the consecrated door-posts of his former house into the sea and follows them for three years—How the Northmen proceeded when they settled—Thorolf brings a carved image of Thor for his temple—Builds a house and temple, sets up an altar to hold the sacred silver ring on which men swore—He prepares the Temple and the Thing—Divides Iceland into districts—Chieftains send to Norway to learn what the old laws were—Ulfljot spends three years in studying the laws—Hakon's Laws—Iceland a Republic—Cruel wars for mastery—State of Norway after Harald's death—Hakon's reign—His subjects refuse to become Christians—Sigard Jarl tries to screen Hakon—He makes sign of cross or Thor's mallet—Hakon's defeat and death—Troubles in Norway—Olaf Trygvasson, his deeds, wars and death—Olaf the Saint—Knud the Great—Olaf's death—Miracles said to have been wrought by Olaf's body—Magnus the Good dies and leaves Denmark to Svend Estridsen—Troubles in Sweden—Erik Sejrsæl—Olaf the Lap-king, first Christian king—Bold language of peasants—Olaf's sons Anund and Edmund—Last of Ynglingar race of Uppsala kings—Erik the Red discovers Greenland—Erik's son Leif brings monks to Greenland, builds Churches—Fate of Greenland—" Black Death "—Hans Egede and his wife go to teach the savage Greenlanders—Leif's wish to make discoveries—He reaches American coasts—Vinland and its grapes—Settlers all murdered by natives—Last notice of Vinland—Columbus re-opens the way.

PART I.

ICELAND.

Early Explorers.—BEFORE we quite leave the time of the Norwegian King Harald Haarfager, we must see how his stern rule, by driving so many of his subjects forth in search of new homes, led to the discovery and settlement in the Northern

Ocean of the island of Iceland, which soon grew to be the most important colony of Norway. This discovery is doubly interesting because it proved the means of encouraging the northern seamen to venture still further westward, till at length they reached the coasts of Greenland, and landed at many spots along the eastern side of the North American Continent. It is true that their discovery of America led to no lasting results, and was forgotten by the other nations of Europe —if it had ever been known to them—till many ages later, when the voyages of Columbus and the other great discoverers of the time drew the attention of learned men to accounts given in the sagas of the early landing of Northmen on the American coasts. But the fact that they did visit the shores of America ought not to be forgotten, and we must now see how the settlement of Iceland and these later and less useful discoveries were brought about.

Iceland was first visited by a Swede, called Gardar, by a Norwegian Nadod, who named the country Snæland (Snowland), and by another Norwegian known as Floki Rafn, who gave the island its present name. These three men all landed in Iceland between the years 861 and 868, and even passed many months at a time there, but it is not certain who among them had been the first to come to the island. On their return to Scandinavia they gave a dreadful account of the land, which according to their report had been cursed by the gods, and given over to the power of horrible giants, who lived hidden within caves and mountains where they kept up a never-ending strife in the midst of liquid fire, boiling water, and burning stones. After the Northmen had heard this report, some years passed before anyone cared to venture upon another visit to a country of which such an alarming character could be given; but when men began to feel the weight of Harald's harsh rule in Norway, they remembered that Floki's companions had not thought so badly of it as he did. Some of the old vikingar then declared that any land must be better than the kingdom over which a Harald Haarfager ruled, while many of the poorer men in Norway said that they did not care for the mountain giants, if only they might reach a spot where neither king nor jarl could have power over them. So all who were able to go, set sail in search of this free land in the far north of which they knew so little.

One of the most important of the expeditions fitted out about this time was that headed by Ingolf the son of a Norwegian Jarl who had slain his foe in a deadly combat known as a "holmgang,"[1] and who, finding that King Harald meant to punish him according to the laws, embarked with all his family and household slaves, and reached Iceland late in the autumn of the year 874. When he caught sight of the land he threw into the sea the consecrated posts of his Norwegian house which he had brought with him, vowing that he would make his home wherever the waves and winds should cast them ashore. They were however drifted away, and for three years Ingolf, attended by his slaves, continued to seek for them, until at length the sacred door-posts were found in a bay on the south-west of the island, where he fixed his abode, and began to build houses on the spot which is now known as Reykiavik, and has always been the chief town of Iceland. Ingolf may thus rank as the first settler on the island, but he was soon followed by so many other Norwegians of noble birth, that in the course of a few years all the habitable parts of Iceland had been peopled by them and their followers, and the usages and laws, as well as the religion and language of the old country, had been carried to this new colony.

Northern Customs.—Among the many old sagas of Norway there is one called the Eyrbyggja Saga, to which we will now refer on account of the light thrown on northern customs in the story of the Jarl Thorolf-Mostrar-Skegg when he went to Iceland after having been outlawed, in 880, by King Harald because he had refused to give up to the king's officer his kinsman Björn, who had been guilty of piracy. It appears that Thorolf, who acted according to the usages practised in such cases by all great Norwegian settlers, carried with him—

---

[1] *Holmgang* meant a fight on an island (*Holm*), and this mode of fighting was one of the most fatal practised by the Northmen. When two men wanted to settle a quarrel by fighting, it was the custom in the Scandinavian lands for them to go to some small and deserted island where they might be free from interruption, and they often fought with such fury that both died from the wounds which they had given each other. Thus a *holmgang* came to be looked upon as the fiercest of all single combats.

when he sailed from Norway with his family and slaves—the image of the god Thor and the earth on which it had stood, together with the greater part of the wood-work of the temple in which he had worshipped in his home. Many friends followed him, and when the vessels drew near to the coasts of Iceland, Thorolf as pontiff, or chief priest of all who had come with him, threw into the sea the columns of the temple on which the image of Thor was carved, and following these sacred objects they entered a bay which from its breadth he called "Breida-Fjord." Here Thorolf landed and took formal possession of the country in the usual manner, which was by walking with a burning fire-brand in his hands round the lands he meant to occupy, and setting fire to the grass along the boundary line. He then built a large house with a temple near it to receive the sacred columns, together with Thor's image and the consecrated earth that he had brought from Norway. In the middle of the temple was a sanctuary or altar, on which was placed a silver ring two pounds in weight, which was worn by the pontiff at all public meetings of the people of his district, and used to give solemnity to an oath. So sacred was this practice held, that the person who perjured himself after swearing upon Thor's ring was looked upon by the Northmen as the vilest of men.

When Thorolf had provided the temple with these sacred objects and with the basins, knives, and other instruments used for making the sacrifices, he prepared niches all round the building for the images of any other northern gods that the people might wish to set up for worship. Next he caused the space around the temple to be enclosed by rows of stones to prepare it for the annual " Herjar-Thing " (the assise), or " assembly of the chiefs," which according to the old northern usage should be held in the open air within sight and sound of the sacrifices. The ground on which the members of the Thing held these meetings was considered as sacred as that on which the temple stood, and was not to be defiled by the shedding of blood in anger nor trodden by the feet of men carrying arms. In the middle of the enclosure one spot was raised higher than the rest, where the jurors and witnesses were to stand forth before a trial began and to take a solemn oath in the presence of all the people that they would decide and speak according to truth, adding "so help me Freje, Njord, Thor, and the All-mighty As (Odin)."[1]

Thorolf divides Iceland.—When Thorolf had thus prepared all things, in order that religion and the laws might be observed in the new country, he divided the colony into three districts which owned him for head pontiff, but were ruled over by separate chiefs, each of whom within his own limits acted much the same as Thorolf had done in regard to his larger share of the island. And the mode of government which he thus set up at his first landing was long followed, and may in the present day still be traced in some matters regarding the administration of the laws in Iceland.

In the space of sixty years after Thorolf's coming to Iceland, all parts of the island that could be dwelt in were occupied by settlers from Norway, in spite of what King Harald Haarfager had tried to do to prevent his subjects leaving the kingdom to settle in this remote and free colony. After a time when the pontiff-chiefs found the inconvenience of having no common high court of law to which they could appeal in case of disputes, they determined to remedy the evil the best way they could. They therefore agreed to trust to the wisdom of one man for whom they all felt respect, and accordingly they applied to Ulfljot, a wise and honest chieftain, and begged him, as he valued the peace and happiness of Iceland, to return to Norway and learn from the wise lawgivers of the old country what were the laws and usages of their forefathers. Ulfljot accepted the charge, and although he was then sixty years of age, he left his home and family and undertook the voyage to Norway,

---

[1] The *Æsir* (sing. *As*, God,) were fabled to have lived in "Asgaard" (Heaven), from whence they crossed the bridge "Bifrost" (Rainbow) to reach "Midgaard" (the Earth). Beyond the sea which encircled Midgaard lay "Jötunheim" or the Giant's Dwelling-place. The Æsir were happy and at peace till they made acquaintance with the giants and giantesses of Jötunheim, when their golden age passed away. Odin cast his spear out in the midst of the world and war began. The Æsir fought with the Vaner (Wends), but finding them too strong to be subdued, they made peace with them and took Njord and his son Freje to be their equals in Asgaard, the former to rule over the sea and the winds, and the latter over peace and plenty.

where he remained from the year 925 till 928. After spending those three years in the study of the laws and in writing down all that Thorleif the Wise, a man skilled in ancient law, could teach him, he came back to Iceland and began to prepare a code of laws, which were read out to the people at an "All-Thing," or general parliament, and approved of by them.

These events happened in the time of the great King Æthelstan, grandson of King Alfred, of whose reign we read so many interesting particulars in the "Old English History." We know, however, little or nothing now of the laws collected by Ulfljot, nor of those drawn up by Thorleif the Wise, and used by Æthelstan's foster-son, King Hakon the Good, in the formation of the ancient code long followed in Norway, and called the Gule-laws, from the Thing at which they were first made public.

For three hundred years after its settlement Iceland was a republic, but it was not a peaceful state, and both before and after the introduction of Christianity the chiefs carried on the most deadly and cruel wars against each other, and few men living on the island were left to enjoy what they owned in quiet. This colony had been settled by men who would not bear one master nor respect the rank of king or jarl, but within a few generations the descendants of those very men were troubled by many masters, and saw their equals striving for more power than any king or jarl in the old country had ever used. For the present, however, we must leave the history of Iceland and return to that of Norway.

PART II.

SWEDEN AND NORWAY.

Hakon, Æthelstan's Foster-son.—On the death of Harald Haarfager in 936, his eldest son, the cruel Erik, " Blod-öxe," or Blood-oxe, so called from his love of shedding blood, began to govern even more harshly than he had done during the three years that he had ruled in his father's lifetime. The people of

Norway growing weary of his cruelty rose against him, and in 938 drove him and his equally wicked queen Gunhild with their children out of the country, and then took Hakon, Æthelstan's foster-son, by the advice of his uncle Sigurd, to be their king. Erik escaped to England, where he offered to become the vassal of Æthelstan, and soon afterwards in return for the services which he rendered the king, he was made ruler over the Danish province of Northumbria, and continued in that office till his death a few years later. Hakon, in the meanwhile, ruled justly over Norway, and besides the Gule-laws of which we have spoken, he collected several other codes to regulate the duties of defending the country and the trading business of his kingdom, and did many other things for the welfare of his people.

His subjects were very grateful to him for all he had done, except in regard to his attempts to put down the old religion, and when he began to urge them to become Christians, the "Bonder," or peasants, came forward at the great annual Thing and declared that they would not forsake the gods who had watched over their fathers through so many ages, adding that unless King Hakon would conduct the services of religion as other kings of Norway had done, they would no longer pay him the duty of subjects. Threats and murmurs resounded on all sides against the king when he was seen to hesitate, and Hakon would probably have lost his crown, had not his uncle Sigurd Jarl, whose wisdom and prudence are praised in the sagas, turned aside the anger of the people. Putting on the robes of a pontiff, which his rank entitled him to wear, Sigurd stepped into the midst of the assembly and said that the king had ordered him to officiate that day in his place, and on that account only had hesitated when the people appealed to him. Then after consecrating the great drinking horn of sacrifice to Odin as the All-Fadir, he held it towards Hakon, standing between him and the assembled people in such a manner as to screen him from notice while he drained the cup. Some persons had seen, however, that the king made the sign of the cross before he drank, and when they told the rest of the people what they had observed, a great tumult arose, and the jarls, priests, and peasants agreed in saying that they would have no Christian for their king. Then Sigurd again came forward, and in a loud voice proclaimed that his nephew King Hakon was a faithful believer in Thor, and that when he was supposed to be making the sign of the Christian's cross, he was only making the sign of the god's mallet.[1] His words, for that once, turned away the suspicions of the people, while Hakon on his side avoided, for a time, all further cause of offence, and even joined in a solemn feast in which all partook of the liver of a horse which had been sacrificed to Odin. This was looked upon as a religious rite, and Hakon repenting of his duplicity in regard to the sacrifices, and of his weakness in having taken part in such a heathen practice, retired for a year to his country house at Mære, to devote himself to acts of penitence; but while he thus withdrew from the management of public affairs his kingdom was being harassed by invasion.

Twice in the course of a few years Norway was invaded by a large fleet of Danish ships which had been sent by Harald Blaatand of Denmark to help the sons of the former Norwegian king, Erik Blod-öxe, to get the crown for themselves. The Norwegians who had suffered greatly under the rule of Erik refused to allow his sons to land, and drove back the ships of the invaders on their first appearance. But when Erik's widow came again with a Danish fleet in 963, King Hakon was surprised and defeated before an army could be collected to repel the enemy, and feeling himself mortally wounded, he sent for his nephews and entreated them to spare all further bloodshed and rule justly in his place. When asked if he wished his body to be sent to England to be buried, Hakon answered, "As a heathen have I lived, and therefore I may not be buried as a Christian."

Olaf Trygvasson.—After the death of Hakon Ethelstan-fostre, Norway for more than half a century endured constant trouble under the rule of Erik Blod-öxe's son, Erik Graafell, and that of Hakon Jarl, the son of King Hakon's uncle, Sigurd, who after securing the throne by the help of the Danish king, Harald Blaatand, in whose name he pretended to rule, threw off the yoke and kept the kingdom for himself. When Hakon Jarl died in 995, Norway was ruled for a few years by Olaf Tryg-

---

[1] Thor's mallet or hammer was the emblem used to give sanctity to oaths and to the vows of marriage, bride and bridegroom either swearing on a hammer, or making the sign of the form of the hammer, which was not unlike that of our Latin cross.

vasson who had taken part with Svend Tveskœg of Denmark in invading England in 994. This prince, who was one of the most daring vikingar of his times, had in the course of his viking visited the coasts of Gaul and Italy, and while he was in the south of Europe he had been signed with the cross, and had soon afterwards renounced paganism. This became the cause of ill-will between Svend and himself, and when Olaf still further offended the Danish king by marrying his sister Thyra against his wishes after she had been divorced by her husband, Prince Burislav of the Wends, a deadly feud sprang up between them. Svend raised a war against his brother-in-law, and Olaf, forsaken by most of his subjects, who were enraged at his attempts to force Christianity upon them, was defeated in a great sea-battle at Svold, on the Pomeranian coast. When the fight was over and all seemed lost, Olaf to escape falling into the hands of his foes sprang overboard in full armour, and was seen no more; but the people of Norway would not believe in his death, thinking that he had escaped and wandered as a pilgrim to the Holy Land, where he lived for many years devoted to works of piety. His widow Thyra starved herself to death, refusing to survive her well-loved Olaf; and his victors, Svend Tveskœg of Denmark, Olaf, the Lap-King of Sweden, and Erik and Svend, the sons of Hakon Jarl, parted his kingdom between them. These princes ruled justly for some years till their power was destroyed by the many great jarls who had grown jealous of them.

Olaf the Saint.—In 1015 Olaf, the son of Harald Grœnske, who was known in later times as "the Saint," freed Norway from her many rulers, and induced the Norwegians to accept Christianity; but the harsh manner in which he forced the new religion upon his people led in the year 1030 to the loss, not only of his crown, but of his life. Knud the Great of Denmark, who wanted to add Norway to his other states, had had a share in bringing about the defeat of Olaf, by the help which he gave to the rebel pagans in the kingdom. The Norwegian king was killed while giving battle to a large body of peasants at Stiklestad in Verdal, and as soon as Knud learnt that Olaf had been slain he sent his own son Svend, a lad of fifteen, to rule in his name as King of Norway. Svend's youth and folly, however, soon made the people of Norway wish their own king back amongst them, for Svend let himself be ruled by bad counsels, and did not obey his father's commands that he should try to win the regard and respect of the nation. It was soon whispered abroad that the corpse of the slain Olaf was working miracles, and these reports took such hold of the minds of the people, that they sent for Olaf's son, Magnus, to be their king, hoping thus to make what amends they could for their sin against the father. In the meanwhile Olaf's body was carefully moved from the battle-field at Stiklestad, where a peasant had buried it after the fight, and carried to the cathedral church at Nidaros, the present town of Throndhjem (Drontheim). Here the remains were laid in a tomb, which then, and for many ages afterwards, was visited by pilgrims from all parts of the Scandinavian lands, in the belief that great miracles were wrought at the spot.[1]

When young Prince Magnus returned from the court of his uncle, Jaroslav Duke of Russia, the Norwegians received him with joy, and Svend of Denmark was forced to leave the kingdom. This was the Magnus who became King of Denmark in 1042 on the death of Knud's son Harthaknud, and who showed great kindness to Knud's nephew, Svend Estridsen, leaving him to rule over the Danish kingdom in his name. As we have read in a former chapter,[2] Magnus having met with a poor return for his friendship, had to go to war with the ungrateful Svend, and was killed in a battle against him near Halsted in the year 1047, after having, with his last breath, begged his people to help Svend to become King of Denmark, while the Danes being

---

[1] St. Olaf was believed by the people of the North in those early times to have possessed many of the powers which had been ascribed to the god Thor, and to have been gifted with his bodily strength and his red beard. St. Olaf's shrine of silver, weighing 3,200 ounces, and inlaid with precious stones, was for many ages carefully preserved at Throndhjem, and carried by sixty men in solemn procession on the Saint's festival, July 29, on the election of a king of Norway, or other great occasions. At length it was seized by the Danes and carried away, and when the Swedes in our Queen Elizabeth's time made war on Denmark and Norway, and took the town of Throndhjem, they found no relics of the Saint but his helmet and spurs. These they took and brought to Stockholm, where they are still preserved in the church of St. Nicholas.

[2] See Chap. iv., p. 57.

willing to receive him, Svend secured the Danish crown for himself through the generous conduct of his former rival.

Sweden.—Before we close this chapter, and begin the story of Svend's reign in Denmark, we must try to get some idea of what had been passing in Sweden during the time that the seamen of Norway and Denmark were spreading themselves far and wide over hitherto unknown lands. There is not much to learn in regard to the Swedish people of old on account of the quarrels between the Svea and the Göta, and the confused state of public affairs. We know, however, that the former people were for some ages ruled over by descendants of Ragnar Lodbrog's son or grandson, Björn Jernside (Ironsides), amongst whom the most noteworthy was Erik Sejrsœl, or the Victorious, who began to reign in the middle of the tenth century, and died in the year 993. This prince in 983 defeated his nephew, Styrbjörn, and a great number of vikingar from the pagan brotherhood of Jomsborg, in a three-days' fight at Fyrisval off the Swedish coast. From that time till his death he is said to have ruled in peace over Sweden, and even at one time to have had Denmark under his power and to have driven the Danish King Svend Tveskœg out of his kingdom. The truth of this account seems very doubtful, but the story is recorded by the writer, Adam of Bremen, who was the friend and scribe of King Svend Estridsen of Denmark. Erik Sejersœl, at his death in 993, left one son Olaf, known as the "Lap-king," because he was an infant in arms when he received the homage of the people. The mother of this young prince was Sigrid, called "Storaade," or the Proud, who after the death of King Erik became the wife of Svend Tveskœg of Denmark, for whom she secured considerable power in Sweden during the childhood of her son, the little King Olaf.

Olaf the Lap-King.—Olaf the Lap-King, who reigned from 993 to 1024, was the first Christian King of Sweden, and is believed to have received baptism about the year 1000. He had been instructed in Christianity by Siegfred, an Englishman who may be called the second apostle of the North. This good man devoted a long life to the work of converting the pagan Swedes, and died at a great age, among the people of Småland, with whom he had begun his labours. But while the Lap-king became a Christian, most of his people remained heathens, and although they allowed Olaf to erect a bishopric at Skara—the mother-see of the North—they forced him to leave them free to follow their own religion, in return for which they gave him the choice of any district in Sweden in which he liked to build Christian churches. He made choice of West Gothland, which thenceforth continued to be the chief seat of Christianity, while "Svithjód," the lands of the Svea, would not receive Christian teachers within their boundaries, or take Christian kings for their rulers for more than a century later.

Olaf the Lap-King's reign was troubled by constant quarrels with Norway, towards whose king, Olaf the Saint, he had borne ill-will since the latter had invaded the coasts of Sweden in the course of a viking cruise. The Swedish peasants of that age had great power in the state, and were not backward in using it; for when the king refused their request that he should make peace with Norway and give his daughter in marriage to the young Norwegian King Olaf, they threatened to dethrone him. In a long speech before the Thing at Uppsala a great Lagman or law-explainer, called Thorgny, set before the king what he was to do, and ended by informing him that, unless he made his acts conform to the wishes of his people, they would do by him what their forefathers had done when five of their kings had, like him, been puffed up with pride and tried to follow their own evil wishes. As these kings had been publicly drowned in a deep morass Olaf had no wish to bring a similar fate upon himself, and he, therefore, in the presence of all the men of the Thing, promised that he would rule his actions by their wishes: "For such," he added, "has ever been the custom with the kings of the Svea." But in spite of his promises Olaf soon afterwards gave his daughter in marriage to the Russian Grand Duke, Jaroslav of Novogorod, who was a near kinsman of his, and this act would certainly have cost him his crown had not the Svea, in their jealousy of the men of Gothland, taken their king's part when the Göta proposed in the year 1022 to put him aside. They declared that as the Göta had always been second to the Svea in olden times, they would not allow them to put themselves first in deciding who should be king over them. The Göta yielded, and the end of the dispute was that Olaf remained king, and his son Anund was made joint ruler with him. After the death of Anund, his brother, Edmund Gammal, or the Old, reigned in Sweden, and with him ended the race of the Uppsala kings, who through Sigurd Ring traced their descent to Odin's pontiff Njord. Edmund was a bad king, who let the Christians be persecuted in the land, and who is believed to have died after a short reign about the year 1055, although the exact date is not known.

PART III.

NORTHERN DISCOVERIES.

Erik the Red.—During the last half of the tenth century, when the people of Norway were struggling to resist Christianity, and their kings were striving to put down the old pagan faith of the country, restless men continued, as they had done under Harald Haarfager, to seek new homes in which they might worship as they liked, and escape falling under the power of the laws. Then it was that a Norwegian, known as Erik "Raudi," or the Red, son of Thorwald Jarl, having been made an outlaw both in Norway and in Iceland on account of a murder of which he had been guilty, set sail in search of some quiet spot, where he might do what pleased him without having to fear the consequences of his acts.

In the course of his cruising in the northern seas, he came to a land which he named "Greenland," in the hope perhaps of making others believe that it was a fruitful country. This discovery of his was made in 983, during the time of our king Æthelred the Unready, and a few years later he induced a number of Icelanders, who like him were tired of living in a land where laws were enforced, to join him in the new country, and thus Greenland was settled by people from Norway and Iceland. Erik Raudi, or the Red, had one son Leif, who in early youth had served under King Olaf Trygvasson and gone with him to Gaul and Italy, and after sharing in many of the daring adventures of the Norwegian prince, had returned with him to Norway and became a Christian. On the death of the king, Leif determined to convert his father's new colony, and in the year 1000 he came back to Greenland, bringing with him several monks, who at once began to baptise the people, till soon there was not a pagan left among them.

This colony of Greenland had a very strange and sad fate, of which we must speak now, although the history of its troubles really belongs to a much later period. Unlike its sister colony, Iceland, it was after a time wholly destroyed, and so thoroughly lost sight of that at the present day it is a matter of doubt whether the settlements made by Erik and his son Leif were on the east or the west coasts of Greenland. It is, however, believed that both the eastern and western shores were early settled, and that they continued to be occupied by a flourishing colony till near the middle of the fourteenth century. Then in the reign of our Edward III., the plague known as the "Black Death," which had been raging for many years in every part of Northern Europe, reached Greenland, and nearly killed all the people. The few persons who escaped the ravages of this frightful disease were soon afterwards cut off by some hostile wild natives, who, taking advantage of their small numbers, fell upon them and killed them. It is supposed that the settlements on the east coasts, known as the "Oestre Bygd," were not quite destroyed at the time that those of the "Vestre Bygd" were cut off, but before the reign of our Edward IV. (in 1460) they too had ceased to exist. For ages afterwards no one made any attempt to explore the coasts on which these old northern settlers had met with so sad an end, but in the early part of last century, when George I. was King of England, a Norwegian clergyman, called Hans Egede, obtained ships and money from the Danish king, Frederick IV., to proceed to Greenland in order that he might try to convert the native Greenlanders, who had been neglected by the Mother-Country since the days of the Black Death of 1350. Hans Egede and his wife Gertude laboured with zeal to convert and civilize the poor neglected natives from the time of their landing in Greenland, in 1721, till the death of Hans in 1736, when their son Paul Egede took up the good work that they had begun.

Since that time the Danes have had settlements in the country, and have opened factories and mission-houses for the benefit of these remote colonies.

Leif's Discoveries.—We must now go back to Leif, who after having seen a church established in Greenland and a bishop appointed to take charge of it, began to wish for some new excitement elsewhere. This soon offered itself to him in the prospect of finding a new land as his father Erik the Red had done, when he discovered Greenland. It happened that in the year 1003 an Icelander, Bjarne, while sailing in search of his father who had gone on a trading voyage to Greenland, was carried far away to the west and south, till he reached a flat country so thickly covered with wood, that he felt certain from the descriptions he had heard of Greenland, it could not be the land of which he was in search. He therefore sailed in a different direction and came safely to Greenland, where he spoke to the settlers of the strange land he had seen. On hearing these accounts Leif became impatient to visit the new country, and buying Bjarne's ship he manned it with thirty-five good seamen, and begged his father Erik to take the command of it. Erik the Red agreed to accompany his son, but being an old man by that time and feeble, he went to the place of embarkation on horseback, when, his horse stumbling, he regarded it as a bad omen and declined to go on board, saying, "I do not believe it is given to me to discover more lands, and here I will abide."

Leif then set sail without his father, and following the course which Bjarne had taken, he reached after a time a long line of coast, at many parts of which he and his men landed, and gathered delicious berries and other fruits, which were unknown to some of them, but which seemed to Leif very like the fruits he had eaten in the south of Europe when serving under Olaf Trygvasson. One day when Leif and some of his men had landed on the unknown coast, he lost sight of his father's servant Tyrker, who was a German. Leif sought him for a long time in the woods, and at length found him gathering bright purple and red bunches of fruit, which the man seemed overjoyed to have found. In his excitement he had forgotten the northern tongue, which he had long used, and began to speak in his own South-German language, and it was some time before he could make his master and his companions understand that he had found grapes, of which in his native country men made wine.

The Northmen spent the winter in this district, which Leif had named "Vinland den Gode," or "Wine-land the Good," and which is believed to have been the present state of Rhode Island, and after cruising along the coasts further south, they returned to Greenland and told their friends of all the strange lands they had seen. This happened about the year 1003, or 1004, and during the next few years Leif and his brothers, Thorwald and Thorstein, made several voyages to the same shores, with the view of settling in Vinland or in one of the many other pleasant spots which they had seen in the far-west. But the settlements which the Northmen attempted to make on those coast-lands, which we know from their position must have been in the Atlantic states of North America, were too small to resist the attacks of the natives, and thus they were one by one cut off and the leaders killed. Leif died in Greenland amongst his own kindred, but Thorwald and Thorstein, and several other great chiefs were early cut down in hand-to-hand fights with the natives, whom the Northmen called "Skrælingar" or dwarfs, and compared to the savages whom they and their fathers had found in Greenland.

The latest notice of Vinland is to be found in the "Eyrbyggia Saga," where it is related that, in the last years of the reign of Olaf the Saint of Norway, who died in 1030, an Icelander named Gudleif, in making a trading voyage to Iceland, was driven far to the south and west till he reached a land where he saw dark-skinned natives on the shore. These men came in great numbers to attack the strangers, and, after seizing them, carried them bound into the country. Here they were met by an old, light-haired chief of tall and commanding stature, who, spoke to Gudleif in Icelandic, and told him that he and his companions might return to their ships, but that if they valued their lives they would make no delay, as the natives were cruel to strangers. He refused to tell his name, but he asked tidings of Snorre Gode, one of the leading men of Iceland, and begged that Gudleif would carry back with him a gold ring for Snorre's sister Thurida and a sword for her son. When Gudleif returned with these gifts, and told the people of Iceland what had befallen him, it was believed by them that the fair-skinned man in Vinland was Björn, a famous Skald, who had loved Thurida in her youth, and who had never been heard of since he had sailed from Iceland in the year 998.

After Gudleif returned in 1030 from his voyage to the farwest, no settlement of the Northmen is known to have been again attempted, although a Saxon priest is said to have sailed from Iceland in 1059 to convert the heathens of Vinland, but he too was murdered by the natives. For nearly four centuries and a half the western world was again wrapped in darkness, until in 1492 the great Genoese seaman, Christopher Columbus, re-opened the ocean-road to its vast territories, and for the first time made them known to the nations of the old eastern world in which we live.

CHAPTER VII.

THE ESTRIDSENS.

The story of Svend Estridsen, the father of all later rulers of Denmark—His wars with Harald Hardraade, King of Norway, called Denmark's Blight—Harald's invasion of England, his death on the field of battle—Svend's message to William the Conqueror, demanding homage from him—The fate of Svend's hostile fleet—Svend's learning; his love of learned men; his friendship for Adam, Canon of Bremen; his intimacy with the English churchman, William, Bishop of Roeskilde—Svend's act of murder—William's way of turning him out of church; Svend's penitence—Why Svend was called "Estridsen"; how he is the ancestor of the Queen as well as of the Princess of Wales—Svend Estridsen the great great forefather of our kings—Svend's death.—The succession of five of his fourteen sons—The reign of Harald Hejn or Whetstone, and why he got that name—The character of his successor Knud, known as the Saint; how he favoured the clergy and oppressed the laity; what came of his conduct—His murder and the fate of his only son Karl—The laws of succession in Denmark—Olaf-Hunger; the troubles of his short reign—Erik Ejegod succeeds; his beauty and great skill in arts and exercises—The canonization of Saint Knud—Erik and his Queen Botilda go to the Holy Land, and die on the way—Niels, the last of the five king-brothers, comes to the throne on the death of Erik—Knud Lavard; his murder by prince Magnus—The vengeance taken by Knud's brother—Magnus is slain, and King Niels takes refuge in Slesvig, where he is killed by Knud's Guild-brothers, about sixty years after the death of Svend Estridsen, his father.

PART I.

SVEND ESTRIDSEN, THE FATHER OF DANISH KINGS.

Svend Estridsen, 1047-1076.—WE have seen how King Magnus the Good did his best before his death to secure to Svend the crown of Denmark; but although in that respect Svend's fortune was better than he had any right to expect, he was not without plenty of troubles. In the first place, King Harald of Norway, the uncle and successor of Magnus, would not leave him at peace, and whenever the Wends and other pagan tribes of the Baltic began to attack one province in Denmark, the King of Norway was sure to fall upon some other part of the kingdom, and thus King Svend was kept in a constant state of unquiet. Once he only saved his life after a lost battle by putting on the dress of a herdsman, and staying in hiding with a peasant called Karl, whose wife not knowing as her husband did the rank of the stranger, roughly told him that she never had seen a man so clumsy and ugly as he was. Although the king was obliged to bear the insult he did not forget it, and some years later when he gave the peasant a large farm in Sjœlland, he forbade him ever to bring his wife there.

For seventeen years after the death of Magnus, Harald returned every summer with his fleet to harass the poor Danes, who in their distress called him the " Lightning of the North," " the Blight of the Danish islands ;" and happy they were when at last Harald, wishing to conquer England and not caring to leave a foe so near home, made peace with Svend in 1064. The fate of King Harald Haardrade, who was defeated and slain by the English at the Battle of Stamford Bridge in 1066, did not deter Svend from following in his steps, and making an attempt to invade and conquer England in the year 1069. First he sent, in 1067, to William the Conqueror to demand homage and tribute from him, and to tell him that he, Svend, as the nephew and heir of Knud the Great, was by right of heritage king of England. William the Conqueror, who had not been many months on the English throne when this message came to him, showed no anger, but returned greetings and handsome gifts to his "friend and cousin," King Svend of Denmark. But when, two years later, Svend despatched a fleet of 240 ships, under the command of his sons, Harald and Knud, to invade England, William very soon proved he was master of his kingdom, and the young princes were forced to return to Denmark without having done any of the great deeds that had been expected of them. It was believed that Svend's brother, Asbjörn, to whose care they had been entrusted by their father, had been bought over to betray and deceive them, and when he came back to Sjœlland with only a remnant of the great fleet, the king met him in anger, and ordered him to leave the country and never more set his foot in Denmark; and so ended this last of all Danish attacks upon England.

Svend's Character.—Svend was not a very good man, but he was an able ruler, and learned for the times in which he lived; for he was well acquainted with Church history, and spoke several languages, amongst others Latin, in which he kept up a correspondence with the great Hildebrand, afterwards known as Pope Gregory VII. But although he was a devout churchman and caused several bishops' sees to be founded in Denmark, he would not obey his friend the Pope when he wrote to require that he should hold his kingdom as a dependency on the Court of Rome. Unlike his father, Jarl Ulf, or his uncle, King Knud, Svend Estridsen is said to have been wanting in good-looks and bodily strength, and to have been a great coward; and he seems to have chosen his friends, not amongst the nobles of his court, but among learned churchmen, for whose pursuits he had more taste than for those of the bold knights and warriors of his time. Svend's friendship for the scholarly Adam, canon of the Bremen Cathedral, has proved of great value to later ages, for by the King's favour this churchman was able to write down in his *Chronicle*[1] many things of interest connected with the history of Svend's forefathers, and to inform us of many particulars in regard to the habits and customs of the Danes in those times, which we should not have otherwise known.

Another of Svend's intimate friends was Bishop William, or Vilhelm, as the Danish writers call him, an English monk to whom the King had given the see of Roeskilde, and whose sturdy independence and firmness often put his sovereign's friendship to a severe test, as we shall see from the following account of the manner in which he is known to have behaved to him. It happened that once on a New Year's Eve, when the king's servants had been making merry in the palace-

---

[1] Adam of Bremen wrote down in the Bremen Chronicle for his bishop, all that King Svend told him of Denmark. His account of the kingdom shows the misery to which the pagan pirates had brought the land. "In Jutland," he says, "men dare not live near the sea-coasts for fear of sea-rovers; and they only till those lands which lie inland, or far up streams."

hall of Roeskilde, and drinking much more than they ought, some among them forgot the respect they owed to their royal master, and began talking of his bad luck and want of courage in battle. Svend overhearing their words, in which there was a great amount of truth, grew very angry, and on pretence that he had reason to suspect treason gave orders for these unwise jokers to be seized and killed, and in accordance with these commands they were cut down on the New Year's Day, while they were at matins in the same church in which his own father, Jarl Ulf, had been slain.

Somewhat later in the morning, Svend, clothed in his royal robes, came into the church and was about to enter the chancel when Bishop Vilhelm, who was preparing to celebrate high mass, barred his entrance. The king tried to push on, but the prelate thrust him back with the end of his crozier and called him a murderer, unworthy to enter a church which he had stained with the blood of his fellow-creatures. The courtiers on hearing Bishop Vilhelm's angry words rushed upon him with drawn swords; but the king, struck by the truth of his reproaches, left the church, and returning to the palace changed his royal robes for the dress of a penitent. He then re-entered the church porch, where, bare-headed and barefooted, he waited till the bishop came to receive his confession and give him absolution. After this Svend came for the third time to the church door, but on this last occasion he again wore his mantle of state and his crown, and thus clothed was led to the altar, when the *Te Deum* was sung and the services of the church completed. Three days afterwards Svend, in the presence of a large number of people, rose and drew near the altar of the church in which mass was being performed. Begging that those present would keep silence and listen to his words, he confessed his sin of causing the death of his servants, and as a proof of his penitence, made an offering to the church of half a *harde* or Hundred of land. This district is said to have included the ground on which stands Copenhagen, the present capital of Denmark, with all its suburbs, and the adjoining little island of Amak. About a hundred years later, these lands were given by Axel, known as Absalon, the warlike bishop of Sjælland of those times, to his king, Valdemar I., and *Ab-*

borg, as the place had been called while it had served as a castle for defending the country against the attacks of sea-robbers, soon became known as the Merchant-haven, or " Kjobenhavn," which we translate *Copenhagen*.

Svend's name "Estridsen."—Svend, who is known in Danish history as Svend Estridsen, or the son of Estrid, was so called in respect to the higher rank of his mother, who was sister of Knud the Great. If he had followed the usual practice of the Northmen and taken the first name of his father Ulf with the addition of *sen*, meaning son, he would be known as Svend " Ulfsen."[1] The Jarl Ulf was nearly related to the royal family of Norway, and therefore his son Svend could boast of a very high descent through both his parents. In speaking of the Great Knud's nephew, Svend Estridsen, we must not forget that our Queen, as well as the present King of Denmark, and therefore the Prince of Wales as well as the Princess of Wales, can claim this king as their common ancestor, and through him may trace their descent back to Gorm the Old. Queen Victoria is descended in a direct line from King James I. of England and VI. of Scotland and his Queen, Anne daughter of King Frederick II. of Denmark, and the latter king, like all the other princes of the house of Oldenburg, traced his descent through the female line back to Svend Estridsen, whose mother Estrid was great-grand-daughter of Gorm. Hence in reading the history of Svend Estridsen and his descendants we must bear in mind that we are reading the history of the common ancestors of the royal families of Great Britain and of Denmark. During three hundred years after the death of Svend Estridsen the Danish crown was worn by princes descended from him in the direct male line, but in 1375, when Valdemar III. " Atterdag " died, leaving no sons, this long line of descent was broken, although the Danish throne was occupied till the middle of the next century by the sons or grandsons of that king's daughters. In 1448 the princes of the house of Oldenburg, who have since then ruled

---

[1] The Swedes add *son* instead of *sen* to the father's name. Thus in Swedish Svend would be known as Ulfsson, or *Estridsson*, and not *Ulfsen* or *Estridsen*, as in Danish.

over Denmark, gained the Danish throne in right of their descent through Princess Rikissa, daughter of King Erik Glipping, and thus Denmark during the thousand years of her history has changed dynasties less frequently than almost any other country of Europe.

PART II.

SVEND ESTRIDSEN'S SONS.

Harald Hejn, 1076-1080.—When Svend Estridsen died, in 1076, he left as many as fourteen sons, and of these five were in turn kings of Denmark. Their reigns did not add much to the comfort of the Danish people, who had little but want, trouble, and war while these princes ruled over them, and as there is not much that is pleasant to tell of these five kings, we need not linger long over the story of their troubled reigns.

Svend's eldest son Harald, who ruled the kingdom of Denmark only four years, from 1076 to 1080, that is, in the time of William I. of England, was surnamed *Hejn*, or Whetstone, from his always giving way when he met with things that were hard to bear. From what we read of him we cannot suppose that his subjects were very sorry when he died and was followed on the throne by his next brother, Knud, a quick-tempered, brave and energetic young prince. This king, however, soon lost the affection of his subjects by his harshness in asking for all kinds of labour from the working classes. When they begged that he would spare them so many forced tasks, he threatened to shut up all the oak-tree forests in which the herdsmen had been used to feed their pigs, and to hinder the fishermen from following their trade in any of the Danish waters, on pretence that every fjord, sound, and bay, no less than every piece of woodland in the kingdom, belonged to him to give or withhold as he pleased. He was very severe to pirates, which in these days we should think was only right and proper, and a very good thing for all honest folks. The Danes, however, had not yet learnt to look upon piracy as anything very bad, and they were rather inclined to regard a daring sea-robber as a very grand kind of adventurer who had nothing in common with a thief on land. Thus it happened that one winter when the king went over to Bornholm, and caused one of the chief men of the island, called Orgil Ragnarsen, who had been caught in the act of robbing and boarding ships at sea, to be hanged in sight of all the islanders, the Danish people took the matter up as a grievance, and made as much clamour about it as if Knud had taken the life of an honest innocent man.

Many of Knud's acts were however very unjust, and the marked favour which he showed to the bishops, by raising them to the rank of the highest nobles in the land, gave great offence. When he tried to enforce the payment of tithes to the clergy, and threatened if the people refused he would make them give to the crown much larger sums of money, there was a general rising and tumult all over the kingdom. "Give us what fines you please," cried the angry peasants at the great meetings of the nation where the king made this demand; "we will pay anything rather than leave to our children such a burden as these tithes that you ask of us!"

The king and the bishops were greatly incensed at the spirit shown by the Danish people, who then and for a long time afterwards, were very distrustful of the clergy. The latter acted with such harshness and cruelty to all the poorer and working classes that a revolt broke out, and King Knud on his progress through his kingdom was everywhere followed by cries of hatred and anger. After treating the peasants of Jutland with much severity, he crossed over to the island of Fyen to get out of the way of their complaints; but this did not save him, for a large body of Jutlanders followed him and overtook him just as he was seeking refuge within St. Alban's Church, in the town of Odense. The citizens now joined the angry Jutlanders, and a crowd soon closed round the church, against whose doors they beat with clubs and staves and stones, calling: "Where is Knud, our God-forsaken king? Let him come forth and show himself! He has carried arms long enough against the rights and property of us Danes! It is full time we made an end of this!" After a long and fierce attack the doors burst under the blows aimed at them, and the enraged peasants rushed with noisy shoutings into the church, where King Knud, feeling that his last hour had come, was kneeling before the altar, while his brothers Benedict and Erik, at the head of a few faithful friends and serving men stood ready to defend him.

"Now King Knud I will pay you for stealing my cows!" cried one. "Take that, in return for robbing me of my oxen and my horses!" shouted another, as one by one they rushed forward and struck wildly at all persons within their reach. Benedict was cut down, and the murderers, pushing aside his body threw themselves on Knud, who without lifting a hand to defend himself, fell dead before the altar struck by a spear which had been thrown at him from a distance. His brother Erik made his escape, but seventeen of the king's servants were slain with him; and thus Knud paid with his life for the unwise eagerness he had shown in raising the power and wealth of the Church at the expense of the laity. The clergy proved their grateful sense of his efforts in their favour by getting the Pope to have him counted as a saint, and they took such pains to make the people believe that miracles were done through his help, that by degrees he came to be honoured as the patron saint of Denmark.[1]

King Knud's only son, Karl, met with a similar fate as his father when he was about the same age. His widowed mother, Queen Adela, had fled from Denmark as soon as she heard of her husband's murder, and had carried the little prince, who was then a boy of three years of age, with her to Bruges, to the court of her brother Count Robert of Flanders. In the course of time the Danish prince was allowed to succeed his uncle as Count of Flanders, where he was known as Charles the Dane, and ruled from 1119 till 1127 in the time of our Henry I.; but having like his father, King Knud, shown too much favour to the clergy and been too strict and harsh to his people, they rose against him, and following him in anger to the church of Our Lady at Bruges, where he had taken refuge, they slew him before the altar.

[1] In the year 1101, Knud was canonized, and his remains were laid within a splendid shrine and kept in St. Knud's church in Odense (Fyen). Soon afterwards guilds or brotherhoods were established in his honour and placed under his protection. These guilds had women as well as men among their members, and at first they were formed only for purposes of religion and charity, but by degrees the brothers and sisters also met together at feasts and merry-makings, which were in general held in honour of the anniversary of the foundation of their society.

PART III.

LAWS OF DENMARK.

Olaf-Hunger, 1086–1095.—According to the old laws of Denmark, the people had the right to choose their kings, and it was usual, although it does not appear that it was necessary, for them to make their choice among the sons, brothers, or nearest male heirs of the former king. They in most cases gave the crown to the next heir, but the eldest son of the sovereign had no right whatever to take the title of king on the death of his father unless the people at the Thing, or National Parliament, had given a promise beforehand that they would have him for their ruler. When Knud was murdered no one seemed to think of choosing his little son, who with his mother was hurrying out of Denmark, and the people at once offered the crown to Knud's brother, Prince Olaf. It is very likely that the murderers of the late king were the more anxious to give the crown to Olaf, because he had once joined the rebels against Knud and his bishops, and on that account had been seized by his brother and forced to leave the country. He had then taken refuge amongst his wife's friends in Flanders, or, as some say, he had been sent to Bruges in chains, and kept a close prisoner by Knud's orders; and he now found great trouble in getting back to Denmark, for Count Robert of Flanders, the uncle of little Prince Karl, refused to release him, but at last the Danes paid a heavy ransom for him, and he was thus enabled to return to his own country.[1]

Olaf's reign, which is counted from Knud's murder in 1086, and lasted till 1095, was a very unhappy one on account

---

[1] The right of choosing a king rested almost wholly at this time in Denmark with the noble-free men and the Bonder, or peasant-free men. The nobles had no titles in Denmark till more than 600 years later. The clergy only by degrees and very slowly gained a voice at the great National Things, and the burgher-class cannot be said to have existed till after this period, for they owed their rise to the formation of guilds of trade, which are not heard of in Danish history till after the time of St. Knud.

of the grievous famine which troubled the land all the years he ruled, and which gained for him the unpleasant surname of "*Hunger.*" The bishops tried to persuade the people that the want and distress in the country were sent direct from God to plague the land on account of the murder of the pious King Knud, and that other kingdoms were not thus cursed. And they and their clergy in their sermons told the Danes that while "for seven heavy years they had seen dry springs and hot summers burn up the grain and straw, and wet autumns hinder the corn from ripening, the Christians of other lands had overflowing crops and rich and early harvests." But these statements were not true, for the real fact was that England, Germany, France, and Italy were at that time visited by the same bad seasons, during which men and beasts died of want and disease; towns and villages were flooded with the overflowing of streams and lakes; and domestic animals and birds, finding the houses deserted and their masters unable to give them food, betook themselves to the woods and moors and grew wild again.

Had Olaf done his best to store up the grain and fruits of the earth, to drain his lands, and keep his people active and sober, he might have saved them and himself much trouble. But he did nothing to turn away the evil of some bad seasons, and spent his time in feasting and drinking, and his money in keeping up more state at his court than any other king had done before his time; and when he died in the year 1095 at an early age, no one seemed to regret him.

Erik Ejegod, 1095-1103.—Prince Erik, who had made his escape from the church of St. Alban in Odense, when his brother King Knud was murdered, was chosen by the people to succeed Olaf. Good seasons came back with the beginning of his reign, and therefore his subjects looked upon him with feelings of love and respect. His great beauty, which gained for him the name of Ejegod, or "good for the eyes," made him a special favourite among the Danes, who felt proud of their tall handsome king. Erik had the blue eyes and long, flowing light hair, which were praised in the folk-lore of the North as having always belonged to the noblest of the vikingar of old. He was noted for his strength and his skill in warlike exercises, and for his knowledge of the eight arts which were required of a well-born, accomplished Northern knight and warrior. These eight arts were: riding, swimming, skating, steering, throwing javelins, playing chess, playing the harp, and composing verses. To these Erik added the gift of speaking many languages, so that when he journeyed through different lands on his way to Rome, he could converse with the natives of each country in their own tongue. And as he was also very friendly in his manners, free in giving to the poor, quick of tongue, and merry of heart, we need not wonder that this king, who was moreover handsomer and taller than any of his subjects, and had the strength of four ordinary men, should have been the idol of his people. He ruled justly for the most part, and defended his country from the Wends and other pagan pirates, who had for many years before his time sorely plagued the poor Danes, and obliged them to forsake their lands near the sea, and retire beyond the thick woods into the interior.

On Erik's first pilgrimage to Rome in 1098, he secured from the pope, Urban II., a promise that his brother King Knud should be counted as a saint, and on his return to Denmark the ceremonies of his canonization took place with great pomp at Odense, in the church known since then as St. Knud's. The year after this event (in 1102) King Erik went for the second time on a pilgrimage, in order that he might make atonement for the murder of one of his servants. His subjects had begged him to remain at home, and had even offered to give to the third of their substance for a blood fine, and for the masses which he wished to purchase at Rome and Jerusalem, but he was resolved to go himself, and so he and his queen Botilda set forth, but neither lived to enter the Holy City. King Erik died in 1103 in the isle of Cyprus, and the queen soon afterwards within sight of the gates of Jerusalem, near which she was buried.

Great was the grief of the Danes on hearing of the death of their much-loved king. For a time they would not believe that he could be dead, but when there remained no further doubt of it, they made choice of his brother Niels to succeed him, setting aside an elder son of Svend Estridsen on account of his weakness, and passing by the sons of Erik Ejegod. Some of the latter were still very young, and the eldest, called Harald Kesia, who had ruled the kingdom during his father's absence, had shown himself so cruel and unjust, that the people feared to choose him or any of his brothers.

PART IV.

REVENGE OF THE GUILD-BROTHERS.

Niels, 1104-1134.—Niels, who reigned from 1104 to 1134, in the time of our King Henry I., was a poor weak ruler; and as he could not keep his kingdom free from pirates, he gave Slesvig, or South Jutland as it was then called, to his nephew Knud, the son of Erik Ejegod, who was known as Knud *Lavard*, or *Hlaford*, the old northern word for chief lord, or master.[1] Under this warlike prince, the Wends were so thoroughly beaten that during his life Denmark had peace from these cruel foes. Knud had been trained to arms at the court of Lothaire, duke of Saxony, and when the latter prince was chosen Emperor of Germany, he gave him in reward for his defence of the Holstein lands from the attacks of the pagan Wends, the title of King of the Obotrites, and with his own hands placed the crown upon his head. These honours roused the envy of his cousin Magnus, the son of King Niels, who feared that on the death of his father the people might pass him over, and choose Knud to reign over them. To avoid this danger, Magnus made up his mind to put Knud out of the way; and in order to effect this purpose, he persuaded his father, Niels, to invite him to spend the Yule-tide with them in the royal castle of Roeskilde. Knud, who did not suspect the evil intentions of his kinsmen, came at their request, bringing with him only a small retinue of men-at-arms; and after spending the Yule-week in the feasts and games usual in those

[1] This Knud married Ingeborg, a daughter of Mistislav, Grand-Duke of Novogorod, and their only son, who was born about the time of Knud's murder (Jan. 1131), received the name Vladimir from his Russian great-grandfather. This name was softened by the Danes into Voldemar or Valdemar.

times he took friendly leave of the king, and set forth on his way home. Then Magnus, on pretence of wishing to consult him on some family matters, rode after him with a large band of armed men, and, attacking him as he was resting in a wood near the town of Ringsted, killed him before he could lift a hand to defend himself.

Erik Emun's Vengeance. — This deed brought no good to Magnus or his father, for as soon as Knud's brother, Erik, known afterwards as Erik Emun, or the Boaster, heard of the murder he made an appeal to the people at the great Thing, and begged them to give him men and money to make war on his false uncle, King Niels. The Danes, as well as the men of the Slesvig and Holstein provinces, had always held the brave Knud "Lavard" in great esteem, and they therefore took up arms and willingly gave Prince Erik all the help he needed to punish the murderers of his brother, so that he soon found himself strong enough to offer battle to the royal troops. The two armies met at Fodevig in Skaania, in the spring of 1134, when Prince Magnus was slain, and all the bishops and priests who had come into the field with him were either killed or made captive. King Niels himself barely escaped falling into the hands of the victors; and, in the hurry of his flight he let himself be persuaded to cross the Belt to Slesvig, not thinking of the danger that would befall him in a town where Knud Lavard had held his court, and where he was well known and much beloved by the citizens.

Knud Lavard had, moreover, been head-master of St. Knud's Guild, or Company, which had a law that no brother must leave the death of another member of his brotherhood unrevenged. When the King was begged to bear in mind this well-known law, he laughed and said: "It would be a shame if Svend Estridsen's son, King Niels, should have a fear of cobblers and brewers!" and with these words he rode boldly into the courtyard of the royal palace.

But soon King Niels was made to feel that cobblers and brewers could prove as fierce foes as kings and princes, for no sooner had he and his men come into the castle-hall than they heard the outer gates closed behind them, and a ringing of bells from every belfry and tower in the town. The watch-word of the guild-brothers passed from street to street, and soon the market-place outside the castle swarmed with noisy, angry and fierce armed men, who were all eager to take vengeance on the father of Prince Magnus, for whom, although he was their king, they cared very much less than for their slain guild-brother, the brave Knud Lavard. The clergy, who wished to prevent bloodshed, came forth from their churches robed in their state vestments and bearing on high the host, but the guild-brothers sternly thrust them aside, and, making good their entrance into the palace, slew King Niels and all who stood by him. And thus died, in the year 1134, the last of Svend Estridsen's five king-sons, about sixty years after the death of that father and ancestor of all later Danish rulers.

CHAPTER VIII.

THE VALDEMARS.

The time of the Valdemars—The troubles that had come upon Denmark after the death of Niels—Valdemar the Great; his early training; his want of courage in his youth; his great bravery in later years; his campaigns against the pagans in the island of Rygen—The downfall of the temple of the great god Svanteveit at Arcona; the trick by which the place was taken; the demon that the Danes said they saw—Bishop Absalon; his love of his king and the church, and his contempt for peasants; his quarrels with the people—King Valdemar's death—Grief of Danes, and sorrow of Absalon—Knud VI.; his bold defiance of the Emperor; his successes—Absalon's activity; the monks of Sorö – Knud's death—Valdemar II. receives the homage of the German princes.

PART I.

TROUBLES BEFORE THE VALDEMARS.

Troubled Times from 1131 *to* 1157.—THE age of the Valdemars, which began with Knud Lavard's only son Valdemar, is the most brilliant period of the history of Denmark, and the Danish people from those early times to the present day have continued to love the name and memory of Valdemar I. and of his sons Knud and Valdemar, and to look back to those princes as the greatest and best rulers they have ever had. Young Valdemar grew up in the midst of civil wars, troubles, and sorrows of all kinds, for the kingdom was in a wretched state during the latter part of King Niels' reign as well as after his murder in 1134, when his nephew Erik Emun was raised to the throne. Erik was a brave man, and kept the country free from the attacks of the Wendish pirates, which, as we have seen, had long proved a heavy scourge to the people living on the coasts; but his cruelty in causing his brother Harald Kezia together with his ten sons to be murdered, made the Danes hate and fear him. His nephew, Erik the Lamb, who was chosen king after him, let his kingdom be overrun by sea-robbers and spent his time with the monks, leaving his poor subjects to defend themselves until they came to despise him as much as they had dreaded his uncle. When Erik the Lamb died in 1147, after having taken the vows of a monk in St. Knud's Abbey in Odense, a great civil war broke out which lasted ten years. During this time the Bonder, or peasants, suffered severely, and when a Thing was called in 1157 to discuss the question of choosing a king, they had become so poor and powerless that the nobles and bishops did not think of consulting them, when they made choice of Knud Lavard's son Prince Valdemar to be their ruler. There were other changes, too, in the manner of proclaiming the new king which showed how much power the higher classes had gained. In former times when a Danish king had been chosen to reign over the people, it was the custom that he should go from town to town, from hundred to hundred, and from province to province, to show himself and receive the homage of all his subjects. But Valdemar who had been abroad, and liked German and foreign fashions, despised making this kind of royal progress, and instead of it he caused himself to be crowned in a church by the bishops, after having been anointed with holy oil, decked in royal robes of state, adorned with a finely jewelled cap on his head, and invested with a golden sceptre.

Valdemar, 1157-1182.—When Valdemar I. came to the throne he found no money, no soldiers, no trade, and no order in the kingdom.[1] But when he died he left to his son a flourishing, well defended, busy, and peaceful monarchy, to

---

[1] It is stated by some writers that to secure support from the side of Germany, he made an alliance with the Emperor Frederick Barbarossa, and recognized him as his suzerain, doing homage to him as his vassal when he visited his court in 1162. Valdemar's friend Axel Hvide, known as Bishop Absalon, had implored the king not to take this step, which did not, however, entail upon Valdemar any of the usual duties of a vassal, and must therefore have been more of a ceremony than a formal act of submission.

which he had added large tracts of land on the pagan shores of the Baltic, where the Wends and Esthonians had been made to submit to him, and to receive Christian teachers and renounce their cruel heathen practices.

In the course of his reign Valdemar made as many as twenty great expeditions against these heathen pirates, at all seasons of the year, not sparing himself from any labour or hardship. In the earliest of these expeditions he did not, however, show much bravery; and he so often turned back on some pretence or other that the sailors in his fleet had begun to think him a coward, and once he had heard some of these rough men laugh at him as "a knight who wore his spurs on his toes, only to help him to run away the faster!" These taunts made him very angry, but when he found that even his friend and foster-brother Axel Hvide, who was known later as Bishop Absalon, felt contempt for his want of courage, he all at once began to face danger bravely, and from that time till the very close of his life he was never again known to shun any risk.

Absalon was more of a sailor or a soldier than a churchman, and seemed to like nothing better than to stand on the deck of his own ship and give his commands to the seamen, or to lead them on shore against an armed foe, and pursue with a few followers some fierce band of sea-rovers. From his castle Axelborg, on the present site of Copenhagen, he kept a sharp look-out for pirates, and it was not often that this fortress was without a row of heads set up in proof of the vengeance that he took on robbers, and as a warning to others of the fate they would meet with if they chanced to fall into the hands of King Valdemar's zealous friend, Bishop Absalon. The war against the fierce pagans of the Baltic ended in 1168 with the taking of the town of Arcona, on the island of Rygen, and the complete destruction of the great temple of the god of the Slaves, Svanteveit, whose monstrous four-headed image was torn down from its stand and burnt in the presence of the islanders.

This great event was brought about by the clever trick of a young Danish man-at-arms, who while the army lay encamped on the sea-beach of the Island of Rygen, below the town of Arcona, had noticed that the high cliffs on which the temple was built were honey-combed by a number of holes or caves, which could not be seen from the ramparts above, but were easily perceived by looking from below at the steep wall of rocks. One day the idea of turning these holes to good account struck the young man, and without losing a moment he arranged with some of his fellow-soldiers what was to be done to carry out his plans. Setting to work, these young men brought together as much dry straw and as many sticks as they could collect, and under pretence of playing at a game of pitch and toss which the sentries above might watch if they liked, they filled a number of the holes in the rock with the sticks and the straw. One of their number then clambered up the side of the steep wall by using spears and stones for a ladder, and set light to the trains. In a few minutes to their great joy they heard the cracking sound of fire, and saw columns of smoke and flame rise up the face of the rock and close round the wooden spikes and palings at its summit, which were soon in a blaze.

Arcona taken.—The pagans trembled with horror and fright when they first noticed flames circling round the high mast, from which floated the banner of their great god Svanteveit, but before they could rally, the Danes, headed by Bishop Absalon, rushed to the assault and made themselves masters of Arcona. Then began the ceremony of baptizing the heathens. Attended by his monks, Bishop Absalon laboured for two days and two nights in the work, and only ceased when almost blinded with want of sleep he dropped down before the altar that had been set up beside the fonts, at which the converts were received and signed with the cross.

When all were baptized, King Valdemar caused the huge wooden image of the god to be dragged amid loud war-music to the open plain beyond the town, where it was cut up for firewood by the serving-men of the army. Although the islanders had been forced to receive Christian baptism, they had not ceased to fear their old gods, and nothing could persuade them to take part in the removal and destruction of the idol, for in their ignorance they expected every moment to see lightning descend from heaven to destroy the Danes, and to punish their own neglect of their god Svanteveit. The Christians were hardly more sensible, for they pretended that when the image was being carried out of the temple-gates, a horrible monster, spitting fire and brimstone, burst from the roof and hurled itself with wrathful howls from the high cliffs into the sea below, which opened to receive the demon, and closed over his head in loud bubbling waves of flame and smoke!

PART II.

DEATH OF VALDEMAR AND ABSALON.

Absalon.—After these wars against the heathens Bishop Absalon continued to serve King Valdemar as a loving friend and faithful servant. He was not, however, always a good and just master to those who were placed under his power, and the poor peasants on the estates which belonged to him in Skaania, while he was primate of Denmark, had great reason to complain of his harsh rule. It is said that his bailiffs forced the wives and daughters of the peasants on his lands to drag stones and timber through the forests in the midst of a hard winter, while the men were busy building up a fine house for his use. At last the people, nearly worn out with their labours, refused to work any longer; and then Absalon, finding that he could not compel them to obey the orders of his officers, crossed over the Sound, and went to the king's court at Vordingborg in Sjælland to beg him to come with an army to punish the disobedient peasants. Valdemar tried to make his archbishop act with more mercy, but when he saw that Absalon would not listen to reason, he set sail with a number of troops for the primate's estates in Skaania, declaring that no one should ever say King Valdemar had refused to give help to his friend Absalon when he asked for it. On his arrival, the king, who was of a kind and loving nature and not willing to make war on his own people, again tried to restore peace between the primate and his peasants. Had Absalon been as merciful as his royal master things might have come right without the shedding of blood, but he was proud and could not forgive the poor peasants for daring to oppose him, since he was high-born and they were only serfs. To punish them, he caused all the churches to be

closed, and forbade the clergy from doing any of the services of
religion as long as the people should refuse to perform the work
he had set them to do. This made them more angry than ever,
and when King Valdemar landed in Skaania with Absalon, he
found a great crowd of peasants drawn up in battle array, on
and near the bridge over the little river Dysia, which emptied
itself into the sea close to the archbishop's chief city of Lund.[1]
The rebels were only armed with scythes, wood-axes, clubs and
any rude weapons that they could lay their hands on, and when
Absalon observed their shabby and disorderly appearance, he
cried out in a proud defiant tone, "This beggarly rabble is unworthy of being cut down by the swords of nobles and knights,
it will be best to hunt the pack with whip and lash!"

On hearing this unseemly remark, King Valdemar reproved
the haughty churchman by saying, "You forget, good friend,
that we are dealing with men, and not with dogs!"

The fight was hard and long notwithstanding the poor arms
and humble rank of the bishop's foes, but it ended at last in the
complete defeat of the peasants of Skaania, who saw themselves
forced to pay tithes to the church, which they had long
looked upon as a cruel injustice and striven to resist.[2] Soon
after these events the good King Valdemar I. died at the age
of fifty-one, in the spring-tide of the year, 1182, at the moment
that his restless prelate was stirring up new troubles.

Knud VI. 1182-1202.—Valdemar I. like many of his forefathers was buried in the church of Ringsted, and as the funeral
procession headed by Bishop Absalon drew near, a crowd of
peasants met it and begged, with tears and loud cries of grief,
to be allowed to carry the remains of their beloved king to his

---

[1] This great churchman is known in Danish History as "Bishop
Absalon," and is seldom spoken of under his higher rank of archbishop.
He had been appointed to the primacy during the life-time of the former
archbishop, Eskil, when the latter gave up all his dignities and retired to
the monastery of Claravalle in France in the year 1177. The primate
Eskil took this step from grief at the treason of his grandsons, the princes
Knud and Karl, who on their father's side were related to the royal family
and who had joined in a revolt against King Valdemar.

[2] The Danish people for many ages strove to resist the payment of tithes
and to force the clergy to marry, as they, like the other Northern nations,
had a great dislike to the monkish system of the church.

last resting-place. When the bishop began to read the service for the dead his voice failed him, and he wept and trembled so much that he had to be held up by two of the assistant monks, and after all was over the people went sorrowfully away, saying that now Denmark's shield and the pagan's scourge had been taken from them, the country would soon again be overrun by the fierce heathen Wends.

But Absalon ordered all things so well for the young prince Knud, Valdemar's eldest son, who at the age of twenty had been proclaimed king, that Denmark was able to maintain a bold front against all foes, whether pagan or Christian, and the Danish people had cause to feel proud of their gallant king. When Knud came to the throne, the Emperor of Germany, Frederick Barbarossa, demanded that he should appear at the imperial court at Ratisbon and receive the crown of Denmark as a gift of the empire. But so changed were the power and credit of the Danish monarchy since the time when Valdemar the Great, much against Absalon's wishes, had been forced to obey a summons of the same kind, that Knud VI. was able with bold words to defy the power of the empire. "Tell your master," said Knud to the envoy who brought the emperor's command that the Danish king should appear at Ratisbon to receive the crown from his hands, "I am as much monarch in my own realm as the kaiser is in his, and if he has a fancy for giving away my crown, he had better first find the prince bold enough to come and take it from me!"

After that daring speech nothing more was said for a long time about giving or taking the Danish crown, and Frederick Barbarossa, who had more foes in Italy and elsewhere than he well knew how to deal with, was forced to let the question rest for the time, but he neither forgave nor forgot the insult, and he never lost a chance during the rest of his life of stirring up strife against Denmark. In 1184 he helped the pagan princes of Pomerania to invade the Danish islands with a fleet of five hundred ships, and the land would again have been overrun by the fierce heathen Wends, if old Bishop Absalon had not boldly attacked and beaten off their vessels before they reached the coasts of Sjælland. In this encounter the pagans were so thoroughly routed, that when the heavy fog cleared away by which the Danes had been able, unseen, to approach the enemy, only thirty-five of their ships remained fit to keep out at sea, although they had brought five hundred great well-armed vessels into the fight. The king gave an account of Absalon's great victory to the people at the National Thing, and the fame of his exploits was made the subject of songs and tales in every part of Scandinavia, and even among the Vœringjar at Miklagaard.

Knud's Successes.—After this great victory, which brought all Pomerania and some of Eastern Prussia under the power of Denmark, Knud took for himself and all his successors the title of "King of the Wends and other Slaves," and from that time to the end of his reign, Knud by the help of his warlike brother, Duke Valdemar, went on adding one district after the other to his old dominions until he had made himself master of Hamburgh, Lübeck, and all the country of Holstein, Lauenburg and Mecklenburg. Not content with these great successes, Knud was anxious to extend his conquests, and he next turned his arms against the pagan lands of the Esthonians and Livonians. As long as his Danish troops were in the country, he found it an easy matter to make the people declare themselves to be Christians, and attend the churches which he had caused to be built; but no sooner were his armies withdrawn than the natives returned to their old heathen practices, and thus little progress was made towards the spread of Christianity in those pagan lands on the south of the Baltic.

In the meanwhile there was no lack of trouble at home while the Danish flag was being planted on foreign ground. The emperor had found it easy to raise foes in Denmark against King Knud, and by his help a very serious rebellion was soon kindled in Slesvig, the object of which was to set on the throne Valdemar, Bishop of Slesvig, who was a grandson of that Prince Magnus who had slain Knud Lavard, the grandfather of King Knud and of his brother Prince Valdemar. The latter had been made governor of all South Jutland, and to him the task was now given of putting down the Slesvig rebels, which he did so quickly and so thoroughly, that all the schemes of the emperor to injure the Danish monarch failed. Bishop Valdemar was taken captive by his active young namesake, and was treated by him with great cruelty, for he was chained and thrown into the dungeon of Söborg Castle, where he was kept for many years in painful and close confinement, an act of injustice and cruelty, which, as we shall see, brought a bitter return to Prince Valdemar. Bishop Valdemar's ally Count Adolf of Holstein was also forced to submit, and his land was seized on by Duke Valdemar who threw the unhappy count into the dungeons of Söborg.

The latter years of Knud were disturbed by disputes with Philip Augustus of France, whose cruel conduct to his queen, Ingeborg, the Danish king's sister, gave rise to much trouble both in France and in Denmark and led the pope more than once to excommunicate the French monarch and his people. Bishop Absalon went on to the last days of his life working for the good of King Knud and his brother Valdemar, whom he had loved and cared for from their childhood. These princes owed to him much of the skill in knightly arts for which they were noted, but he had taken care that they should be adepts in the learning as well as the warlike exercises and athletic sports of their age, and had caused them to be instructed in all the historical knowledge which could be gained in those times. Absalon was a kind friend to those who cared for learning, and he encouraged Saxo Grammaticus and his friend Svend Aagesen to collect all the popular Danish traditions and historical tales that could be learnt among the old Skalds and poets; giving money to them and to the other monks in Sorö monastery to enable them to carry out their search for these remains.[1]

Absalon died in the year 1201, and a few months later the death of Knud VI. opened the path to the throne to his brother Prince Valdemar, who was now the nearest heir, as the late

---

[1] See Chapter II. Bishop Absalon, who had studied at the University of Paris, was learned for the age in which he lived. He spent all his large fortune in enriching the monasteries of Esrom, Vitsköl, Ringsted and Oem, which had been founded under his predecessor, the primate Eskil, who had been the first to call Cistercian monks into Denmark. Under Eskil and Absalon the Danish Church acquired special canonical laws, and the chapters first claimed the right of choosing their bishops, independently of the sovereign's wishes and only subject to the pope's approval.

king had left no children. Valdemar was in Northern Germany at the time he heard of his brother's death, and so great had been his success over his enemies, that the princes of Holstein, Lauenburg, Pomerania, Rygen and Mecklenburg, without waiting to see on whom the choice of the Danish Thing would fall, at once did homage to him in a solemn court, held at Lübeck, where the Hanse Leaguers joined them in accepting Valdemar for their sovereign lord.

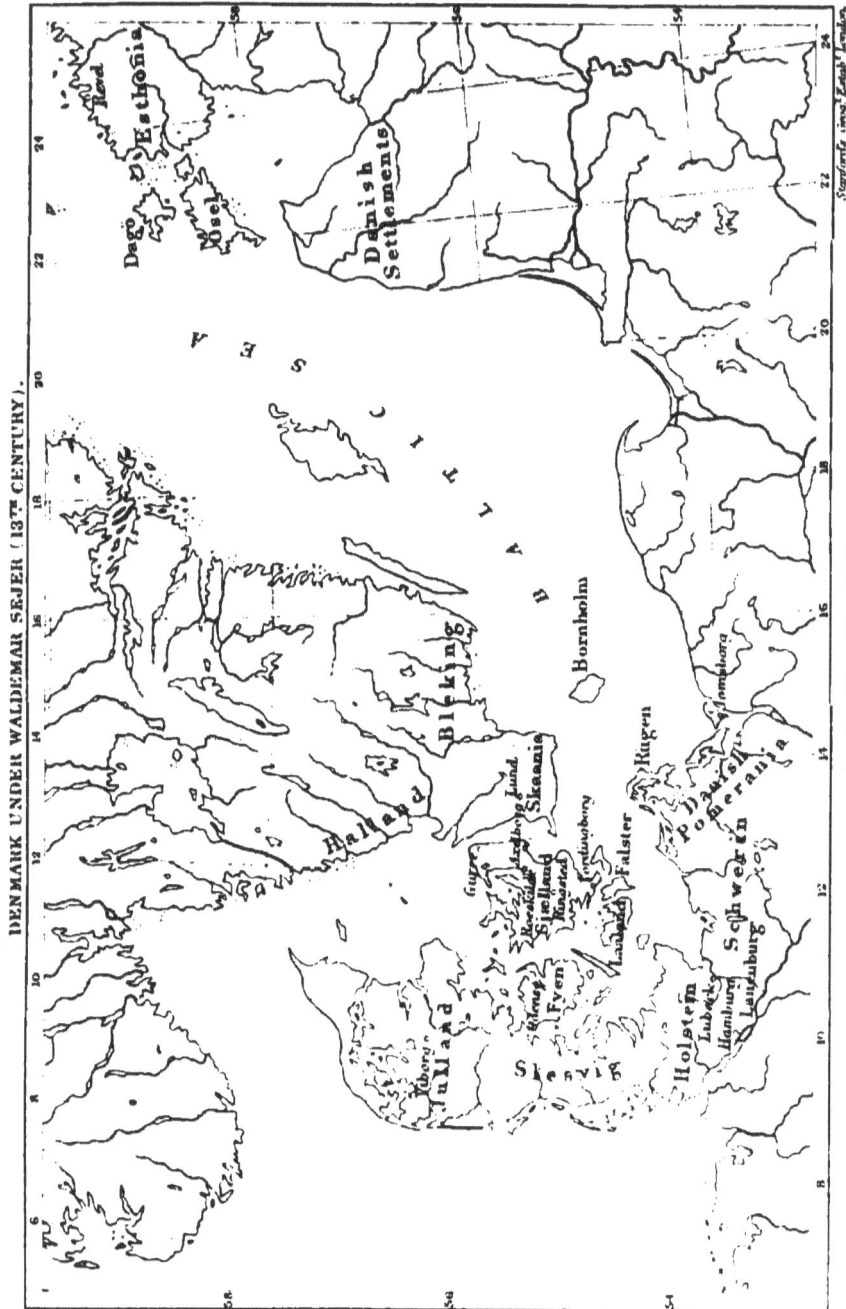

CHAPTER IX.

DENMARK FROM 1202 TO 1259.

The greatness of Denmark under Valdemar Sejr; his successes for twenty years—The sudden blow by which all the glory of the Danish Monarchy was thrown down—The fatal hunt on Lyö—Valdemar and his son gagged, bound, and carried away by night—They are kept captive in Germany for three years—Their hard fate—Cruelty of Black Henry; Count Albert of Orlamunde tries to rescue them; is defeated and put in the same dungeon with Valdemar—Valdemar's return to Denmark; nearly made captive a second time; his merits in peace; his lawbooks; his death; his two wives; their sons; the fame of Valdemar among the Danes—The troubles under Valdemar's sons and grandsons—Erik; his disputes with his brothers; his wars; his nickname Plovpeng; his visit to Slesvig—The conversation of the brothers—Abel's rage—Erik murdered; his body sunk in the Slie—Abel's false oath of innocence; his choice as King; his murder—The recovery of Erik's body—Christopher I.; his disputes with the clergy; excommunicated; conduct of people; Christopher's murder.

PART I.

DENMARK UNDER VALDEMAR II. (SEJR) AND HIS SONS.

Valdemar II. 1202–1241.—NEVER in the whole period of her existence had Denmark been in so prosperous and glorious a condition as under the earlier part of Valdemar II.'s rule. His many conquests gained for him the well-merited title of "Sejr," the conqueror, and his great merits as a lawgiver and a ruler secured him the love of the Danish people, who, not only in his own times, but to the present day, have looked upon him as the best and noblest of the kings of Denmark. Soon after he came to the throne Valdemar overcame his enemy Adolf, Count-Duke of Holstein, and compelled him to give up his duchy and his other lands, which were at once granted by the king to his own nephew, Albert of Orlamunde, who under the title of Duke of North-Albingia ruled over the Slesvig-Holstein dominions, and kept the Danish frontiers well protected from German invaders. Valdemar also subdued and annexed Pomerania, and in 1217 the German emperor with the sanction of the pope rewarded the Danish king's devotion, by giving to him and future kings of Denmark all the territories north of the Elbe and the Elde, and thus made him actual master of great part of Northern Germany.

The princes of the German Empire were indignant with the emperor for thus extending the power of the Danish king at their expense, and they formed conspiracies against him and tried to oppose him, but without effect, and one by one the different princes were forced to submit. The most vindictive of Valdemar's many enemies was his kinsman and namesake, Valdemar, Bishop of Slesvig, who after being defeated when heading a rebellion in Knud's reign, and having been kept in close captivity for fourteen years, had been released in 1206 at the earnest entreaties of Valdemar's gentle queen, Dagmar. This man, who had become archbishop of Bremen after his release, although for a time subdued, and compelled by the victorious Valdemar to retreat to the monastery of Loccum in Hanover, was concerned in every plot against the Danish king, and never ceased to labour against the prosperity of Denmark.

Valdemar's success in Germany had led him early in his reign to attempt to extend his power to Norway and Sweden, but in neither kingdom were his efforts followed by any lasting results, and after having taken part with the banished prince, Sverker Karlsson, against Erik Knudsson, he had to withdraw his troops from Sweden after a signal defeat, and ended by making peace with King Erik, and giving him his sister Rikissa in marriage. His zeal for the Church and his love of adventure led him in 1219 to set on foot, with the pope's special sanction, a crusade against the pagans in Esthonia. Armed with a papal bull which gave him the sovereignty of all lands which he might convert, Valdemar entered upon this undertaking with an army of 60,000 men and a fleet of 1,400 ships, and soon completely overran the whole of Esthonia, and caused great numbers of the people to be baptized. The Danes, however, found powerful rivals in the Livonian Knights of the Sword, who declared that no other Christians had the right of converting these pagans, and soon fierce battles were fought and much blood shed in the effort made by each party to secure the greater number of converts. It is to these religious wars in Esthonia that the Danes refer the first appearance and use among them of the Dannebrog, or national standard, which, according to the legend, suddenly fell down from heaven while the primate Andreas Sunesön, Absalon's successor, was praying on a high hill with uplifted hands for victory. It is not improbable that the pope may have sent a consecrated banner bearing the white cross on a blood-red field to King Valdemar as a token of his favour, and that its sudden appearance, when the Danes were beginning to waver before the pagan ranks, gave the victory, which in later times was believed to have been gained through the primate's prayers.

Valdemar's Downfall.—When Valdemar returned with the victorious Dannebrog from Esthonia, he was at the very summit of his power, and could not have dreamed of the terrible vengeance which one of his least dreaded enemies would inflict upon him. Fear alone kept his vassals submissive, and it was believed that even the pope and the emperor, who seemed to favour him, would rejoice in seeing the downfall of the supremacy of Denmark in Scandinavia and Northern Germany. Some among the German princes whose lands he had seized never concealed their hatred of him, but others, disguising their feelings of anger and jealousy, pretended to be on friendly terms with him, took favours from him, and shared in his wars abroad and his amusements at home, at the very time that they were helping in every secret plot that was made against him. Amongst these false friends there was no one who seemed more attached to King Valdemar than the Count-Duke of Schwerin, and no one who hated him more strongly. The king was of an open frank nature, and although he had often been warned against the count, who, both on account of his complexion and his evil nature, was known in his own country as "Black Henry," he would not listen to any such warnings, and went on treating him like a faithful friend.

Count Henry was, therefore, able to learn all that he wished to know of the king's habits and mode of life, and often gave secret help to some traitor who wanted to injure Valdemar; but after a time, when he saw that all the plots laid for the Danish monarch's ruin failed, he resolved to act for himself. The king's trust in him soon gave him the chance of carrying out his evil purposes; and when Valdemar in the spring of the year 1233 invited him to come and hunt for two days with him in the woods of Lyö, he said he much regretted that he could not join him, as he was lamed by a fall and could not rise off his couch. But instead of keeping his bed, Count Henry was scouring the country over by night to prepare all things for the plot he had in hand, which was no less than to make a prisoner of his trusting friend the king. This was easier for him to accomplish than it would have been for many others, as he knew the island well. Accordingly, when he learnt from his spies that the king, with his eldest son, Valdemar, had landed at Lyö with only a few servants, he prepared to carry out the design he had long had in view.

At the close of a hard day's hunt, when Valdemar and his son were sleeping within the rude unguarded tent that had been put up for their use, and the few attendants and huntsmen were scattered about, lying under the shelter of trees and rocks, Count Henry's men landed and crept cautiously into the midst of the tired sleepers. Then, entering the royal tent, they gagged and disabled their victims while they were yet buried in profound sleep, and before either could utter a sound or make any effort to resist them, they drew sacks of wool and straw over their heads and faces, nearly choking them, and passed strong cords round their bodies to compress their legs and arms. Thus gagged and crippled, the tall and strong king and his young son were carried through the midst of their own people to the strand, and laid like helpless logs in the bottom of the boat which was waiting for them, and which, with muffled oars, shot quickly across the narrow strait to the opposite shore of Fyen. There the men transferred their precious freight to the fast-sailing yacht which was to carry the captives to a German port. The wind favoured their passage, and on the following day, almost before the royal attendants at Lyö had discovered their loss, the lately dreaded and powerful King of Denmark was landed in Germany at a lonely part of the coast, and, still gagged and bound, was placed on a horse and tightly secured to the saddle, after which he was hurried on at full gallop, with no longer stoppage than was necessary to change the armed escort. In this manner father and son were conveyed to the castle of Danneberg in Hanover, which had been lent for the purpose to Count Henry, as he himself had no fortress which was deemed by the conspirators strong enough to receive the royal captives. Prince Valdemar, who was the only son of King Valdemar's first queen, Margrete of Bohemia, and who resembled his mother both in her feebleness and her beauty, was nearly killed by the rough treatment he had received, and when his bonds were removed on his arrival at Danneberg, the blood flowed from every part of his body. But without paying any regard to his tender youth and sufferings, Count Henry caused him and his royal father to be shut up in a cold, dark dungeon, fed on the poorest and coarsest food, and left without a change of clothing.

PART II.

VALDEMAR'S CLOSING YEARS.

Valdemar's Fate.—It gives us a very striking idea of the cruelty and lawless state of those times when we think of poor King Valdemar's fate, and bear in mind that for three years he was left to endure the pangs of hunger and cold and the bonds of a felon, although the pope and emperor threatened Count Henry with all the penalties that the church and empire had decreed against those who raised their hands against a prince, anointed by the Bishops of Rome and holding lands under the imperial crown. Count Henry gave ready promises that he would without delay attend to the commands which he had received to release King Valdemar and his son; but he evaded the fulfilment of his promises, knowing that Rome and Ratisbon were too far from Danneberg to give him real cause for alarm, and feeling that all the other princes of Northern

Germany would help him to keep their common enemy safe in prison as long as there was anything to dread from him. From Denmark there was not much to be feared either, for although the Danish nation thirsted for vengeance, and eagerly demanded to be led to the rescue of their beloved king, there was no prince among them able or willing to do anything to deliver the captives. The king's sons were children in age, and all the more distant kinsmen of the royal family had been banished, or were dead; and thus there was no one with the power or right to take the control of public affairs. For some time even the people remained ignorant of the fate of their king, but at length the whole sad story became known, and then Valdemar's nephew Albert, Count of Orlamunde, who had been on his way to Rome when the news of his uncle's capture reached him, returned in haste to Denmark, and collecting an army marched into Hanover and gave battle to the German princes who had brought their forces to aid Count Henry in defending Danneberg. The poor Danes, who had not been well prepared for the war, were, however, very soon defeated by the Germans, while their leader Count Albert was taken prisoner and thrown into the same dungeon as the king and prince. The poor captives were now in a worse state than before any attempt had been made for their rescue; and King Valdemar, seeing no other chance of escape from captivity, agreed to the terms of release offered him by Black Henry, which were that he should pay a ransom of 45,000 silver marks for himself and his son Valdemar, and let his three younger sons be brought to Danneberg and kept in prison with Count Albert till all the money was paid.[1]

On these terms the royal captives were set free, and they at once returned to Denmark, where the kingdom was in a fearful state, while the people of almost all King Valdemar's former dominions in Germany had thrown off their allegiance to him, and done homage to their own princes. Poor Valdemar, humbled and crushed in spirit, found himself thus deprived

---

[1] Count Henry also required that the king should give him all the jewels of the late Queen Berengaria which had not already been bestowed on churches and monasteries, and send him 100 men-at-arms, with horses and weapons for their use.

of all the power which had been won by his great valour, and that of his father Valdemar I. and his brother Knud VI. In his grief at the thought of dooming his sons to the fate from which he had just escaped, he wrote an earnest letter to the pope, praying him to use the power, which all good churchmen of those times believed he had, of absolving him from his oath to let his children go into captivity. The pope taking pity on him, granted his prayer, and sent one of his bishops to Count Henry of Schwerin to tell him that if he tried to enforce this wrong against the King of Denmark, who had appealed to the Church of Rome, he should be deprived of all the services of religion and be made to pay a heavy fine to the papal throne.

When first Valdemar returned to Denmark he was too much cast down and too full of sorrow to attempt to get back any of his old conquests. After a time, however, his spirit revived, and when in 1227 the peasants of the Ditmarshes refused to pay the tribute which the Danish crown had long claimed from them, he could not bear the insult, and putting himself at the head of his army marched into their lands. But fortune had left him, as it now seemed, for ever, and after seeing 4,000 of his troops killed by the rebels, who had been strongly helped by the German princes of Holstein, and being wounded in the eye by an arrow which struck him to the ground, he only escaped a second capture through the timely aid of a German knight. This friendly foe had in former times been in Valdemar's service, and when he saw his old master helpless and bleeding, he lifted him to his saddle and carried him from the field of battle at Bornhöved in Holstein, to Kiel where his wounds were tended, and means were found to convey him to his country palace, Vordingborg in Sjælland.[1]

Valdemar's Merits in Peace.—After this campaign King Valdemar lived at peace with his neighbours, and the remaining

---

[1] According to the legend of Bornhöved, Count Adolf of Holstein owed his victory over the Danes to the Virgin, who, having heard the vows which he made at the close of a long summer-day's fight to build churches and convents, and take upon himself the vows of a monk if he were successful, placed herself before the sun to prevent his rays from dazzling the eyes of the Germans. By these means Count Adolf was able to bring his men in the rear of the Danes and cut them down before they could rally in their own defence.

fourteen years of his reign were devoted to the cares of government and to the preparation of several codes of laws for the various provinces of the kingdom, for there were not in that age any general laws for the whole monarchy. In 1241 Valdemar laid the Jutish code before the Thing of Jutland, which met at Viborg, and before the Sjælland Thing at Vordingborg.[1] These laws, which had been revised by the learned Bishop Gunner, and were soon extended to South Jutland (or Slesvig) and to Fyen, continued to be in force for nearly 450 years, when the Danish King Christian V., in 1687, caused new laws to be framed, although even then all the provisions of Valdemar's famous code were not wholly set aside. Under these old laws the people continued, as in more ancient times, to decide upon ordinary cases of dispute by juries of which there were several kinds, one consisting of "eight good and true men" chosen by the king, and another of twelve jurors chosen by the community, who were all bound to tender an oath to the royal bailiff before the Thing that they would determine according to "what was most right and most true." In many cases where in older times the ordeal by a red-hot iron had been in use, the oaths of twelve men were accepted in proof of the innocence of an accused person. The royal bailiff of the Danish Things had no judicial power, but was called upon to see the judgments of the juries carried out, to keep order, receive oaths, and see that everything was arranged according to prescribed custom during the sitting of the Thing, which met in the open air within a space enclosed by a ring of stones. The laws were lenient, and most crimes could be atoned for by money, or other fines; compensation to the sufferer being more considered among the Scandinavians than vengeance on the offender.

Valdemar's Children.—Three days after the Jutish laws were read and approved of before the Thing of Vordingborg, King Valdemar died at the age of seventy-one, leaving three sons, Erik, Abel, and Christopher, who all in turn ruled after him, and who were the children of his second queen, Berangaria,

---

[1] Ten years earlier the king had caused a *Jorde bog*, or "Book of Lands," to be drawn up, which gave an account of the value, produce and ownership of every farm and estate in his kingdom.

daughter of King Sancho V. of Portugal. His eldest son, Valdemar, who had been crowned joint king with himself to secure his succession when he was only six years old, and who as we have seen shared his captivity at Danneberg, had died in 1231, at the early age of twenty-three, from a stab in the foot received when hunting. As the prince's wife and infant son had been carried off shortly before his death by some sudden disease, or as the people thought by poison, there was no descendant left of Valdemar's first queen, Margrete of Bohemia, whom the Danes, in their fond admiration of her gentleness and beauty, called Dagmar, "Day's maiden."

This queen long continued to be a special favourite with the people of Denmark, amongst whom the fame of her virtues was kept alive in many of the most popular of their national rhyming verses, known as Kæmpeviser, where King Valdemar's Dagmar is represented as a fair, fragile, golden-haired princess, gentle and pure as a saint. According to one of these old ballads, when she lay on her death-bed and her chaplain urged her to confess, she could recall no sin but that of having decked herself in her best new boddice and plaited her long hair with bright ribbons before she went to mass. But while the Danes thus took delight in trying to extol the virtues and beauties of their favourite, there was nothing too bad for them to relate of Valdemar's second queen, the tall, black-haired Berangaria, whose name they turned into "Bengjœrd," which from that time forth became a by-word for any vile woman. The superstitious peasants even believed that fierce and loud cries of rage and terror might be heard from her tomb in Ringsted Abbey by those who passed near it at midnight, while at the same moment the softest strains of heavenly music floated over the neighbouring grave of Valdemar's first and best loved queen, Dagmar.

The memory of Valdemar II. has always been especially cherished by the Danes, who regard him as the greatest of their conquerors, and the most patriotic of their early kings. In his own age and in those immediately succeeding his death, he was looked upon as the perfect model of a noble knight and royal hero, and while he was honoured for his gallant and successful efforts to raise Denmark to a height of power which it had never before reached, he won the love and pity of the people on account of the miseries and degradation brought upon him in return for those very efforts to exalt the greatness of the Monarchy.

PART III.

A CENTURY OF TROUBLES.

Erik, 1241–1250.—Nearly one hundred years separates the beginning of the first Valdemar's reign in 1157 from the close of his son Valdemar Sejr's reign in 1241; and that century marks the rapid rise and decline of the power of Denmark in Northern Europe. But whether in its successes or its losses, it was an age of glory of which the people have cause to be proud. It was very different, however, in regard to the following century, from 1241 to 1340, which was filled up with the reigns of Valdemar Sejr's three sons and their immediate descendants, for during that period the Monarchy was gradually stripped of all its domains and seemed for a time nearly blotted out, while the people rapidly lost their national independence and ceased to exhibit the daring spirit for which they had once been noted.

Valdemar's excessive love for his children had been the first cause of the terrible disasters and civil wars which followed quickly upon his death; for in order to make provisions for his younger sons he had given Slesvig with the title of duke to Abel, and Laaland and Falster to Christopher, while he bestowed Bleking and Halland on his grandson, Nikolaus. When, therefore, Erik became king, he found that little more than the title of royalty was left to him, for his brothers on the plea that their father had given them full sovereignty over their lands, refused to do homage to the Crown. The disputes which sprang up when Erik tried to enforce his rights soon ended in fierce civil war, and cost the lives and properties of a great number of the Danish and Slesvig peasants, who cared nothing for the quarrels of their princes, and only wanted to be left to till their fields and earn their living in peace. Erik was not a bad ruler, and whenever his brothers gave him the chance, he lived on friendly terms with them; but he brought ill-will upon himself amongst the people by going to war with the pagans in Esthonia, and levying a tax to meet the expenses which gained for him the nickname of "Plov-peng"—plough-money—because it was laid upon the peasants in accordance with the number of ploughs that each man used on his land.

Quarrel between the Brothers.—On his return from Esthonia, where the Danish king reaped some glory but no profit, he wished to make friends with his brother Duke Abel, and therefore went to pay him a visit in his castle of Slesvig. The duke received the king very well and made a feast for him, but he bore hatred in his heart, and when after dinner they were amusing themselves according to the fashion of the day, with playing chess, he began to complain of all the troubles and the losses which he and his family had suffered at the hands of the king's soldiers in the last war. Erik begged him to "*let bygones be bygones*," and not rake up old grievances, but this only seemed to make him more angry, and he cried out "No! King Erik, I am not going to '*let bygones be bygones!*' I cannot forget that my two daughters had to run for their lives from your soldiers when they laid siege to this castle, and that the poor children, barefooted and bareheaded, had to hurry out of my gates and take shelter in a mean burgher's house!"

"I am truly grieved, dear brother," said the king good-naturedly; "and though I am not, God knows, as rich as I could wish to be, I have surely enough left in my treasury to buy shoes and hoods for my pretty nieces."

This speech did not appease Duke Abel, and rushing forth into the outer hall, he called to him two knights, Lave Gudmundsen and Tyge Post, who had lived in his service since they had been outlawed by the king. Reminding them of all the wrongs that King Erik had done them, he bade them go into the inner chamber and do with him what they liked, so that they took care no one should see him again, living or dead. The knights waited for no further orders, and arming themselves, they hastened to the hall where the king had thrown himself on a couch to rest a while till his brother returned, whose anger had given him no concern, as he knew of old that his temper was hasty. Here they fell upon him unawares, and having bound and gagged him, put him into a boat, and rowing with him out upon the river Slie, which flowed close to the castle walls, they cut off his head and threw his body, round which they had passed heavy chains, into the middle of the stream.

Abel, 1250–1252.—When Abel learnt how his brother had met his death by the hands of the knights, he sent off messengers to the Danish Islands to announce that Erik was dead, and to offer himself to the people as their king. But as he found that they accused him of being his brother's murderer, and would not believe his statement that King Erik had been drowned while fishing in the river, by leaning too far over the side of the boat and losing his balance, he took a solemn oath before the great Thing that he was guiltless, and brought twenty-four nobles to swear to the truth of his words. This practice of swearing for another man was an ancient northern custom, seldom made use of in those days. But although it always had been looked upon as a very solemn way of proving the truth, it did not now deceive the nation; yet, for the sake of the memory of their old king, Valdemar Sejr, the Danes would not withhold the crown from his eldest living son, although they knew that Abel was guilty of his brother's death, and looked upon him with distrust and fear. These events took place in the year 1250, but two years later, when the people had begun to find peace under King Abel and to benefit by his brave defence of the country against the attacks of pirates, he was murdered on his retreat from an unsuccessful campaign against the unruly Ditmarshers. Abel owed his death to the vengeance of a wheelwright, known in the marshes as Hans of Pelvorm, whom he had wronged on a former occasion, and who, having sworn to take the king's life, watched his opportunity, and when Abel was riding along a narrow road, by the great Milderdam, sprang forward and struck him dead with a blow of his sledge-hammer. Then lifting the body of the king off his horse, while the few royal attendants who had witnessed the deed fled in terror, he threw it into the bog near by, where it rapidly sank below the surface of the deep turf.

Erik's body recovered.—By a strange accident, about the very time that King Abel was murdered and his dead body left without burial in the Frisian marshes, the headless trunk of his slain brother, King Erik, was raised to the surface of the waters by the shifting of the under currents of the Slie, and the manner of his death was thus made known. The monks of Slesvig abbey had been the first to discover the body, and recognizing it to be that of the late king, they took the remains, and laid them in a grave near the spot on which they had been found. Soon a report was spread abroad that miracles were being done and marvellous cures wrought at King Erik's grave, and for a long time the abbey derived large revenues from the money paid by pilgrims who flocked to the spot. But although Erik was looked upon as a saint and a martyr, he was never canonized.

Abel's short reign is worthy of special note for being the first in which the burgher classes were permitted as a distinct body in the state to send representatives to the "Danehof," or yearly national assembly. They were also allowed to have their own courts of justice in the towns, and to settle their affairs in civic or town-councils, presided over by a mayor, or chief burgher-master, although every town had its own royal bailiff who in the king's name enforced obedience to the laws of the country, and the payment of all proper taxes to the crown. After a time the town-councils in all the larger cities of the kingdom were left free to frame their own codes of laws, but about one hundred and fifty years later, under Queen Margaret, these civic by-laws were almost all done away with and replaced by one general body of laws, binding on town and country alike.

King Abel, at his death in 1252, left several sons, but as they were young, and his brother Duke Christopher was a man in the prime of life, the Danes chose him for their king. It was not uncommon in the Middle Ages for young heirs to be set aside in that manner, in favour of some older kinsman. The crown of Denmark was, moreover, then and for a long time afterwards elective and not hereditary, that is to say, the nobles, clergy and burghers had the right of deciding which one of the late king's heirs should succeed him, although they generally chose the eldest son or nearest heir. So in this case the electors only used their just rights, and one reason that had great weight with them in passing over Abel's sons was that they were under the care of their mother's brothers, the Counts of Holstein, whom the Danes looked upon as enemies; and it must be owned that those princes never lost a chance of showing their ill-will to the people of Denmark.

Dawn of Slesvig-Holstein Wars.—The first act of the Holstein princes after Christopher was made king was to insist that he should confirm to his and their young nephews all the rights over the duchy of Slesvig, which Abel had claimed in Erik's lifetime as due to him in accordance with the intentions of their father, the late king, Valdemar Sejr. When Christopher refused, the Holsteiners made war on Denmark, and after much fighting King Abel's son, Valdemar of Slesvig, was allowed to hold the duchy, but on what terms both parties purposely left to be settled at some other time. And thus the seeds of dispute about that richest of all the Danish crown lands found a good soil, in which to multiply into an abundant harvest of troubles for future generations.

Differences between Church and State.—This was the first reign in which the king and prelates had not been on friendly terms, and Christopher soon fell into serious disputes with his primate, Jakob Erlandsen, a man of great learning, who had been a fellow student in Rome of the pope, Innocent IV., and was so devoted to the Romish Church that he considered his duty as a subject much less binding on his conscience than his obligations as one of the clergy. Christopher, finding that the Danish bishops were gaining more power and greater riches than the highest nobles of the land, threatened to call them to account for their exercise of seignorial rights, and their defiance of the laws, on which Erlandsen declared that unless the king ceased his attempts to curtail the privileges of the clergy, the kingdom should be laid under an interdict. This so enraged Christopher that he caused the primate to be seized in his own palace and carried, chained like a common felon, to one of the royal castles.

This act, as might have been expected, brought the anger of Rome on the kingdom of Denmark, which was laid under an interdict, and a sentence of excommunication passed on the king and all who had taken part in the seizure and ill-treatment of the primate. The people, however, at first, paid little heed to these acts, and as the clergy in Jutland and some of the islands refused obedience to the papal decrees, the services of the Church were still carried on in many parts of the kingdom. At the moment, however, when Christopher was about to seize upon some of the crown lands held by the bishops, his sudden death while he was receiving the communion in the cathedral of Ribe, from the hands of the abbot, Arnfast, plunged Denmark into greater troubles than any it had yet known. The suspicions generally current amongst the people that the king had died from the effects of a poisoned wafer given him by Arnfast became still stronger when shortly afterwards the abbot, who was known to be a secret friend of Erlandsen, was raised to the rank of Bishop of Aarhus.

CHAPTER X.

DENMARK FROM 1259 TO 1387.

Erik Glipping; his minority; the Queen-Regent; his quarrels with Slesvig and with the Church; settlement of disputes; his evil habits; civil war; conspiracy; his murder in a barn; fifty-six conspirators—his son Erik Menved's reign a repetition of his own—The Queen-Mother—War—anarchy—Disputes with clergy—Rebels swarm over the country—The young King's mode of education, love of war and tournaments, want of money; he pawns crown lands—Hansers secure fisheries and forbid royal servants to fish—Treatment of Primate Grand—Consequences of the outrage—Interdict—Conduct of people—Erik's domestic troubles in losing fourteen children; his advice to his nobles; his death—Christopher II.—Magna Charta of Danish barons—Perfidy of the King—Civil wars—Struggles—Geert of Holstein rules and sets up a puppet-King—Geert's murder; revenge of his sons on Niels Ebbeson—Valdemar returns from Germany and is chosen King; his brother Otto's fate—Valdemar's marriage; his conduct; his recovery of crown lands; his taking of Wisby; his contempt for Hansers—Wars with Germany; seizes on Elizabeth of Holstein; marries his daughter Margaret to the heir of Sweden—Enemies close round Valdemar; his subjects do not help him; his defeat, flight and humiliation—Hansers' arrogance—Valdemar's merits; people's hatred of him—"Valdemar the Bad"; his death—"Atterdag," its meaning; his family; his heirs—Olaf—Queen Margaret's regency—Hakon's death—Olaf's death—Margaret's mistaken policy.

PART I.

AN AGE OF TROUBLES.

Erik Glipping, 1259–1286.—On the death of Christopher I., the last of Valdemar Sejr's sons, there seemed some chance that the crown of Denmark would pass away from his descendants, for the clergy, who enjoyed excessive power in the state resolved to use their influence in preventing the son of the former king from being chosen as his successor. But the nobles, together with the burgher-classes who had begun to make their power felt, refused to set aside the old dynasty, and in spite of the opposition of the prelates chose the young prince Erik, son of Christopher I., to be king.

Erik, surnamed "Glipping," or the Blinker, was only ten years of age when he was crowned King of Denmark, and his mother, the widowed Queen Margaret of Pomerania, therefore ruled in his name during his childhood. Her first act was to release the primate Erlandsen, whose captivity had brought such troubles on the land during the former reign, but he refused to be reconciled with the royal family, and availed himself of his newly-gained freedom to hasten to Rome in order that he might appeal to the papal chair. In the meanwhile Denmark continued to be disturbed by a civil war, excited by the late King Abel's grandson, Duke Erik of Slesvig, who on one occasion defeated the royal troops and seized on the persons of the Queen Regent and the young king, the latter of whom was kept a prisoner in Nordborg Castle by his daring vassal for three years, and only released on his pledging himself to acknowledge the hereditary rights of the descendants of King Abel to the duchy of Slesvig. The differences between the king and primate were not finally settled till 1273, when Erik Glipping was forced to pay a fine of 15,000 marks silver to the archbishop to atone for the wrongs inflicted upon him by King Christopher, on which the interdict was removed from the kingdom, after having been enforced in name if not in fact for fourteen years.

The king had tried to evade the fulfilment of his promises to Duke Erik as soon as he found himself safe out of his power, but the question of the terms on which the duchy of Slesvig was held was at last laid before the imperial court at Ratisbon, and that too was decided against Denmark. In consequence of the decision of the Emperor and the commands of the Pope, young Valdemar, the heir of Duke Erik, was in 1283 formally put in possession of the lands claimed for him, but which the Danes regarded as part of the crown domains, not to be separated from the monarchy

K

except as feudal fiefs to be held by a vassal of the Danish King.

After these questions were settled and all excuse for war was at an end, Erik might have given his kingdom some rest, and tried to repair the evils of past years. But he was a weak, vicious man, so fond of pleasure and of indulging his own evil passions, that he wasted on himself the money that ought to have been spent for the good of the country, and raised up a band of formidable enemies. At length, after having done many private wrongs to men who had served him well in the times of his troubles, a plot was formed against him by some of the highest nobles of the land. After several attempts against his life which failed, the conspirators carried out their purpose of slaying him, in the autumn of 1286, when fifty-six of their number, disguising themselves as monks, fell upon him in his sleep and slew him in a barn where he was resting after a long day's hunt. The king who had always feared violence had caused the doors to be barred and guarded before he lay down, but by the treachery of his page, or chamberlain, Rane Jonsen, the conspirators were admitted, when, rushing upon their unarmed king they all struck at him with their swords, and after completing their work by leaving fifty-six wounds on the body, hurried away, and dispersed before Erik's friends could detect or secure them.

PART II.

DECLINE OF THE ROYAL POWER.

Erik Menved, 1286-1319.—The early part of the reign of the young king Erik Menved, "With a But."[1] must have seemed to those who could remember his father Erik Glipping's childhood as a coming back of that older time of trouble. There was again a boy-king under the care of a foreign mother and Queen Regent, who could not speak the language of the

---

[1] He was so called, it is said, because he never made up his mind to anything.

country which she was called upon to rule. There was again the same want of loyalty among the nobles and richer clergy, who thought the times favourable to their own increase of power; and there were rebels swarming over the country and keeping up ill-will against the royal family. A few brave knights and nobles, headed by the learned chancellor Martinus de Dacia, whose fame had spread to every part of Europe, proved themselves true friends to their young king and his mother, and it was chiefly by their help that Queen Agnes of Brandenburg was able to keep up any show of power. She was bent upon punishing the murderers of her husband, but it was not very easy to lay hands upon them, for the king of Sweden, although he had married a sister of Erik Glipping, gave them his support and helped them to get ships and men, so that they were able to do great damage to the lands near the Danish shores. Each of the leaders of the rebel murderers of the late king seized upon some strong point, and then kept a part of the coast for his own special pillage-ground, and many years passed before the kingdom was relieved from the attacks of these traitors. But when their fiercest chiefs, the Marshal Stig and Rane Jonsen, were no longer at the head of this pirate-like war—the former having died in 1293, and the latter having been taken and broken on the wheel in the same year—this frightful scourge ceased.

The young king and his brother, Prince Christopher, were in the meanwhile being very carefully trained in all knightly exercises under the Marshal, or Drost Peder, and they became brave and accomplished princes; but unfortunately Erik when he was a boy had learnt to take such great delight in trying his skill in all kinds of mimic warfare, that when he grew to be a man he was not happy till he could make war in earnest. So in spite of all the distress and want in Denmark he entered upon costly and useless campaigns against the christian, as well as the pagan lands of eastern Germany. In later years when his poor subjects were no longer able to supply money for these foolish schemes, or for the splendid tournaments which he held in honour of his empty success in Pomerania and Esthonia, he pawned or sold nearly all the crown-lands, till at last there was scarcely any dominion remaining to the monarchy. Amongst other districts Erik had sold to the German Hanse traders a long line of coast land with all the herring fisheries in the Danish seas.

By these and other acts of folly and wastefulness, this king of Denmark had sunk so low that at one time the Hansers had power enough to forbid the servants of his household from fishing more than one day in the year off the Danish coast of Skaania; while they kept armed boats to enforce their orders that the Danes should leave the fishing ground as soon as they had salted one day's haul of herrings for the royal kitchen. Notwithstanding these and many other proofs of the abject condition of the sovereignty at this period, Erik plunged his kingdom into fresh troubles by his quarrels with Johan Grand, the successor of the primate Jakob Erlandsen. The young king and his mother, who had good reason for believing that Grand, together with the Duke Valdemar of Slesvig, had given their support to the murderers of Erik Glipping, even if they had not been present when he was slain, felt that the raising of this man to the primacy was an insult to themselves, more especially as they had informed the Danish clergy generally of the grounds of their objections to his being chosen to be Archbishop of Lund. Grand was nevertheless elected, and for a time he and the king avoided giving open proof of their mutual ill-will, but soon the primate's arrogance and the young king's hastiness of temper led to a rupture between them. Then Erik, losing patience, allowed his brother Prince Christopher to arrest the primate as a traitor, and to shut him up in the castle of Söborg, where he was kept for eight months in close confinement. The harshness and even inhumanity with which young Prince Christopher had carried out his brother's orders made this outrage the more unpardonable in the eyes of the pope. Boniface VIII., who, when he heard of the indignity that had been inflicted on the primate, excommunicated the royal brothers and laid the Danish kingdom under an interdict. In the meanwhile Grand, whose health never recovered from the bodily injuries which he had received in having been carried in a storm of rain and hail in an open boat by night to his prison, escaped from Söborg by the help of some of his monks and made his way to Rome, where he did his utmost to keep the Danish king out of favour with the Church and the pope.

Denmark under an Interdict.—As in former times the interdict could only be imperfectly enforced in Denmark where the people took the part of their king, and braved the authority of the Court of Rome. They even refused to suffer the penances enjoined upon them, and when the clergy tried to close the doors of the churches, the peasants rushed to arms and forced their priests at the peril of their lives to perform all the services of religion for them. But although this resolute conduct on the part of the Danes took away some of the evil effects of the interdict, it did not save the king from the consequences of his unjust act towards the archbishop. At the end of five years Erik was forced to write a humble letter to the pope praying for pardon, and to pay a fine of 10,000 silver marks to the papal treasury; and thus the Church gained another victory at the expense of the nation.

King Erik was as unhappy in his family concerns as he was in public affairs, for he had the misfortune to lose all his fourteen children in their infancy. His Queen Ingeborg of Sweden was so deeply distressed at the death of her youngest son, who was killed by falling off her lap while she was driving with him in an open carriage, that she went into a convent in 1317, and died there two years later and only a few months before the king. When Erik found himself left childless he felt great concern in regard to the choice of his successor, and knowing the ambitious and deceitful character of his only brother Duke Christopher, he called together the nobles and prelates of Denmark, and telling them that he feared his own life was near its close, he begged them to take counsel together, and settle upon some prince for their future king who would prove a just ruler. At that time, however, there was no other heir of the royal house whom the people cared to choose, and therefore on the death of Erik Menved in 1319, the Council of State proclaimed Duke Christopher king; but as they had no better opinion of him than his brother had expressed, and saw a good chance of increasing their own power, they drew up a very hard agreement which they made him sign before they would permit him to be crowned.

Christopher II., 1319—1332.—In this charter, which may be called the *Magna Charta* of the Danish barons, the nobles and prelates took such good care of their own interests that little or no power was left to the king, and as it freed them from all taxes, the crown was deprived of the revenues that it had formerly had under its command. Amongst other points, the nobles had claimed the right of refusing to carry arms for their king beyond the limits of their own country, while he had to bind himself that he would pay their ransom if they were taken captive in war. Christopher made no objections to the hard terms imposed upon him, because he had resolved from the first that he would disregard them as soon as he was able to bid defiance to his council; but as he had neither power nor money, he found this less easy than he had expected, yet he nevertheless plunged his kingdom into civil wars which brought misery to both parties.

After a time of great trouble, the end of the long strife between him and his unruly nobles was that in 1325 they called in a strong neighbour, Count Gerhard of Holstein, to help them. This prince, known in Denmark as " Black Geert," routed the king's troops and took his eldest son Prince Erik captive, and instead of letting Christopher have a share in the guardianship of young Valdemar of Slesvig, which the Danish king had claimed as a right, he drove the king himself out of his kingdom, and after persuading the Danes to declare the throne vacant, he set his nephew, this boy Duke Valdemar, in his place.[1] For fourteen years Black Geert was the real king of Denmark, of whose lands and people he disposed pretty much as he liked, while Christopher and his sons, although sometimes able to make head for a time against their strong foes, were seldom left very long in the enjoyment of power.

Christopher's death in 1332 did not alter things very much, and for eight years longer the Danes were at the mercy of the Counts of Holstein, which was the more galling to them as they had always regarded those princes as of far lower degree than their old rulers. In the year 1340, Denmark was freed from her stern master by the daring act of a Jutlander of rank,

---

[1] Valdemar of Slesvig, crowned King of Denmark as Valdemar III., was the cousin of King Christopher II.

called Niels Ebbesön, who with sixty-three serving men forced his way into the castle of Randers, and slew Count Geert in the midst of his own people and with his army of newly levied Germans lying encamped around him.

The effect of this daring deed was to scatter the great Holstein army, which seemed at once to melt away and disappear on the death of its leader. The Jutlanders rose in a body, and placing themselves under the command of Niels Ebbesön, stormed the German forts and after carrying everything before them, drove the Holsteiners back to their own territory. Soon however new armies led on by Geert's son Henry, known from his unflinching courage as the "Iron Count," appeared in Jutland, and defeated Niels Ebbesön in a fierce battle at Skandersborg, where the latter fell, together with two of his own sons and a large number of his men. The Iron Count did not care to continue the war after he had thus taken vengeance on his father's murderer, and withdrawing his troops after his victory at Skandersborg, he left his cousin Valdemar of Slesvig and the Danish princes to decide as they liked upon the fate of Denmark. King Christopher had died some years before these events, so thoroughly neglected by his own subjects and despised by his enemies, that on one occasion, when two nobles, thinking to find favour with the Holstein princes, attacked the house in Saxkjöbing in which the fugitive monarch had found refuge, and brought him to Count Johan of Holstein, that prince would not be troubled with him, and left him free to go where he liked. Soon after this humiliation, Christopher II. ended his useless and unhappy life in neglect at Nykjöbing, and thus in 1332 Denmark was freed from one of the worst and most contemptible kings who ever occupied the throne. From the moment Christopher obtained the crown till the murder of Geert in 1340, the country had been torn by civil war, brought on either by the treachery of the king, or the ambition of the Holstein prince, and while a few of the nobles made themselves rich at the expense of the crown, many old families were reduced to beggary, trade was destroyed, and the peasants were so crushed that they fell into a state that was little better than slavery

PART III.

THE CREDIT OF DENMARK REVIVES.

Valdemar Atterdag, 1340-1375.—The Danes in their joy at the death of Geert of Holstein forgot all the evils which they had suffered under their own king before the Holsteiners drove him out of the country, and determined to restore the old dynasty. At Christopher's death in 1332 he left only two sons, the eldest, Prince Erik, having died some years before in a useless attempt to recover the crown for him. Otto, the second son, was a prisoner in Holstein, while the youngest, Valdemar, was living in peace at the court of the Emperor Louis of Bavaria, who had given him a kind reception, when after the defeat of his father and brothers he had fled to Germany. This young prince who had been spending his time in jousting and other amusements while his native country was being brought to ruin by its enemies, was the one on whom the choice of the Danes fell when by the murder of Count Geert they found themselves free to elect a king. Valdemar of Slesvig was still regarded by the Holsteiners and other Germans as the rightful monarch of Denmark, but the Danish nobles looked upon him simply as the puppet king of his uncle Geert, and, after the Count's death, they paid no attention to their Slesvig sovereign. Valdemar himself had no wish to retain the crown, and on the arrival of the young Danish Prince Valdemar from Germany he entered into a friendly compact with him, and not only refused to oppose his election to the throne, but gave him his sister Hedwig in marriage, with a dowry of 24,000 silver marks. He then retired to his own Slesvig territories, well pleased as it would appear to be free of the trouble of ruling such an unhappy and poor kingdom as Denmark. Nothing now stood in the way of Valdemar's success, and after he had forced his brother Otto to renounce all claim to the throne and to enter the Monastic Order of the German Knights as the price of his liberty, he felt he had no other rival to fear.

Valdemar, from the moment he became king of Denmark in 1340, when he was twenty-five years old till his death in 1375, at the age of sixty, made money the chief object of his desire, not because he cared for hoarding wealth but because he was most eager to get back the lost crown-lands; and he knew very well that there was no way of doing this except by buying them one by one from those who held them in pawn. It is said that he never loved his wife Princess Hedwig of Slesvig, but he had shown himself eager to marry her on account of her dowry of 24,000 silver marks. As soon as the money was in his power he used it to redeem a large part of Jutland, and soon afterwards bought back more of the old Danish monarchy with the 19,000 silver marks, which he got from the German Knights in return for the province of Esthonia which they wanted, and which was in truth of little value to the Danes. The people were very well pleased to see the old Danish provinces again under the power of the crown, and as long as the king raised money without asking them for it, they did not very much care how he got it, but when he began to levy taxes for the purpose they were not so well pleased. The general ill-will and grumbling soon grew into open rebellion. Foreign princes brought help to the men of Jutland, who had risen against the king's tax-collectors, and in the civil wars which followed, Valdemar's subjects in their anger at the demands made upon them forgot all that he had done for them.

Valdemar looks about for money.—The king, however, did not pay much heed to what others thought of him, and as he wanted to secure money at any cost, he made up his mind in 1360 to attack the rich Hanse-town of Wisby in the island of Gothland. He had no cause of quarrel with the Hanse-traders at the time, and had only just signed a treaty in which he had pledged himself to respect their rights and to give due notice if ever he meant to make war on any one of their cities. These treaties, however, made little difference to Valdemar, and having cast longing eyes on the stores of money, rich silks, furs and other costly wares that were housed away in Wisby to be sent on to the ports of the Northern Seas, he resolved to seize upon them if he could. Without giving any notice he attacked the island with a great fleet, and forced the Gothlanders to submit. After he had made himself master of the place he refused to pass through the gates of Wisby, and ordering a breach or, opening to be made in the wall he rode in state into the town, after the manner of the great conquerors in olden times. Then loading his ships with gold, silver and an immense booty of all kinds, he sailed back to Denmark in great glee, and from that time forth called himself king of the Goths as well as of the Danes.

But he was not left to enjoy his success very long, for the Hansers and the Swedes were equally enraged at this act of treachery and cruelty, and although the latter did no more than threaten, the former made war in good earnest against Valdemar. When the German heralds came in great state to the castle of Vordingborg, where the king was then holding his court, and began to read aloud their formal notice of war, he made sport of them and bade them go back to the seventy-seven German towns in whose name they had come. It is said that Valdemar, to show his contempt for the traders, sent them a letter in rhyme of which the following was one of the least coarse and offensive verses:—

> "If seventy-seven ganders
> Come cackling, come cackling at me ;
> If seventy seven Hansers
> Come crowing, come crowing at me ;
> Do you think I care two stivers?
> Not I ! I care not two stivers !"

The Germans were beaten both at sea and on land in the beginning of this war, and Valdemar caused his prisoners to be shut up in one of the towers of Vordingborg Castle, over which he set a gilt goose as an insult to the traders, whose name of Hansers was in common use for cocks or ganders, and was often applied in those times to a foolish boastful fellow. The German traders grew more bitter than ever against the Danish king after these insults, and they made great efforts to collect so large a fleet, that the Danes might have no chance of beating them a second time ; besides which they made common cause with the Counts of Holstein and with Albert of Mecklenburg, who had private quarrels of their own to avenge on Valdemar. The Holstein princes were very angry just at that time because the Danish king had seized upon their sister, the Princess Elizabeth of Holstein Gottorp, when she was on her way to

Sweden to marry Hakon, heir to the Swedish and Norwegian crowns, and had kept her closely guarded in his own palace on pretence that her health would not allow her to cross the sea at that stormy season of the year.

Valdemar's real motive, however, had been to prevent the marriage of Elizabeth with the Swedish prince, as he had set his heart upon seeing his own little daughter Margaret married to the future king of Sweden and Norway. When therefore the ship in which Elizabeth was making the voyage ran ashore on the coast of Sjælland, he resolved not to lose so unlooked for a chance of carrying out this scheme. And sending an urgent message to the King and Queen of Sweden to beg that they would bring their son to spend the Yule-tide with him, he made all things ready, and when they arrived he persuaded them to consent to the marriage of Prince Hakon with his daughter Margaret, and let the wedding be celebrated at once. It is said that during this visit Valdemar induced his foolish royal guest to give up the bonds and charters by which he held in pawn Skaania and the other old Danish provinces, pledged to Sweden by King Christopher, and that he at once burnt the deeds. There was great rejoicing at Copenhagen on account of this event and of the marriage, and feasting and jousting went on day after day for the entertainment of the Swedish princes, but before the close of all this merry-making the Queen Blanka of Sweden was taken ill and died, and then her husband, King Magnus Smek offered to take the Holstein princess to be his second wife, if he could be sure of getting her large dowry. Poor Elizabeth felt that this was a cruel insult, and having refused with anger to listen to the king's offers, she sent trusted messengers to inform her brothers of the shameful manner in which she had been treated, and to entreat that they would avenge the wrongs she had suffered at King Valdemar's hands.

Valdemar in trouble.—These events had taken place soon after the Hansers' first defeat by the Danes, and when they heard of the close alliance that their enemy had formed with Sweden and Norway, they felt still more anxious in regard to themselves, and made such great efforts to raise forces and excite enemies against the king before he could find time to prepare another expedition like the one he had carried on against Wisby, that he was soon beset on all sides. Valdemar did not see the full danger till it was too late, and when the Counts of Holstein, who were eager to avenge the insult offered to their sister, induced several German princes to join them and the Leaguers against the Danish king, he was forced, after a short but fierce war, to submit, and to secure terms of peace by giving up Skaania and the other old Danish provinces. These lands he had recovered, as we have seen, from Magnus Smek, and the Danes who had rejoiced at their restoration to the Danish monarchy were now equally mortified at their rapid loss, while the Council of State and all the richest nobles began openly to murmur at their king, and gladly made his conduct an excuse for refusing him help to carry on the war. Under these circumstances Valdemar could do nothing to defend himself, and in 1368 he left Denmark, carrying with him his family, and, according to some writers, all the gold and silver that he could collect, and went to seek help from his friends and kinsmen in Germany.

For more than four years Denmark remained without a king, and her people, either from feebleness or indifference, allowed the Germans and Holsteiners to manage public affairs as they liked. So completely had the Hansers made themselves masters of the Danish kingdom, that Valdemar had to buy peace and secure the right of resuming the regal power at the terms offered by these traders. Before he could return to his own dominions, he was forced to promise for himself and all his descendants that the traders of the German Hanse League should have a voice with the Danish nobles, prelates and burghers in the election of future kings of Denmark. Thus humbled, Valdemar came back to Denmark in 1372, and during the remaining three years of his life he had the good sense to refrain from all attempts to make war on his old enemies, and to devote himself to the good of his people. In spite, however, of all his efforts to benefit them, his subjects never liked him, and in the songs and tales invented about him, and repeated among the Danish peasants from one generation after the other, till almost our own times, he is always spoken of as a hard, crafty prince, ready to barter his very soul for money, and willing to sell the lives and comfort of those nearest to him to gratify his own ambition. The superstitious country-people long continued to give proof of the fear and hatred in which this stern but able king had been held in his own times, for among all their national tales, " Valdemar the Bad" was made to play the part of Satan or one of his favourite spirits, and when in the winter night's storm they heard a sudden rush of wind and a howling of the tempest, they were wont to say that King Valdemar was driving his hounds with lash and spur through the air to the hunting grounds on lake Esrom in North Sjælland, near his palace at Gurre, which he was reported to have said would be dearer to him after death than heaven itself.

Valdemar was surnamed *Atterdag*, "Again a day," in allusion to his favourite maxim that men should bide their time, and hope that if one day brought trouble another day would come in which a lost chance might be recovered, and he certainly almost always acted up to this precept. The death in 1374 of Henry, Duke of Slesvig, the last direct descendant of King Abel, had given Valdemar the hope of bringing that much-coveted province back to the crown; but before he could take formal possession of the duchy as a lapsed fief, he himself died suddenly at the age of sixty. With him ended the last direct male representative of the Valdemars, and thus the two main branches of the Svend Estridsen line of descent became extinct at the same time. Valdemar's only son had died some years earlier leaving no family, and his nearest male heirs were, therefore, the sons of his daughters Ingeborg and Margaret. The elder of these princesses had married Count Albert of Mecklenburg, and at her death she had left one son Albert. The younger of his daughters, Margaret, had been given in marriage when quite a child, as we have already seen, to Hakon King of Norway in his own right, and son of Magnus King of Sweden, and she too had one son, Olaf, who succeeded his grandfather Valdemar on the throne of Denmark.

Olaf, 1375-1387.—On the death of King Valdemar, the Council of State and the nobles were divided in their opinions in regard to the claims of his grandsons. Most persons felt that Albert of Mecklenburg, as the son of the late king's eldest daughter, had the best right to the throne, but the Danes hated all Germans, and were just then especially distrustful of the Mecklenburg family, owing to the close alliance into which those princes had entered with Denmark's hereditary enemies, the Counts of Holstein. For these reasons, and because the Danes had strong feelings of loyalty and affection towards the young Queen Margaret of Norway, they passed over the elder branch and gave the crown to her son Olaf, who was proclaimed king in the same year, 1375. As the little prince was only five years old at the time, his parents, Hakon and Margaret, took the oaths for him, and signed in his name a charter which secured to the nobles the same rights which they had demanded from Christopher II.

King Hakon died in 1380, and was succeeded by young Olaf, who thus again united Denmark and Norway under one ruler, but the death of that prince at the age of seventeen in 1387, before he had exercised independent power, destroyed the hopes that had been raised by his early talents and good disposition. His mother Queen Margaret had ruled over both kingdoms in his name since the death of her father and husband, and by her tact and ability had succeeded in gaining the confidence of the Danish and Norwegian nobles, and in restoring some degree of order into the countries under her sway. The only act of her government which proved a source of future evil was her granting South Jutland, or Slesvig, as an hereditary fief to Count Gerhard VI. of Holstein in 1386. This step she had been unwillingly led to take in order to hinder the formation of an alliance then threatening against Denmark, between the Holstein princes and her enemies, the Counts of Mecklenburg, who were already supported by the Hanse League and other German powers. But in the end it brought troubles, which were far worse than any it prevented, both to Queen Margaret and to Denmark long after her time.

CHAPTER XI.

SWEDEN IN EARLY TIMES.

Sweden in early Christian times—Upsala—A hundred years of murder and trouble among the Swedish kings—Sverker Karlsson—Better times—Erik the "Saint"; his laws in favour of women—Erik's crusades; his death; becomes patron Saint of Sweden—A century of troubles to the end of Bondar race of kings in 1250—Sweden less civilized than Denmark—Danish princess Rikissa—Swedish women refuse to follow Danish habits of luxury—Norway after the death of Magnus the Good in 1047—Harald Haardraade; his wish to invade Denmark; his adventures in the East; his escape from prison; his marriage; his invasion of England in 1066; his death—Olaf reigns in Norway; his son Magnus, the kilt-wearer—The three brother-kings—Sigurd goes to Jerusalem; gives away his ships and returns to Norway over-land—Murder and trouble—Norway's age of mis-rule—The "Birch Legs" and the "Croziers" disturb the kingdom—Many claimants of the crown—Hakon IV. a great king who restores Norway to some credit, and begins a new course of order—Crown declared to be a Fief of St. Olaf—Increased influence of Church.

PART I.

FIRST CHRISTIAN KINGS.

Sweden in early times.—WHILE the sons and direct descendants of King Svend Estridsen had continued to maintain the doctrines of the Church of Rome in Denmark, and almost without exception to favour the Romish clergy and enrich them at the expense of other orders of the state, Christianity was still struggling for tolerance, if not for existence in Sweden.

After Olaf Sköt Konning, the " Lap King," had established the Christian faith in about the year 1000, it again began to decline under his eldest son Anund Jacob, and was so neglected under his younger son Edmund Gammal, that before the death of that prince about the year 1056, it seemed to have been nearly driven out of the land.

Upsala, which from the time of Frey Ingve had been the seat of the king and chief priests of the Svea, continued for a long time after those princes had become Christians to be looked upon as the most sacred spot in their dominions. Here Christian as well as pagan kings received the homage of the people, standing on the king's stone of Upsala, within sight of the hill on which the first temple to Odin was built by the old rulers of the Svea. Here too, the people met to discuss public affairs long after they had become Christians, as their forefathers had done when they held their yearly Thing in the plain on which Odin's temple stood. The control of this sacred spot was the chief cause of the respect paid by the people of Southern Sweden or Gautland (Gothland) to the rulers of Svithjod, and when Edmund Gammal, the last of the Ynglingar or Upsala race, died leaving no children, a fierce struggle broke out between the two nations, which ended in the men of West-Gautland proving themselves stronger than the Svea and able to set up a Christian King Stenkil. one of their own people, to rule over all Sweden. During his reign from 1056 to 1066 the pagans and Christians lived together in peace, and there was a short rest from warfare. After the death of Stenkil, who had been Jarl of Vestergötland before he came to the throne, and was descended through his mother from the old Ynglingar race of kings, several of his sons and near kinsmen were in turn made kings. But Sweden was equally disturbed under all the successive rulers who occupied the throne for nearly a century. Religious wars raged with violence for the greater part of that period, and the country was so torn by factions, that at last all the princes of the royal race were slain together with a great number of the chieftains. In this state of disorder no bishops ventured to remain in Sweden, and there would have been no Christian churches left, if a few monks had not come from Skaania and kept alive some knowledge of their religion among the people. At one time both Svea and Gauta obeyed a pagan king, and after setting aside Christianity joined together in offering sacrifices to Odin, and partaking of horse-flesh, which was looked upon as a kind of solemn sacrament in the worship of the god. At another time there was no king, either among the Svea or the Gauta; and then the chief law-explainers in Svithjod and in Gautland ruled each in his own district.

First dawn of better times.—The first prince under whom these troubles began to lessen was a Christian called Sverker Karlsson. This king, who reigned from about 1135 to 1155, and whose rule fell, therefore, within the same period as that of Stephen in England, built churches and monasteries, and invited monks of the order of St. Bernard, from Clairvaux in France, to come and take charge of these houses. He even sent messengers to the pope, praying that bishops might be settled in Sweden, and a place chosen for the see of a primate, that the Swedes might no longer have to be under the power of a foreign church; for up to that time all Scandinavia was included in the see of the Danish Archbishop of Lund. The pope, in 1152, sent his friend, Cardinal Nicholaus Albinensis, to Sweden to see if King Sverker's wishes could be complied with, but as it was found that the Svea and the Gauta were too jealous of each other to agree upon the choice of a district for the primate's see, the matter was dropped for the time. The cardinal[1] was able, however, before he left the country to secure for the Court of Rome the promise of the payment from the Swedish people of the tax known as St. Peter's pence. Thus for the first time in her history Sweden gave public proof of her union with the Church of Rome. Sverker's old age was troubled by civil wars, in which his son Johan took an active part, and was at length slain by a band of peasants, who had been enraged by the vicious and headstrong conduct of the young prince. At this moment the Danes attacked the Swedish coasts, but were beaten off by the men of Smaaland, who could obtain no help from their unwarlike old king; and the angry feelings which had been roused by Sverker's want of courage led in 1155 to

---

[1] Nicholas Breakspear, afterwards Adrian IV., the first and only English pope.

his murder at the hands of his own servants, while he was on his way to church to hear mass on Christmas Eve.

The Bondar, or freemen of Svithjod, met together at Upsala to choose a new king as soon as the death of Sverker was made known, and they were soon joined by the men of West-Gautland, but as usual they could not agree. While the Svea declared they would have none other than Erik Jedvardsson to sit upon the king's seat at Upsala, the Gauta refused to have any king but Sverker's son Karl. The former were, however, the stronger of the two, and Erik became king. This prince, who was a first cousin of the late King Sverker, belonged through his father Jedvard to the peasant or bondar class, from which his descendants took the name of the Bondar race, and for more than a hundred years the throne of Sweden was filled by one of this family, or by a prince of the Sverker line. Murder was in general the means by which each party got rid of a king of the opposite race to the one which they upheld, and thus the disputes which began when Erik, instead of Sverker's son Karl, was chosen king, were handed down from one age to another and grew more fierce with time.

Erik the Saint, 1155–1160.—Erik, who after his death gained for himself the title of "Saint," worked hard during his short reign of five years to improve the state of the country. There were three things, the old sagas tell us, which King Erik the Saint laid to heart, and these were :—" To build churches and to improve the services of religion, to rule his people according to law and right, and to overpower the enemies of his faith and realm." He was known in history not only as the Saint, but also as Erik "Lag-gifware," or the Law-giver, and is said to have won the love and grateful respect of all the women of Sweden by the laws which he passed to secure to them many rights, of which these three were the most important, viz., that every wife should have equal power with her husband over locks, bolts and bars; that she might claim half his bed during his life; and that she might enjoy one-third of his substance after his death.

Erik was the first king who erected a church at Upsala, where up to his time the worship of Odin had been kept up by force, at the cost of Christians as well as of pagans. Now, however, a primate's see rose at Gamla (old) Upsala, and a learned and pious man named Henrik was appointed to be the first archbishop. This prelate went with King Erik on a crusade against the pagan Finns, who had long been a scourge to the poor people of the eastern coasts of Sweden, burning and plundering their homesteads with as little mercy as the Northern Vikingar had in bygone ages shown their victims. Archbishop Henrik paid with his life for his zeal in trying to convert these heathen pirates, but his efforts and those of the king had the effect of bringing Finland under the power of Sweden, with which it remained united for many ages. Erik owed his death to the attack of a Danish prince, Magnus Henriksen, who, thinking that the troubled state of Upper Sweden might be favourable to the claims which he pretended to have on the Swedish throne, made a sudden attack on Upsala while Erik was hearing mass in Trinity Church. When the alarm was given and the king was warned of the approach of Magnus, he refused to leave the church till the close of the service, but then rushing forward at the head of his men he met the Danes, and after a fierce fight was cut down and slain by the invaders.

Erik's virtues and piety gained for him the love of his people, who worshipped him as their patron saint, although he was never canonized, on account of the greater favour in which the rival house of the Sverkers had for many years been held by the papal court.[1]

PART II.

TROUBLED TIMES.

The Bondar.—The century which divided the first and last of the Bondar race was marked by one constant struggle, in which

---

[1] The remains of St. Erik were for many ages preserved in the cathedral of Upsala and honoured as holy relics. His arms were emblazoned on the National Flag of Sweden, and a figure of the sainted king appears also on the banner and seal of the town of Stockholm.

no class except the clergy increased in power, or even kept their old position in the state. Erik, the first of the Bondar, died in 1160, and Erik Eriksson Læspe, the last of the race, died in 1250, a period that included nearly all the years of the reigns of the first four of our Plantagenet kings, viz., Henry II., Richard I., John, and Henry III.; for Henry II. came to the throne in 1154, and his grandson Henry III. ended his long reign of fifty-six years in 1272. Yet in all that long period, there is little or nothing to record of affairs in Sweden but the quarrels, wars, and murders of many kings, and the disorder and misery of the whole country. The only class of men who did anything to lessen these evils were the monks, many of whom had come from England. These zealous men first taught the Swedes how to till the ground and plant gardens, to prepare salt, to build and work water-mills, and to make roads and bridges. Besides this they also strove to make them give up some of the many evil pagan practices to which they still clung, as for instance divorcing their wives whenever they grew tired of them and marrying others according to old heathen forms; and thrusting their children out, or exposing infants in desert places to perish from cold and want when they did not care to be burdened with them. The greater number of the monks who came over to Sweden in those early times met their death by violence, but their memory has lingered nearly to the present day in the different districts in which they carried on their labours. Thus the people of Westmanland long honoured the Irish monk David as a saint, while in Sudermanland and Norland the names of the English martyrs, St. Bothurd, St. Askill, and St. Stephen, were for many ages held in great esteem, and their relics guarded with much care. During this troubled period in Sweden, when the country was laid waste by the civil wars between the Bondar and Sverker races of kings, Denmark often took an active share in these disputes, and gave refuge to the defeated princes of both parties in turn. Thus when Sverker Karlsson had murdered all but one of the grandsons of St. Erik, and the Swedish people threatened to take vengeance for these acts of cruelty, he escaped from their fury by fleeing to Denmark, where he was well received and helped by the Danish king, Valdemar II., who sent him back to Sweden with a fleet and an army. Sverker's defeat by his former subjects in a battle, fought at Lena in West Gothland in 1208, in which he was slain, forced the Danish king to withdraw his troops without having done anything to add to the fame of Denmark in Sweden; and as soon as Erik Knutsson, the grandson of Erik the Saint, proved himself strong enough to seize upon the throne, Valdemar II. made peace with him, and even gave him his sister Rikissa in marriage.

Erik Knutsson, 1210-1216.—Erik Knutsson, who reigned from 1210 to 1216, was the first king of Sweden who was crowned at the hands of the clergy within a church, for before his time the Swedish kings were simply proclaimed in public. It is related that Sweden was still much less civilized than Denmark, and that when the young Princess Rikissa landed in West Gothland to be married to King Erik, she found that there were no carriages of any kind, and that she had to make the long journey to her husband's court on horseback. When she complained of this, the Swedish women cried out angrily against the young queen's love of ease, saying, "We will have none of your new-fangled Danish fashions, our queens have never yet been too weak to sit upon a horse." So after that Rikissa had to try to make the best of what she found in Sweden, but as soon as her husband Erik died, she returned to Denmark, taking with her her little son Erik, called "Læspe," or the Halt.

This prince was raised to the throne in 1222 on the death of the last of the Sverker race, Johan Sverkersson, and his reign lasted till 1250, when the Bondar line of kings died out with him. He had not been suffered to rule in peace, and more than once this last of the Bondar kings had to flee from his kingdom and take refuge with his mother's kinsmen in Denmark. A new race, known as the "Folkungar," came into power during his reign, and gained such a footing in the state, that Erik Læspe, against his will, had to give the title of "Jarl of the Swedes and Goths" to the rich and powerful Birger Brosa, who was at that time head of this great family. The rank of Jarl and duke gave Birger much power, while his wealth helped him to live in a princely style. The clergy showed him marked favour in return for the aid he gave them in trying to

have church-assemblies made free of control from the state;
and he won the good-will of all devout churchmen by setting
on foot a crusade against the pagan Finns, whom he forced at
the point of the sword to renounce their old faith and receive
baptism. The Jarl had not returned from Finland when Erik
Læspe died in 1250, and the Swedish Council being anxious
to act independently of him, proceeded to elect a new king in
his absence. After a long and stormy debate, their choice fell
upon Jarl Birger's eldest son, Valdemar, who through his mother
was closely related to the royal families of Sweden and Denmark,
she being sister of the late King Erik Læspe and niece of the
Danish kings Knud VI. and Valdemar II. Their choice of
Valdemar gave offence to his father, who was indignant when
he learnt that his wife's claims on the succession had been
thought better than his own.

We will, however, leave for another chapter the story of
young Valdemar of Sweden and his father Birger Jarl, and
proceed at once to the history of Norway, which we must
resume from the time of Harald Haardraade, the ablest and
most powerful ruler in Northern Europe during the middle of
the eleventh century.

PART III.

THE EARLY TROUBLES OF NORWAY.

Harald II.—We have seen that when King Magnus of
Norway died in 1047, and gave the kingdom of Denmark to
Knud the Great's nephew, Svend Estridsen, he left his Norwegian crown to his uncle Harald. This prince known in
history as Harald Haardraade, and to the Danes of his own
and later times as "Denmark's Blight," and the "Lightning of
the North," was by no means satisfied with his nephew's way of
disposing of his crowns, and was eager to go to war with Svend
almost before the breath was out of King Magnus's body. But
the Norwegians refused to fight for him, declaring in the first
Thing held after the death of their king, that they "would rather
follow the dead Magnus than the living Harald," and the new
king had therefore to content himself with his one crown.

Harald had in his earlier days gone through many strange adventures at the court of Byzantium, where he was for some time chief captain of the Væringjar; and the story of the Empress Zoe's love for him, and his daring escape by night from the prison where he had been put through her jealous desire to prevent his departure, was made the subject of many romances during his own and later times. After his escape with all the other Northmen from "Miklagaard," or Constantinople, with vast treasures in gold and precious stones, he had gone to Russia and married his cousin Elizabeth, daughter of Jarislav of Novogorod, and returned with her and all his soldiers and slaves to Norway, where he had done his best to stir up strife and raise wars against his nephew, King Magnus. When he came to the throne he at once plunged into vikings and quarrels with his neighbours, and as we know through our Old English History, it was this king, who at the request of Tostig, brother of Harald King of England, invaded our island and was defeated and slain at Stamford Bridge on the 25th of September, 1066.[1]

Olaf Kyrre, 1066-1093.—Olaf, the eldest son of Harald Haardraade, who had come to England with his father, made a treaty with Harald King of England after the battle of Stamford Bridge, in accordance with which he was allowed to depart in peace with his men and ships. On his return to Norway, he became king in the place of his father, and unlike him gained the love of his people, who called him Olaf "Kyrre," or the Peaceful, because in his time they were not plagued with wars. We are told that in this reign, the Norwegians began to enjoy comforts which their forefathers had never known, and that houses were now first built with windows

---

[1] It is related that before the fight King Harald of England sent to offer Tostig terms, promising that if he would lay down his arms and join him, he would give him the third of England for his share;—"And what will Harald of England give Harald of Norway, my friend and ally?" asked the earl. "Seven feet of England's earth for a grave," answered the English king's messenger, "or a foot more may be, since his length of body exceeds that of other men!" "Then ride back to your master, and tell him to arm for the fight," cried Tostig, "for it shall never be told in Norway that Tostig of Northumbria forsook King Harald in the land of his foes. Together we will conquer England, or die with honour."

instead of mere holes to let in air and light, and with closed-in stoves in the place of rude open hearths. Olaf loved show and company, and he kept a court with officers of state like the kings of other lands, and did all he could to teach his people the more polished manners he had seen among the southern nations of Europe.

When Olaf died in 1093, his son Magnus Barfod became king, and this prince who was very much like his grandfather, Harald Haardraade, was as fond of war as his father Olaf had been of peace. He soon got into a quarrel with the Swedish king, in regard to the boundary-line between their kingdoms, but in 1101 a peace was made, in which it was agreed that Magnus should marry the Swedish princess, Margrete, who on that account was known as *Fred Kulla*, or the "Peace-Maiden." Magnus next turned his arms against the Western Islands and Scotland, and after forcing the natives to pay him tribute, he went to the Isles of Man and Anglesea, both of which he subdued. His last attempt was to conquer Ireland, but having gone too far inland, he was cut off from his ships by a large band of Irish peasants, and he and all his men were slain. It is said that he took his name "Barfod," "Bare-legs," from his habit of wearing a kilt like the men of Cantyre, amongst whom he had spent some time. When the people of Norway first saw their king with naked legs and short skirts they laughed at him, but Magnus was not a man to trouble himself about his subjects' laughter, and he kept to the highland dress to the end of his days.

The Three Kings.—When the news of Magnus' death reached Norway in 1103, the people chose his three sons, Ejsten, Sigurd and Olaf to be their joint kings. Olaf's death while he was still a child, and Sigurd's absence for some years in the Holy Land, left Ejsten for a time sole King of Norway, but when Sigurd came back from the crusades, he ruled jointly with his brother. Ejsten was of a quiet gentle nature, but Sigurd was so restless and wayward, that one might almost suppose him to have been insane. He had gone to the Holy Land with a large fleet, which he used to put down pirates in the Mediterranean, and after making his way to Jerusalem and helping to take Sidon from the Infidels, he paid a visit to the Greek emperor, Alexius, at Constantinople. There he stayed some time, and in return for the costly presents made to him by the emperor, he gave him as a parting gift all his ships, and returned to Norway by way of Hungary, Germany and Denmark. After this great adventure, he took the name of "Jorsalafar," or "the Jerusalemite," and on his return to his own kingdom, he did all he could to raise the power of the clergy, and induce his people to follow some of the practices of the Christian churches in the South of Europe which had not before been known in Norway. As soon as he became sole King of Norway on the death of his brother Ejsten in 1123, he put down many of the old forms of law, and ordered that doubtful cases should always be decided by means of the ordeal of a red-hot iron. This new practice proved a very unlucky one to Sigurd himself, for it happened that towards the end of his life a man came to Norway from Ireland, who claimed to be a son of the king's father Magnus Barfod, and demanded to have the truth of his words tested by ordeal. The king gave his consent, and this man, who was believed to be an impostor, but who called himself Harald Gille Magnusson, went through the ordeal in the presence of Sigurd and a large number of people, and was at once owned by the king as his brother. On the death of Sigurd, his son Magnus, who was a very vicious prince, tried to drive the new claimant out of the country, but the people of Norway who had by that time learnt to think him more fitted to be their king than Magnus, would not suffer him to be set aside, and in the end they chose both these princes to rule jointly over the kingdom.

Magnus and Harald did not long remain good friends, and the Danes as usual were not slow to take part in the civil war, which very quickly broke out in the kingdom. When Harald was beaten by his rival he took refuge in Denmark, from which he returned with an army; and while he was making war in one part of Norway, the Wends were pillaging other portions of the country.

Norway's age of troubles.—Norway, like the other northern kingdoms, was doomed to pass through a century of civil wars. No other country has perhaps ever been troubled by so many claimants of the throne in so short a time, and from before the middle of the twelfth to the middle of the thirteenth century, that is from the reign of our Henry I. to the twenty-fourth year of Henry III., there was no peace for the kingdom from these pretenders. Some of these men had perhaps real claims to the throne, but whether true or false, the claimants for the most part lost their lives by violence. Harald Gille's first act had been to blind his fellow-king Magnus, and in the next year he was himself strangled in his bed at Bergen by Sigurd, a man who claimed to be also a son of Magnus Barfod, and who after killing Harald Gille, took the blind king Magnus out of the prison in which he had been thrown, and set him on the throne. Then a new war broke out, and Sigurd and Magnus the Blind were both killed in battle.

Many parties now sprang up in the country, known by a great number of names, and of these the strongest were *Birkebenerne*, "the Birch Legs," and *Baglerne*, or "the Croziers." The former took their name from the birch-bark sandals or leggings, which they were forced to wear for want of proper shoes, and the latter from the word "bagall," the latin *baculus*, a crozier, because their first leader had been Nicholaus, Bishop of Oslö. The greatest leader of the "Birch Legs" was Sverre, who in 1176 gave himself out to be a son of King Sigurd II., but was believed by most persons to be the son of a brush-maker of Trondhjem, who had received some learning in order that he might become a priest. His success against the other claimants of the throne was so great that in the year 1184 he secured the homage of the Norwegian people, and was crowned at Bergen. He was a very able ruler, but there were so many parties in the state against him that he had no chance of doing much for the good of the kingdom, and he died in 1202, worn out by constant war. The clergy, headed by the Archbishop Erik of Trondhjem, were his worst foes, and as usual the Danes were ready to help in keeping up strife in the sister-kingdom, so whenever Sverre's subjects rose against him, they were certain of aid from Denmark, which always gave them a retreat in case of need. Sverre's only son, Hakon III., reigned no more than two years, and his sudden death at Bergen in 1204, most likely by poison said to have been given him by his stepmother, Margaret, daughter of St. Erik of Sweden, opened the way to new claimants.

Then the "Birch Legs" crowned a little child called Guttorm, a grandson of Sverre, and ruled the kingdom in his name till his death a few months later. After that they gave the crown to Inge Baardsen, a nephew of the great Sverre, who during his thirteen years' reign had to contend with four or five rivals, who in turn laid claim to the throne, and were sometimes able by the help of the Danes to drive out Inge, and set themselves up in his place for a short time.

Hakon IV., 1217-1263.—On the death of Inge, in 1217, Hakon, a boy of thirteen who had been brought up at his court and was said to be a son of Hakon III., was set upon the throne by the "Birch Legs."

During these times of trouble the clergy had gained great power in the state, and taken upon themselves the sole right of choosing the king, for although according to law the eldest son was to succeed his father, this was only to be allowed in cases where the bishops could be certain that the claimant " had not fallen away from the doctrines of Christianity and the Church." In 1162, the crown of Norway had been declared to be a "fief of St. Olaf," and only to be held by the prince who had received it at the hands of the pope's chief servant in Norway, namely, the Archbishop of Trondhjem, and accordingly from that time forth, the Norwegian kings were crowned in a church with all the ceremonies usual in other countries at royal coronations, and the simple forms of the old northern courts were quite done away with.

CHAPTER XII.

SWEDEN FROM 1250 TO 1400.

Birger Jarl, Father of Kings; his expectations of the Crown—Choice of his son Valdemar in his absence—Ivar Blaa's conduct—Valdemar's "Erik Course"—Birger's anger—Ivar's retorts—Birger submits; his rule in Sweden; the laws he passed in favour of women—Valdemar's incapacity—Quarrels between brothers—Magnus seizes on Valdemar—The reign of Magnus; his merits as a law giver; his nickname Barnlock—New order of nobles; the Unfree and Free; nobles and cavaliers—Three sons of Magnus—Torkel Knutsson's influence for good; troubles after his death; civil war; King Birger throws his brothers in a dungeon and starves them to death; feelings of people against him; consequences of his acts—Magnus, son of murdered Duke Erik, made king; his minority; his vicious conduct and weakness; his queen; his son Erik killed—Hakon made king of Norway—Friendship for Valdemar Atterdag of Denmark; gives up Skaania and other provinces—Hakon promises to marry Elizabeth of Holstein; his marriage to Margaret of Denmark—Death of Queen Blanka—Magnus insults Elizabeth—Valdemar promises him help—Magnus outlaws twenty-four nobles; what they do; fate of Magnus—Albert of Mecklenburg, King of Sweden; Albert's reign; his weakness and wars—Bo Jonsson; his great power—State of kingdom—Bo Jonsson's heirs invite Margaret to take the crown; her conduct—Albert's defeat and unhappy end—Margaret's success—Union of Calmar—Erik of Pomerania accepted as future king of Sweden.

PART I.

THE FOLKUNGAR KINGS.

Birger, the Father of Kings.—THE Folkungar race, which ruled over Sweden from the time of our Henry III. to the close of the reign of Edward III., numbered amongst its members kings of great talent. Birger Jarl, "the father of kings" and the founder of this family's influence in the state,

although he never wore the crown himself, may be said to
have been more of a king than some among his descendants
who bore the regal title. Birger, as we have seen in a former
chapter, was absent from Sweden when his brother-in-law, Erik
Læspe, the last of the Bondar race died, and when he returned
from the crusade which he had been carrying on in Finland,
he was very angry to find that the Swedish Council of State
had taken advantage of his absence to choose his young son
Valdemar to be king. Some of the Councillors had opposed
Valdemar's election on the ground that as the son of Birger
Jarl he would be completely under the control of that ambitious chieftain, but their objections had been set aside by
Ivar Blaa, a noble knight, related through his mother to the
Bondar family, who leading the little Valdemar into the
Council Chamber, presented him to his brother-nobles as the
only one able to save them from having Birger raised to be
king and master of Sweden. That argument removed their
objections against Valdemar, for knowing the character of
Birger, the Council foresaw that the Jarl would dispute the
crown with any stranger, and accordingly they conducted the
youth in great state to Upsala, and presenting him at the Mora
Stone to the people, secured for him the homage of all the
different orders of the Thing, and carried him on his
" Erik's course," [1] or royal progress before his father's return
to Sweden.

When on his arrival Birger learnt what had been done, he
gave vent to threats of vengeance against the Council, and
tried, but without avail, to induce the people to set aside
Valdemar's election, on the ground that it was not according to
law, since it had been settled without his knowledge and consent as Jarl of Sweden.

"Who was the traitor that dared to elect a king in my
absence?" asked the Jarl, when he first met the Councillors of
State. "I was the man, Birger Jarl," cried the knight Ivar,
"and if my choice does not please you, we can all see
now where we could have found a king more to your mind!"

---

[1] An ancient custom, which required of a newly elected king that he
should drive through every province of the kingdom to show himself and
receive the homage of the people.

Birger was silent for a moment on receiving this reply which showed that the Council saw he had been disappointed at not getting the crown for himself, and then he asked, " Who would you choose if you set my boy aside ? "

" We will think about that," answered Ivar, " but there is no lack of choice. Sweden might find a king to suit her under this cloak of mine ! "

After that, Birger Jarl let well alone, and took his place as chief seneschal at the splendid coronation of his little son in 1251 at Linköping. From that time till his death in 1266. the Jarl, although not a king in name, ruled Sweden with a vigour and prudence that very few of the earlier kings had shown. He kept the nobles in check, and made them respect the laws, encouraged knightly training, and did away with trial by ordeal; and he also won the gratitude of the women by the laws which he caused to be passed in their favour, and which gave them the right to half as much as their brothers of the property of their parents. Before Birger's time the daughters of wealthy men could not claim any share in their fathers' possessions as long as they had brothers living; for as the law put it, " where the hat comes in, the cap goes out." Birger is said either to have founded the town of Stockholm, or at any rate to have fortified it, and raised it to the rank of an important stronghold, and thenceforth it became one of the best defences against the attacks of Finnish pirates.

Valdemar, 1250-1279.—As soon as Birger died, his son King Valdemar began to quarrel with his brothers, Duke Magnus and Prince Erik, to whom their father had given provinces some years before his death. Valdemar's evil conduct in preferring his sister-in-law, the lovely nun Jutta, to his queen Sofia,[1] brought the anger of the clergy upon him, and in 1274, he was forced to send away Jutta, and by way of penance to make a pilgrimage to Rome. During his absence, Magnus was looked upon as king, but on his return there was a meeting of the three brothers, and Valdemar was left to rule as before.

For a short time, things seemed to go on more smoothly, but in the next year Erik Glipping, King of Denmark, gave men

[1] Daughters of the Danish king, Erik Plovpeng.

and money to the princes to rise against Valdemar, who was surprised with his queen and his son while they were resting in a wood, and barely escaped from the pursuit of his brothers. After staying a short time in Norway, where he had taken refuge, he ventured to come back to Sweden, but he was soon taken and shut up by Duke Magnus, who forced him to renounce the crown of Sweden and content himself with the province of East Gothland. Valdemar soon afterwards went over to Denmark, but on his return to Sweden in 1288, he was seized by order of his brother, and kept under mild restraint in the castle of Nyköping until his death, which took place in 1302. His only son, Prince Erik, was then released from the prison in which he had long been kept, and spent the rest of his life in the service of the Swedish kings without making any attempt to gain the crown for himself.

Magnus, 1279–1290.—In the meanwhile, Magnus, who had been crowned King of the Svea and Gauta, in 1279, proved himself an able ruler. For some years, he had a hard task in putting down all the revolts which were stirred up by his own wealthy and unruly kinsmen of the Folkungar family, but by his firmness he succeeded in crushing their power, and then he set to work to complete the task which his father Birger had begun in making the laws more just towards the poor. He owed his name "*Ladu-laas*," Barn-lock, to a law which he caused to be passed in favour of the peasants, and which ordered that travellers of noble birth should pay like other persons for the straw and corn that they used on their journeying from place to place. "No Roman emperor could wish himself a nobler name than *Ladu-laas*," says the writer of the Old Swedish Chronicle, "and very few could have laid claim to it, for the name of '*Ladu-Brott*,' Barn-breaker, would suit most rulers much better."

The reign of Magnus Ladulaas marks a great crisis in the history of Sweden, for he first settled by law the kind of service to the crown which made men rank as *Frälse*, free, instead of being classed as *Ofrälse*, not free. The difference between the two classes was merely in regard to freedom from taxes, and had nothing to do with freedom of person or property, which might exist as fully amongst the *Ofrälse* as amongst the

Frälse, free. But Magnus, who was very anxious to augment the power of the crown, granted freedom from taxation to all who would serve with horses and men against the enemies of the king, and thus established a kind of nobility by service, known by the name of *russ-tjenst*, and this in the course of time came in Sweden to be an order of knights or cavalier-nobles, who were expected to be foremost in the field when the king was at war, and nearest his person as office-bearers at his court in times of peace.[1]

King Magnus kept a brilliant court, and encouraged the nobles in following all the practices of knighthood which were common in the Southern Countries of Europe. He was also one of the best supporters that the church and clergy had ever had among the Swedish kings, and in the course of his reign he caused five monasteries to be founded, and gave large sums to many of the churches in his kingdom. At his death in 1290, his body, by his own desire, was placed in the Franciscan monastery, which he had founded in Stockholm, "in the hope," as he said in his will, "that his memory might not pass away with the sound of his funeral bells."

PART II.

THE THREE UNFRIENDLY BROTHERS.

Birger, 1290-1319.—Magnus left three sons, Birger, Erik and Valdemar, whose unhappy quarrels brought misery and death upon themselves and many of their nearest kindred and friends. Birger was crowned king when only nine years of age, and as long as his father's friend, the Marschal Torkel Knutsson, governed for him, all went well in Sweden. The Finns were again brought under subjection to the Swedish crown, after having fallen away from the Christian religion; a new and complete code of laws was laid before the people at the Great Thing of 1295, and approved of by them; and many things were done during this period for the good of the country.

---

[1] This service with men and horses was known as *russ-tjenst*, horse service, from the old northern word *rus* or *ros*, a horse, and *tjenst*, service.

SWEDEN FROM 1250 TO 1400.

But as soon as Birger began to reign by himself all went wrong. After long quarrels with his brothers, he made friends with them, and at length in 1306, yielded to their wishes that he should allow them to have the faithful Torkel Knutsson tried for treason, and put to death. As soon as Erik and Valdemar had thus freed themselves from the restraint of the Marschal's influence in the state, they seized upon the person of the king and kept him shut up till he had signed a treaty by which they were left to govern their provinces as if they were free sovereigns. Some years now passed in seeming peace, but the dukes joined with the kings of Norway and Denmark against their brother, and they and their friends laid waste his kingdom in every part, until the unhappy peasants were scarcely able to keep corn enough to feed themselves, and whole districts were stripped of everything that could serve for food for men or cattle.

Then it was that King Birger, by the advice, it is said, of his Danish queen, Marta, daughter of Erik Glipping of Denmark, made up his mind to revenge himself upon his brothers. In the autumn of the year 1317, when Edward II. had been ten years King of England, the King and Queen of Sweden were keeping their court at the castle of Nyköping, and having learnt that Duke Valdemar was on his way from Oeland to Stockholm, they invited him and his brother Duke Erik, to spend the Yule-tide with them. The two princes came, and were welcomed with every appearance of friendship by the king, who expressed his regret that the smallness of the castle would not allow of their servants being housed with them. But as soon as the men had left to take up their quarters in the town, the bridges were raised and the gates locked, and when the king learnt that his brothers were asleep, he gave orders to have them chained, and thrown into the lowest dungeon of the castle. Two of the knights to whom Birger had committed this charge showed unwillingness to obey him; but when they were put into irons on the spot, no one else attempted to evade his orders. The king looked on while his brothers were being chained to rings fastened for the purpose to the wall of the dungeon, and then, wild with excitement, he

M

rushed up to the queen, and cried out : " Now all will be right ! At last I have Sweden in my own hands !"

Slow Death of Princes.—For four months the prisoners were left in their wretched prison, while King Birger and Queen Marta lived in the same building, and refused in any way to lessen the misery of their captives. At length the friends and followers of the prisoners clamoured so loudly for their release, and threatened the life of the king so fiercely, that Birger found it would not be possible for him to remain longer at Nyköping. He and the queen then quitted the castle, after they had seen the prison tower made fast, and the keys thrown into the water, leaving the princes to die of hunger. The sad fate of the brothers became a favourite subject for the popular tales and songs in which the northern nations in that age took such great delight, and in the Swedish Rhyming Chronicle it is related that Duke Erik, who had been sharply wounded when put into the dungeon, lived only three days after the door of his prison was locked for the last time, while Valdemar lingered a full week longer than his brother.

The news of Birger's treatment of the princes raised all Sweden against him. Stockholm closed its gates when he drew near, and the people of Nyköping refused to let him enter the castle, and threatened to take his life unless he produced his brothers. Then the captain of the fort had the dead bodies of the princes wrapped in robes of golden tissue, and laid on biers outside the castle-gates, that the people might see that those for whom they had taken up arms were no longer living. At the sight of their wounded starved bodies the rage and grief of the besiegers knew no bounds ; and, rushing forward, they attacked the castle of Nyköping, and razed it to the ground.

Birger for a time had help from Denmark, where his son Magnus had been kept in safety by his brother-in-law, King Erik Menved ; but at length he gave up the attempt to struggle against his people, and fled in 1319 with his queen and daughter to the Danish Court. In the following year young Magnus was taken by his father's foes, and in spite of the pledges of safety given him if he would lay down his arms and disband his Danish soldiers, he was publicly beheaded at

Stockholm. The death of this son, a brave and promising youth, caused much sorrow to King Birger, who died in the following year, bowed down by grief, and was buried at Ringsted Abbey, which contains the graves of many of the early Danish kings.

PART III.

HALF A CENTURY OF TROUBLES.

Magnus Smek, 1319.—In Sweden in the meanwhile the people were gathering loyally round the gallant knight, Mats Ketilmundsson, who on Midsummer's Day, 1319, had appeared before the assembly of the Thing at Upsala, and holding up in his arms Duke Erik's little son Magnus, a child scarcely three years of age, had begged the people to receive him as their king. This they pledged themselves they would do, and the next year a number of the highest members of the Thing went into Norway to demand the homage of that kingdom for their little prince, who through his mother, Ingeborg, daughter of Hakon V., was the nearest heir to the Norwegian crown, which his grandfather, the late King Hakon, had caused to be settled upon the children of his daughter.

The people of Norway were well pleased to receive Magnus as their king, and a Council of State was chosen there as well as in Sweden to govern until the young king grew to be a man. This was a happy time for both kingdoms, and there was great rejoicing in Sweden when, in the year 1332, representatives came from the provinces of Skaania, Halland, and Bleking,—which had been pawned by Erik Menved and the weak Christopher II. of Denmark to the Swedish Council of State,—and offering to take oaths of allegiance to King Magnus on behalf of themselves and their countrymen, prayed to be joined with the Swedish kingdom. But when Magnus began to rule for himself after the death of his true friend and adviser, Mats Ketilmundsson, in 1336, there was an end of the prosperity of the kingdom and everything seemed to go wrong, for he and his queen, Blanka of Namur, showed such a taste for pleasure, and such a liking for bad favourites, that the people in both countries soon lost all their love and respect for them.[1]

Things went on from bad to worse until at last, in the year 1350, the king's elder son, Prince Erik, put himself at the head of a large army of the best men in the kingdom of Sweden, and demanded that his parents should send away their unworthy favourite, Bengl Algotsson. At the same time the Norwegians demanded to have Hakon, the second son of King Magnus, to govern them; and thus the people in both kingdoms showed how glad they would be to get rid of their weak king. The sudden death of Prince Erik caused very great sorrow amongst the Swedes, who thought that he had died by poison given to him by his mother, Queen Blanka. Magnus in the meanwhile still further enraged his subjects by the friendship he showed towards King Valdemar Atterdag of Denmark, who had had the craft to regain the provinces of Skaania, Halland, and Bleking in return for a promise of help against the Swedish Council of State, and thus Sweden lost those valuable districts, which the people had hoped would remain for ever united with the Swedish crown lands. When it was known that Valdemar had induced Magnus to agree to a marriage between his little daughter Margaret and Hakon, heir to Norway and Sweden, the Council of State did their best to prevent it, and at first it seemed as if the plans of the Danish king would all be thwarted, for by their advice, young King Hakon withdrew his consent to marry Margaret, and offered to take Elizabeth of Holstein, as his people wished, to be his queen. But soon after this marriage appeared to be settled, everything was again upset, and Hakon became reconciled to his mother and his father, and went to Copenhagen to marry the little Princess Margaret. In the meanwhile, as we have seen in a former chapter, poor Elizabeth, who had set sail for Sweden, lost both husband and freedom; for having been driven by stress of weather into a Danish port, she was detained there, on some pretence or other, for a long time by King Valdemar, and at last she

---

[1] The nickname *Smek* was given to Magnus to betoken his low vicious habits.

had to send for help to her brothers before she could regain her liberty. After the marriage of his son and the little Danish princess King Magnus, thinking he might now take his own way, ordered twenty-four of the first nobles of Sweden, against whom he had some ill-will, to leave the kingdom without delay, and not return till he gave them permission, on pain of being outlawed.

The outlawed nobles made haste to leave Sweden, but it was only to betake themselves to the court of Mecklenburg, where they offered the Swedish crown to Albert, Count of Mecklenburg, son of King Magnus's only sister Euphemia. The count accepted their offer with joy, and in the autumn of the same year, 1363, he landed in Sweden, together with the twenty-four banished nobles, and was at once chosen king by the Great Thing, which at the same time declared that Magnus and Hakon had both forfeited the allegiance of the people on account of their want of good faith to their own subjects, and their friendly conduct to the enemies of the kingdom. In a battle fought between the rival kings at Enköping in 1365, Magnus was taken captive, and not again set free till 1371, when by a treaty between Albert of Sweden and Hakon of Norway, it was settled that he might enjoy certain revenues and remain with his son, on condition that he made no attempt to regain the Swedish crown. His death in the year 1374 freed Albert of Mecklenburg from the chief cause of disturbance in his new possessions, for King Hakon never showed any wish to get back the Swedish crown for himself.

PART IV.

SWEDEN UNDER FOREIGN RULE.

Albert, 1363-1389.—Albert had been chosen by the nobles of Sweden under the idea that he would be a mere puppet in their hands, but they found that his obstinacy made him less easy to manage than they had supposed; and their anger was soon turned against the crowd of Germans who had followed him into Sweden, and to whom he had given all the offices of state that he could dispose of. Hatred of the foreigners made many of the knights and lesser nobles join the Bondar in an attempt to bring back King Magnus, and they all united together in an appeal to the Council of State, praying them to relieve the nation of their heavy burdens. But the great nobles cared very little about the troubles of the poorer people, and so in spite of their own causes of discontent against the king, they did nothing to help their countrymen. What made matters worse was that the Hansers gave their support to the German king, and in return for great privileges in their trade, guarded the shores of Sweden for him and kept him free from all attacks by sea.

Bo Jonsson rules.—After a time, however, the Council of State took offence at Albert's conduct, and they made him understand that, if he wished to keep the crown of Sweden, he must not put his German friends into the command of the royal fortresses, or attempt to raise them above the Swedish nobles; indeed, they even threatened to depose him at once if he did not obey their directions. Then King Albert to save himself, made choice in 1371 of Bo Jonsson, the richest noble in Sweden, to be his "*all powerful Helper*," as he called it, and to rule for him "over his court, his house, his lands, his officers, and servants, to choose the members of the Council of State when any should be removed by death, and in all things to enjoy the same power as himself." From that time till his death, in 1385, Bo Jonsson "ruled the land with a glance of his eye," as the Rhyming Chronicle of those times expresses it; but nothing could exceed the licence of the nobles at this period, for they and the knights and bishops carried on their private quarrels without any regard to the laws. Bo Jonsson himself on one occasion followed his foe, the knight Karl Nilsson, into the church of the Franciscans at Stockholm, and hacked him to pieces before the high altar. Where the great men of the land could do such deeds without being punished for them, the poorer classes had little chance of meeting with right and justice.

When Bo Jonsson died, King Albert thought that there was a good chance for him to free himself from the power of the nobles, but the latter were not so easily put down, and after a fierce civil war and much trouble the heirs of Bo Jonsson, to whom he had left by will all his power in the state, as if it were his own to dispose of, made an offer of the throne to Queen Margaret of Denmark and Norway.

This act was the signal for new wars and fresh troubles of every kind. The Hansers and some of the German princes sent ships and troops to Sweden to help King Albert, and a small number of Swedes still held to him, but this they did less from regard for his person, than from the hatred which they bore to Denmark, and the fear they had of having a Danish ruler over them. Between pirates and armed foes threatening the coasts, and war on land, with bad crops, famine and disease in all parts of the kingdom, few nations could have been in a worse state than the Swedes at that time.

Margaret in Sweden.—Margaret proved a far more dangerous foe to King Albert than any he had ever had to deal with, as he found to his cost, in spite of his folly in despising her. As soon as she had formally accepted the offer of the Swedish crown made to her by Bo Jonsson's heirs and some of their friends, she lost no time in sending an army into Sweden, which gave Albert's German troops battle at Falköping and defeated them; after which she kept Albert and his son shut up in prison till the year 1395. When he was set free, King Albert found he could no longer stay in Sweden, and he then returned to his old home in Mecklenburg, where he spent the rest of his days, in neglect and want, and died, it is said, in the same year as Queen Margaret. As his only son had lost his life in 1397, there was no one of the family left to dispute the claims of Margaret's adopted son and heir, Erik of Pomerania, to be king of Sweden after her.

Queen Margaret ruled the Swedish kingdom so ably, and managed the nobles so cleverly, that none of them seemed to have thought of going against her wishes, although she called upon them to pay taxes, and to give back the castles and lands which they held in pawn, and to do many other things which former kings of Sweden had never asked of their subjects without getting themselves into trouble, and running the risk of losing the crown. Margaret even persuaded the Swedes in

1396—although much against their will—to crown her nephew Erik, and to do homage to him as joint king with herself. Not content with this, she induced them in the following year to consent to the union of the kingdom of Sweden with Norway and Denmark under one ruler. But although as long as she lived she kept the Swedish people quiet, and content to have a foreign ruler over them, it was very different when she was no longer at hand to maintain peace amongst them.

CHAPTER XIII.

NORWAY FROM 1217 TO 1400.

Hakon IV.; his character; his wars—Skule Baardsson; his defeat and death—Hakon's reputation among foreign princes—Iceland: its condition; the causes of its downfall—Snorre Sturlasson murdered—Iceland subdued—Greenland—Invasion of Scotland; defeat at Largs—Hakon dies—Magnus, the Law-betterer; his reign—Erik Priest-hater—Troubles—Maid of Norway—Hakon V.; his successor—Magnus Smek of Sweden—Black Death—The Partridge—Olaf succeeds Hakon VI.—Margaret's Regency—Olaf's death—Erik of Pomerania—Margaret's popularity—Olaf's funeral; his heart carried to Denmark—Albert's pretensions—Things of Denmark choose Margaret as their "Master" and sole Ruler—Norway makes choice of her for its Queen; her adoption of Erik; her love for him—Opinion of foreigners—Lübeck Chronicle—Troubles in Sweden—Albert's hatred of her; she accepts the Crown of Sweden; defeats Albert; his imprisonment and humiliation; put on the rack—Stockholm resists the Queen—The *Vitalien*—Margaret's success—Albert ransomed—Women of Mecklenburg—Queen and young Erik enter Stockholm—Erik crowned—Act of Union of Calmar—Erik's incapacity; his character—Execution of Brodersen—Troubled times; wars with Holstein; causes of war—Regent-Countess—Margaret's meeting with the Countess—Margaret's death.

PART I.

NORWAY'S BEST TIME.

Hakon IV., 1217–1262.—Hakon IV. is the only king of Norway who made himself much known or respected in his own times beyond the limits of the Scandinavian lands. But he was no ordinary man, and from the moment when in 1217, at the age of thirteen, he was chosen by the party of the

"Birch Legs" to be king, till his death in 1262, while engaged in hostilities with the Scottish King Alexander III., he never relaxed his efforts to extend and secure the power of the crown. In his youth he defeated one hostile faction after the other, and when at length he found that Skule Baardsson, who was his father-in-law and the brother of his predecessor, Inge Baardsson, aimed at nothing short of equal power with himself in the state, he turned his arms with success against him also. In the early part of his reign, Hakon had derived great help from Skule, and after marrying his daughter Margrete, he gave proof of his gratitude and affection for his old friend by raising him to the rank of Jarl and Duke of Norway, and entrusting one-third of the kingdom to him to govern in his name. Not content with these honours, Skule in 1240 caused himself to be proclaimed king, and advanced on Trondhjem at the head of his partizans, among whom were many chieftains of great power; but before he could reach the Norwegian capital he was met by Hakon at Oslö, where the rebel army was completely routed, and he himself forced to take refuge within the walls of a monastery.

Skule's death by violence soon after his defeat at Oslö secured to Norway a greater degree of peace than it had known for a hundred years. At the same time Hakon showed great ability in restoring order to his kingdom, while his fame for valour and piety spread to distant lands, and so strongly excited the admiration of foreign princes, that Louis IX. of France (known as the Saint) sent a special embassy to Norway to entreat his help in a crusade, and the pope proposed that he should extend his reputation by taking arms against the emperor, Frederick II. But Hakon was wise enough to escape entering into distant conflicts which did not concern him, and had also the tact to avoid giving offence by his refusal. The king had, in fact, objects in view much nearer home, for he had long been anxious to reduce Iceland to the condition of a mere province of Norway, and to put an end to the independence of that colony, which seemed always ready to give a welcome to everyone wishing to escape from the laws of the mother-country.

Iceland ceases to be free.—The Icelanders had enjoyed their freedom since the days of Harald Haarfaager, when the island was first settled, and they had continued to live under equal and just laws, which made provision for the sick, aged, and suffering, and appeared in every way suited to secure personal freedom, and maintain the rights of every individual in the state. But unfortunately the jealousies and rivalries of the great families of the island, after gradually weakening their own power and embroiling all classes in strife, ended in destroying the independence of the republic, and reducing Iceland to the rank of a mere province of Norway. This event was mainly due to the ambition of the powerful family of the Sturlas, the chief of whom, Snorre Sturlasson, who was at the head of public affairs in Iceland, had raised such a host of enemies around him by his arrogant conduct, that Hakon found no difficulty in stirring up a revolt against him. After long wars, Snorre was murdered in his own house in 1241 by his son-in-law, Gissur, and the Icelanders were a few years later brought completely under the power of the Norwegian crown.

His success in this matter, and in his attempts to unite the colony of Greenland with the mother-county, encouraged Hakon in the hope that he might recover the lands which the Norwegians at one time held in Scotland; and towards the close of his reign he invaded the Scottish kingdom with a powerful fleet. The accounts given of this event by the Scotch and Norwegian chroniclers vary so much that it is not very easy to make them agree. It seems, however, to be beyond dispute that King Alexander III. of Scotland surprised the Norwegians while they were landing on the coast of Ayr; and in a battle fought at Largs, about 1261, so thoroughly defeated them that the small remnant left were glad to take to their ships, and sail in all haste to the Orkneys. There Hakon was seized with illness, and after spending the winter in much suffering, he died in the spring of the year 1262 at Kirkwall. His son Magnus, according to the Norwegian account, sold the Hebrides to Alexander of Scotland for a large sum of money; but according to the Scotch report of these events, Magnus of Norway was forced to renounce all claims to the islands without receiving any money in return.

Whatever the state of the case might have been, we know at all events that Magnus and Alexander continued to be good friends as long as they lived, and that the latter gave his daughter in marriage to Erik, the eldest son and successor of Magnus of Norway. Magnus, who reigned over Norway from 1262 to 1280, was a good and able ruler, who gained for himself the honourable name of *Laga-bæter*, or "Law-betterer," in return for the care which he took to collect and settle the best laws of the land, and to do away with those older laws which had become useless in the course of time.

PART II.

THE LAST OF THE HAKONS.

Erik Priest-hater, 1280–1299.— Erik, known as *Præstehader*, or the "priest-hater," ruled from 1280 to 1299. Although neither a bad man nor a harsh king, he did not succeed in gaining the love of his people, and was moreover always at war either with the Danes, on account of his mother Queen Ingeborg's dowry which had never been paid, or with the Scotch on account of the heritage of his daughter, Margrete. Then he also had disputes with the Hansers, whose trading rights he tried to curtail, and with his clergy, whose freedom from paying taxes he would not admit. Between all these causes of difference Erik had a troubled reign, but the worst of all his misfortunes was the death of his daughter Margrete, called by the Scotch the "Maid of Norway." The little princess who was heiress to the crowns of Scotland and Norway died at sea, while on her way in a well-guarded ship to claim the Scottish throne on the death of her maternal grandfather, Alexander III. This last trouble weighed heavily upon Erik, who never again attempted in any way to secure influence for himself or his family in Scotland.

Hakon V., 1299–1319.—On Erik's death in 1299, without leaving any sons, his only brother Hakon, who had governed Southern Norway with the title of duke during his brother's reign, became king. Hakon V. was a good ruler, and his subjects, who had much love for him, were glad to agree to his wish of letting the crown be settled on the children of his daughters, as he had no sons. Thus it came to pass that at his death in 1319 the people of Norway willingly received as their king the little Magnus of Sweden, son of King Hakon's daughter, Ingeborg, by her marriage with Erik, Duke of Sodermanland, who, as we have seen in Chapter XII., was left to die of hunger by his brother, King Birger of Sweden. Long after the Swedes had grown tired of Magnus on account of his weak love for his queen Blanka of Namur and his many favourites, the Norwegians continued to prove their respect and regard for this king, who was always known in Norway as the " Good Magnus." When at last, in 1350, King Magnus gave up the Norwegian throne to his second son, Hakon, known as Hakon VI., who had married Margaret of Denmark, the people did not forget him; and after he had fallen into trouble and lost the throne of Sweden, they begged their young king to secure his freedom, with permission for him to live in Norway for the rest of his days. Thus Magnus "*Smek*," or the " Favourite Lover," as the Swedes called him, was not quite without friends amongst his subjects.

Norway and Sweden, like the other countries of Europe, were fearfully plagued between 1350 and 1360 by the pest, known as the *Black Death*. Some Norwegian parishes were nearly rendered desolate by this scourge, and in one place among the hills it was said that all the inhabitants had been cut off by the plague except one little girl, who ran into the woods, and lived so long alone, feeding only on roots and berries, that when she was found she had almost forgotten how to talk, and had grown so wild that she could not bear to be looked at or spoken to. No one could learn her name, and she was thenceforth always known as the " Rybe," Partridge, and when she married and had a family, her children joined the name " Rybe " to their father's name of "Jorgerssen."

Olaf in Norway.—We have seen in a former chapter that when King Hakon died in 1380, his son Olaf, who five years before had been chosen King of Denmark under the regency of his mother, Margaret, succeeded to the throne of Norway.

As the young prince was only ten years of age when this second northern crown was placed upon his head, it was of course necessary to choose some one to govern in his name ; and the great skill Queen Margaret had shown in ruling Denmark for her son now made the Norwegian people entrust the regency, with full regal powers, to her during the minority of her son. Olaf's death in 1387, at the age of seventeen, and before he had begun to exercise any authority in the state, seemed for the moment to threaten the peace of the kingdom. But the confidence which the nation had learnt to place in Queen Margaret led the Council of State, without any long delay, to follow the example set by the Danes, in begging her to retain the regal power, and continue to rule the kingdom with the rank of an independent sovereign. She was solemnly proclaimed Queen of Norway at Oslö in 1388, and from that time till her death in 1412, the Norwegians had little reason to repent of their choice, for while she kept the country free from enemies abroad, she caused the laws to be carried out with equal justice against rich and poor, and brought the kingdom into a condition of peace and order, which it had not known for ages. Her popularity in Norway led the Norwegian Council of State to agree to the plans which she had most at heart in regard to the choice of a successor, and the union of the three northern kingdoms under one sovereign ; although in both these important matters the wishes and hopes of the nation at large were entirely opposed to her own. Yet so great was the influence of Margaret, that while she lived the Norwegians allowed themselves to be governed by Erik of Pomerania, for whom she had secured the three northern crowns, conjointly with herself; and after her death, in respect for her memory, they long continued true to him, although by his folly and weakness he had forfeited all claim to their respect and loyalty.

PART III.

THE TRIPLE-CROWNED QUEEN.

Margaret, 1387-1397.—Before we close this chapter we must enter somewhat more fully into the story of Olaf's death, and the events which led his subjects to choose Queen Margaret to succeed him. Olaf had died suddenly in 1387, while staying with Queen Margaret at Falsterbo, and the common people, as was often the case in that age, supposed that he had been poisoned, while many years afterwards her enemies spread a report that he had not died in his youth, as was supposed, but had been carried away out of Norway by his mother's orders. This absurd story led to a plot being formed against her in the year 1402, when an impostor appeared at Danzig, who gave himself out to be King Olaf, but the falseness of his claims was soon brought to light; and he was given up to the queen, who caused him to be burnt in the market-place at Falsterbo.

The real Olaf, of whose death there was no doubt, had received a solemn funeral at Lund in Skaania, after having lain in state for some days, wrapped in his royal robes, and wearing the crown on his head, while his heart, embalmed and enclosed in a silver shrine, was carried across the Sound to Denmark, where it was deposited in the abbey church at Sorö. As soon as Olaf's death was known, Albert the Elder, King of Sweden, appealed to the Danish people for their support, and as the heir of his nephew, Albert the Younger, grandson of Valdemar III., demanded the crown of Denmark, but the Danes paid no attention to his demands, and ten days after Olaf had been laid in his grave, the Thing of Skaania made choice of "their dearly loved, high-born princess and lady, Margaret, to be sole and independent ruler of Denmark." The Things of the Islands and of Jutland fully concurred in this choice, and all agreed in declaring that they had taken the unusual step of choosing a woman instead of a man to be their ruler, not so much because the Lady Margaret was the nearest heir of her father, the late King Valdemar III., but chiefly on account of her great, many, and well-tried merits. "They then did homage to her as their "true king and master," promising to serve and obey her all their days, unless she of her own accord should wish to give them a king to rule over the land.

In the following year the Norwegians followed the example of the Danes, and at the diet which met in 1388 at Oslö, Margaret was proclaimed Queen of Norway, and by her own wish the little prince, Erik of Pomerania, grandson of her sister Ingeborg, was chosen as her successor. Margaret had adopted this boy soon after her son's death, and from the moment that the little prince, who was only five years old at the time, came to Denmark from his home in Germany, she acted towards him in all respects as if he had been her own child, causing him to be treated with the greatest respect by her officers and attendants, and to be instructed in all the learning and accomplishments befitting a prince. By her special desire, the Danes acknowledged the little Erik as her successor on the throne of Denmark; and when she had secured to him the heritage of the Danish and Norwegian crowns, she seemed to feel as if she were merely to govern as a regent for him. Although as long as she lived all power in both kingdoms rested in her hands, she professed to reign in Erik's name during his childhood; and when he was declared of age, she caused him to take his place by her side on the throne, and tried in all ways to push him forward and make him appear to be the real sovereign. Her subjects seem, however, to have been well aware that it was to her alone to whom they owed the order which prevailed during her reign in Denmark and Norway, while her fame soon spread far beyond the northern kingdoms. We are told by the writers of the great Chronicle of Lübeck, that "when men saw the wisdom and strength that were in this royal lady, wonder and fear filled their hearts. She made peace with old foes, and kept good order over her people, gaining to her side both nobles and peasants. She went from castle to castle, and received the homage and faithful service of the great; she journeyed from province to province, and looked well into matters of law and of right, until all obeyed and served her; justice was done in the land, and even the high-born sea-robbers, who so long had plagued the kingdom and defied the laws, were seized with terror, and were glad to come forward and give surety in money for their future good conduct." The writers of the same chronicle who bear this testimony to Margaret's talents for ruling, tell us that " great marvel it is to think that a lady, who, when she began to govern for her son found a troubled kingdom, in which she owned not money or credit enough to secure a meal without the aid of friends, had made herself so feared and loved in the short term of three months, that nothing in all the land was any longer withheld from her and her son."

PART IV.

SWEDEN UNDER A QUEEN.

Margaret receives a third Crown.—While Denmark and Norway were thus enjoying greater security and quiet than either kingdom had known for many generations, Sweden continued in an unsettled state, owing to the discontent of the people with the king, Albert the Elder of Mecklenburg, whom they had themselves chosen to replace their former feeble ruler, Magnus Smek. Albert, although unable to govern the one kingdom that had so unexpectedly been put under him, was eager to secure Denmark as well; and when his nephew Albert the Younger, grandson of Valdemar III. died, he had, as we have seen, pretended that this young prince's claims on the Danish crown had passed to him. He found, however, that the Danes would not listen to his pretensions, and that his attempted invasion of the Danish kingdom had only brought loss and disgrace upon himself, which made him conceive the greatest hatred for the successful Margaret, whom he tried to bring into ridicule in every possible way. This conduct on his part roused the Queen's anger against him, and made her the more ready to listen to those Swedish nobles who, soon after she became ruler of Denmark and Norway, had come to entreat that she would accept the crown of Sweden, and try to restore order in that kingdom as she had done in the other Scandinavian lands. It was a pity that Queen Margaret had not contented herself with the two crowns which were already hers, for three were surely too much for any woman, especially as the greater number of her predecessors had found it no easy matter to bear the burden of one northern crown.

As soon as it was known that Margaret intended to take possession of Sweden, Albert raised an army of hired German troops, and prepared to take the field against her. She in the meanwhile had collected a large force, consisting of Danes, under her general, Ivar Lykke; Norwegians under the knight, Henrik Parrow; and Swedes, under Erik Kettlesson; and in the first battle which was fought between them the Swedish king was completely defeated. The hostile armies met at Leahy, a little hamlet between Falköping and Jonköping, on the 24th February, 1389, where the greater number of Albert's German troops were cut down or drowned while they were trying to force their way over the morasses, which lay between them and the queen's forces. Albert himself and his son, together with many knights, were taken captive before they could make their escape from the boggy ground which gave way under their heavily-weighted horses; and being led into the presence of the Queen, who had awaited the result of the battle within the castle of Bohus, the unhappy father and son were made to atone on the rack and by a long imprisonment for the many insulting words and acts of which they had been guilty towards Margaret.

Albert punished for his insults.—The rhyming chronicles of those times relate that King Albert had insulted the Queen by sending her a long gown and an apron, with a whetstone to sharpen her needles, and had spoken of her as the "unbreeched king" and "the monks' wife," in allusion to the favour which she showed the prelates, and had tried in every way to bring ridicule and discredit upon her. It is said that when Albert fell into her power, she avenged herself for these insults by causing him to be dressed in a long gown, bib and tucker, and by having a fool's cap put on his head with a tail dangling from it which was nineteen ells in length. Then after letting her servants keep him on the rack till he had promised to give orders that all the frontier-castles should be surrendered to her,[1] she had him and his son shut up in prison within the tower of Lindholm castle, where they were left for seven years to repent of their rudeness to her.

After these events nearly all the castles of Sweden which were held by the royal troops opened their gates to her. Stockholm, the chief city, however, held out year after year, until she agreed to release her prisoners on the payment of a ransom. The Swedes themselves showed no wish to oppose the Queen, and would gladly have given Stockholm into her hands, but the city was held by a band of Germans in the service of Albert, who would not submit. These men brought great misery on the land by engaging the help of a large number of their countrymen, known as the *Vitalen*, or *Victualling* Brotherhood, because their chief duty was to keep the town and fortress of Stockholm well supplied with *victuals*. They cared very little how they got them, or how heavily they taxed the poor country people to furnish what they needed.

King Albert and his son were kept in prison till 1395, when, in accordance with a treaty made with Queen Margaret on their behalf by the Hanse Leaguers and other German powers, they were released on the payment of 60,000 marks—silver. The Hansers who had advanced this sum had taken Stockholm as a security for three years, at the end of which time the city was to be given up to the Queen if the money were not paid back to them. It is said that the women of Mecklenburg gave up all their gold and silver ornaments to enable the deposed king to repay the ransom, but Albert, with his usual want of principle, spent the money on his own pleasures, and left Stockholm to fall into Margaret's hands. In the year 1398 she made a solemn entry into the Swedish capital, accompanied by her young nephew, Erik of Pomerania, who was then presented to the people as their future king. Shortly afterwards, Erik was crowned with great state at Calmar by the

---

[1] "And thus," says the chronicler who relates the circumstance, "was King Albert tortured in one night out of his two castles of Axelwald and Rummelberg, and would by the like means have been robbed of a third, Orebro, if the governor, who was a German, had not defied Queen Margaret's power and kept himself and his men shut up in the fort."

Archbishops of Lund and Upsala, and proclaimed King of the three northern monarchies, and on this occasion the remarkable Act, known as the Calmar Act of Union, was first made known to the Scandinavian peoples. By this Act, which had been drawn up at Calmar in 1397, and signed by the Queen and seventeen deputies of the several councils of state of the three northern kingdoms, Denmark, Sweden, and Norway were declared to be for ever united, and to be ruled over by one king only, while each state was to retain its own laws, rights, and usages. The king of this triple monarchy was to be chosen conjointly by all three nations, but nothing was said in regard to the manner in which the election to the throne was to be carried on, and hence from the very first this scheme for Scandinavian unity was beset with doubts and difficulties, which could not fail to create troubles in the future.[1]

Margaret and Erik, 1397-1412.—After the union of the three northern kingdoms had been settled, Queen Margaret withdrew more and more from public affairs, as if to show that Erik, since his coronation in 1397, had become sole King of the Scandinavian lands. But in fact she was as much the actual sovereign as ever, for Erik's incapacity forced her to retain her hold upon the regal power. As long as she lived, the people scarcely knew how feeble a ruler she had given them in the person of this young German prince, for she was almost always at hand to advise and control him, and he was thus generally prevented from showing his want of talent for governing, or commanding troops. Erik was not without a certain kind of ability, and he was learned and accomplished for the age in which he lived, but he seems to have been wholly wanting in good sense, and to

---

[1] If Margaret could have been certain of being followed on the throne by rulers as able and just as she had been, this Act of the Union of Calmar might have worked for the good of the three kingdoms. For it was quite true, as the Queen said, that each one alone was a poor weak state, open to danger from every side, but that the three united would make a monarchy, strong enough to defy the attacks and schemes of the Hanse traders and all foes from the side of Germany, and would keep the Baltic clear of danger from foreigners. There was however no ruler who came after Queen Margaret equal to her, as there had been none before her to be compared to her.

have been very vain, headstrong, and obstinate, besides which
his wonderful fortune in being chosen to rule over three kingdoms made him conceited and haughty, while at the same
time he was ungrateful to her to whom he owed everything.
In spite of all her watchfulness he was often led by his own
wilfulness to betray his incapacity to his subjects, and shortly
before Margaret's death in 1412, he gave proof of his injustice,
and his indifference to her feelings, by ordering the execution
of her intimate friend and counsellor, Abraham Brodersen, on
pretence that it was owing to this nobleman's fault that the
war, which Erik was then carrying on against the Counts of
Holstein, had proved unsuccessful.

This act must have shown the Queen how unworthy her
nephew was of the confidence and affection she had lavished
upon him, and according to some authorities it gave her a
shock from which she never recovered. The two years that
passed between Brodersen's execution and Margaret's death
were marked by great disturbances in Denmark, where the
people were heavily taxed to keep up the war which Erik was
waging against Holstein, and which had broken out soon after
the death of the former count, Gerhard VI., to whom Queen
Margaret had in earlier times ceded the duchy of Slesvig.
This prince had fallen in an attack against the Ditmarshers in
1402, leaving three infant sons, the Counts Henrik, Adolf,
and Gerhard, and the widowed countess, Elizabeth of Holstein,
had at first sought help from Margaret against her husband's brother, Bishop Henrik of Osnabrück, but after a time,
fearing that the Danish Queen might keep the strongholds in
Slesvig which had been garrisoned with Danes, she made
friends with her brother-in-law. Upon this a war soon broke
out, and it was in the midst of these troubles that Margaret,
seeing how ill King Erik understood how to conduct public
affairs in times of difficulty, resolved to try to bring about
a peace with Holstein. Accordingly, in the spring of the year
1412, she left Sjælland in her ship, " Trinity," and sailing to the
coast of Slesvig, invited the Countess Elizabeth to confer
with her.

Three days after these royal ladies had settled the terms
of an agreement which it was hoped would restore quiet to

the provinces, Margaret died suddenly at the age of sixty-three, and almost before the sound of her funeral bells ceased, the three kingdoms had begun to resound with the noise of active preparations for war.

"Death," says a Swedish writer, "made an end of Queen Margaret's life, but it could not make an end of her fame, which will endure through all ages. Under her hands the three kingdoms enjoyed a degree of strength and order, to which they had long been strangers before her time, and which neither of the three regained till long after her."

CHAPTER XIV.

DENMARK FROM 1412 TO 1448.

Erik rules alone—Trouble of people at loss of Margaret; her tact; her difficulties—Erik's incompetency; makes war for twenty-five years on Holstein; rest of monarchy neglected; his want of success—Men of Femern; decision of Sigismund, Erik's cousin—Erik's pilgrimage; capture—Philippa of England; her abilities; the bad coinage—Close of Holstein War—Engelbrechtsson; the rebellion; his conduct to the Bishops—Nobles side with Erik—Karl Knudsson—Erik's deposition; his piracy; his return to Germany—Christopher of Bavaria; his claims; his character; proclaimed King of Norway and Sweden; his conduct to Knudsson—his Queen Dorothea; their stay in Stockholm—Christopher's troubles; his easy temper—A revolt in Jutland; peasants defeated—Christopher's schemes for raising money; his death—Search for a new king—Christian of Oldenburg—Queen Dorothea's dowry; what became of her—Sweden under Christopher and Karl Knudsson—Christopher's conduct to the Swedish people—Trial of Swedish heretics—Karl crowned king of Sweden, and soon afterwards made king of Norway; frequently deposed—Alternation of fortune—Enemies of Karl; Karl in banishment—Christian I. of Denmark made king of Sweden; Christian's defeat—Karl dies king, and appoints Sten Sture marshal at his death; Sten Sture's successful rule of Sweden—Prosperity of country—Founding of Universities at Upsala and Copenhagen.

PART I.

ERIK LOSES THREE CROWNS.

Erik, 1412-1439.—THE news of Queen Margaret's death spread like wild-fire through the three Northern kingdoms. Everywhere men were disturbed when they thought of the future; for, the little that was known of Erik's character and conduct was fitted to excite fear and dislike of him in the minds of his subjects. Margaret had possessed great tact in keeping the nobles under subjection, while she never lost their affection, and she had secured the goodwill of the clergy by her liberality to the Church and her deference to their counsels. Her greatest difficulties had been to reconcile the national jealousies of the three kingdoms, and although her policy in giving offices of trust to Danes in Sweden, and to Swedes in Denmark, had not proved as successful as she had hoped, and each people grumbled over the heavy taxes imposed upon themselves for the common benefit of the three kingdoms, no real opposition was ever offered to her authority, and as long as she lived peace was preserved in all the Scandinavian states. But after her death everything was changed. Erik might perhaps have made a respectable ruler over the small and half-uncivilized territory of his Pomeranian forefathers, but he was quite unfit to rule over a great empire. Although the master of three kingdoms, he could not assert his authority over one feeble vassal like the young Count of Holstein, and instead of attending to the affairs of his monarchy, he spent twenty-five years in an useless war to decide the terms on which that prince was to hold the Duchy of Slesvig, while the rest of his dominions were left at the mercy of his German favourites, many of whom were men of low birth, who knew nothing whatever of public affairs and could not even speak the language of the people.

King Erik was generally unsuccessful in his warfare, as he laid siege to strong fortresses, and attacked the enemy without plans of any kind and in a headstrong reckless manner; and wherever he made war he laid waste the country and burnt out the people, more like a fierce Pagan freebooter than a Christian king. Thus year by year his subjects learnt to despise and fear him more and more. He had treated the men of the island of Femern with great cruelty because they had sided with the Counts of Holstein, but his conduct instead of leading them to submit to his power, made them fight all the more fiercely, and when in 1426 they gave him battle at Immervad, and beat his troops, they had gone into the field singing loud enough for him to hear a song which ended with these words—

"When the cow in her stall
Will give us flax to spin,
Then the king in his hall
May hope our land to win!"

Erik's Appeal to the Emperor.—A truce had been agreed upon in 1423 between Erik and the Holstein princes for a year, but before that term was out, seeing that he could not gain his point in any other way, he went to Germany, and laid his case before his cousin, the Emperor Sigismund. Judgment was given in his favour, and an order was issued by the Imperial Council to the Counts of Holstein to resign the Duchy of Slesvig within a limited time to the King of Denmark. But even then, when he may be said to have had everything in his own hands, instead of returning to Denmark, and forcing the Counts of Holstein to give up the Duchy to him, he set off on a pilgrimage to the Holy Land. At that time, although he was still master of three kingdoms, he could only afford to take a retinue of forty men and horses with him. On reaching Venice he found himself short of money, and having put on the dress of a serving-man, he, with a few followers, joined a Venetian trader and with him went to Jerusalem, where, however, he was recognized and taken captive by some Greeks, who would not set him free till they had obtained a heavy ransom for him.

Erik's English Queen.—During Erik's absence his Queen Philippa, the daughter of our Henry IV., did her best to keep order, and she is said to have entered into a treaty with the Hanse-traders and other German companies for bringing the coinage of Danish money into some order. Much trouble and confusion had arisen in the Northern kingdoms owing to the false weights which King Erik had allowed to be used in coining money during his reign. Queen Philippa induced the Councils of State of the three kingdoms to agree to her plan for settling the true value of the money, but as soon as King Erik returned, the old cheating began again, and during the rest of his reign money was coined in his mints which did not contain the proper quantity of gold and silver, and which therefore was looked upon with great distrust by the traders of other countries, and brought discredit upon himself and his people.

In 1428 the Hansers and other Germans made an attack on Copenhagen, which did not succeed owing to the able means of defence taken by Queen Philippa. At length, in 1435, Erik was forced to make peace with Holstein and give up the Duchy of Slesvig to Count Adolf, the only one of the princes of the family who had outlived the long war. The three kingdoms had all suffered much during this great struggle, but Sweden seems to have been the most weighed down by taxes and burdens of all kinds, and was so badly treated by King Erik's servants and officers, that it was no wonder the people were easily led to revolt against his power. The chief leader of the rebels was an honest Dalesman, called Engelbrecht Engelbrechtsson, who, being anxious to free his country, had gone through the districts of Dalekarlia and Westmannland, stirring up the people against the king. At his appeal they rushed to arms and followed him in large bands. The Swedes had good cause for their hatred of King Erik, who seldom troubled himself to come amongst them, and who seems to have cared for none of his dominions except the Danish Islands, where he had spent his childhood and youth. The most hated of his officers was the royal bailiff, Jossen Ericksson, or Jens Erichsen, as the Danes call him, who, amongst other cruel deeds laid to his charge, was accused of having caused men to be hung up over blazing fires, and women to be harnessed to heavily-laden waggons. Engelbrecht drew up a deed in which he set forth a list of these and many other wrongs that the Swedish people had suffered during the reign of King Erik, and, taking this paper with him, he marched with a large band of followers to Stockholm, where he laid it before the Council of State, praying them that they would restore to the kingdom its old rights, and depose Erik. When the bishops and nobles, who were members of the Council, bade him bear in mind the oath which he, as well as they, had taken to honour and obey the king, Engelbreckt without saying another word caught up one of the prelates by the back of his neck, and holding him out of the window, threatened to throw him and all the others down into the armed crowd below, unless they would, without further delay, fulfil the wishes of the nation. After that the Council did as he required, and drew up and signed a deed which set forth that since King Erik had broken his oath to the Swedish nation, they would no longer serve him as his subjects.

Nobles side with Erik.—The nobles, however, had no liking for the peasants, and in their hatred of this class they overlooked much that they did not approve of in the king, and leaving the former to shift for themselves, they agreed in 1436 to a new act of union with Denmark and Norway, and renewed their homage to Erik. If this prince had been less false and changeable, he might have kept his Swedish crown, for the Swedes had a great respect for their rulers, and were never very eager to oppose the authority of those who were set over them. But nothing seemed to teach King Erik that honesty is always the best policy; and he so often broke faith with his subjects, that at last they no longer felt any scruples in breaking faith with him. He had chosen a young Swedish nobleman, called Karl Knudsson Bondar, to be marshal or viceroy of Sweden, and to govern the kingdom for him. And for a short time he seemed to act openly and fairly by him, but very soon Knudsson found out that Erik had planned his disgrace and ruin, and as he was fond of power and not much more loyal to his word than the king, he at once began to lay schemes for gaining the crown for himself. About this time Engelbreckt Engelbrecktsson was murdered by one of the marshal's friends, and the peasants, who had no other leader in whom they trusted, were then easily gained over by Karl Knudsson. and made to renounce their allegiance to King Erik. The Swedish Council of State also took up Karl's cause, and proclaimed him King of Sweden, after deposing Erik in the year 1439. When the Danes heard of what the Swedes had done, they also declared that they would no longer have Erik of Pomerania for their king.

At that moment King Erik was on his way to Gothland, where he had intended to remain till his Councils of State should submit to his wishes, and declare his young cousin, Bugislav of Pomerania, heir to the three kingdoms. When he heard of the steps which his subjects had taken against him in his absence, he prepared to return to Denmark, threatening to punish their conduct with extreme severity.

But he was not allowed to land at any port, and when all his money was spent and he failed to gain funds by piracy, he went to Pomerania, where he spent the last ten years of his life in neglect and even poverty, and died in 1459 without ever having set his foot again on any of his former dominions.

PART II.

THE OLDENBURG LINE BEGINS.

Christopher, 1439-1448. — In the year 1438, the Danish Council of State, after declaring that King Erik had forfeited all claim to the allegiance of the Danes, offered the crown to his nephew, Christopher, son of Duke John of Bavaria and of Catherine of Pomerania, only sister of the late king. This young prince joyfully agreed to all the terms proposed by the Council, and on his first arrival in Denmark, he contented himself with the title of regent of the kingdom, and pledged himself to govern according to their advice, but he soon took the title of king, and in 1439 he was crowned at Viborg, in Jutland, where the nobles and clergy did homage to him. The ancient laws of the land required that the peasants should take an equal part with the higher classes in the choice of the king, but this branch of the nation had sunk so low that the Councils of State no longer thought of consulting them in any way. Yet although they were not allowed to have any share in offering the crown to Christopher of Bavaria, they were well pleased to have him for their king, for in the earlier visits which he had made to his uncle's court he had gained the goodwill of the nation at large, and by his easy temper, cheerfulnesss and general kindness of manner, had made himself a great favourite among the Danes.

As soon as Christopher was crowned king of Denmark, he began to strive to secure the thrones of Sweden and Norway, and left public affairs in the Danish kingdom to be settled by the Council of State, while he turned his mind to win over the Swedes and Norwegians. At first there seemed little chance that he would succeed, for in Norway most men still looked upon Erik as their rightful king, and in Sweden the marshal and regent, Karl Knudsson, who wanted the crown for himself, had a strong party in his favour. Margaret's scheme for uniting the three kingdoms under one crown was thus thwarted on the first attempt to carry it out, but in 1442, after much trouble and long suspense, Christopher was proclaimed king both in Norway and Sweden. The Swedes had been the first to submit to him, chiefly through the persuasions of their clergy, to whom Christopher had promised special privileges, and whom he won over by so many gifts that the bondar class, who never cared much for this German prince, called him the "bishops' king." Christopher had to pay a heavy price for the Swedish crown, for besides the clergy he had to buy over the marshal, Karl Knudsson, who would not receive him as king until he had secured for himself the duchy of Finland as an hereditary fief, and the island of Oeland for a term of years, besides a large sum of money in payment of his outlay while regent of the kingdom. Knudsson had also obtained from the king a written promise that he should never in any way be called to account for his acts, or for the manner in which he had spent the public money while he ruled the kingdom, but in spite of this, heavy demands were soon made upon him for lands and moneys which his enemies charged him with having taken on false pretences, and he was forced to give up Oeland and great part of Finland. His brother-nobles, who had always been jealous of him, did their utmost to keep up ill-will between him and the king, and during this short reign the marshal had no share in the government, and was even seldom seen at the Swedish court.

Christopher's Queen.—In the year 1446, King Christopher brought his young bride, Dorothea of Brandenburg, to Stockholm to be crowned Queen of Sweden. The time was not well chosen for wedding festivities, for, besides many other causes of trouble in the land, there was almost a famine owing to the bad seasons of the previous year. And the people, enraged at the lavish waste of the Court and the quantity of corn used at Stockholm to feed the horses in the royal stables, collected in large bodies around the palace, uttering cries of anger against Christopher, whom they called the "bark-bread," and "famine" king, and threatening to set Karl Knudsson on the throne in his place. This state of things made Sweden hateful to the king and his young queen, and they were glad to get away from the country as soon as they could, but they fared scarcely better in their other kingdoms, for in Norway King Erik was still held in greater favour than Christopher, and in Denmark the people grumbled over their high taxes and hard living nearly as loudly as the Swedes. Poor King Christopher cannot have had a very happy life after he had won the three crowns which he had so much coveted, for everything that went wrong in any one of his kingdoms was always laid to his charge, and he had constantly to listen to a long list of grievances set forth by one or another of his three Councils of State. On the whole he seems to have had an easy temper, and a way of trying to make the best of troubles which he could not mend. On one occasion a body of Swedish nobles came to his Danish court at Viborg to complain that the coasts of Sweden were being troubled by pirates, who were believed to be in the pay of the late King Erik, and to demand that they should be pursued and punished without mercy. "Well!" answered the king, "it certainly is a pity that my uncle cannot find a more honest way of getting his living, but after robbing him of his three kingdoms, I do not think we ought to be very hard upon him if he snatches a dinner now and then without paying for it. A man cannot live on nothing, you know!"

Revolt in Jutland. — The Swedes were very angry at Christopher's indifference to their troubles, and when the peasants of Jutland raised a revolt in favour of King Erik, they would not supply him with the men and money which he wanted them to give him, and it was some time before he was able to collect an army and advance against the rebels. This was in fact the very worst peasant war that any Danish king ever had to meet. At one time there were 35,000 men in arms against the royal troops, and once when they gained the day in a great battle, they seized upon the king's general, Æske Brock, and put him and twelve other nobles to death. The Jutlanders had gained over to their side a leader of noble birth, called Henrik Tagesöns, and for a time it seemed as if the rebels would suceeed in putting down the power of the king and nobles in Jutland. Everywhere the rich were pursued and slain, their houses burnt, and their lands seized and parted among the peasants, who were however at last thoroughly defeated in a battle fought near Aagard in Jutland, and from that time forth they were forced to pay heavy fines to the crown and the great landowners, and to give tithes to the clergy, which was more hateful to them than any other obligation that could have been laid upon them.

Ways of Raising Money.—Christopher, who was always in want of money, tried in the course of his reign various shabby ways of obtaining it. In Sweden he sold the crown-fiefs to the highest bidders, and sometimes, as it was said, his officers took money from two or more buyers of one fief, and then left them to settle by fighting between themselves who was to be the owner. In 1447 he seems to have taken a lesson from his uncle, the pirate king Erik, for he sent ships to waylay a number of Dutch and English trading vessels as they were passing through the Sound, and seized upon all the money which they had received in return for the goods sold by them to his own subjects in Denmark, Sweden and Norway. In the following year this ignoble king planned another money-raid, and on pretence of wishing to go on a pilgrimage to the church of Wilsnak in Brandenburg, demanded a free passage for himself and his retinue through the Hanse-towns. His real object, however, was the attack and plunder of the rich trading port of Lybeck, where a number of German princes, who were in league with him, had assembled as if by chance, bringing with them arms which they had hid in empty wine casks. The breaking out of a fire in the night, which was mistaken by the Danes and their friends for the signal of attack, saved the city, for the citizens on finding out the treachery of their guests sounded the alarm bells, and, gathering together in large numbers, drove the strangers out and forced Christopher to leave the harbour with all his ships and men. On reaching Helsingborg the king found himself too ill to proceed further, and after a few days' suffering he died in the first week of the year 1448, from the bursting of a malignant tumour, which was ascribed to poison, according to a common mode of explaining diseases not understood by the surgeons of those times.

Council in search of a King.—As Christopher died leaving no children, the Councils of State found themselves again called upon to look about them for some prince of the royal blood to whom they might offer their crowns. The Danish Council at once fixed upon Adolf, Duke of Holstein, and not waiting for the burial of the king, they sent to offer the throne to that prince, hoping that by this choice they might again unite Slesvig with Denmark. But Duke Adolf, who had no children and who loved his ease, would not trouble himself to accept the crown which was offered to him. He told them, however, that if they were in want of a king from his family, he thought they could not do better than take his nephew, Count Christian of Oldenburg, who, like himself, could trace his descent from the old royal Danish house through Rikissa, daughter of Erik Glipping. The council followed Count Adolf's advice, and as the young Oldenburg prince at once accepted the offer which they made him of the Danish crown, no time was lost in settling who was to succeed King Christopher. The Council next had to think what was to be done in regard to the widowed Queen Dorothea, whose large dowry had all been spent, and would now have to be refunded. But here again Count Christian helped them out of their difficulty, for he made himself so agreeable to this young widow of seventeen, that she consented to marry him as soon as her term of mourning was past, and thus saved the Danes the hard task of raising a large sum of money to repay to her father the ample fortune, which her late husband had spent on his unlucky wars.

PART III.

SWEDEN UNDER DANISH RULERS.

Sweden from 1434.—Before we close this chapter, we must take a glance at what had been going on in Sweden and Norway since the days when Engelbrecht Engelbrechtsson ha[d] so boldly come before King Erik of Denmark to demand justice for his fellow-countrymen. Engelbrecht's first visit to the Danish court was made in 1434, and from that time till Erik was deposed in 1439 one congress after the other met to consult about public affairs in Sweden; but no lasting good was effected by all these meetings, and public affairs were as much disturbed as ever. The great men of the land fought and struggled among themselves for freedom from all restraint but that of their own will, and the peasants were made to pay heavily in the way of taxes and forced labour for the little liberty that they could still claim. Change of rulers did not make much difference to the lower classes, but still they agreed generally with the nobles in hating Danish rule, although fear or interest often made them offer to do homage to Danish kings. Party spirit ran high in Sweden at the time when Christopher of Bavaria was elected King of Denmark in 1440. And although the diet which met that year at Arboga had passed a solemn decree that the union of Calmar should never be renewed, and no foreign king should ever again be chosen in Sweden, the Marshal Karl Knudsson was able in the same year to persuade the electors to proclaim Christopher king, in return for which, as we have seen, he secured to himself the fief of Finland, and received Oeland in pledge for the moneys which, according to his own statement, he had spent in the public service. At the moment Karl was thus apparently serving the cause of the King of Denmark, it was reported by his friends that a pious man had foretold that he would be crowned King of Sweden at Upsala, and that a little child had even seen the crown sparkling on his head. These rumours made a great impression on the superstitious and the ignorant, and when his tall and handsome person was seen by the side of the short and stout King Christopher, the Stockholmers ran after them crying out: "The marshal ought to be king. Our crown would better suit him than that stumpy little German!" Christopher could not have been very well pleased with these remarks, but he was a good-natured man, and only observed that "the Swedes were a free-spoken people."

It was the clergy, as we have seen in a former part of this chapter, who had the greatest share in securing the crown of

Sweden for King Christopher of Denmark; and to reward them, he granted their order greater freedom than they had ever enjoyed in the kingdom. During his stay in Sweden Christopher took part in the first trial against heretics that had been witnessed by the Swedes, and looked on while a poor half-witted peasant was made to do public penance for the opinions he had expressed, and sentence was read aloud against all who might in future repeat the offence for which he was punished. The nobles rose against Karl Knudsson as soon as he left Stockholm to take possession of his fief, and King Christopher, who was always in want of money, seized upon the occasion to extort fines from the Marshal in defiance of his promises to him, and to offer his lands to anyone who would bid the highest for them. While these things were going on among the great men of the kingdom, the poor were dying off under the evil effects of murrain among the cattle, famine, and the plague.

The news of King Christopher's death in 1448 recalled Karl Knudsson from Finland, and in the following year he entered Stockholm with a great array of troops, and after some months of disturbance and conflict, he was proclaimed king at the Mora Stone amid great cheering on the part of all the people, and soon afterwards crowned, together with his wife, at Upsala.[1] When the news of these events reached Norway, the Norwegians showed a strong desire to take Karl for their king, and they sent messengers to Christian of Oldenburg to announce to him that they were resolved never again to submit to be ruled by a Danish monarch, after which Karl was crowned King of Norway in the cathedral of Trondhjem. But Karl had not the power of retaining what had been given him, and soon the Norwegians found themselves in the midst of a civil war, which had been stirred up in the country by Christopher's successor, King Christian of Denmark, who had friends amongst the upper classes. The Swedish and Danish kings both sent

---

[1] The Swedish *Rhyming Chronicle* says of her:—
   "Af alla de Fruer man kan leta
   Skal man aldrig skonare quinna veta."

   Of all the ladies one may see,
   Ne'er was a fairer dame than she.

hostile armies into the kingdom, and Norway was made a battle-ground for foreign hired troops, who cared for neither party, and only strove to secure booty for themselves. In the course of this war Danes were found fighting in Karl's ranks, and Swedes on the side of King Christian, and men seemed to care very little for their country in comparison with their private interests. It must be owned, however, that many persons had family connections in all three kingdoms, and therefore, it might have been a hard matter to decide on which side one ought to take up arms.

Karl Knudsson made King of Sweden, 1457.—Karl Knudsson did not make as good a king as might have been expected from his former conduct; and from a brave and daring party-leader he became a weak and suspicious monarch. His officers, whom he chose from the lower classes, behaved quite as ill, or worse than the foreigners who had been employed under Danish or German rulers; and very soon both poor and rich agreed in disliking their old favourite, while the clergy were especially opposed to him on account of the laws which he had caused to be passed to prevent the Church being enriched by gifts from persons on their death-beds.

The Archbishop, Jöns Bengtsson, had also long and private causes of anger against the Swedish king, and in 1457 this primate at length ceased to keep up any pretence of good-will towards him, and having with solemn state laid his mitre, staff, and pallium, or cloak, on the high altar of the cathedral of Upsala, he put on armour, and sword in hand advanced to the church door on which he caused to be posted up a declaration of war against the king. Karl made only a faint attempt to resist the rebels, and finding, as the old chronicler, Olaus Petri, says, that "his primate was in right good earnest and had no idea of playing at war," he embarked in haste and secresy by night with as much of his wealth in gold and silver as he could carry away with him, and betook himself to Dantzig, where he remained for seven years. Then it was that Christian I. of Denmark was able to secure the crown of Sweden for himself, with the promise that his eldest son Hans should succeed him, but the people soon began their old complaints against Danish rule. For a time all had seemed to promise well, but when in the year 1463 a report was spread that Karl was coming back from his exile, it gave the Swedes courage to express their discontent at the heavy taxes which the Archbishop, on behalf of King Christian, had been levying upon them; and rising in numbers all over the country, they threatened to renounce their allegiance to him unless these burdens were removed. The primate to restore quiet agreed to their demands, which so enraged Christian that he ordered the arrest of Jöns Bengtsson, whose enemies in the Council caused the words "*the Archbishop is a traitor*" to be written in large letters upon all the public buildings and churches of Stockholm. The peasants, who looked upon the primate as a martyr in their cause, took up arms, and advanced towards the capital for his rescue, but they and the citizens who took part with them were soon quite routed by the Marshal Thure Thuresson, who gained for himself the name of "the Peasants' Butcher," on account of his great severity towards them. It was said of him that he had spared neither air, water, nor land in his thirst for gold, as he had pulled the gilt weather-cock from the highest tower in Stockholm, broken down walls, and drained lakes in search of treasures. Still the peasants kept up the strife, and in the winter of 1464 King Christian I. of Denmark had to come back to Sweden to quell the tumult. He had left the Archbishop shut up in a Danish prison, and he now appeared at the head of an army to chastise the rebels. But the peasants of Dalekarlia still defied him, and leading him by false information to advance into a thick wood in Westmannland they gave him battle, defeated him, and forced him to return to Denmark without having gained any footing in Sweden. Then a war-cry was raised all over the land : "Sweden is a kingdom, not a farm or a parish to be ruled over by bailiffs, and we will have no Danish overseers to plague us, but a true-born Swede for our king." On this the Council of State had to yield to the wishes of the people, and recall the exiled king, who, however, once again for a period of many months was forced to leave his kingdom and give place to Christian.

Karl's successors, 1467-1470.—In 1467, Karl Knudsson for the third time recovered the throne which he retained till his death three years later, and with his last breath he entrusted the government of the kingdom to his nephew, Sten Sture, while he earnestly prayed him never to attempt to gain the throne for himself. After some hesitation on the part of the Council of State, Sten Sture was formally proclaimed Regent and Marshal of Sweden in the spring of 1471. Six months later, King Christian I. of Denmark, landed near Stockholm with a large army of German hired troops, who boasted of all the disgrace which they would bring upon men and maidens throughout the land, while Christian in his contempt for Sten Sture called him a conceited puppy, who needed a sound thrashing to make him know his right place. But the result of the day's fight at Brunkebjerg, when Sten Sture's wife and other noble ladies looked down from the castle walls on the combatants below, was very different from what the invaders expected, and their complete defeat freed Sweden for some years from further attacks on the part of the Danes. King Christian I. never again set his foot on Swedish ground, and for a short time the kingdom enjoyed greater quiet and prosperity under Sten Sture than it had known during the whole of the century. Amongst other blessings, the people owed to the marshal the revival of trade and agriculture, while schools and learned men were encouraged, and the University of Upsala was founded and opened with great state two years before Copenhagen could boast of a similar institution in 1479.

CHAPTER XV.

DENMARK AND SWEDEN FROM 1450.

Christian of Oldenburg father of the present line of Danish kings—His character—His nickname of *"Stringless Purse"* well merited—His efforts to secure the crowns of Sweden and Norway—His defeat in Sweden in 1471 after many successes—His schemes for getting money—His conduct in regard to Slesvig—Secures the duchy and gains the title of Count of Holstein—What he sacrificed for these provinces—His daughter Margaret's dowry—Loses the Shetlands and Orkneys—The University of Copenhagen—His dislike of Denmark—His son Hans succeeds him—Hans' troubles to secure the three kingdoms and two provinces—Prince Frederick's bad advice and ambition—Conquest and loss of Sweden—Campaign against the Ditmarshers—Hans defeated—Only one successful war in this reign—Affairs in Sweden since 1434—Karl Knudsson the marshal made king—Christopher of Bavaria laughed at by the Swedes—The troubles with the primate Jöns Bengtsson—Sten Sture and his conduct to Christian I.—Hans in Sweden—Sten Sture's speech to him, and Hans' reply—Hemming Gade—His hatred of Denmark—Svante Sture the adopted heir of Sten Sture—His love of war and soldiers—His bravery—Svante's sudden death—Sten Sture the bravest of the Stures—Christian II., his treachery to the Swedish hostages—Gustaf Vasa carried to Denmark and thrown into prison—Sweden laid under an interdict—Sten Sture excommunicated; he dies in 1520, and Christian II. makes himself master of Sweden.

PART I.

THE FATHER OF THE OLDENBURG KINGS.

Christian I., 1448-1481.—LOYAL Danes have always shown themselves very ready to excuse the faults and extol the merits of Christian I., the founder of the long line of kings who have ruled over Denmark for more than four hundred years. It is true that he was a brave man, of a cheerful and amiable disposition, but he was selfish and wasteful, and cared very little for the troubles and burdens which his useless wars brought upon his subjects. He might have proved a very good king to the Danes if he had been content with the one crown which they had given him, but he would not rest till he had added to it the crowns of Sweden and Norway. As neither the Swedes nor the Norwegians wished to have him for their king, and were anxious to annul the Act of Union, which Queen Margaret had forced them to make with Denmark, Christian did not effect his purpose very easily ; and for twenty years of his reign the lives and property of his subjects were wasted in unprofitable struggles. During this time public affairs in Denmark were neglected, and the unhappy Danes were nearly ruined by the heavy taxes, loans and gifts demanded of them to carry on war, or to defray the cost of the many journeys, which Christian made to Germany and to Rome for the purpose of seeking help from the Emperor or Pope. Christian's sudden change of fortune might perhaps at first have served as an excuse for his ignorance of the use and value of money, but to the end of his life he continued to waste and want, meriting the nickname of "Stringless Purse," given to him by the Danes, who said that "silver slipped through King Christian's fingers like grain through a sieve."

Christian crowned in Norway.—In Norway the Council of State agreed as early as the year 1450 to accept Christian as their king, and to renew the Act of Union with Denmark. This they did not do from any love to the Danish king, but because the Norwegians, who were a peace-loving people, had hoped in this manner to secure for their country the quiet which they so much prized. They, however, quickly found out their mistake, for as soon as Christian had been crowned at Trondhjem, the people were ordered to arm themselves for a general attack of the Swedish frontiers. The Norwegians did not venture to disobey their new king's orders altogether, but they performed their duties so carelessly, that the Swedes had very little to fear from them, and, therefore, although Christian sometimes brought great armies into Sweden, and called upon the men of Norway to join their ranks, he was never able to get a secure footing in the country. The Marshal Karl Knudsson was indeed more than once driven out of Sweden by Christian's troops, but he as often regained his power, and was at length crowned king in the year 1464. On the death of Karl, the Danish king made another attempt in 1471 to gain the Swedish crown for himself, but (as we have seen in the last chapter) his army was so thoroughly beaten by the Swedes in a battle, fought at Brunkebjerg, near Stockholm, that he lost all further desire of invading Sweden, and never again turned his arms against that kingdom.

Christian's want of money often led him to do things unworthy of a king; and his neighbours and allies soon found that there was scarcely any favour he would not grant to those who could pay well for what they wanted of him. Thus the Hanse-traders were allowed, in return for a large sum of money, to keep the trade of the Baltic in their own hands, and to drive off Danish vessels as if they had no right to carry foreign goods into their own native ports, and in this manner the Germans were made rich at the expense of the Danes. Besides getting money by these and many other unjust means, King Christian had the bad habit of spending on his own pleasures what had been granted to him for other purposes, while he never scrupled to call upon his people to pay extra taxes, whenever he was more than usually in want of money.

Union of Slesvig and Holstein.—The old royal line of Slesvig-Holstein died out in 1459 with the Count-Duke Adolf, whose numerous kinsmen at once began to dispute among themselves in regard to the manner in which his heritage should be disposed of. King Christian sent troops into Slesvig, and claimed the right of taking the duchy on the ground that as his mother's brother, Count Adolf, had died without leaving any children or direct heirs in the male line, the fief had lapsed, or fallen back to the crown, by which it had been granted in former times. These claims were not disputed, and Christian had thus the good fortune of recovering without bloodshed a province, whose possession had for many ages been made a subject of dispute between the kings of Denmark and the dukes who had held it. But instead of resting satisfied with what he had thus easily obtained, he wanted also to make himself master of Holstein.

That province was, however, a fief of the German empire,

and as Christian could not hope to secure it unless he could induce the nobles and knights of Holstein to propose to the Emperor that he should receive the investiture, he resolved to buy their favour at any price. They were not slow to avail themselves of this opportunity to increase their own power, and accordingly they took care to make themselves almost independent of their future ruler before they would promise him their support. The terms to which he agreed were that in return for the title of Count of Holstein the nobles and knights of the province and their heirs after them should be free from paying taxes to the Danish crown, and should not be called upon to give to the kings of Denmark any aid in money or men unless with their own entire free-will. Besides granting these and other privileges, Christian promised for himself and all his successors that the provinces of Holstein and Slesvig should remain for ever united; and that on his death the electors should be held free to choose a successor from among any one of his heirs, and were not to be bound to take the next king of Denmark to be Count-Duke of the united provinces.

The Danes were indignant when they heard the terms on which the king had gained the empty title of ruler of Holstein, and their vexation was increased on finding that they were to be made answerable for his rash promises of paying off in money all other claims on his uncle's heritage. Amongst others Count Otto of Schaumburg, who was a kinsman of the late Count-Duke Adolf, had demanded 40,000 florins before he would give up his pretensions to the Holstein lands, while the king's three brothers had each required the same amount with one-third of the Oldenburg and Delmenhorst patrimony of their family. The Danes after much grumbling and delay paid the required sums of money to their king, who, as usual, spent them on his own pleasures, and left the poor Jutlanders to be pillaged by Count Otto's troops, and to buy off future attacks by heavy fines.

Christian loses the Shetlands and Orkneys.—King Christian's bad habits of thus misapplying the money entrusted to him by his people had in one instance a very important influence upon territories now forming part of the British empire. It happened that when his daughter Margaret at the early age of fifteen was married, in the year 1469, to the almost equally young king, James III. of Scotland, her dowry was fixed at 60,000 florins. The Danes, who were much pleased with the marriage, gave King Christian the money, of which James III. received only 2,000 florins. When the advisers of the young Scottish king demanded the remainder of the dowry, King Christian, to save himself from further trouble, gave them the Shetland and Orkney Isles to be held in pawn till he should be able to redeem them by paying 58,000 florins. But as the time never came when the Danish king was master of so large a sum of money these old Norwegian provinces were lost to Norway, and have since formed a part of Scotland.

The same misuse of money continued to the end of his reign to bring Christian into discredit with all classes of his subjects; and he gave special offence to the clergy by his conduct in regard to the University of Copenhagen, which was not opened till 1479, although he had five years earlier taken the money which they had supplied for the purpose, and obtained the necessary charter from the Pope, Sixtus IV. When at length Christian caused the university to be opened, he could only endow three chairs, and therefore all students who wished to learn anything more than divinity, law, and physic, were still forced to go abroad and seek instruction in some foreign school of learning. Hence the University of Copenhagen did not prove of much use to the Danes at that time, and it was not till the Reformation that its teachers could obtain any help from the State, or that students could receive proper instruction within its walls.

King Christian and his queen Dorothea never took the trouble to learn Danish, or to follow the habits of the country over which they ruled, and during the reign of this founder of the German house of Oldenburg, the higher classes in Denmark began to adopt the manners and customs of Germany, and almost gave up the use of their own tongue.

PART II.

CROWN BARTERED FOR FAVOURS.

Hans,—1481-1513.—On the death of King Christian I., in 1481, the nobles and knights of Slesvig and Holstein used their rights of election in regard to the succession, by declaring that they were not prepared to receive his eldest son and heir, Hans, as Count-Duke of their united provinces; and they showed such a marked leaning in favour of the second brother, Prince Frederick, that Hans had to submit to hard terms before he could secure their votes. The Danish nobles treated the young prince nearly as badly, and although the common people in Denmark were anxious to give him the crown immediately on his father's death, he was not allowed to ascend the throne till he had signed a very hard compact, by which the higher classes assured to themselves all the privileges they cared to possess. As soon as Hans had been crowned king of Denmark, he began, like his father, to try to obtain the other Scandinavian thrones; and although, as in Christian's case, the Norwegians were anxious to have nothing more to do with Danish rulers, they had no native princes of their own, and therefore for want of knowing what else to do, they agreed to receive Hans as their king. This king was a great favourite with his Danish subjects on account of his preference for the customs of the country, and for his use of the Danish language, which he spoke like a true-born Dane; while his parents and his brother, Prince Frederick, openly boasted of their German descent, and never concealed their contempt for the Danish people.

Frederick's ambition.—Although King Hans loved peace, the disturbed state of his dominions when he came to the throne, and the ambition of his brother, drew him into many wars during his long reign. The Queen-mother had always shown great partiality for her younger son, Prince Frederick, and not content with securing for him, on the death of Christian, a promise from the nobles and prelates of Slesvig and Holstein that he should be proclaimed joint ruler with his brother, King

Hans, over the duchies, she obtained for him the right of choosing which part of Slesvig he should hold as his own. The duchy had been divided in the year 1480 into two parts, the Segeberg and the Gottorp lands, but after choosing the latter he had grown dissatisfied with his choice, and been allowed by his brother to change it for the Segeberg portion of Slesvig. This indulgence only made Frederick bolder in asking for greater favours, and at last he demanded, as a right, that he should be allowed to rule over the islands of Laaland, Falster, and Moen, and be crowned joint king over Norway. These demands were, however, too much even for the indulgent Hans, and refusing to listen to his brother's request, he called together a diet, or meeting of the Lands-Thing at Kallunborg, and with the full assent of the members formally rejected Frederick's pretensions, and threatened him, in case he should ever renew them, with the forfeiture of the lands which he held in Slesvig. Prince Frederick was forced after this to be more careful in his conduct, but his restless, discontented nature led him to foment troubles and excite wars whenever he was allowed to use his influence with his brother. Thus it was chiefly by his persuasions, but against the advice of the Queen-mother, that the king resolved upon trying to gain the Swedish throne by force. He had for many years let himself be satisfied by the promises of the Swedish Regent and his Council of State, and believed their declarations that they would offer him the throne whenever they saw that the moment had arrived for proclaiming his authority in the kingdom. Fourteen years passed without bringing King Hans the crown he coveted, and then losing all patience, he listened to the advice of his brother and sent a large army of German hired troops into Sweden. Success attended him everywhere, and after defeating the Regent-Marshal Sten Sture, and forcing him to lay down his offices and give account of his government, Hans was, in 1495, crowned King of Sweden, and his son Christian proclaimed as his successor.

This easy conquest of Sweden did not, however, prove very lasting, for when in the year 1500 Hans suffered a signal defeat in the Ditmarshes, the Swedish nobles seized the opportunity of freeing themselves from the power of Denmark, and having taken Sten Sture for their leader, they drove the Danes out of Stockholm, renounced their allegiance to King Hans, and kept his queen, Christina of Saxony, a prisoner for three years. The hatred of the Swedes towards the Danes now showed itself in all parts of the kingdom, and was as great amongst the higher as amongst the lower classes. The sudden death of the Marshal Sten Sture in 1503, when he was returning from Denmark after escorting the released Queen Christina to her husband's court, was ascribed to poison given to him, it was said, by the orders of Prince Frederick, and this event increased the general feeling of bitter hatred. When Hemming Gade, Bishop of Linköping, addressed the people at Upsala after Sten Sture's death, he ended his speech with these words : " The Danes are a nation of murderers and thieves and have been so from all time, but let us not despair, for the Almighty, who has saved seven parishes in the Ditmarshes from their hands, will not fail to rescue a whole kingdom ! "

When King Hans heard what had happened in Sweden he appealed to the Emperor and Pope to punish the rebels ; but this had little effect in changing the feelings of the people towards him, and as he was unable to send any more armies into the country, he was obliged to submit, and he never again renewed the attempt to gain the Swedish crown by force.

PART III.

THE BRAVE DITMARSHERS.

Defeat of Danes.—The losses of King Hans in the Ditmarsh campaign, to which we must now return, had, moreover, been so great, that he had no wish after that inglorious defeat to enter on new wars. The inhabitants of the Ditmarshes, which adjoined the Holstein lands, were not pure Germans, but belonged to those Frisian tribes occupying the north-western parts of Germany and Holland and the islands near the Slesvig-Holstein coasts, who were descended from the ancient Frisii, known to the Romans for their bravery and love of freedom. The same spirit had always animated these people, and they had age after age made many a gallant stand against the neighbouring princes who had attempted to subdue them. Geert the Great and other rulers of Slesvig and Holstein had from time to time suffered defeat at their hands, and although the Emperor Frederick had formally given over their lands to Christian I. of Denmark to be joined with the Holstein territory, the Marshmen had refused to own themselves subject to the power of Denmark. When Prince Frederick obtained the title of Duke of Slesvig-Holstein he had called upon the Ditmarshers to pay taxes to him, and to do homage for their lands; and on their neglecting to attend to his summons, he had induced his brother, King Hans, to invade the Marshes in the winter of the year 1500.

The royal army, which was commanded by the king and the Slesvig-Holstein duke, was composed of an unusually large proportion of nobles and knights, who showed their contempt for their peasant foes by going to the attack clad in their ordinary hunting costume, and carrying only light arms. But they soon found how ill they had judged the Marshmen, for instead of submitting to them, as they had expected, these men fought desperately whenever they came in contact with the royal troops; and although Meldorf, the chief town of the Marshes, was taken and sacked, and the inhabitants killed with great cruelty, only a small number of the Danes and Germans who had formed part of the invading army escaped alive from the Marshes. They were on their way from Meldorf to Hejde, on the afternoon of a cold winter's day in the year 1500, when they found their advance checked by a line of earthworks thrown up against a dyke, known as "Dusind Dyvel's Werff," near Hemmingstedt, and defended by 500 Ditmarshers under their leader, Wolf Isebrand. The royal German guard rushed to the attack, shouting "Back, churls, the guards are coming!" and three times forced the Marshmen to retreat, but they as often rallied. At that moment the wind changed, bringing a thaw with it, and as the troops were struggling on, blinded with the sleet and snow and benumbed with cold, the sluices were suddenly opened by the peasants, when the water, driven on by the rising tide, soon covered the marshes and swept everything before it. Then the Ditmarshers, who were accustomed to make their way quickly through the marshes by the help of their poles and stilts, threw themselves upon the invaders, and cut them down, or pierced them dead with their long spears. Six thousand men perished in this way, and an immense booty fell into the hands of the victors, including seven banners, of which the most noteworthy was the Danish national standard Dannebrog, which was carried in triumph to Oldenwörden, and hung up in the church as the greatest trophy of the victory.

The king and Duke Frederick barely escaped falling into the hands of the Marshmen, and they and the other leaders rated their loses in money, stores, and ammunition, in that afternoon's defeat, at 200,000 florins or guldens. King Hans may be said to have owed the loss of Sweden to his evil fortune in the Marshes, while his power in Norway was threatened by the same cause; for the Norwegians under a leader, called Knud Alfson, made several attempts to throw off their allegiance to Denmark after they learnt the result of the king's campaign against the Marshmen. Hans had earnestly begged his brother for help to put down the rebels, but when the duke refused to aid him unless he would promise to have him proclaimed as joint King of Norway, he sent his young son, Christian, to quell the disturbance, and refused to listen to Frederick's demands. Prince Christian performed his task so thoroughly that in the course of a few months order was restored, but he at the same time used his powers with such great cruelty, that before he left the kingdom he had nearly rooted out all the old Norwegian nobles.

The only war undertaken in this reign, which brought any good results to the Danes, was that carried on against the Lübeck Traders, who had shown great insolence to King Hans when they learned that he had granted rights of trading in his dominions to English merchants as well as to the German Hansers. The Lübeckers, trusting to the strength of their ships, attacked the Danish fleet without waiting for its advance, but the admirals, Sören Norby and Otte Rud, beat them back, and so thoroughly routed them, that they were glad to accept peace at the cost of paying 30,000 gulden to defray the expenses of the war. Soon after this one successful event, Hans died at Aalborg, in the year 1513. With the Danes he had always been a great favourite, and even among the Swedes and Norwegians he was personally liked in spite of their hatred of the Danish rule. His many good qualities were marred by violent fits of passion, but these occurred only rarely, and were thought by his subjects to be due to short, but uncontrollable attacks of insanity.

PART IV.

THE FALL OF THE STURES.

Sweden under Sten Sture.—We have seen[1] that while Christian I. of Denmark was always wasting and wanting money, and little or nothing was done during his reign to improve the condition of the Danes, the Swedes enjoyed peace and prosperity for some years under the rule of their marshal or chief governor, Sten Sture, the nephew of King Karl Knudsson. This better state of things was, however, at length interrupted by a succession of bad seasons and many public calamities, while the death of Christian I., in 1481, also gave rise to much disquiet and disturbance in the country, since his eldest son and successor, Hans, laid claim to the crowns of Sweden and Norway as soon as he had made himself master of that of Denmark. The Norwegians, who had kept themselves as quiet as they could under the constant turmoil and dissensions of Christian's reign, came forward at his death to propose to their Swedish neighbours that the two ancient kingdoms should unite together, and that counsel should be taken as to the terms under which the Union of Calmar might be revived without bringing the same miseries as before upon the northern lands. But these negotiations were not followed by any active results, and soon afterwards the Norwegians allowed themselves to be persuaded to accept Hans as their king. The Swedish nobles had by that time become dissatisfied with Sten Sture, whose popularity with some of the lower classes had also been weakened on account of the many evils which had befallen the kingdom during the latter part of his rule, through destructive storms, droughts and other troubles, as the plague,

[1] See Chapter xiv.

&c., for which he was in no way answerable. Year after year the Council of State threatened to call in King Hans of Denmark, and in 1497 they carried out their threats by proclaiming him king in Stockholm and Upsala, when Sten Sture, after having for a short time been supported by the peasants of Dalekarlia, had to submit and to receive the Danish king as his master. Hans made his solemn entry into Stockholm, leaning on the arm of Sture, who, when the king asked him jocosely, "If he, like a faithful steward, had prepared all things for his coming," answered, pointing with his finger to the Swedish nobles gathered round them, "*They* can answer that best, for they have done all the baking and brewing here to their own liking!" At these words King Hans seemed suddenly to be seized with one of the attacks of rage to which he sometimes gave way, and answered angrily, "And you, Sten Sture, have in the meanwhile left me an evil heritage in Sweden, for the peasants, whom God made to be our slaves, you have raised into masters, and those who ought to be lords, you have tried to enslave."

When Hans was crowned king of Sweden, at Stockholm, in 1499, he conferred knighthood on all the nobles who had taken part in his proclamation, and it was said that his success had been mainly due to the eagerness with which the wives of these nobles had sought to obtain for their husbands the gold chain, which was the badge of their knightly rank, and could only be given by the hands of the sovereign.

The Stures rule Sweden.—Sten Sture, who was hated by the nobles and supported by the peasants, was at the head of every outbreak which disturbed the rule of Hans, and when the Danish king was defeated by the Ditmarshers in 1500, it was he who, in the name of the people, declared Sweden to be independent of Denmark. At the death of Sten Sture in 1503, his adopted heir, Svante Sture, was in accordance with his wishes, made marshal and regent of the kingdom. This knight was of a daring, frank nature, and it was said of him, that he would take no man into his service who winked his eyes at the stroke of a battle-axe, and that he would rather strip his coat off his back than leave a friend and brother-warrior unrewarded. He cared more for his soldiers than for any other class of the nation, and as long as he governed Sweden there was nothing but war. He and his learned friend Hemming Gade, Bishop of Linköping, who may be said to have ruled the land between them, seemed only to think how they might show their hatred to Denmark, and although during this time there were constant meetings between the nobles of the two countries to settle their differences, neither people had any rest from the hostile and piratical attacks of the other. The Hanse traders sided sometimes with the one, and sometimes with the other party, and there was neither peace nor safety to the poor in any one of the three northern kingdoms.

On the sudden death of Svante Sture in 1512, his son, Sten Sture "the Younger," was chosen to fill his place. This Sten was the noblest and best of the Sture race, and his efforts to relieve the people as far as he could from the taxes which weighed so heavily upon them, and his gallant attempts to secure the freedom of the country, endeared him very greatly to the Swedes. He had, however, a rival and foe in the archbishop, Gustaf Trolle, who through hatred of the Stures, proved himself a traitor to his country, and brought about worse troubles than any that had yet fallen upon the unhappy land. In 1518, Sten Sture defeated the army which Christian II. of Denmark had brought before the walls of Stockholm in the hope of forcing the Swedes to acknowledge his claim to the Swedish throne. After the battle Christian sought an interview with the regent, and demanded, in proof of his good faith, that several Swedish hostages should be sent on board a Danish ship of war to remain there until he had returned in safety from the meeting. The regent agreed to this, and made choice by their own consent of the bishop, Hemming Gade, and five other persons of noble birth, one of whom was young Gustaf Ericksson Vasa, the future King of Sweden, who had served in the recent war and borne the royal standard of Sweden in the battle of Stockholm. While the meeting between the king and regent was taking place, the Danish ship, according to the king's orders, weighed anchor and sailed to Denmark, where the hostages were kept in prison on pretence that they were rebels. Christian, on his return to Copenhagen, obtained a bull from the Pope to lay Sweden under an interdict, and to excommunicate Sten Sture and all who had taken part with him, and thus ended Christian's pretended wish to be reconciled with the regent. A Danish army under the command of Otte Krumpe, was sent into Sweden with orders to affix to all church doors through the land copies of these papal decrees; and although the Danes were defeated with much loss by the Swedes on the Aase Sound, their greater forces prevailed after a time, until Sten Sture's death in 1520 placed the kingdom completely at the mercy of Christian II. of Denmark.

CHAPTER XVI.

DENMARK FROM 1500.

Christian II. of Denmark—His birth—Nearly killed by an ape—Strange mode of bringing up—Placed with Metzenheim Bogbinder—His tutors—His singing in the choirs of Copenhagen—His knowledge of Latin—His father's use of the rod—Christian sent into Norway—His mode of ruling that kingdom—His love of the poorer classes—Death of Sten Sture in 1520 makes Christian master of Sweden—His cruel massacre of ninety Swedish nobles—Swedes give him the name of "Tyrant"—Some of his good works, as the opening of poor-schools, post-offices, inns, &c.—Puts down Strand rights—Tells the bishops to read their Catechism—Favours the cultivation of flowers and fruits—Amager Island peopled by Flemings—Encourages Reformed faith for a time—Danish nobles alarmed for their safety—King's Dutch favourite, Mother Sigbrit—Dyveke the Dove—The dish of cherries—Torbe Oxe put to death—Nobles send in paper announcing that they depose Christian ; he goes to Holland in haste—The war with the new king Frederick I.—Christian taken prisoner; put in a dungeon with a dwarf—His death 17 years later—Frederick I. ; his conduct and reign—The Reformers' first Danish versions of Scriptures—Persecutions, struggles—Counts' Feud for three years after Frederick's death—Christian III. succeeds to thrones of Denmark and Norway—Puts down Catholic Church in Denmark—Establishes the Lutheran faith—Persecutions of Calvinists—Christian's death—Progress of country during his reign.

PART I.

CHRISTIAN'S BRINGING UP.

Christian II., 1513-1523. CHRISTIAN II. of Denmark, who was the only son of King Hans and his queen, Christina of Saxony, was born at Nyborg in 1481. This prince, whose capacity was as great as his cruelty, and whose learning and knowledge of business far exceeded those of most men of his rank and times, was brought up in a strange manner, considering that he had been early crowned joint king with, and successor to his father, and was looked upon by most Danes as the rightful heir to the thrones of Norway and Sweden, as well as to that of Denmark. We are told that one day when he was sleeping in his cradle, a tame ape lifted him up and ran with him to the flat roof of the castle, where the creature was seen dangling and tossing the infant up and down. The royal servants were in great alarm, but they dared not call out or follow the animal lest he might throw the child to the ground, and so they waited till the ape of its own accord brought him within reach of his nurse.

The king and queen were often absent on long journeys, going from place to place to visit the different provinces of their kingdoms; and in order to provide for their little son during their frequent absences from the Danish capital, they—strange to say—removed him from the court and the care of their own attendants, and placed him in the house of a tradesman of Copenhagen, named Hans Metzenheim *Bogbinder*. The latter name is thought by some writers to have been only a surname, and by others to have been used to show that Metzenheim's business was that of a book-binder. He was, however, a man of standing in the city, a burgomaster and councillor of state, and he and his wife, who had no children of their own, showed great love for their charge.

They took care that his learning should be well attended to by engaging the services of a good scholar, the Canon George Hinze, under whom Christian studied daily for several hours. When he grew older, the king placed him altogether under the care of Hinze, who, finding that he could not trust the wild little prince when he was absent, thought it would be best never to let him out of his sight, and he therefore took him with him into church whenever he was doing duty. As Christian had a good ear for music, and a fine voice, he was made to sing among the choristers at matins and vespers. But when King Hans was told that the heir to the three northern kingdoms was singing in every choir of Copenhagen, he flew into a great rage, and said very bad things of and to the canon. The poor man pleaded in his excuse, that being only a low-born peasant and a priest, he did not know what was the right thing to do for a prince, and was in constant terror lest some harm would befall the royal boy when he saw him taking part in the rough games in which he had great delight. The king forgave the canon, but he wrote an earnest letter to his kinsman, the Elector Joachim of Brandenburg, begging him to send to Denmark, without fail, a stern and learned man who would know how to manage the unruly young prince. The Elector looked about him for the right kind of man, and soon a great scholar, known as the Magister, or Master Conrad, came from Germany, and taught his pupil to such good effect, that Christian for the rest of his days spoke and wrote in Latin as well as the most learned university-professors of his times. But although the young prince loved learning and made good progress, he loved his own amusements better; and we are told as a proof how well King Hans followed Solomon's precept not to spare the rod, that when he found his son was in the habit of bribing the palace-watch to let him pass freely in and out whenever he wanted to join the entertainments of the citizens, he used a horse-whip so sharply on Christian's back and shoulders as to force him to go on his knees and promise amendment. But at last the time came when the father could no longer use the rod, and in 1501 Hans sent Prince Christian into Norway as independent governor, or viceroy of that kingdom.

Christian in Norway.—It was here that the prince first showed the resolution and cruelty of which he was capable, for although he was only twenty years old at the time, he put down every attempt at rebellion with such quickness and sternness, that the nation was soon nearly crushed, and almost every Norwegian noble or knight of standing killed or banished. He seems from his boyhood to have had a hatred of the nobility generally, and although he knew how to win over the Danish nobles and prelates, when he required their support at the death of his father King Hans, in 1513, to confirm his early election to the throne, he usually avoided their society, and chose his friends and officers from among the lower classes. The hard terms which the Danish Council of State imposed upon him as the price of his crown, estranged him still more from the nobles, who, in the new charter signed by Christian at his coronation, had secured for themselves so many privileges as to leave the king no real power in the state.

Christian on his accession made the crown of Sweden the great object of his ambition. His cause was supported by Gustaf Trolle, the primate of Upsala, and many others belonging to the ancient nobility, who, in their jealousy of the power enjoyed by the Sture family, were ready to proclaim Christian King of Sweden. But the greater number of the Swedes were devoted to their ruler, Sten Sture the younger, and looked upon the Danes with hatred and jealousy, and from the moment King Hans died the people showed very clearly that they would never submit willingly to a Danish ruler. During the war which broke out between Sture and the archbishop's party, Christian sent his armies year after year into the country, but he gained no footing there till 1520, when his general, Otte Krumpe, surprised Sten Sture by marching along the frozen streams and lakes till he came unawares upon the Swedes, and gave them battle on the ice, at Aasund in West Gothland. The Danes beat the Swedish army, which dispersed when it became known that their leader Sten Sture had died on the road to Stockholm, from the severe wounds which he had received at Aasund. His brave widow then closed the gates of Stockholm against the Danes, but treachery on the part of the townspeople forced her to submit, and then by the help of the Swedish bishops Christian was able to make himself master of the throne, which he had been so eager to win.

PART II.

THE SWEDISH CROWN LOST.

The Blood Bath.—In the autumn of 1520 Christian was crowned at Stockholm with great pomp; and by the grace and affability of his manners he charmed all the Swedes who took part in the festivities, which were held in honour of his coronation. At the moment, however, when the Swedish nobles thought their troubles at an end, the king's chief officers of state, the Westphalian Didrik Slaghoek and Jens Beldenak, Bishop of Odensee, stepped forward before Christian while he was surrounded by his court, and in the name of the primate, Gustaf Trolle, demanded reparation for the wrongs which it was pretended the archbishop had suffered at the hands of Sten Sture the younger, and his councillors, in having been deprived of his see. Christian, on pretence of upholding the dignity of the Church, required to know the name of all who had signed the act of deposition, which, as he well knew, had been passed in consequence of the primate's treason in fighting with him in former years against his own countrymen. The document was produced, and all whose names were attached to it were arrested on the spot, although it was shown that they had merely acted in conformity with the orders of the national diet. The next morning early they were brought before a court, composed of twelve ecclesiastics, who were all Swedes excepting Beldenak, and were asked one question only : whether men who had raised their hands against the Pope and the Holy Roman Church were heretics? As they were forced to reply in the affirmative, they were told that they had passed judgment of death on themselves.

At noon on the same day, the 8th of November, 1520, ninety persons, belonging chiefly to the nobility, but including a few burghers, were led forth into the great market-place of Stockholm, where, closely guarded by Danish troops, they were beheaded one by one before the eyes of the terror-stricken citizens. The first who suffered was Bishop Mads of Strangnæs, who, as the axe was falling on his head, cried aloud, " The king is a traitor, and God will avenge this wrong ! " When Erik Johansson Vasa, the father of the future kings of Sweden, was led out, a messenger from Christian came to him to offer him pardon and grace. " No," he cried, " for God's sake let me die with all these honest men, my brethren ! " and he laid his head on the block.

A heavy storm of rain fell at the close of this frightful butchery, and the blood streamed along the streets, and gurgled and splashed up from the wet and muddy market-place. Then Christian, turning his back on the scene of this ghastly spectacle, left Stockholm in the full belief that nothing would hinder the scheme he had at heart, of raising the burghers and peasants to be as firm supports to the throne, as they had been in olden times. But the lower classes, for whose welfare he pretended he had caused the death of the nobles, stunned by the horror of the deed, and seeing no prospect of good to themselves in such a frightful outbreak of fury, slunk back to their homes, with feelings of hatred and fear of the king, whom they and all Swedes since their time have remembered only as "the Tyrant." It has been well said that the "Union of Calmar was drowned in the blood bath" of the 8th of November, 1520, for from that day till the spring of 1523, when Gustaf Vasa was crowned king of Sweden, the Swedes never gave up their determination to release themselves from their Danish bonds.

Christian II. of Denmark had some great and noble qualities, which in the eyes of many of his subjects more than atoned for his occasional outbreaks of cruel fury. He not only caused several new and good laws to be passed in favour of the trading and working classes of the country, but he showed himself at all times anxious to diffuse education amongst the very lowest of his subjects, and was in fact the first king in Northern Europe who opened poor-schools in his dominions. In his earnest desire to promote the education of his people he went so far as to order the burghers of Copenhagen and all other large cities in the three Scandinavian kingdoms, under penalties of heavy money fines, to compel their children to learn to read, write, and cipher, and when they grew older to see that they were instructed in some trade. He also caused better books to be prepared and printed for the public schools; while he ordered that the children, who were intended for the learned professions, should not be boarded with unlearned persons, lest in their earlier years they might be taught evil, which they could never again forget. He made the first attempt at having post-offices in the country by forming a band of post runners, who both winter and summer passed between Copenhagen and the chief towns, carrying letters for which they were paid according to the number of miles they had brought them. Then he caused way-side inns to be built at certain distances along the roads, and ordered that if travellers received damage from the badness of the public roads, the parishes in which they lay should be made to pay for it. He forbade the nobles and higher clergy to use strand rights, or to seize, as they had hitherto done, on wrecks; and when the bishops of Jutland, who drew good incomes from this practice, laid complaints before him of their heavy losses, saying there was "nothing in the bible against taking stranded goods," his only answer was, "Let the Lord-prelates go back and learn the eighth commandment by heart!" In the same manner when the clergy begged that for the good of the Church he would allow witches and wizards to be burnt as in the olden times, and not be let off with a whipping as he had decreed, he asked them if they had ever read the sixth commandment? It was a pity that a king who knew so well how to reprove others had not taken that and other commandments to heart.

Christian did much for his navy, for he built good ships, put down pirates on the Baltic, and made the Hansers of Lübeck respect his authority. He caused equal weights and measures to be used in all towns, and passed many laws in favour of the peasants, to whom he granted the right to leave the lord on whose lands they worked whenever they wished it and could prove that they had been treated unjustly. He also put down the cruel custom of selling the poor peasants with the land, like beasts of the field, and punished masters for ill-treating their servants. The growth of flowers and vegetables was made the great object of his care; and, to teach the Danes how to manage gardens and orchards, he, by the advice of his queen, Elizabeth, sister of Emperor Charles V., sent for Flemish gardeners who were then the best in Europe. These men came to Denmark in 1516 and settled in Amager, a small island in the harbour of Copenhagen, which they soon changed into a blooming garden, and where, from that time forth they and their descendants lived. The Amager peasants still enjoy the rights that Christian gave them, and even to the present day they retain the dress and habits of the Flemish homes of their forefathers, brightening up the old market-place of Copenhagen with their quaint, highly-coloured costumes, and supplying the citizens with the finest fruits, flowers, and vegetables that can be raised in the long cold winters and short hot summers of Danish Sjælland.

PART III.

KING CHRISTIAN LOSES ALL.

Reformers in Denmark.—Christian II. gave great offence to the Danish nobles as well as to the clergy by the favour which he showed towards the teachers of the Reformed faith, and in 1520, his uncle, Frederick the Wise of Saxony, sent to Copenhagen at his request a learned doctor named Martin Reinhard, to preach the gospel to the people. As, however, this preacher could not speak Danish, his sermons had to be translated from German before they could be understood, and therefore made so little impression upon the hearers that King Christian wrote again to his uncle, begging for another preacher, and asking whether Luther himself would not come to Denmark and settle a new Reformed Church for him. But the great Reformer had other things to do, and after a time Christian seemed to lose his interest in the new faith. At any rate, as soon as he found that a Nuncio was coming from Rome to inquire into the justice of the sentences passed upon the Swedish nobles who had been put to death at Stockholm by his orders, he wrote to the Pope to promise that he would punish heretics in his kingdom; and seemed ready to pledge himself to any measure demanded of him if he thought that it might ward off the anger of Rome, of which he stood in great awe.

The Danish nobles rejoiced at the downfall of the Reformed party, but they put little trust in the king's promises, and feared that his great love for the society and counsels of persons of low birth would some day bring upon themselves the same fate as that which had befallen their Swedish brethren. They knew that his chief adviser, a Dutchwoman, commonly called Mother Sigbrit,[1] hated all persons of high rank, and they

[1] This woman, who had first made Christian's acquaintance when she and her young daughter Dyveke kept a tavern at Bergen during the prince's viceroyalty, had unbounded influence at the Danish Court, and to show her contempt for the nobles, she would keep the highest officers of State waiting for hours in the cold in the depth of winter, while she amused herself by watching their discomfort from the windows of her own well-warmed rooms in the palace.

felt that as long as she and her kindred, with their Dutch
notions of freedom and equal rights for all classes, kept their
power over the king, there was no safety to be hoped for by
the nobles of the land. This Sigbrit, who had for years been
as great a favourite with the Flemish queen as with Christian
himself, was the mother of a lovely young girl known as
Dyveke, or the Dove, whom the king had dearly loved, and
whose death he had deeply mourned. As Dyveke had died
suddenly, it was said she must have been poisoned, and some
persons even thought that she owed her death to eating a dish
of cherries, sent to her by a nobleman, Torbe Oxe, who it was
known had once wished to marry her. The king did not rest
till he had had poor Torbe brought to trial on this and other
charges, and when the council declared they could see no just
cause of offence against him, Christian swore that " in spite of
all they said, Oxe should lose his head, if it were ten times as
hard to cut off as a bullock's." True to his word, the king
refused to listen to any appeals in Oxe's favour, and caused
him to be brought to the block and executed. After this
event Mother Sigbrit rose to still higher power, and the
Danish nobles began to look about them to see how they
could best secure their own safety. Neither they nor the
bishops liked to risk their persons by attending the annual
Things, and soon a compact was made between these two
Orders of the State to renounce their allegiance to the tyrant.

Fatal glove.—One day in the April of the year 1523 Christian found in a glove which he was about to draw on a
rumpled paper, in which his nobles made known to him their
purpose to call in his uncle, Duke Frederick of Holstein, to
be their king. Strange to say, Christian's courage failed him
at that moment when he most needed it, and although the
city of Copenhagen, together with the peasants and burghers
in all parts of Denmark and even of Norway were in his
favour, he fled in haste, and setting sail with his family and all
his belongings, betook himself to Holland, where he remained
for some years, and where three years later his gentle queen
died among her own countrymen at the early age of twenty-six.

Had Christian stayed amongst his subjects he would perhaps have put down the rebellion raised against him; for even among the nobles he had devoted friends, and for many years his able commanders, Henrik Gjö, Sören Norby, and others, made a brave stand for him. In Norway, too, where he landed in 1531 with an army of Dutch and Germans, he was hailed with joy, but at that moment, his uncle Frederick made a treaty with Sweden and Lübeck, both of which powers dreaded Christian's return to Denmark. By their joint forces his troops were beaten, and at last in 1532 the unhappy king, on a promise of safety, gave himself up to his uncle's commander, Knud Gyldenstjerne, who, instead of setting him at liberty as he had promised, carried him to the Castle of Sonderborg on the island Als, and had him confined in a dark dungeon below the tower. In this wretched prison, to which light and air could only penetrate through a small grated window, that served at the same time for the passage of the scanty food given to him, Christian spent seventeen years of his life with a half-witted Norwegian dwarf for his sole companion.

On the death of Frederick I., his son, Christian III., showed a wish to release the unhappy captive, on condition of his pledging himself to retire to Germany. But the Danish nobles were still too much in dread of Christian II. to suffer him to be set at liberty, and all that this more merciful king could do was to have the prisoner removed to Kallundborg Castle, where he was permitted to pass the last ten years of his life in comparative comfort, and where he died in 1559, within a few months of the death of his cousin and namesake, Christian III.

Frederick I., 1523-1533.—We must now go back to the time when Christian II. left Denmark, and the nobles found themselves free to choose another king more to their mind than the one whom they had put down. They soon made choice, as we have seen, of Christian's uncle, Duke Frederick, who did not hesitate a moment in accepting the crown that was offered to him by the Council of State, and as soon as he felt secure of the support of the nobles of the Danish islands and of the duchies he called upon the Swedes and Norwegians to proclaim him king. The former replied that they had already chosen a king for themselves, viz. Gustaf Ericksson Vasa; but the Norwegians after a time consented to do homage to him, and in return Frederick declared Norway a free elective monarchy. From the moment Frederick I. became king of Denmark and Norway he began to undo everything that his nephew, Christian II., had done, and one of his first acts was to give orders that all the laws which had been passed in the last reign in favour of the peasants should be publicly burnt in his presence. The poor-schools were closed all over the kingdom, the newly-printed books burnt, and the Reformed preachers driven out of the towns and forbidden to preach the doctrines of Luther, or to read the bible to the people. The Danish and Holstein nobles rejoiced in having a king who agreed with them in thinking that it was "contrary to good order and morality" to raise the condition of the peasants; and the poorer classes found themselves worse treated and more crushed than they had been before King Christian II. tried to lift them out of their misery. Frederick and the nobles looked upon them as mere slaves, fit only to work like the beasts of the field; and at Court, German manners and the German language had quite taken the place of the national customs and form of speech.

Frederick was not equally successful in his measures against the Reformers, whose influence increased rapidly during this reign, and was mainly due to the effect produced by the preaching of the doctrines of Luther in Denmark, in the year 1520, when Hermann Tast, a learned priest of Husum in Jutland, stood forth in the market-place of that town, and explained many passages of the Scripture to the people in accordance with the new teaching of the German Reformers. A few years later, another priest, named Hans Tausen, preached with such force against the Church of Rome, that the Danish clergy took alarm, and tried by all means in their power to put down this learned and dangerous man. But each time that he was shut up by his bishop the people flew to arms and clamoured till they secured his freedom. At length, in 1530, the burghers in Copenhagen and the other large Danish towns began in their turn seriously to ill-use the monks, and to destroy the images and ornaments of the churches, until the soldiers were sent to put an end to the riots. But at that time the people at large had been made acquainted with the Scriptures, for in 1524 a translation of the New Testament into Danish had been published at Antwerp by Hans Mikkelsen, a learned man who had left his home and lost his all to follow King Christian II., and in 1529 a second and better version was given to the Danes by their countryman Kristen Pedersen, who also translated the Psalms into Danish. The Romish clergy had called meetings to decide what was to be done to put down these doctrines, and had taken strong measures against the preachers, but all to no purpose, and the whole Danish nation very soon adopted the Reformed faith, although it was not till the year 1536 that this form of religion was established by law in Denmark.

The Count's Feud.—There had been many troubles in the land on the death of Frederick I. in 1533, and for three years after that event the country was without a king, and a state of great disorder reigned in the land. This period is known as the time of "the Count's Feud," for it was taken up with the wars carried on under the command of Count Christopher of Oldenburg to recover the Danish throne for his cousin, the poor captive king, Christian II. But besides this cause of trouble there were other reasons why a new king was not chosen at once on the death of Frederick I. The nobles and the clergy could not agree on the question of religion; the former wishing to take Frederick's eldest son, Christian, to be their king, and the latter wanting to have him passed over as a heretic, and the younger son, Prince Hans chosen, who was only a little child at the time, and whom the bishops hoped they might bring up in their own faith. Gustaf Vasa, King of Sweden, gave much help to Prince Christian by carrying on war against the Lübeckers, who had taken the part of the count, chiefly because they were always glad to have an excuse to fight against Denmark; but when they found that Count Christopher was often beaten by the Swedes and by Prince Christian's friend and chief commander, Johan Rantzau, they hastened to make peace, and leave the poor deposed king, Christian II., to his fate.

PART IV.

DENMARK ACCEPTS THE PROTESTANT FAITH.

Christian III., 1536–1559.—In the year 1536 Count Christopher found that he could no longer keep up the feud, and the nobles and clergy, after taking good care of their own interests, agreed to offer the crown to Christian, who in the summer of that year made his solemn entry into Copenhagen, and was proclaimed king under the title of Christian III. We may here notice that from the time of Frederick I. it has been the custom in Denmark to have no names but these two, Frederick and Christian, in the succession; each new king dropping any other first name that he might have had given him in his baptism, and taking up either that of Frederick or Christian. Christian's first act was to summon the Council of State and engage the members of that body to stand by him in the execution of the plans, which he laid before them for putting down the power of the Romish Church. The bishops were then all placed under arrest in one day, but those who pledged themselves not to oppose the king's measures were soon released. A great Thing, or general diet, was called in the autumn of 1536, at which the Lutheran faith was proclaimed to be the established belief of Denmark, and the Roman Catholic bishops were deprived of their rank, titles, and lands. The Lutheran clergy, who were placed at the head of the new church, were known at first by the name of "over-seers," but after a time they were called by the old title of "bishop." Every parish was allowed to choose its own pastor, or vicar, the vicars were left to choose their provost, and the provosts in their turn were free to make choice of their own bishop. By these measures the Pope lost all power in the Danish kingdom. The nobles on the other hand gained a great increase of wealth and influence in the land, for on one pretence or other they obtained a large number of the estates which had been held by the Church, while at the same time they kept down the clergy, and by degrees came to treat them as persons much inferior to themselves in rank. Chris tian III. was a just, kind-hearted man, who tried to do his best for the welfare of his subjects, and he showed himself anxious to have the wealth of the Romish Church used to endow schools for the clergy and poorer laity, but the nobles had left him so little power in the state that he could not effect the good he had so much at heart. A few Latin schools were opened for poor scholars, and the University of Copenhagen now first acquired honour and credit on account of the learning of its teachers. Neither the king nor his people had, however, learnt much charity by changing their faith, and very soon the Lutheran Danes proved themselves to be quite as cruel to all who differed from them in religion as the Catholics had been. Whenever a Calvinist or other Reformed teacher, who did not belong to the Church of Luther, came to Denmark and began to preach, he was hunted out of the land without mercy, as if he had been some wicked malefactor, instead of a minister of the Church of Christ.

Progress in the kingdom.—When Christian III. died on New Year's Day 1559, in the first year of our Queen Elizabeth's reign, Denmark was in a more settled state as to the religious, foreign, and home affairs of the nation, than it had been for a very long time. The troubles in the Church seemed to be at an end, and in every parish in the country the doctrines of Luther were preached from the pulpits, and all men and women from the highest to the lowest could read their bibles in their own tongue. The convents and monasteries were indeed still held by the nuns and monks, who had not been willing to leave them, for King Christian had shown a tender regard to the feelings of those who desired to end their days within the walls of the cloisters, in which they had taken their vows before the establishment of the Lutheran religion in the kingdom. But by degrees one convent after the other was closed, and Denmark, like Sweden and Norway, became a thoroughly Protestant land.

Great progress had been made in learning during Christian's reign. The laws had been revised with much care; equal weights and measures were brought into use in Norway and

Q

Denmark; one form of money was made legal for both countries, and a more just standard was fixed for the amount of silver to be put into the coinage. Trade began to flourish again, and the Danes now went in their own ships to buy the wares in foreign ports, which for a long time had been brought to them by the rich German traders of Hamburgh and Lübeck.

CHAPTER XVII.

SWEDEN BETWEEN 1520 AND 1568.

Gustaf Eriksson, known as Vasa—His birth, family, early school life—His treatment as a hostage—His escape—His wanderings among the miners of Dalekarlia—His various dangers and adventures—His ill-treatment at the hands of the peasants—Their repentance and subsequent choice of him for the "Chief Man"—The beginning of his army—His first flag made of the silk of the Danish traders—His troops encounter the Danes—Bishop Beldenak's surprise at their hardiness—Defeat of the Danes—Gustaf's letter to the princes of Europe—The fate of his mother and sisters—Christian II. tries to avenge himself—Norby's conduct to his prisoners—Complete submission of Sweden to the authority of Gustaf, who is crowned king in 1523—State of Stockholm—Gustaf's want of money—His conduct to the clergy—Favours the Reformers—Puts down the power of the Romish Church—Seizes on its revenues and lands—The peasants support him against nobles and prelates—Submission of all classes—Gustaf's restless activity in controlling the affairs of all his subjects—His troubles in his family—His division of his kingdom—Erik succeeds—Erik's strange character and conduct—His extravagance and caprice—His suit to Queen Elizabeth—His gifts to her—His intentions towards Earl Leicester—War with Denmark—Erik's cruelty to the Stures—His fits of insanity—His submission to Karren Mannsdatter—His marriage with her—His deposition—His imprisonment and the cruel usage he met with—His sufferings—His death by poison—The fate of his wife and children.

PART I.

GUSTAF VASA FREES SWEDEN.

Gustavus Vasa, 1523-1560.—AFTER the Blood Bath at Stockholm, in 1520, Christian II. returned to Denmark in full confidence that he had nothing further to fear in Sweden. His course had everywhere been marked by cruelty. At Jonköping he ordered the captain of the castle to be executed, together with his children; and at Nydala he caused the abbot and some of the servitors of his abbey to be drowned.

No open resistance had followed these acts, but at the very moment that Christian thought himself most secure in his power over Sweden Gustaf Eriksson Vasa,[1] the future deliverer of his country, was already undermining the Danish dominion. This remarkable man, who was born in 1496, was the son of Erik Johansson, one of the victims in the Blood Bath of Stockholm, and had, as we have seen in a former chapter, been unjustly made captive and carried to Denmark by the orders of Christian when he fell into his power as a hostage during the king's conference with Sten Sture the younger. Gustaf had been kept a prisoner for more than a year at Kallö in Jutland, under the custody of his own kinsman, Erik Bauer; and after his escape in 1519, he for a time found safety at Lübeck. In the spring of 1520 he ventured to return to Sweden, where he was forced to assume various disguises, and to labour on farms and in the mines of Dalekarlia, to escape the notice of the Danish authorities, by whom a price had been set on his head. The Swedish peasants themselves at first often threatened his life, declaring that they meant to be true to the king as long as "he left them herrings and salt enough for themselves and their families." But by degrees friends and supporters sprang up around him, and his confidence in his countrymen was seldom abused.[2] Even when

---

[1] This king, known to foreigners as Gustavus, was called Gustaf by his own countrymen. The name *Vasa* was never used by Gustaf himself, nor had it belonged to any of his ancestors, surnames not having been adopted by the Swedish nobles at that period. Some writers have derived the name from the estate of Vasa in Upland; but others, with apparently better reason, believe it to have been taken from the arms of the family, which were a fascine (or vase), such as was used in storming; the black colour of which was changed by King Gustaf into gold (or), which led to the idea that his cognizance had been a sheaf of ripe corn.

[2] Once he only escaped falling into the hands of the Danes by concealing himself under a load of hay, and when the soldiers thrust their spears into the mass and wounded him in the side, he still kept silence, while his faithful guide, to account for the appearance of the blood which had trickled from his wound to the frozen snow-covered road, cut his horse in the leg. The barn at Ranköhytta in Dalekarlia, where he t... ...; the spot in the woods near Marnaas, where he lay t... day ... ... concealed under a felled pine trunk, and was fed by the p... ...s of the district; and many other places rendered memorable by his l... ...urs, are still preserved and honoured in Sweden.

the peasants refused to listen to the first public appeal which he made to them at the Mora Stone, they did not betray him; and when, soon after he had left the district by their request, the particulars of the Blood Bath were related to them by a noble of Upland, named Jon Michelsson, they repented of their conduct, and wished Gustaf Eriksson were amongst them again. By Michelsson's advice they sent swift "Skid"-runners or skaters to seek Gustaf by night and by day, and soon these men traced him to a mountain pass between Sweden and Norway, just as he was about to cross the frontier, and brought him back to Mora, where at the King's Stone peasants from all the neighbouring districts assembled and elected him to be their "chief man in the kingdom." The superstitious country people regarded it as a favourable omen that whenever Gustaf had addressed them the wind had blown from the north, which had always been looked upon in Sweden as a proof that "God would give the matter a good ending." Sixteen powerful men were then chosen for his body-guard, and soon a few hundreds more Dalesmen offered him their services as foot-followers. From this small beginning of power the Swedish chroniclers date the commencement of his reign, although the Danes and their adherents in Stockholm continued long after these events to reckon Gustaf Eriksson and his followers as a company of lawless rebels. In the spring of 1521 he suddenly made his appearance at the Royal Copper Mines above Rättwik, where he seized upon the money belonging to the crown and on the wares of the Danish traders settled there, and carried off the royal bailiff, Christopher Olsson, whom he entrusted to the safe-keeping of one of his faithful Dalesmen. He then divided the money and goods among his followers, who made their first flag out of a piece of silk taken from the Danes; and presenting himself before the miners while they were attending mass, he made them a long address, in which he told them of all the evil that the Danes were working in the land, and obtained a promise of support from them, as well as from the Dalesmen of Dalekarlia.

The Danes finally driven out.—In the meantime the authority of the Danish king was maintained at Stockholm, where Didrik Slaghœk ruled under the name of Regent of Sweden, and was supported by the influence of the archbishop, Gustaf Trolle, and some of the Swedish nobles and chief citizens. As soon as they learnt what had been going on among the Dalesmen, they sent an army of 8,000 Germans to attack Gustaf's followers, whom they found assembled on the banks of the Dal, near the Brunnbäk's Ferry. When the Danish commander, Bishop Beldenak, saw the Dalesmen pouring a shower of arrows with a strong and steady aim across the little stream, he inquired where all these men had come from, and where they could get food in such a desolate region? On hearing that they were so hardy that they drank water only, and if necessary could make shift to live on bark-bread, he is reported by the chroniclers to have said: "If this be so, my comrades, let us retreat while we may, for the devil himself, let alone ordinary mortals, could never subdue a people who can live on wood and water!" The victory at the Brunnbäk, while it dispirited the Danes, gave the turning-point to Gustaf's fortunes; and by encouraging the peasantry to declare themselves for him, actually placed the whole of Northern Sweden in his power: and soon 20,000 men were gathered round his standard at Vesteraas, where the Dalesmen with their long pikes killed a large number of the horses and men of the enemy. But the moral effect of their success was even greater than the havoc which they wrought in the Danish ranks, for the news of the defeat which the Danes met with in trying to defend the town depressed the king's troops and brought fresh support to Gustaf's cause. One castle after another was taken by force or stratagem, and soon there was no Danish leader left in Sweden to fear but Christian's able commander, Severin or Sören Norby, who by his gallant defence of Stockholm gave a temporary check to Gustaf's arms. The feeling against the Danes in Sweden had, however, risen so high that nothing could any longer resist the determination of the people to free themselves. Christian II. had never paused in his course of cruel persecution; and when the news reached Sweden in 1522 that many of the widows and children of the victims in the Blood Bath had died in the horrible dungeons in which the king had thrown them when he carried them to Denmark, the fury of the Swedes knew no bounds. Gutsaf Eriksson's mother and his two sisters had been among the first who sank under the cruel treatment to which they were subjected; and in the letter which he addressed to the Pope, the Emperor, and all Christian princes, in 1522, in explanation of the reasons that had induced him and his followers to rise against the power of the King of Denmark, Gustaf openly accused the king of having poisoned the unhappy Swedish ladies who had died in the Danish prisons. When Christian learnt the purport of Gustaf's appeal, he sent orders to Norby to murder every Swedish noble whom he could seize upon, but the Danish commander let his prisoners escape whenever he could, saying it was "better that men should have a chance of getting a knock on the head in battle than to wring their necks as if they were chickens."

Other Danes had not such scruples, and the Junker Thomas, commandant of Abo, obeyed his king's orders so exactly that he was able to send a report to Denmark of the success with which he had celebrated another Blood Bath. This officer, however, met his own death in the following year, when in making an attempt to relieve Stockholm he and all his ships fell into the hands of Gustaf, and he was hanged on a tree in sight of his own men. The news of King Christian's deposition and flight from Denmark in April 1523 was followed in Sweden by a meeting of the diet at Strängnäs, where on the 23rd June in that year Gustaf Eriksson was proclaimed king of Sweden, and the union with Denmark, which had existed for one hundred and twenty-six years, for ever dissolved. During that short interval between the deposition of Christian and the proclamation of Gustaf, one town after the other had been relieved of its Danish garrison, Calmar and Stockholm were taken, and the provinces of Skaania, Blekingen, and Halland included by force of arms and through the help of treaties in the kingdom of Sweden, of which they formed an integral part, both by their geographical position and the national character of the people. Before the close of the year Finland had declared its willingness to receive Gustaf as its king, and thus all the Swedish dominions were brought under the power of the one man who centred in himself the wishes and hopes of the entire nation.

PART II.

GUSTAF RULES WITH A STRONG HAND.

Gustaf Vasa crowned.—When Gustaf made his entry into Stockholm in the midsummer of 1523, he found a ruined and desolate capital in which half the houses were destroyed, and where the people were broken down by the miseries of the past siege and the effects of foreign rule. There was no money to carry on the expenses of government, while the nobles and prelates, who were the only classes able to help, had made themselves free of all taxation and service to the crown except in cases of foreign invasion. The Hanse leaguers, who had also secured to themselves entire freedom of trade in return for the services which they had rendered the Swedes against Denmark, pressed their claims for payment on account of the arms and provisions which they had given Gustaf during his siege of Stockholm, and whichever way he looked, money difficulties seemed to oppose his efforts to put order into the affairs of the kingdom. Then it was that he determined at one blow to crush the power of the higher clergy —who had made themselves hateful to the people by their wish to uphold the union with Denmark— and to relieve his own wants and those of the State at the expense of the Church.

Gustaf had early acquainted himself with the nature of the new doctrines preached by Luther, and when the brothers Olaus and Laurentius Petri, who had studied at Wittenberg, returned to Sweden in 1519, and began teaching the people the Reformed faith, he had given them his support as far as he was able. When he became king he appointed Olaus to a church at Stockholm, and made the younger brother professor at Upsala, and soon afterwards chose for his chancellor the provost Laurentius Andreæ, who had renounced Catholicism and translated the New Testament into Swedish. He also caused a public disputation to be held between the supporters of the old and the new dogmas, and paid no attention to the Papal letter presented to him by Bishop Brask, in which Adrian II. ordered a court of inquisition to be opened in every bishopric of Sweden for the punishment of heretics and the condemnation of Luther's works. Gustaf's attempt to exact the payment of taxes for the purpose of defraying the expenses of the late war, led to disturbances, and he had several times to quell considerable revolts which had arisen out of his determination to put down the power of the Church. Two Anabaptists, called Knipperdolling and Rink, had caused great disorders in Stockholm, where they had led their followers on to destroy the images in the churches and ill-treat the clergy, but Gustaf ordered them to be driven out of Sweden; and when the people declared that they wished to keep to the faith of their fathers, he assured them that he had no desire to set up new doctrines, and that all he wanted was to do away with abuses. He nevertheless completely crushed the power of the Romish clergy at the diet held at Vesteraas in 1527, when in the opening address, read by the chancellor, Laurentius Andreæ, he laid before them a statement of the necessities of the kingdom, and made the members clearly understand that unless money was freely given by the nobles and the rich prelates, he would at once resign the regal title and retire into private life. "It was impossible," the king said in this speech, "to govern a people who threatened to come out against him with battle-axe and bent bow whenever he began to inquire into any act of treason, and who sent the bound and scorched staff from house to house to summon men to take up arms, as had been the custom of their forefathers in Sweden in bygone times, whenever their kings had done anything that displeased them.[1] After pointing out all that the people owed to Gustaf, and setting before the assembly the disorders of the kingdom, the chancellor inquired of the prelates what they had to say in reply. Then Bishop Brask on behalf of the clergy answered that he and all his brethren knew the duty that they owed the king, but they could not forget that they were bound in all spiritual matters to obey the Pope, without whose express command they could allow of no changes in regard to reli-

---

[1] It had been customary in olden times to call together all the able-bodied fighting men of a district by sending from house to house a charred branch, to which was hung a loop of cord for fastening it to the house-door.

gious teaching nor consent to any lessening of the rights and revenues of the Church; and concluded by saying that if in this respect any evil-minded men had taught heretical doctrines or given bad advice they must be put to silence and punished."

When the bishop had ended his speech, Gustaf demanded whether the Council of State and the nobles considered this a proper reply to his demands? On hearing from Ture Jönsson, who was chosen to speak for them, that they knew of nothing better to say, he sprang to his feet, exclaiming— "Then I will no longer be your king. If such are your thoughts I do not wonder at the treason and discontent of the common people, who blame me if they do not get rain or sunshine when they want either. Your aim, as I see, is to be my masters, and to set monks, priests, and other creatures of the Pope over my head. Who would be your king on such terms, think you? not the worst soul out of hell! So see to it; give me back what I have spent of my own fortune, and I will go away from you all, and never return to my ungrateful country." At the end of this angry speech Gustaf paused, and bursting into tears, rushed from the hall.

Effect of Gustaf's threat.—There was great confusion in the district when it was known that King Gustaf threatened to leave Sweden, and the peasants, collecting in large numbers, cried out that "if the lords could not make up their minds what ought to be done, the Bondar would find a way to help themselves." The bishops were the first to give in, and on the third day Magnus Sommar, Bishop of Strängnäs, came forward and said that "the servants of the Church had no wish to be protected at the risk of destroying the peace of the kingdom." The nobles under Ture Jönsson held out till the Bondar threatened to go to the king, and propose to him that they should all be sent back to their own castles; and then they too came in a deputation to the palace with promises of submission. But Gustaf returned only hard answers to the messages sent to him, and it was not until all his proposals had been agreed to by each order of the diet that he yielded. The bishops, who from that time forth were never again admitted into the Council of State in Sweden, where they had before taken the highest places, drew up a protest against these attacks on the rights of the Church, in a meeting held with locked doors in the church of St. Ægidius, and concealed the writing under the stone floor of the chancel, where it was accidentally found many years afterwards. At the same time they all signed publicly a memorial in which they said "they were content to be poor or rich according to the king's good pleasure."

Conduct to the Clergy.—Gustaf carried out the Resolutions passed at Vesteraas with much severity, taking castles and lands from the prelates, and visiting harshly every act of hesitation on their part in giving them up. Reformed teachers were permitted to preach in Swedish to the people, "as long as they used the Scriptures only, and had nothing to do with false miracles and such-like fables." As soon as he had thus secured the disposal of church property, and received the submission of the nobles, Gustaf celebrated his coronation, and took active steps to put down the disturbances which had broken out amongst the Dalesmen, whose leaders he punished with death. The outbreak had in the first place been caused by the king having taken one bell from every church for the payment of the debt still due to the Lübeckers on account of their help against the Danes, but by degrees other causes of dissatisfaction were added; and for fifteen years his government was disturbed by opposition to the new faith, by attempts on the part of Christian II. and his friends to recover the northern crowns, which led more than once to friendly alliances between Gustaf of Sweden and Frederick I. of Denmark, and by the treachery and discontent of the nobles. But in 1542 the king so thoroughly crushed the rebels in Smaaland that after the murder of their leader, the peasant, Nils Dacke, peace was never again disturbed during his reign. And so firmly was the power of the crown established, that in 1544 Gustaf found himself able to secure the passing of a law by which the throne was declared hereditary in his family.

Gustaf's restless activity.— From that time till the end of his life he never ceased his labours for the improvement of his kingdom, and so untiring was his industry and his determination to be master in all things, that there was no subject, however trivial, that he did not consider, or even decide upon. He put such order in the finances of the kingdom that he left at his death a rich treasury, with a standing army of 15,000 men, and a well-appointed fleet. He overlooked everything himself; writing with his own hands letters to the clergy in regard to the management of their houses and lands, and even rating them soundly for any proceeding in their parishes of which he did not approve. He corresponded with the overseers of the mines and forests in regard to their expenses and the best ways of controlling the works under their care ; with the nobles in regard to the management of their estates ; with the peasants as to the proper manner in which they should rule their houses and families, plough their land and tend their cattle ; and with his own relations and personal attendants on the subject of their dress and domestic affairs. In regard to religious matters he had early shown himself very jealous of interference from anyone, whether Pope, bishop, or noble ; but when he had crushed the clergy and the nobles he proved himself the hardest taskmaster the Church had ever yet known in Sweden. Thus, whenever the Reformed clergy showed any sign of independence, he threatened to deprive them of all rank and power in the State ; and while he exacted the tithes to the utmost, he kept the parish priests well provided with useful directions for making the greatest profit out of the land which they were allowed to hold under the crown.

Swedish trade owed its origin to him, and when he found that the people living in the sea-ports did not take an active part in the American and Indian trade which he desired to encourage, he sent them harsh reproofs, and threatened to come himself and see what they were doing. No kind of business or trade escaped his notice, and he enjoined upon the master-workmen, on penalty of a fine, to engage apprentices and to teach them with care and patience. He drew up regulations for the maintenance of greater cleanliness in the towns, and ordered roads to be made from north to south through the kingdom. He took pains to see that schools were maintained in the several parishes, and gave a new character to the university teaching at Upsala. And he even caused a new rhyming chronicle to be drawn up, for the sake, as he himself said, of " giving a true account of the events recorded by the Danish chroniclers, and to keep up in the minds of his people the remembrance of the conduct of the Danes during their rule in Sweden."

Family Troubles.—This good and great king, to whom his family owed its reputation, and Sweden the place which it afterwards acquired among the other nations, was troubled in his later years by the quarrels and evil conduct of his sons, and the frequent insurrections of his subjects. He had been three times married, and Erik, the eldest and only son of his first queen, Katherine of Saxe Lauenburg, had by his half-insane and excitable acts caused him the greatest anxiety. Knowing the violence and caprice of Erik's nature, Gustaf determined to make his younger sons independent of him, and by his will he left, as hereditary duchies, Finland to Johan the next in age, Ostgothland to Magnus, and Sœdermanland and Værmland to his youngest son Karl, who was then a child. Soon after the king had received the sanction of his council and the diet for this subdivision of the kingdom, he died, at the age of sixty-four, worn out with care; and, in accordance with the wishes which he had expressed, he was buried within the chancel of the cathedral church of Upsala.

PART III.

QUEEN ELIZABETH'S SUITOR.

Erik. 1560-1568.—At the time of Gustaf's death, his eldest son and heir, Erik, was about to start on a voyage to England to make a formal suit to our Queen Elizabeth. He had caused a large fleet and a number of men-at-arms to be given to him, in order, as he said, that he might make a gallant appearance at the English Court, but many persons thought that Erik had only wanted an excuse for securing a powerful force with which he might attempt to seize upon the crown of Sweden without waiting till it came to him by heritage. The news of his father's sudden death reached him while he was reviewing his ships and men at Elfsborg, and, disbanding the troops, he hurried back to Stockholm and caused himself to be proclaimed king. Erik was at that time twenty-seven years of age, handsome, graceful, eloquent, accomplished in manly exercises, a good linguist, able to write well in Latin as well as Swedish, a poet, musician, and painter, and skilled in astrology and the mathematical sciences of his times. But all these advantages were marred by a strangely capricious disposition, and by sudden and violent outbursts of temper, which at times amounted to insanity.

Erik soon began to quarrel with his brother Johan, who had married Katerina Jagellonica, sister of King Sigismund II. of Poland. In consequence of these disputes Johan retired to Poland and took part with that country in a war against Sweden, during which he was made a prisoner and carried back to his own country, where King Erik caused him and his wife to be shut up in the castle of Gripsholm, where they were kept for four years under close, although not harsh, constraint.

During the first few years of his reign Erik wasted all the money that his father had left in the treasury in preparations for his coronation, and in his various absurd missions in search of a wife. Besides the new regalia which he ordered from London and Antwerp, and chests of jewels and ornaments of all kinds, he caused a number of strange animals, which had never before been seen in Sweden, to be brought into the country for the public games with which he intended to amuse the people. We learn from the lists given of these animals that rabbits were at that time unknown, or still uncommon in Sweden, for they are included with lions and camels among the rare and curious creatures to be exhibited.

Erik's Wooing.—As soon as his coronation was over, Erik resumed his preparations for gaining the hand of Queen Elizabeth, to whom he sent ambassadors with costly gifts, amongst which we hear of eighteen piebald horses, and several chests of uncoined bars of gold and silver, strings of oriental pearls, and many valuable furs. Besides making these presents he gave money to his envoy, Gyllenstjerna, with orders to bribe the English Councillors of State, and to " have the queen's favourite, Earl Leicester, put out of the way, even if it should cost 10,000 dollars." During the preceding year his intentions towards the earl had been more honourable, for he then directed Gyllenstjerna to inform Leicester that "his king was ready to offer him battle in his own royal person either in Scotland or France." The English courtiers were thrown into great perplexity when they heard that King Erik had embarked with a great fleet from Sweden, and was coming to press his suit. But they might have spared themselves all anxiety, for Erik, with a changeableness that had already begun to assume the character of insanity, suddenly gave up his plan of going to England. At the same time he sent one messenger to Scotland to see if Queen Mary was as handsome as people had reported, another with a betrothal ring to Princess Renata of Lorraine, the grand-daughter of Christian II. of Denmark, and a third with a contract of marriage already drawn up to the Princess Christina of Hesse, for whose hand he had more than once sued. Lest Queen Elizabeth should feel herself aggrieved by these proceedings, he sent another embassy to England to assure her that the cares of his State had alone kept him away, and that he was not in earnest in regard to the offers of marriage which he had made to the Hessian princess. The queen accepted his apologies and kept his gifts, and so ended this Swedish wooing, to the relief of Elizabeth and her advisers.

War between Sweden and Denmark.—While Erik was indulging in all this folly and extravagance, new wars were springing up in all directions. From 1563 to 1570 Sweden and Denmark were engaged in a very disastrous contest, both by sea and land, which had taken its origin in the foolish vanity of the two rival young kings, Erik XIV. and Frederick II., who had each assumed the three northern crowns in their national arms. This Scandinavian Seven Years' War was marked by great atrocities on both sides. The Danes were seldom the victors at sea, although they had good commanders, but during the latter part of the struggle they often met with signal successes on land after their able general, Daniel Rantzau, led them on. Rantzau's death, while besieging Varberg in 1569, put an end to this war, which cost both parties nearly an equal number of lives, and embittered the mutual jealousy of the two nations, which under Gustaf had begun to diminish.

Erik's insane suspicion led him to destroy his best friends, and on pretence that the losses which the Swedes had sustained in the war were due to the treason of Nils Sture, who had the chief command of the army, he deprived that noble of all his dignities and had him publicly proclaimed a traitor. After this he for a time took him back into favour and even sent him on a second mission to the Princess of Lorraine, but he soon afterwards caused him and all the other surviving members of the family of the great Stures to be tried at Upsala and condemned to death on the charge of treason. It is believed, however, that Nils Sture was innocent, as all the documents connected with the trial were destroyed by the king's evil adviser, Göran Persson.

Erik's Insanity.—Before the council had signed the death warrant, Erik, in a fit of insane fury, rushed into the prison of Nils and stabbed him to the heart, and after looking on while his soldiers completed the murder, he ran to the cell in which the aged Svante Sture and some members of his family were confined, and, throwing himself on his knees before him, cried out, "For God's sake forgive me what I have done!" "I will forgive all except the taking of my son's life; if any wrong comes to him you must answer for it to me before God," replied the old man. "Then," cried King Erik, "you too must be cut down;" and rushing forth, followed only by a few of his soldiers, he made his way towards the neighbouring woods. One of these men soon returned with a message that all the prisoners except the knight Sten were to be put to death. There were two persons who bore this name, and owing to the doubt as to whom the order referred to, both escaped the fate which fell upon their comrades in prison. Göran Persson, after these murders were completed, sought and obtained the signatures of the Council of State to death warrants against all who were slain, and then first made known what had happened. Erik in the meanwhile wandered about the woods in a state of wild fury, no one daring to try and induce him to take food or rest, but at the end of three days, a poor girl, named Karren or Katherine Magnsdatter, who had more influence over him than any other person and whom he afterwards married, persuaded him to return to Upsala. A fortnight later he made his public entry into Stockholm, repeating peni tential psalms with clasped hands, and with his eyes turned towards heaven.

Erik marries Karen.—A prolonged fit of insanity followed this outbreak, and Erik tried by gifts to the families of his victims to make atonement for the evil he had done. In 1567, whilst the war was going on against Denmark and Poland, and the Swedes were being beaten in Livonia, the king married Katherina Mannsdatter, and caused her to be crowned with great pomp. About this time Duke Magnus went out of his mind on being forced by the king to sign the death-warrant of their brother Johan, and for the rest of his life had to be kept in confinement. But the duke escaped the fate intended for him, and soon he and Karl took up arms against Erik, demanding the surrender to them of his unworthy favourite, Göran Persson, who was known to have been the king's chief adviser and helper in all the acts of cruelty of which he had been guilty. The dukes advanced on Stockholm, and soon made themselves masters of all the approaches to the castle, where Erik had shut himself up with his queen and their children. Göran, who was also there, was seized by the king's own bodyguard and given over to the dukes, and after a short trial was put to death, after having undergone the most horrible tortures that his enemies could inflict upon him. When Erik learnt the fate of his favourite, he surrendered, and was by the order of his brothers brought to trial before the assembled states. He conducted his own defence, and when his brother Johan interrupted his harangue against the nobles, with the remark that he was out of his senses, Erik turned sharply upon him and said : " Yes, once and only once have I been out of my mind, and that was when I set you and your intriguing wife free ! " The states, in spite of his defence, declared that he had forfeited the crown for himself and his children, and condemned him to perpetual confinement, with the attendance and personal consideration due to a royal prisoner. Duke Johan did not, however, in those particulars obey the orders of the states, for although he spared his brother's life, he suffered him to be tortured by the most cruel usage at the hands of his gaolers, who not unfrequently beat and wounded him.

R

His Miseries and Death.—During the eight years that he lived after his deposition in 1569, he was carried from one prison to another on pretence that his presence had excited insurrection, and always under the guardianship of men who had been made his enemies by some former act of injustice or cruelty on his part. He addressed frequent appeals for mercy to his brother, begging piteously to be allowed to retire to some foreign land, where he might enjoy the happiness of having his wife and children with him. "Surely," he once wrote, "the world is large enough to yield a spot where distance may deaden the force of a brother's hatred." His threats, his indignant protests against his brother's usurpation, and every attempt made by his friends to rescue him, were visited upon him with an increase of harshness. In his calmer moments he amused himself with reading and with music, and by writing long treatises in his own justification. In 1575 the Council of State, at the request of Johan, signed a warrant in which power was given to Erik's keepers to put him out of the way if in consequence of any attempt at his rescue they might not be certain of being able to retain him in safe custody. For two years no one could be found to act on the hint, and Johan being determined to wait no longer, sent his secretary, Johan Heinriksson, to Oerbyhuus, where Erik then was, giving him a letter, written with his own hand, in which the commandant, Erik Andersson, was enjoined to administer to his prisoner sufficient arsenic or opium to kill him within a few hours. But in case he should refuse to take it, he was to be bound to a strong bench and bled in the hands and feet till he was dead, or laid forcibly on his bed and choked with bolsters and pillows. Care was to be taken, however, that he had first properly received the Holy Communion. As Erik Andersson hesitated to accept the fearful charge committed to him, Heinriksson undertook this cruel labour, and mixing poison in a plate of pea-soup, he forced the unhappy king to swallow it, and after many hours of suffering Erik died in the night of the 26th of February, 1577, in the forty-fourth year of his age. His body was laid in a simple grave in the cathedral of Vesteraas, and covered with a stone bearing this inscription in Latin from 1st Kings, chapter ii. verse 15:

"The kingdom is turned about, and is become my brother's: for it was his from the Lord."

Erik's love for the humbly born Karen Mannsdatter had been so great that the common people ascribed it to sorcery. She alone had ever had power to calm his fury and turn away his anger, and throughout his wretched captivity she never ceased to avail herself of every chance permitted to her of giving him assurances of her faithful love; and those, as he himself asserts in his numerous writings, were the only alleviations he had to his misery. Of their two children, the elder, Sigrid, married early, when at the court of Johan's queen, and became the ancestress of the ducal family, Thott. The younger, a son, named Gustaf, after being sent out of Sweden in childhood, and forced to earn his own living by teaching, was for a time kindly treated and helped by the Emperor Rudolph, under whose protection he studied alchemy. His strange and chequered life, which has often been made the subject of romance, was rendered more unhappy by the frequent attempts of the discontented in Sweden to set up his claims against his uncle Johan. Hence he was never suffered to remain long in quiet, and wherever he went the Swedish king's jealous suspicions followed him. At length he died in 1607, at an obscure country place in Russia, worn out with poverty and disease, and with his brain weakened by too close a study of alchemy and astrology.

CHAPTER XVIII.

DENMARK FROM 1559 TO 1648.

Christian III. of Denmark followed by Frederick II.—The Ditmarsh campaign—The Danish victory at Hejde—The Danish and Swedish kings both assume the three crowns in their arms—The war that sprang up from this assumption—Bad fortune of the Danes—Peace favourable to Denmark—Frederick's intolerance in religion—The persecution of Calvinists—The great men of this reign—Vedel and the Kæmpeviser—Tycho Brahe, his island observatories—His merits—His fate—Christian IV.—His minority—His amusements in his boyhood—His love of the sea—His visit to his English relations—The report of King James's courtiers—Christian's talents and acquirements—His war with Sweden and the Imperialists in Germany in the Thirty Years' War—The superiority of the Swedes—Gallantry and death of Gustavus Adolphus of Sweden—Christian's jealousy of the Swedes—Fresh wars with Sweden—Conduct of the Danish nobles and Council of State—Christian's valour—He loses an eye in battle—The national anthem of Denmark—Kirstine Munk and her fate—Eleanore Kirstine Ulfeld and her husband—Their influence over King Christian—His death—The love of the Danes for this king.

PART I.

WAR BETWEEN SWEDEN AND DENMARK.

Frederick II., 1559-1588.—CHRISTIAN III. of Denmark, who died in 1559, was succeeded by his eldest son, Frederick II. As soon as he had been proclaimed king, this young monarch took part with his uncles, the Counts Hans and Adolf, in an incursion into the lands of the Ditmarshers, who had excited their anger by refusing to pay certain taxes claimed from them by the Holstein princes. The king entered all the more readily

into his uncles' plans because he was anxious to wipe out the
disgrace of the defeat which the Danes had suffered under his
great-uncle, King Hans, and his grandfather, Frederick I.,
when they attacked the Marshmen in the year 1500.

The Danish and Holstein armies, amounting to 20,000 men,
were under the command of the old Count Johan Rantzau,
and by his skill and activity the campaign was brought to a
close in less than a month by the complete subjection of the
Marshmen, notwithstanding the desperate manner in which
they and even their wives and daughters tried to resist the
advance of the invaders. The young Danish king returned in
triumph to Copenhagen in 1560, after having received the
homage of the 4,000 survivors of the great defeat inflicted by
the royal troops on the Ditmarshers at Hejde. His coronation
took place as soon as he had pledged himself to a new and
stringent compact with the nobles, who secured to themselves
the sole right of selling fish and cattle to home and foreign
traders, and obtained many other advantages in addition to
their old privileges, which were all confirmed to them. His
early success had made Frederick confident in the strength of
his own power; and without regard to consequences he continued to bear the three northern crowns in the national
standard of Denmark, which, as we have seen, brought him
into disputes with the young King of Sweden, Erik XIV., who
with equal vanity and with no pretence of right whatever, had
done precisely the same thing in regard to the Swedish arms,
and joined the Danish and Norwegian colours to his own.

We have read in a former chapter of the war which sprang
up between the two nations, chiefly in consequence of this
act of foolish vanity on the part of their respective sovereigns,
and we have also seen how disastrous this Seven Years' Northern
War proved to both parties. The Swedes, however, suffered
less than the Danes, for Gustaf Vasa had left his kingdom in so
prosperous a state, that they did not feel the burdens of war
as much as the people of Denmark, where the king's power was
entirely crippled by the nobles, who often withheld men and
money from their sovereign at the very moment that he most
needed them. Besides the trivial question as to the right of
bearing the three northern crowns on the national arms, the

more important one of the King of Denmark's claim to the
sovereignty of Slesvig and Holstein had been in part the
cause of the war; for Frederick, to evade dividing those provinces with his brothers, who claimed the right of governing
independently of the King of Denmark, had given the island
of Oesel and Courland as an equivalent to his younger brother
Magnus. This prince was for a time supported by the influence of the Russian tyrant, Ivan Vasilievitsch II., but when
Ivan, with his usual caprice, sided with Erik of Sweden,
who had sent an army into Livonia to maintain the supremacy
which he claimed for Sweden in those lands, Magnus was
deprived of all his possessions. Soon after these events, and
partly in consequence of them, war broke out between Sweden
and Denmark in 1563. The Danes in the course of this
contest were generally unsuccessful at sea, although they had
very able commanders; and until the old generals, Otte
Krumpen and Johan Rantzau, took the place of Count
Gunther of Schwartzburg in the command of the army, they
were almost equally unlucky by land, for the German count
left his troops inactive while he busied himself in sending to
Germany the herds of cattle that he had driven off the rich
Holstein and Slesvig lands in which he lay encamped. In
1565 Krumpen and Rantzau gave a new turn to the war, and
during the three years that they continued their aggressions in
Sweden they defeated one Swedish army after the other, and
laid waste a great part of Vestgotland, Smaaland, and Ostgotland. King Erik of Sweden, in his rage and mortification,
visited every defeat on his soldiers as well as on their leaders;
at one time ordering a number of men-at-arms to be cut down
in his presence, and at another hanging up an unsuccessful
commander before the eyes of his soldiers. In return for the
damage done by the Danes in Vestgotland, he caused the old
Danish province of Blekingen to be so cruelly laid waste that
there were only a few poor peasants left in it, and when these
unhappy men begged humbly for the king's protection, he said
he did not want Danish traitors but true-born Swedes for his
subjects; and he forthwith sent a notice to the men of Smaaland
that "they might go and take what they could find in the
Blekingers' homes."

Frederick's Intolerance.—The peace which was concluded between the two countries at Stettin, in 1570, was on the whole very favourable to Denmark, since in return for giving up her pretensions to Sweden, which could never have been established, she secured her own rights over Norway, Skaania, Halland, and Blekingen. The remaining part of the reign of Frederick II. was prosperous, while he left public affairs under the direction of his able minister, Peder Oxe, who restored order in the finances, encouraged learning and trade, and did what he could to improve the condition of his serfs. To him his countrymen are indebted for the introduction of many fruits, vegetables, and flowers, hitherto unknown in Denmark, while he also stocked the lakes and streams with carp and other fish. Frederick was an able, well-disposed man, and in most respects he agreed readily to all that his minister proposed for the national welfare. He was, however, intolerant in matters of religion, and especially opposed to the doctrines of Calvin, whose adherents were persecuted with the greatest severity through the influence of the Lutheran divine, Jacob Andreæ, professor at Tübingen, who had been sent to Denmark by Frederick's brother-in-law, the Elector August of Saxony, to advise the Danish king in regard to questions of faith. At his suggestion twenty-five articles of belief were drawn up, to which everyone who wished to reside in the Danish territories was compelled to give his adhesion. Persecution prevailed in every part of the Danish territories, and fell with almost equal severity on the clergy and the laity. Among the former, the most distinguished victim of the king's intolerance was Nils Hemmingen, the friend and pupil of Melancthon, who held the chair of theology in the University of Copenhagen, and who was deprived of his office and interdicted from teaching on account of his presumed leaning towards some of the doctrines of Calvin. The pastor Niels Mikkelsen was even more severely treated, being ordered to leave the kingdom on account of having preached what was condemned as "the damnable heresy that by God's grace even heathens might be saved." Another pastor, Ivar Berthelsen, had to think himself very fortunate in having the sentence of death which had been passed upon him commuted into a long imprisonment, on account of his having omitted to read the words of the renunciation of the devil, which formed part of the baptismal service.

The great men of this reign.—In this state of things there could scarcely be any great progress in learning, which was moreover also much hindered by severe and foolish laws against liberty of the press; but nevertheless during this reign many public institutions were established in different parts of the kingdom; the schools of Sorö and Skovskloster were opened, and learned men were encouraged, provided they proved themselves orthodox Lutherans. One of the most distinguished of these was Anders Sörensen Vedel, to whom Frederick committed the labour of drawing up a new History of Denmark. Vedel never completed this task, although in connection with it he translated the Latin History of Denmark, written by the old monk of Sorö, Saxo Grammaticus, and collected all the national ballads and historical songs which were still current in Denmark, and which were generally included under the name of *Kæmpeviser.* These compositions, which are far more ancient than the art of printing, had been handed down by word of mouth from one generation to another, and are of the greatest importance, because in many cases they are our only sources of information in regard to many highly interesting events in the history of Denmark. Another and a far more widely celebrated man belonging to this period was Tycho Brahe, the great astronomer, who had early in life secured the respect and admiration of the learned of his times by his writings on the "New Star,"[1] which had suddenly appeared in the heavens in 1572, and then after continuing to shine for eighteen months had ceased to be visible. Frederick II. always showed great interest in Tycho's researches, and to enable him to pursue his observations unmolested, he bestowed upon him the little island Hven, near Copenhagen. Tycho built a great observatory, known as Uranienborg, and remarkable in those times for the number of ingenious instruments which it contained, and for the subterranean observatory attached to it, in which through a nar-

---

[1] *De Nova Stella;* published in 1572 in a separate paper, but afterwards included with other treatises in one volume, *Progymnasmata.*

row slit far above the observer's head the stars might be seen in broad daylight. When King Frederick died, Tycho Brahe's relations, who belonged to the oldest nobility, and had long resented his devotion to scientific research as a disgrace to their rank, used all their influence with the regents to bring him under suspicion of treason and heresy; and at length, to escape being shut up for life as a traitor or a madman, he was forced to seek safety abroad. At the earnest invitation of the Emperor Rudolph II. of Germany, he sent in 1598 for all his instruments from Denmark, and settled at Prague, where he died in 1601, while engaged with his friend Kepler in composing from his numerous observations at Uranienborg those astronomical tables, which are known as the Rudolphine. To Tycho Brahe, as the first man who since the days of the ancient astronomers, Ptolemy and Hipparchus, had been able to detect the errors of the old systems, and construct more correct instruments, modern astronomy owes a large share of the important results which were secured to it by the subsequent labours of Kepler and Newton.

The memory of Frederick II. of Denmark and his highly-gifted queen Sophia possesses a special interest to Englishmen, since as the parents of Anne, wife of James I. of England and VI. of Scotland, they rank among the direct ancestors of our Queen.

PART II.

THE GREATEST OF THE OLDENBURG PRINCES.

Christian IV., 1588–1648.—When Frederick II. died, in the year 1588, his son and successor, Christian IV., was not more than eleven years of age. According to the will of the late king, his queen Sophia of Mecklenburg was to act as regent for her son till he attained the age of eighteen, but the Council of State refused to confirm the regency, and appointed four members of their own body to conduct the affairs of the government, and to have charge of the person of the young king. Still further to promote their own interests, they decreed that Christian's minority should continue till his twentieth year, and they drew up a number of strict rules of conduct which were to be observed by the young prince in his intercourse with his guardians. These were, however, able men, under whose care King Christian grew up to be an accomplished and even learned ruler. He early showed great capacity for mathematics and mechanics, and pains were taken by the chancellor, Niels Kaas, to provide him with competent teachers in these and other branches of learning; while his love for the sea was gratified by another of his guardians, the Chief Admiral, Peder Munk, who caused a beautiful little frigate to be built expressly for him, and launched upon the lake by his palace of Skanderborg, where expert sailors taught him how to manage his toy man-of-war, and shipbuilders instructed him in all the details of their craft. This kind of training strengthened his natural taste for a seaman's life, and one of the first things he did after he became his own master was to explore all the fjords of the Norwegian coast as far as Lapland, where he witnessed the striking sight of the sun continuing above the horizon for nearly all the twenty-four hours of a midsummer's day.

This king paid a visit to England in 1606 to see his sister Anne, who had married James I.; and we are told that he took his young nephews, the princes Henry, Charles and James, for a cruise with him in the Channel, on board his own ship, the *Trefoldighed* or *Trinity*, for which he had himself given the model. There was much feasting and merry-making during this visit, and when he left, the courtiers of James I. expressed their astonishment at the quantity of beer and wine that the royal guest could take. They were, however, even more astonished at the learning of this northern king, who spoke many languages with equal facility, could fence and fight, ride and drive, and swim and leap with the best of them, and who seemed to know something of every subject, asked questions about everything he saw, was well acquainted with the science of his times, and knew all that was needed to plan the building of a ship, a church, or a palace. Christian very possibly inherited some of his talent and love of knowledge from his mother, Sophia of Mecklenburg, who was said to have been the most learned queen of her age, and who, when the nobles and Council of State would not let her act as regent for her son, retired to a quiet place in the country, where she spent her time in the study of chemistry, astronomy, and other sciences.

War with Sweden.—It would have been well for Denmark if her king had devoted his great talents to the duties of governing his kingdom quietly, and had kept at peace with his neighbours. But Christian's reign was seldom free from war with Sweden or Germany, and hence his subjects were never left for any length of time to benefit by his excellent laws, and the able measures which he took to promote the industry and welfare of his kingdom. The first outbreak of war between Denmark and Sweden was due to the determination with which the Swedish king, Charles IX., tried to shut out the Danes from all share in the trade with Courland and Livonia, and to exact tribute from the Lapps, whom Christian IV. claimed as his own subjects on the ground that Lapland belonged to Norway. The Swedes were anxious for peace, and offered to negotiate, but Christian, who would listen to no explanations, entered Sweden in 1611 at the head of 16,000 men, and after several small but fierce encounters, in which young Gustavus Adolphus of Sweden gained his first experience of war, he made himself master of Calmar through the treachery of the commandant. The Danes carried on the war with great cruelty in Vestgotland, whilst the Swedes, under their young king Gustavus, who soon after the taking of Calmar succeeded his father at the age of seventeen, laid waste the Danish territories in Skaania. In this campaign both kings were often in great peril. On one occasion Christian's life was only saved by the devotion of one of his officers, Kristen Barnekov, who gave him his own horse, and then turned to receive the enemy's attack while the king escaped; at another time when young Gustavus fell through the ice on Lake Vide in Skaania, he would have been drowned or captured by the advancing Danes, if a Swedish knight had not rescued him at the risk of his own life. Both kingdoms suffered severely in this war, and both showed an equal readiness to enter into a treaty of peace, which was concluded in 1613, when Sweden gave up her claims on Norwegian Lapland for six years, after which time that district and the port of

Alfsborg, if not redeemed by the Swedes for one million silver dollars, were to be united for ever with Denmark. The Danes had confidently looked forward to their possession of these districts, as they did not believe it possible for the Swedes to collect so large a sum in the time, but to their disappointment the money was paid and the lands redeemed.

Christian's great merits.—Christian's merits as a ruler were great. To him Denmark owed the establishment of trading companies in Iceland, Greenland, America, and the East Indies; the opening of the first line of post-roads from Copenhagen to the various sea-ports; the erection of numerous bridges, fortifications and other means of national defence; the enlistment of the first standing Danish army; the careful organization of the fleet and navy, and the foundation of several military and naval colleges. He encouraged home trade by bringing skilled artificers from abroad to teach the Danish workmen, aided master tradesmen in building manufactories and workshops, and employed men skilled in science to superintend the royal silver and copper mines in Norway, and give advice to the inspectors of the crown lands, woods, and lakes. His love of display and taste for building tended greatly to improve and embellish his capital; and the splendid castles of Fredericksborg and Rosenborg near Copenhagen, together with the Round Tower, the Royal Exchange, and one or two churches which have escaped the effects of the numerous great fires and bombardments, from which the Danish capital has suffered in the last two hundred years, still attest the artistic skill and creative genius of this king, who in most cases himself drew the models and plans of the buildings which he erected.

Christian IV. applied himself with great diligence and sagacity to the task of revising the laws of Denmark and Norway, and making alterations in them suited to the changed condition of society; and here, as in the measures which he took to improve the higher schools, he showed a strong leaning towards principles of equality. The effect of all the changes which he brought about in the laws was to subject the nobles to the same legal control as the classes below them, while the extension which he gave to university teaching in his kingdoms was designed to benefit poorer students. He also showed his wish to improve the younger members of the nobility by founding in 1623, an academy at Sorö, near Copenhagen, which was intended solely to give them instruction suited to their rank before they left their own country to travel abroad for the sake of amusement. His constant endeavour to lessen the power of the nobles over their serfs, and check their encroachments on the rights of the crown, made him unpopular with the higher classes, and in return they thwarted him in every possible way, and took vengeance for his disregard of their prerogatives by withholding the money supplies which he required to carry on operations against the Imperialists in the Thirty Years' War. This war, which began in 1618, and gradually embroiled all the princes of Northern Europe before its close in 1648, had spread to the Baltic lands early in the year 1625, and then it was that the Protestant princes of North Germany appealed to Christian IV. for help against the Imperialist generals, Wallenstein and Tilly, who, after laying waste every Protestant district of Southern Germany, had thrown their armies into Pomerania. Christian IV. brought a large number of troops into Germany, and for three years he did good service in the cause of the Protestants in Pomerania, the Mark-lands, and Brunswick; but while he was fighting abroad, his enemies were carrying the war behind his back into his own country, and slaying and plundering wherever they appeared. In Holstein and Slesvig, the duke Frederick III. had opened those provinces to Wallenstein, and given up to him all his fortresses, in defiance of the king, whose vassal he was. This act roused Christian's anger, and was the cause of strengthening the feelings of ill-will which they had long felt towards each other, and which the Holstein princes showed by taking part against Denmark on every possible occasion.

PART III.

DENMARK'S DECLINE.

Christian's Troubles.—In 1629 Christian IV. withdrew from the German war, and by the treaty of Lübeck he regained the lands which had been seized by the emperor's generals, pledging himself never again to take up arms for the German Protestant princes against the Imperial power. Denmark had suffered so severely in this war, and the finances were so thoroughly exhausted, that the king found it a hard task to try to restore order to his kingdom; and while he was struggling at home against his nobles, who always refused help when he most needed it, and thwarted all his measures, he had the mortification of seeing his rival, Gustavus Adolphus, winning renown abroad, and supported by the liberal aid of his subjects. After the glorious death of Gustavus at the battle of Lützen in 1632, the fame of Sweden was gallantly maintained in Germany by his generals, and the welfare of his kingdom was well cared for by the regents who ruled during the minority of his infant daughter, Christina. These successes excited the jealousy of Christian, while they made the Swedish regents arrogant in their bearing towards him; and hence very slight causes proved sufficient to stir up a war between the northern kingdoms. Hostilities began in 1643 with an incursion of the Swedish troops, under Torstenson, into Slesvig, whence they spread themselves all over the peninsula on pretence of seeking winter quarters. King Christian had foreseen this attack, and repeatedly appealed to his Council of State for men and money to form an army of defence, but they would do nothing to help their king, and seemed only to care for their private interests. Christian was therefore forced to make peace on any terms, and in the year 1645 hostilities ceased in accordance with the treaty of Bromsebro, which gave to Sweden the islands of Gothland and Oesel and other Danish territories for thirty years, after which these lands might be redeemed for money by Denmark. At the same time the Swedes secured entire freedom from all the long-established tolls in the Sound, and obtained so great a diminution of these dues for their allies, the Dutch, that the revenue lost more than 200,000 dollars from this source of income.

Christian's gallantry.—It was in this war that Christian, while commanding the fleet from his own ship *Trefoldighed*, or *Trinity*, lost his eye and was otherwise severely injured by the splinter of a mast, which struck him in the face as he was giving the word of command. The king, who was then upwards of seventy years old, continued to direct the movements of his fleet, and remained on deck till the increasing darkness forced the Swedes to take shelter in the Bay of Kiele off the island of Femern. The following day he drew a line of ships across the entrance of the bay, and leaving his admiral, Peder Galt, to watch the Swedish fleet, returned to Copenhagen to seek the rest which he so much needed. To Christian's great mortification, Galt allowed the Swedes to escape, an act of carelessness which the unfortunate admiral had to expiate with his life, for the king had him brought before a court-martial, by whose sentence he was condemned to death.[1]

Denmark was left in a miserable condition after the peace of Bromsebro, and when the old king in his perplexity tried to secure money by commuting for a fine the service with men and horses which the nobles owed to the crown, the Council of State threatened to pass over his sons in the succession, and elect a prince of the Holstein-Gottorp family to be his successor. Thus poor Christian's last days were clouded with many cares and troubles, and at his death in 1648 the kingdom bore very few marks of the care and ability which he had devoted to the government. After the loss of his first queen. Anna Katherina of Brandenburg, in 1612, Christian had married Kirstine Munk, a lady of noble family, to whom he gave the title of Countess of Slesvig-Holstein, as her want of royal birth prevented her being raised to the rank of his queen.

---

[1] King Christian's personal valour in this engagement has been made the subject of a poem by J. Ewald, who died in 1781, and was one of the greatest Danish writers of lyrics. During the present century this song, beginning with the words *Kong Christian stod ved højen mast*, "King Christian stood beside the high mast," has been set to music and used as the national anthem of Denmark.

The king lived for many years happily with this lady, and showed great affection to their large family, but after a time he became distrustful of her, and caused her conduct to be made the subject of judicial inquiry before the Council, and banished her to Jutland, where she ended her days. The most highly gifted of their daughters was Eleanore Kirstine, who married a Danish nobleman, Korfitz Ulfeld, and, together with her ambitious young husband, exerted a very great influence over the king during his latter years, and thus excited the envy of her own relations, and the suspicions of the courtiers.

With the Danish people the memory of Christian IV. has been cherished with devoted loyalty from one generation to another, and they look upon him as the greatest king they have had since the time of the Valdemars, ascribing the good of his reign to himself, and the evil to the nobles by whom he was held in such galling bondage.

CHAPTER XIX.

SWEDEN BETWEEN 1568 AND 1611.

Johan, son of Gustaf Eriksson Vasa, crowned king on the forced abdication of his brother, King Erik XIV.—Johan's suspicion of his brother, Duke Karl—Karl's superior abilities—His zeal for Protestantism—Johan's learning—His religion and bigotry.—His methods and devices for spreading Catholicism—Jesuits aid him—Pope's condemnation of their conduct—His liturgy, known as *Röda Boken*—His terms of reproach against the Reformers—His second marriage with the young Gunilla Bjelke—His change of views—The many miseries of his reign—His wars—His son Sigismund succeeds to the Polish crown—Sigismund's wish to return to Sweden.—Conduct of Council—Johan and Duke Karl reconciled—Johan's death-bed penitence and resolution—His death—The Queen's conduct—Karl's anger at her avarice—He conducts the government—Summons the Assembly at Upsala—Resolutions to uphold Lutheran faith—Importance of Upsala Resolutions—The Russians and their barbarism—Sigismund's arrival in Sweden—His conduct—Quarrels with his uncle, but has to submit to his terms—Religious dissensions—The coronation—Sigismund returns to Poland—Karl's rule—The Duke's subjection of Finland, and cruelty to nobles—Civil war—Sigismund's abdication—Claims of young Duke Johan put aside voluntarily—Karl, or Charles, as he is called, is crowned king—His learning, character, and conduct to the nobles and the lower classes in his kingdom—His zeal for Protestantism—His internal improvements—His constant wars abroad—His effort to establish friendly relations of policy with other States—His will—His two wives—His daughter—Her learning—Her marriage—She becomes ancestress of future kings of Sweden—King Charles's friendship with Henry of Navarre.

PART I.

THE SONS OF GUSTAF VASA.

Johan, 1568-1592: *His zeal for Catholicism.*—IN Chapter xvii. we followed the history of Sweden from the time that the power of the Danes under their king Christian II. was entirely crushed, and the Swedish monarchy was raised to the rank of an independent and prosperous state under its great deliverer, Gustaf Eriksson Vasa. We shall now have to take up the thread of the narrative from the year 1568, when Gustaf Vasa's son and successor, Erik XIV., was deposed by his brothers Johan and Karl, the former of whom was crowned King of Sweden under the title of Johan III., while the unhappy Erik, after nine years' cruel captivity, was, as we have seen, murdered at Oerbyhus in the winter of 1577.

In all the proceedings carried on by the dukes against their elder brother, the name of Karl had always been associated with that of Johan; but when the insane king was securely set aside, Duke Johan asserted his right to be crowned sole king, and began at once to show a suspicion of his younger brother Karl, which compelled that prince to exercise great caution in his conduct. Duke Karl was the ablest of Gustaf Vasa's sons; and as he was a zealous Protestant, a large portion of the nation who were opposed to the re-establishment of the Catholic faith looked to him as a champion in the cause of their religion, and made his dominions of Södermanland, Närike, and Värmland a centre of opposition against the arbitrary power of King Johan. But in spite of his own ambition and the many opportunities presented to him of gaining the goodwill of the people, Duke Karl remained loyal both to his brother and to his nephew Sigismund. Johan, like King Erik, was a learned man, and during his imprisonment he had devoted himself to study. He had, however, at the same time been induced by his wife, Katerina Jagellonica, who shared his prison with him, to renounce Protestantism and declare himself a Catholic, and during her lifetime he never ceased his labours to re-establish the power of the Romish church in Sweden. The death in 1573 of Laurentius Petri, the first Lutheran archbishop of Sweden, gave Johan the opportunity of testifying publicly the views which he had long been trying secretly to promote, and the new primate, Gothus, a weak and visionary man, was easily persuaded to give his sanction to a church law for the restoration of monasteries, the worship of saints, prayers for the dead, and the use of various ceremonies. Jesuits were sent for to lecture in Stockholm, but were expressly ordered to conceal their religion, and to hold disputations nominally in the defence of the Reformers. When Pope Gregory XIII. learned the acts of duplicity in which these Jesuit teachers had been engaged, he strongly condemned their conduct, and enjoined upon the king boldly to proclaim his adhesion to the Church of Rome, and to use no further deceit in the matter. Some years later he even caused Father Laurentius Norvegicus to be summoned before the General of the Order of Jesuits at Rome, to answer for his conduct in pretending to uphold doctrines which he believed to be false. The liturgy which Johan had drawn up with a view of reconciling the new with the old faith, and which had been severely condemned by the Papal Court, was known as *Röda Boken*, the red book. The king's determination to enforce this form of prayer on his subjects was the cause of great discontent in the country, and soon the court of Duke Karl, who had refused to allow it to be introduced in his duchy, became the recognized asylum for all persons threatened with persecution for their adhesion to the doctrines of the reformers. The Pope's disapproval of Johan's conduct and the death of his queen, Katerina Jagellonica, had the effect of estranging him completely from the Catholics, but for a time he insisted all the more strongly upon the use of his liturgy, punishing all preachers and teachers who opposed its adoption as "ignorant blockheads, obstinate asses, and wicked devils." After Johan's marriage in 1585 with Gunilla Bjelke, a young girl of sixteen, and daughter of the Councillor, Johan Bjelke, he gradually yielded to the influence of his wife's family, who were zealous Lutherans, and allowed the Catholic party to be thwarted in all the schemes which he had himself urged them to enter upon. Johan was a man of unstable will, possessed with extravagant ideas of his own dignity and of the sacredness of his royal power, but his weakness and vanity led him to be easily guided by those about his person; and after his second marriage he identified himself more and more with the interests of the Swedish nobles, as the Bjelkes, Sparres, Bauer, and others with whom he had become related. In his anxiety to secure the steadfast adhesion of these and other powerful families, he established new privileges of nobility, and bestowed estates and certain manorial rights in connection with the title of count and baron, which had not hitherto belonged to them.

Miseries of this reign.—This reign was unfortunate in almost every respect, for while religious differences had been allowed to disturb the kingdom, and the army and navy had been neglected, bad seasons, murrain, famine and pestilence had pressed heavily upon the working classes, and the finances had been exhausted by those wars with Russia and Poland in which Johan had frequently taken part, in order to enforce his son's claims to the Polish crown. The differences with Denmark had been settled by the peace of Stettin in 1570, by which the dissolution of the union of the two kingdoms was formally recognized, the right of both kings to assume the three crowns in the royal arms was admitted, and Sweden was allowed to take Elfsborg back on the payment to Denmark of a fine of 150,000 rix dollars—a sum of money which is nearly equivalent to two and a half million rix dollars in our own days. In 1587 Prince Sigismund, the only son of Johan and Katerina, was elected to the vacant throne of Poland. He was received by the Poles with every mark of respect and affection, but the cares of government and the independence of the nobles made the young king very soon regret that he had accepted the Polish crown, and separated himself from his own family. King Johan was equally sorry that he had allowed the prince to leave him, and at a meeting held between them in 1589, father and son determined to renounce all claim on the throne of Poland, and to go back together to Sweden as soon as Sigismund's resignation had been accepted. This plan, however, met with so much opposition among Johan's councillors and officers, that the kings had to submit and return separately to their respective capitals. The Swedish king, enraged with his council, caused the greater number of its members to be arrested, and called upon them to defend themselves on the charge of treason, while he effected a complete reconciliation with his brother, Duke Karl, and resigned to him the chief power in the State. The disgraced councillors, Erik Sparre, Thure Bjelke, and Sten Bauer, were deprived of all their tenures of land and dignities, and although no act of treason could be proved against them, they were kept in close confinement till the year 1592, when

Johan, feeling himself to be on his death-bed, released them. He at the same time declared that he regretted having tried to enforce his liturgy, since it had caused so much misery and dissent in the kingdom, and promised if it should please God to prolong his life that he would allow freedom of faith to all persons in his dominions.

Johan's death and Karl's conduct.—The king's death, which took place in the autumn of 1592 at his palace in Stockholm, was concealed for three days by his queen, Gunilla Bjelke, who, together with her kinsmen, the Councillors Clas Bjelke and Goran Posse, was suspected of having employed the interval in removing all the valuables on which she could lay her hands. When Duke Karl on his arrival at Stockholm discovered what had happened, and found that the royal corpse had been put aside, unguarded in an outer office, he gave vent to the fiercest expressions of rage against his sister-in-law and all her family, ordering her to give him a list of everything in her keeping, and to leave the spot before nightfall. The queen, however, was able to produce a document in which Johan had declared that she was not to be called upon to give account to anyone for her possessions, and the duke was, therefore, forced to let the matter rest. He caused his brother's body to be laid in state, and deposited in the royal chapel till his public funeral could be solemnised, and he at once assumed the direction of affairs until the wishes of Sigismund could be known. In this respect he was simply continuing to retain the power which had been confided to him by King Johan, three years before; but foreseeing the policy that his Catholic nephew would probably pursue in regard to questions of religion, he determined to settle the government of the Swedish church before Sigismund's arrival. A meeting of the clergy and representatives of the other orders of the State was, therefore, called at Upsala in 1593, in which after prolonged and stormy discussions the Augsburg confession of faith, adopted by the Lutherans of Germany, was recognized as the established religion of Sweden. All present promised to spend their blood, and their life if necessary, to uphold their faith, and joined with a loud voice in the words with which the president closed his address, saying, " Now Sweden is as *one* man, and we all have *one* God." This meeting is regarded as one of the most important events in the religious history of Sweden, and the centenary of the day on which its resolutions were finally adopted was solemnized by services of thanksgiving in the Swedish churches in 1693 and in 1793, in accordance with the prescribed regulations for its commemoration.

Russians show their power.—During the reign of Johan we hear for the first time of the Russians as formidable neighbours and foes of Sweden. Before the accession in 1533 of Ivan II., who was crowned Czar of Muscovy in 1545, the year before Edward VI. ascended the English throne, the savage tribes of Russia had scarcely been heard of beyond the boundaries of their vast dominions; but under that ferocious tyrant they began to be trained to make war on the neighbouring states. Ivan had however formed a sort of friendly alliance with Erik XIV. of Sweden, who as a proof of his goodwill had agreed to help him in securing for himself the wife of Duke Johan, Katerina Jagellonica, whom the Czar wished to marry. After Erik's abdication, Russian envoys appeared at Stockholm to demand the person of Katerina, and the rage of the people on learning the insult which had been thus offered to their queen was so great that it required the personal interference of King Johan himself and of Duke Karl to save them from being killed on the spot. The ambassadors were however allowed to return to Russia, and in 1570 a Swedish embassy was sent to negotiate with Ivan in regard to the settlement of a boundary question. In defiance of his pledges of safe conduct, the Czar treated these envoys with savage cruelty, and after detaining them for two years in confinement, he sent them back to Sweden with the message that he intended to make himself master of Livonia. This was the signal of war, and till Ivan's death in 1584, the people of Finland, Livonia, and the neighbouring districts were subjected to the most fearful tortures at the hands of their barbarous foes, who burnt their prisoners alive, and spared neither women nor children. Sweden suffered heavily in these wars until the gallant French nobleman, Ponte de la Gardie, who commanded a troop of free lances in the Swedish service, gave a new turn to the course of events, and together with the Swedish captains, Henrik and Clas Horn, recovered

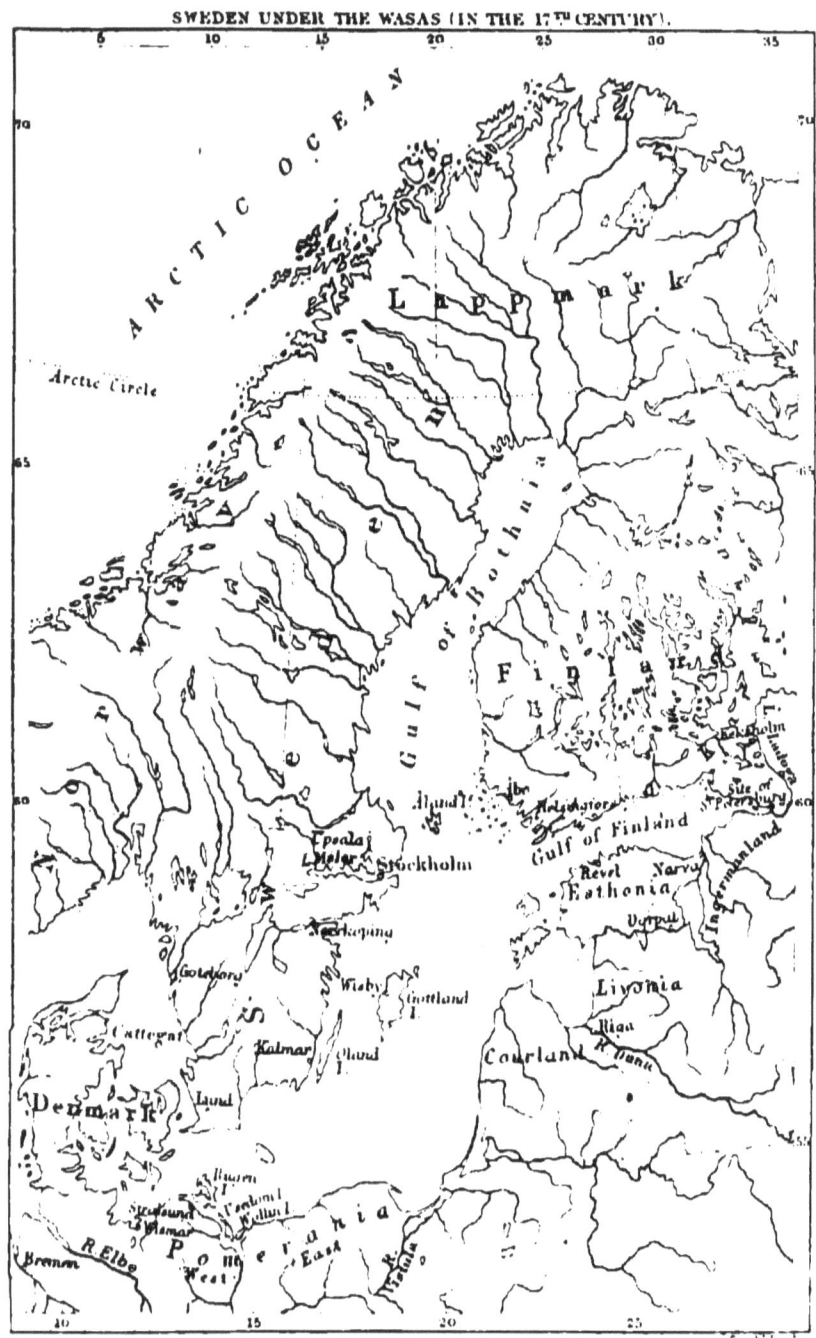

Livonia, and carried his victorious army across the Russian frontier. Ivan on his deathbed had counselled his son Feodor to make peace with Sweden, whose warlike tactics the Russians had learnt to respect, but Johan refused to agree to any terms, and thus entailed upon his kingdom during the rest of his reign a costly and destructive war.

PART II.

RELIGIOUS TROUBLES IN SWEDEN.

Sigismund, 1592-1599.—After great opposition, the Polish Estates consented, on the death of Johan, to let their king Sigismund return to Sweden to assume the crown, and voted a sum of 200,000 gulden in order that he might accomplish the journey with the state befitting his rank. After a tedious and stormy voyage from Dantzic, where Klas Fleming, the powerful governor of Finland, met him with a squadron of Swedish vessels, Sigismund and his queen reached Stockholm in September 1593, attended by a brilliant retinue of Polish gentlemen, and accompanied by the Papal legate, Mala-Spina. Duke Karl stood ready on the castle bridge to welcome the young king, and by his side was Abraham Angermannus, the newly-elected Lutheran primate of Sweden, whose former zealous opposition to Johan's liturgy made his appearance as unwelcome to the king and his friends as the sight of a Romish prelate was to the Swedes. Differences soon broke out between the uncle and nephew, and the duke, returning in haste to his own dominions, left the council to manage as they best could with the king, who rarely called them to his presence, and kept himself almost entirely to the society of his Polish friends and Jesuit admirers. Some of the Swedish nobles, as Klas Fleming, Axel Lejonhufvud, and others, who were at feud with Duke Karl, attended his court, and a few even professed their adhesion to the king's religion; but the mass of the people looked with vexation and distrust at the Roman Catholic ceremonials which were introduced into some of the churches of

Stockholm; and on the occasion of a solemn mass for the repose of the soul of the late king, the Swedes and Poles came to blows, and blood was shed within the church. Foreign Jesuits and Swedish Lutherans preached against each other in the different pulpits of the capital, and while Sigismund refused to ratify the resolutions of Upsala, or to confirm the election of Angermannus as primate of Sweden, the Council insisted upon these points as the condition on which alone they would grant supplies for the king's coronation, and the Estates assembled at Upsala forbade the Papal legate to take part in any public ceremonial, and threatened the Jesuits with death, if they entered within the cathedral doors. Sigismund replied defiantly that the Estates would have to learn the difference between an hereditary and an elective crown, and that his conscience forbade him to change his religion. As the monarch of an hereditary kingdom, professing a different faith from his own, he would not however molest that faith, he said, till he knew what the States would do to secure the liberty of those who believed the same as he did.

In the spring of 1594 Sigismund met the Estates at Upsala, and was crowned with much ceremony in the cathedral church, but not until he had been forced by his uncle and the Council to sign a charter, confirming the religious liberty that had been secured by the Assembly at Upsala in the previous year. Sigismund, with his habitual weakness and insincerity, agreed to everything demanded of him at Upsala, yet almost as soon as he reached Stockholm he began to evade all the obligations which he had assumed. Catholic schools and churches were opened, the Protestant services were interfered with, and the safety of those who attended them was so much endangered as to make it necessary to go armed to church. No redress could be obtained from the king, who, after appointing Catholic governors over every province, returned to Poland. There everything was in disorder, for the Polish nobles, regarding themselves as all of equal rank, refused obedience to the officers appointed to maintain the laws. The Council at Stockholm in the meanwhile declared that no Swedish king could govern from abroad, and that unless Sigismund returned to Sweden without delay, a regent must be named to act for him. Thus urged, the king reluctantly appointed his uncle to govern in concert with the Council of State, but at the same time he sent secret orders to Klas Fleming and all the Catholic provincial governors not to obey his government. Duke Karl, disregarding their opposition, continued to conduct public affairs with great vigour, and in 1595 he settled a favourable peace with Russia, by which Esthonia and Narva were secured to Sweden, while Kexholm and some other spots on the confines of Finland were to be given back to the Russian Czar. Klas Fleming, whose troopers were quartered at Kexholm, and who liked war from the excuse it afforded him of keeping up an army in Finland, evaded the surrender of this place, and his men and the Duke's forces soon fell into hostilities, which only ended with the death of Klas in 1597, when the territory was surrendered to Russia.

Karl as Regent.—The duke and the Council did not long go on in unity, and before the surrender of Kexholm there had been an open rupture between them, and Karl had appealed to the general diet, and been at once named by them Governor-General of Sweden, and all his acts approved of and confirmed. From that moment he appeared as the representative of the bondar and lower landowners of the kingdom, while the higher nobles, whose excessive power he tried to crush, were compelled either to submit or to leave the kingdom, and carry their grievances to the Polish court. By his tact and abilities the Duke broke down all opposition, and after having effectually suppressed the rebellion of the peasantry in Finland, known as the War of Clubs (*Klubbekriget*), and rooted out Catholicism, he found himself strong enough to meet and overcome the Polish army which Sigismund, in 1598, brought to Sweden for the purpose of compelling him to resign his power. At Stångebro, near Linköping, the rival forces met, and after a fierce engagement the royal army was completely routed, and Sigismund was forced to agree to the terms proposed by his uncle, who insisted upon the disbanding and dismissal of his Polish troops, the surrender of all the disaffected Swedish nobles who had taken refuge in Poland, and the summons, within a period of four months, of a diet of the Estates of Sweden, by whose decision the future government of the kingdom was to be regulated. As soon as Sigismund found himself safe out of his uncle's hands, he left the country in haste, and returned to Poland, leaving his friends to fight and suffer in his cause, without supporting them with the strong armament which he had promised to send for their relief as soon as he reached his Polish kingdom.

In the following year, 1600, the Council and Estates of Sweden sent envoys to Poland, demanding the immediate return of Sigismund, in default of which they declared him to have forfeited the Swedish throne, and requiring that in that case he should send his son Vladislav to Sweden, within a period of six months, to be brought up in the Lutheran faith, in preparation of his future acceptance as their king. During this interval the duke advanced with an army into Finland, where Sigismund had powerful friends among the great nobles, and in a short campaign reduced the province to complete submission, avenging the enmity which the nobility had shown towards him by the summary execution, on a charge of treason, of twenty-nine of their leaders, who were brought to the scaffold in Karl's presence at Abo, and put to death with a cruelty that reminds one of the narrative of Christian II.'s Blood Bath at Stockholm. As Sigismund had taken no notice of the demands of the Council and Estates of the Realm, he and his heirs were declared to have no further claims on the allegiance of the Swedish people, and the rights of Duke Johan of Ostgotland, as the younger son of the late King Johan, were taken into consideration; but when that prince declined to be brought forward as a candidate for the throne, no obstacle stood any longer in the way of the succession of Duke Karl, who, however, was not proclaimed king until the diet met at Norköping in 1604. Sigismund, in the meanwhile, continued till his death in 1632 to reign over Poland, whose national credit and prosperity were severely injured by his incapacity for government and his bigoted intolerance. He left two sons, Vladislav and John Kasimir, both of whom became in turn kings of Poland.

PART III.

THE RISE OF SWEDISH POWER.

Charles IX., 1599-1611.—Karl, or *Charles*, IX. of Sweden, as we should rather call him, was the only one of Gustaf Vasa's sons who inherited his good sense and steadiness of purpose, as well as his abilities. All the brothers had been learned, able men, but Karl, the youngest, alone knew how to make good use of his learning, and how to turn his great talents to account. He was a stern and cruel foe, and never knew how to forgive, but he was just and forbearing to his friends and relatives. Like his father, he combined the power of looking closely into details, and keeping watch over the management and expenditure of the smallest sums of money in his own household, with the capacity for laying vast plans for the future greatness of his kingdom. It is related that he carried his economy so far as to direct that his queen herself should measure out the yarn and thread used by her maidens in weaving and sewing. On the other hand, his history shows that from the very beginning of his struggles with Sigismund, he had resolved to risk his fortune and even his life in the effort to make Sweden a Protestant state, while the great object that he had in view during his latter years was to support the Protestant cause in Germany, and aid in crippling the power of Austria, which he foresaw would in time gather the Catholic German states around her, and make a desperate effort to trample down the Reformed faith. In his will he enjoined upon his wife, son, and nephew carefully to maintain the friendly relations which he had entered into with the Elector Palatine, Frederick V., the Landgraf Moritz of Hesse, and other evangelical princes of Germany; and the idea that Sweden would be called upon to prove her devotion to the cause, which those princes upheld, seemed ever present to his mind.

In Charles IX. the Swedes found a second and even greater

founder of their national glory than in Gustaf Vasa, and his struggle with Sigismund is looked upon as the most important turning point of their religious history. At the death of Johan, Sweden was hovering between Catholicism and Protestantism, and if the regent-duke had not settled all further dissent by the resolutions passed at Upsala, in 1593, Sweden would probably have been numbered among the Catholic states of Europe. In all that he did, Charles had always had the lower classes on his side, and he well knew that it was from the nobles alone that he would have any opposition to dread. He had long suspected that a party existed in the state which desired to see an elective monarchy established in the place of succession to the throne by heritage, which his father had secured for the Vasas, and at the diet of Linköping, in 1600, he had caused a number of those nobles who had been surrendered to him by Sigismund to be tried for treason to the state, and for disobedience to his orders while he was regent of the kingdom. A few of these men confessed that they had wished to subvert the Lutheran religion, and were otherwise guilty of the charges brought against them, and they were pardoned; but others, including the heads of the great families of Sparré, Bjelke, and Bauér, were condemned to death, in spite of the tears and prayers of their wives and children, who threw themselves on their knees before the duke and begged for mercy. After the beheading of these men, others of equal rank were imprisoned, and their lands taken from them, while some were banished from the kingdom, and the duke thus found an opportunity of crushing his private foes under the same fate that was awarded to the enemies of the state.

Females allowed to reign.—The first act of Charles IX. after he became king was to allow men of burgher and peasant rank to have a legal and clearly-defined share in the deliberations of the Estates of the diet, and he succeeded in having a change made in the laws of succession, by which the crown was declared hereditary in the persons of his *female*, as well as of his male descendants. His care for the interests of the lower classes won for him the name of "Bondarkonungen," the Peasants' King, which was well merited, inasmuch as he appears to have been always on the alert to defend this order of his subjects from wrong at the hands of the higher classes. On one occasion when the widow of a clergyman was proved to have had an injustice done her in a lawsuit, he wrote to the unjust judge, telling him that unless the poor woman at once received what was her right, "his stick should soon be made to dance the polka on his back." He encouraged trade, and by laying the foundation of the ports of Karlstad in Værmeland, and of Göteborg on the west coast of Sweden, he may be said to have created the foreign commerce of the kingdom. In regard to the working of the Swedish silver and copper mines, this king made great improvements, and there was not a branch of industry, or a department in the government which did not feel the benefit of his able supervision. But while he restored order to his disturbed kingdom, he kept his subjects constantly at war, either with Poland, Russia, or Denmark, and sometimes with all three states at once.

Swedes in Russia.—In 1609 King Charles sent a Swedish army, under Pontusson de la Gardie and Evert Horn, to relieve Moscow from the assault of the impostor, Demetrius, who was aided by Poland, and to secure the succession of the Czar Vasielievitz Schuisky. In both these objects the generals were successful, but a mutiny having broken out among their men when they did not receive the pay promised them by the Russians, and many foreign auxiliaries having gone over to the enemy, De la Gardie and Horn were forced to fall back. With only 400 men they effected a successful retreat through the lands of their enemies, and without any further loss made their way to the Swedish frontiers. Charles, in no way discouraged, sent another army into Russia in 1611, which took Novogorod by storm, and forced the Russians to sign a treaty, by which they pledged themselves not to obey any of the various pretenders, including Sigismund's son, Vladislav, but to acknowledge the Swedish prince, Karl Philip, as their czar.

The Calmar War, 1611: *Charles' death.*—When the news of this success reached Sweden, Charles IX. was on his death-bed, and the kingdom was engaged in the contest with Denmark, which is usually known as the *Calmar* War, in consequence of its having been fought in the neighbourhood of the town of that name. This war was mainly brought about by the haste and ambition of the young Danish king, Christian IV., who thought that, considering the old age and feebleness of Charles, and the youth and want of experience of his son and heir, Gustaf Adolf, the moment was favourable for retaliating on Sweden the losses which Denmark had suffered through the Swedish king's monopoly of the trade of Riga. But King Christian had formed a wrong idea of Sweden and her princes, and the result of the war was not one for which he or Denmark had cause for satisfaction. King Charles IX. died at the age of sixty, in 1611, at Nyköping, on his return from Calmar, after the settlement of a short armistice with Christian IV., and thenceforth the conduct of the war was left to Gustaf Adolf, the future hero of so many glorious victories. At the time of his death, Charles IX. was engaged in friendly alliances with all the great Protestant powers. He had promised to send 1,000 horse and foot soldiers to the Netherlands in the event of the continuance of the war against Spain, in return for which he demanded the right to export salt free of duty from their ports ; and in 1610 he had sent an embassy to England to demand a continuance from James I. of the same friendly relations that had existed between him and Queen Elizabeth, who from the time of his brother Johan's death had shown her goodwill towards him and approved his policy. He also wished James to join him in one common alliance with the Netherlands and France against Austria and Spain ; and envoys were on their way to France to secure the goodwill of the King, Henry IV., when the news of his murder by Ravaillac stopped them. Thus for the first time in her history Sweden had been brought into political relations of friendship with the other more powerful European states, and had taken an independent position among them. With this king, moreover, began the system of personal influence which during the next century and a half the Swedish monarchs exercised over their people, until at length the history of the king became actually that of his kingdom.

Charles IX. was distinguished as a poet and author of no mean ability. He wrote Latin poems, composed numerous hymns and prayers, which were long in use, and left several treatises on political subjects, accounts of his reign, and various journals, which were made ample use of by his son in the history which he drew up of the events of his father's time. Charles was twice married. By his first wife, Maria of the Palatinate, he had one daughter, Katerina, the ancestress of the later Princes Palatine, and of the Palatinate branch of the Vasa line in Sweden; and by his second wife, Kristina of Holstein-Gottorp, he had two sons, Gustaf Adolf and Karl Philip. The Princess Katerina, like her brothers, was a good classic, and when Henry IV. of France demanded her hand in marriage for his friend, Prince Henry of Rohan, she returned a courteous reply in an elegant Latin letter, composed by herself and written with her own hand, in which she referred the matter to her father's decision, and begged her suitor's acceptance of some sable-skins in return for his gifts. Charles's refusal to give his daughter to the Prince of Rohan made no difference in the friendship of King Henry, who offered his services to mediate between Poland and Sweden, and continued to apply to the Swedish government for nearly all the cannons, balls, and steel required by him in his wars.

CHAPTER XX.

SWEDEN FROM 1611 TO 1644.

Gustavus Adolphus; his birth, mode of education, learning, and early practice of government—His investiture with sword and shield—The Calmar War—His first exploits—His succession—The Regency resign their power—Peace with Denmark—War with Russia—Treaty with Russians—St. Petersburg on Swedish ground—Peace—Internal Government—Great things done by Gustavus—The increase of power of nobles—Riddarhuset—Talented men at his court—His great generals—His Polish campaigns—His narrow escapes—The war in Germany—The Danish king's share in the Thirty Years' War—Magdeburg—Its siege—His solemn leaving-taking of his Diet—His little daughter confided to the Council—His departure—His war cry—France gives secret aid—Wallenstein—Gustavus advances on Lützen—His preparations—The battle—King's wounds, his death—Victory of Swedes—The body of the slain king recovered—Its removal—Body embalmed—Heart enclosed in casket and kept by the Queen—The "Schwedenstein"—The monument erected in its place—Personal appearance of King—Generals and friends of Gustavus—Arrangements for government—The campaign of Swedes in Germany—Bernard of Saxe Weimar goes into French service—His death—Johan Bauer—His appearance before Vienna—His masterly retreat—His death—Lennark Torstensson—His great talents—His bodily infirmities—Called "Swedish Lightning"—His career in Germany—His command in Denmark—His resignation—Wrangel succeeds—Peace with Germany—The return for all the sacrifices made by Sweden.

PART I.

THE HERO KING OF SWEDEN.

Gustavus Adolphus, 1611-1632.—GUSTAF II., Adolf, or Gustavus Adolphus, as he is generally called by foreigners, the most accomplished and renowned king of his times, was born in the town of Stockholm in 1594. From the age of ten his father, Charles IX., made him attend Councils of State and the sittings of the diet, and soon afterwards he was taught to receive and reply in Latin, or in some other foreign tongue, to the ambassadors who presented their credentials to the Swedish king. He had been so carefully educated under the learned secretary, Johan Skytte, that before he was fifteen he could speak Latin fluently, and talk German, Dutch, French, and Italian, as well as if each language had been his mother-tongue, while he understood something of Polish and Russian, and had begun to learn Greek. Gustavus to the close of his short but eventful life retained his early love of learning, and whenever he could, he devoted one or two hours daily to the reading of history, politics, and literature with his former tutor Johan Skytte, preferring above all things, as his friend Axel Oxenstjerna tells us, to read in the original, Grotius' "*Tractatus de Jure Belli, et Pacis*," and the works of Xenophon, whom he regarded as the greatest of all *military* historians. When King Charles made his young son Grand Duke of Finland, and Duke of Esthonia and Vestmanland (in 1609), Skytte accompanied him and helped to show him how to conduct public affairs in accordance with the regulations of the Swedish diet, with which the secretary was well acquainted, as he had made the laws and customs of his native country a special subject of study.

While Gustavus was keeping court in his capital, Vesteraas, he underwent a careful training in the art of war, and in all kinds of military exercises and manœuvres; and thinking himself no doubt quite an expert captain, he demanded of his father, as a right belonging to his birth, that he should be commander-in-chief of the forces in the war with Russia. Much to his disappointment, however, the king refused his request, and made him wait till he had reached his sixteenth birthday, after which, in the spring of 1611, he was, in accordance with an old northern custom, declared fit for and worthy of receiving and carrying arms, and with great state presented by his father to the diet, before whom he was solemnly invested with sword and shield. At this moment preparations were being made to meet the young Danish king, Christian IV., who had declared war against Sweden, and was bringing his army forward to besiege Calmar. And the first act of Gustavus after his investiture was to collect the Swedish

T

forces in Vestergothland, and advance to the relief of the beleaguered town.

The Calmar War, which ended with the peace of Knaeröd in 1613, is now chiefly memorable for having served as the school in which Gustavus perfected himself in the art of warfare, and gave the first practical evidence of those great talents which made him in later years one of the most noted commanders the world has seen in modern times. Sweden remained without a king for two months after the death of Charles IX., for in accordance with his will, the queen and his nephew, Duke Johan, with six Councillors of State, were to rule the kingdom till the wishes of the people could be made known. But when the diet, which met at Norköping in December 1611, declared that the Swedes would stand by the promises which they had formerly given King Charles to accept his eldest son for their ruler, Duke Johan again formally renounced all claims on the throne, and he and the queen laid down their powers, although according to Charles' will they might have retained them till Gustavus was eighteen.

Conquests in Russia.—After the conclusion of peace with Denmark, Gustavus carried on the war with renewed vigour against Russia, where the people had chosen a native-born prince for their czar, and refused to receive the Swedish prince, Karl Philip, to whom they had previously offered their crown. Twice Gustavus himself advanced into Russia and gained great advantages over the Russian leaders, until at length the new czar found himself forced to agree to a peace, which was signed in 1617 by him and the great Swedish general, De la Gardie, at Stolbova, a little town on the Ladoga Lake. By this treaty, Sweden obtained Ingermanland and Karelia, with the sum of 20,000 roubles, and recovered all her former rights in Livonia, while Novogorod and all other Swedish conquests in Russia were given up. When Gustavus met the Estates of his kingdom at Stockholm in 1617, he laid before the diet a full report of this treaty, and, after drawing a vivid picture of the power of Russia, and the danger to Sweden of having neighbours on her flanks, whose boundary-line stretched from the Caspian Sea to the frozen ocean, he showed them on a map how by the peace of Stolbova, Russia was now completely shut out from the

Baltic, "and that," he added, "we will hope, by God's help, may always prove too wide a jump even for a Russian." The ground on which St. Petersburg now stands was then Swedish, and on the boundary-line a stone was erected, on which were carved the three crowns of Sweden, surmounted by the following Latin inscription:—

"*Huc regni posuit fines Gustav Adolphus Rex Suconum, fausto numine durct opus. Limites positi an.* 1617."

After this peace Gustavus turned his whole mind to the careful government of his kingdom, and probably no other king ever did so much for the welfare of his people in so short a time; while in all his measures he consulted their wishes, and laid before the national assemblies full reports of his acts. In order that his subjects in all parts of the kingdom might have the opportunity of asserting their rights, he established parliaments, or high courts at Stockholm and Abo, called together the diet every year, and left the four orders into which it was divided, to consider and decide for themselves, in separate assemblies, upon questions in which they were specially interested. He divided the nobility into three classes, consisting (1) of counts, barons, or highest nobles; (2) of the descendants of Councillors of State; and (3) men of noble descent without hereditary titles and lands; and ordered that they should meet in a House of Lords or "Knights' House," known as *Riddarhuset*, on whose books all entitled to a seat were to inscribe their names. He granted many privileges to the noble orders, but in return he required that they should give their services to the state, and thus he secured for the crown faithful supporters among the most influential men in the kingdom. The civil and military services were put upon a regular system, and a stricter discipline and order were introduced into the army than could be found among any other troops in Europe. Gymnasiums, academies, and schools sprang up in every part of the kingdom; the Upsala University was enriched with some valuable mines and lands that formed part of the king's private family property, and several new trading ports, as the present Göteburg, were established. Gustavus had the good fortune of securing the friendship and devotion of talented men in every department of the state, and at the moment when he set forth in 1629, on his fatal but glorious campaign in Germany, his court was celebrated for the number of able military leaders and statesmen who surrounded the person of the king.

After an interval of peace, war broke out again in 1621 between Sweden and Poland, owing to the obstinacy with which Sigismund maintained his pretensions to the Swedish crown. Gustavus in person conducted this war, which began by his conquest of Livonia and Karelia and the taking of Riga, after which he advanced into Polish Prussia and gave battle at Egnen on the Vistula to Sigismund's troops, which were powerfully assisted by an army of Imperialists, commanded by Arnheim, one of Wallenstein's generals. Gustavus gained the victory on this and so many other occasions, that his fame as a successful commander was admitted by foes as well as friends, and the German emperor, Ferdinand II., who through his great generals, Wallenstein, Tilly, and Piccolomini, had nearly crushed the power of the Protestant cause in Germany, saw the danger that threatened the supremacy of the Catholics unless he could arrest the progress of the Swedish king. Large armies were, therefore, thrown into Poland by the emperor, on the pretext of helping his ally, King Sigismund, and Gustavus found himself involved in a fresh war at a time when he was specially anxious for peace. In this fourth and last of his Polish campaigns, he was often in great personal danger; once he only saved his life by leaving his hat and scabbard in the hands of the foes who had surrounded him. Even then he would probably have been made captive if a Swedish soldier, Erik Soop, had not come to his rescue and shot down the trooper, who had seized upon the king's arm and was dragging him by main force towards the enemy's ranks. In writing an account of this feat to his friend and chancellor, Oxenstjerna, Gustavus remarked that he had "never been in a hotter bath." Yet he had had many narrow escapes, for once a ball had carried off the sole of his right boot, and on another occasion a shot had struck him in the stomach. He had moreover repeatedly had his horse shot from under him, and been forced to crawl out from among the dead and dying, and fight on foot till another horse could be brought for him. After the battle of Stuhm, a truce for six years was signed at Altmark in 1629 between Sweden and Poland, which left Livonia and parts of Polish Prussia in the hands of Gustavus.

PART II.

THE DEATH OF THE SWEDISH HERO.

Gustavus in Germany.—The Swedish king now found himself free to give the help which he had long promised to his Protestant allies in Germany. At that time a general European war seemed to be impending. The cause of the German Protestants appeared desperate, and all the other European powers which had adopted the doctrines of the Reformation sympathized with them, while the Catholic states generally, excepting France, which was moved by special interests, sided with the emperor. Christian IV. of Denmark had, as we have seen, helped the German Protestants as well as he could, but when the Imperialists, under Duke Wallenstein, entered Slesvig and seized upon Jutland, he had been forced to accept whatever terms of peace he could secure. Duke Wallenstein had refused to listen to the envoys sent by Gustavus to take part in the negociations for peace opened at Lübeck, and this and other circumstances made the king of Sweden see that there was little chance for him to avoid a war with the emperor. He had, moreover, incurred the anger of Ferdinand II. by opening his kingdom as an asylum to all Protestants who had been persecuted for religion, and by receiving at his court his outlawed kinsmen, the Dukes of Mecklenburg. Wallenstein had been chosen to conduct the war against Mecklenburg, and this great general, who seems to have been excessively jealous of the fame of Gustavus, not content with open hostilities against him, offered to give 35,000 dollars to foment a rising in Sweden, and in his eagerness to make himself master of Stralsund, which opened the passage to the Baltic, he declared that he would never rest till that place was in his hands, " even though it were to be bound tight to heaven with chains of iron."

Gustavus on the other hand felt that if Stralsund were once in the hands of the Imperialists, his career would be closed for ever, and his plans to help the Protestants of Germany rendered of no avail. He, therefore, made the relief of that place his first object, and after sending troops to aid the garrison, prepared to follow in person.

When he had made his preparations for this great and eventful undertaking, Gustavus called together the diet at Stockholm on the 19th of May, 1630, and laid before them a report of the oppression and misery to which their brethren in religion were reduced, and the dangers which threatened Sweden unless the advance of Catholic power could be checked. He then took a touching farewell of them, and raising his little daughter, Christina, a child of five years of age, in his arms, he commended her to their care and fidelity as the heiress of his crown, and closed the meeting with prayer. Each of the several orders of the Estates of the kingdom assured him of their devotion; and having entrusted the government of Sweden to a council of ten, and appointed his brother-in-law, the outlawed Count Palatine, Johan Casimir, to be director-in-chief of all affairs connected with the levying of troops and other preparations for war during his absence, he embarked with all his army, and landed in Germany on Midsummer's Day in 1630.

He brought with him only 15,000 men, and with this small army the Swedish king, trusting in his favourite watchword, *Cum Deo et victricibus armis*, boldly advanced upon his dangerous course. At first circumstances favoured him, for Wallenstein, having fallen into disgrace with the emperor, was no longer among his opponents, while Cardinal Richelieu had pledged himself that as long as the Swedish king could keep an army of 30,000 men on foot against the Imperialists, he should receive an annual subsidy from France of 400,000 rix-dollars. The rapidly rising power of the house of Hapsburg presented so many causes of alarm to France, that Richelieu was glad to avail himself of any opportunity of weakening the empire, and he allowed French soldiers to join the ranks of Gustavus, and gave the latter all the help he could, without actually drawing the French nation into the war. Some of the lesser Protestant German princes openly sided with the Swedish king, but the more powerful, as the Electors of Brandenburg and Saxony who stood in awe of the emperor held aloof, and threw difficulties in the way of the advance of the Swedish army, which in consequence failed to relieve Magdeburg. This unhappy city, after a long and most daring defence, was forced to submit to the Imperialists, the greater number of the citizens having died from starvation, or perished at the hands of the victors, who remorselessly cut down the women and children, or left them to be burnt alive in the flames, which reduced Magdeburg to a heap of ruins. The Elector of Saxony, after having met with the most cruel treatment at the hands of Tilly, entered into a compact with Gustavus, and joined with him in giving battle to that general at Breitenfeld, near Leipzig, where the Swedish king, through the superior discipline and valour of his troops, gained a signal victory in 1631. Tilly, who had never before been defeated, and who had had a very much larger army in the field than Gustavus, fell back upon the Bavarian frontier, where in the following spring, while encamped on the border stream, the Lech, he was again attacked by the indomitable Swedes and forced to meet them in a long and fiercely contested engagement, in the course of which he was mortally wounded.

After the death of Tilly and the defeat of so many of his armies, the emperor resolved to recall Wallenstein, and soon under that great commander's influence fresh armies were enlisted and trained, and strong defences were thrown up against the advancing foe. But neither he nor Gustavus would venture to offer the other battle, and for nine weeks they lay with their armies encamped within sight of each other outside the gates of Nürnberg, which Wallenstein had threatened, and the Swedish king had hastened to protect. At length Gustavus made an assault on Wallenstein's well-defended camp which failed, and, unable to bring his wary foe into the open field, he withdrew to recruit his own sick and hungering army, whilst the Imperialist commander as quickly broke up his camp, and threw his forces into the rich lands of Saxony, where they laid waste everything before them, and the elector in his distress had again to call upon the Swedes for help.

Battle of Lützen.—Gustavus was at Neuburg in Bavaria with his queen when the news of Wallenstein's attempt on Saxony reached him, and he at once took the resolution of forcing Wallenstein to meet him in the field. Ordering all his troops to advance by forced marches to Erfurt, he joined them there on the 28th October, 1632, and rapidly made his final arrangements. On the morning of November 1st, after having passed the night in reading and answering despatches, and sending his instructions to the council in Sweden, he took leave of his wife, whom he commended to the care of the Erfurt citizens, and, mounting his horse, followed his army, which had crossed the Saale on the 30th of October. Gustavus had only 12,000 infantry and 6,500 horsemen under his command at that moment, and Wallenstein, who knew the numbers of the Swedish army, did not believe that the king would venture to meet him with such a small force, and he had therefore gone into winter quarters at Lützen, after sending his general, Pappenheim, to Halle, to watch the movements of the Swedes. The surprise of the Imperialists was great when they found that the Swedish king had brought his army in so incredibly short a time from their quarters near Nürnberg to the plain of Lützen, although the autumn rains and the character of the ground seemed to make the passage of many men and horses almost an impossibility. The greatest confusion prevailed in the camp. Orderlies were riding in all directions to recall the scattered Imperial generals and their brigades. Soldiers were kept at work all night, throwing up entrenchments along the main road between Lützen and Leipzig, on the north side of which Wallenstein had drawn up his men in order of battle. When Gustavus was informed by spies that the Germans were quite unprepared for his attack, he exclaimed, "Now I truly believe that the Lord has given my enemies into my hands," and determined not to delay the assault. His anger against the Imperialists had been strongly excited during his march by the sight of the devastation and misery which they had brought upon the country people. Wherever he passed, ragged, half-famished creatures had crawled forth from their ruined huts or from the poor shelter of the leafless woods, and throwing themselves on their knees, had stretched out their hands towards him. This sight had moved him deeply, and when he noticed their looks of appeal, he had observed to those near him, "These people worship me as a God; I trust I may not be punished for their idolatry."

The morning of the 6th of November, 1632, on which day Gustavus lost his life in the battle of Lützen, dawned in so thick a mist that the two armies could scarcely see beyond their respective vanguards, which were so near, that in reconnoitring their foes they found themselves close to one another. At an early hour, the Swedish army, which was composed of many Scotch as well as German auxiliaries, engaged in prayer and sang Luther's hymn, "*Eine feste Burg ist unser Gott*" ("A tower of strength is our God"), after which Gustavus himself, in a loud voice, gave out his favourite hymn, "*Jesus Christ unser Heiland*" ("Jesus Christ our Salvation"). Clad in his usual overcoat and without armour, which he had almost entirely laid aside for himself and his soldiers, he mounted his horse, and riding along the lines, addressed his Swedes and Finns in their native tongue, telling them that the enemy, who had so long evaded them, was now within their reach, and exhorting them to fight for their God, their country, and their king. "If you fight as I expect of you," he said in conclusion, "you shall have no cause to complain of your reward, but if you do not strike like men, not a bone in your bodies shall ever find its way back to Sweden." To the Germans he spoke strongly and earnestly, calling upon them to follow him bravely, to "trust in God, and to believe that with His help they might that day gain a victory, which should profit them and their latest descendants." "But if you fail me to-day," he added, "your religion, your freedom, your welfare in this world and the next are lost." Wallenstein maintained complete silence, and his men understood from the cold and stern looks with which he scanned their ranks, that they would receive little mercy at his hands if they failed in their duty. Gustavus had expected to be reinforced by Duke George of Lüneburg and the Elector of Saxony, who had both made great protestations of gratitude and devotion, and promised to bring their troops to his aid, but neither of them appeared at Lützen, and he, therefore, had to engage the enemy without their support.

Death of Gustavus.—The king, who himself commanded the right wing of his army, was the foremost of all to advance against the enemy. Waving his drawn sword over his head as the Swedes and Finns responded with the clash of arms and loud cheers to his address, he cried out, "Jesus, Jesus, let us fight this day for thy Holy Name," and giving the word of command, he advanced, while the whole army, as each regiment began to move, caught up the loud cry of the Swedish watchword, "God with us." The enemy awaited the attack on the farther side of a road, skirted by deep ditches, and the Swedish infantry, after crossing, were met with such overwhelming numbers that they wavered and fell back. On perceiving this, Gustavus, who had led his own division over the road, hastened at the head of a troop of his Smaaland cavalry to the help of the infantry. Before he could reach the road, the three brigades under Count Niels Brahe, which formed the Swedish centre, had advanced to the charge with such impetuosity that they took three batteries by storm, and drove back two of the enemy's squares. When the news of this success reached the king, he uncovered his head and uttered a prayer of thanksgiving, and charging at the head of his cavalry, he was soon in the midst of the enemy, with only a few of his personal attendants near him, as the heavy mist, after partially clearing, had become so dense that his troop had not been able to see in which direction he had advanced. At that moment a pistol-shot struck his horse in the neck, a second shattered his left arm, and while he was turning to beg the Duke of Lauenburg to help him off the field, as he was wounded in the foot and unable to dismount, a ball entered his back, and he fell off his horse, which dragged him a short distance with one foot still in the stirrup. The only one of his men near him was a German page, called Lenbelfing, a youth of eighteen, who, when on his deathbed a few days after the battle, made a declaration, written down at the time, and sent to the council in Sweden, by which it appears that when he saw the king fall he had dismounted from his own horse and offered it to his royal master, but Gustavus, unable to raise himself, had stretched his hands towards him, and while he was trying to lift him, some of the enemy's cuirassiers had come up and asked who the wounded man was. When he did not answer, the king himself had told them who he was, on which the men, aiming their pistols at his head, had shot him dead, and stripped the body of everything. This youth, August von Lenbelfing, whose report forms the only authentic account that could ever be obtained in regard to the last moments of the great king, was himself so dangerously wounded in the battle that it was with difficulty he could be carried to Naumberg, where he died five days after the victory of Lützen.

Victory of Swedes.—Dismay spread through the ranks of the Swedes when they saw the king's horse, with empty saddle and bleeding mane, galloping wildly along the road; but soon their terror changed into fury, and demanding eagerly of Duke George of Saxe Weimar to be led on again to the assault, they bore down on the enemy, and after a fierce fight, which was prolonged till nightfall, they gained a brilliant victory, and remained masters of the field, where among the 12,000 dead and wounded that lay around, the body of the slain king was found covered with wounds. The close of the battle had been the fiercest, for at the moment when Duke Bernhard thought that the day was won, Pappenheim appeared on the field, and with his fresh troops attacked the wearied Swedes. But even that unexpected repulse could not long retard their victory, although it thinned their ranks fearfully, and left line upon line of Swedish troops lying dead upon the ground in the order in which they had stood. Pappenheim fell in this closing engagement, and after death, within his doublet the letter was found, saturated with his blood, which Wallenstein had sent, recalling him with his 10,000 men to augment the Imperialist army, which, according to this authority, consisted of upwards of 20,000 men. The victory of Lützen was, therefore, won against double the victor's forces, and it threw into their hands all Wallenstein's artillery and ammunition. The body of the king was carried to the rear the same night, and deposited in the church of the little village of Meuchen, where one of the attendant Swedish officers made a funeral address, after which the schoolmaster of the place read the ordinary form of prayer. The body was, however, found to be too deeply cut and mangled to remain where it was, and was carried to a villager's house and laid by the attendants on a table, while the schoolmaster, who was also a carpenter by trade, put together the rough deal coffin in which it was carried by daybreak the following morning to Weissenfels. Here the body was embalmed, notwithstanding the aversion with which Gustavus was known to have regarded the practice; and after being deposited for a time in the Castle church at Wittenberg, was conveyed to Sweden under the guard of the 400 survivors of the Smaaland cavalry, at the head of which the king had fallen. In the summer of 1634 the remains were laid with great solemnity within the grave that Gustavus had caused to be prepared for himself in Riddarholms' church. His queen, Maria Eleanore, who had been passionately attached to her husband, had caused his heart to be placed within a golden shrine, which she always carried with her, and reverenced with such devotion, that her conduct in this respect more than once drew upon her the reproof of the Swedish clergy. The day after the battle a heavy stone, known to the present day as the *Schwedenstein*, was dragged by some peasants, under the direction of the king's groom, Jacob Eriksson, from a neighbouring height to mark the place where Gustavus fell; but, unable to move it further, they left it within forty paces of the exact spot beside the bank of a field, where it remained till it was replaced, in 1832, by the monument erected by the German people in grateful remembrance of their champion.

Although the Imperialists experienced a most decisive defeat at Lützen, the joy of the Catholics on learning that their most dreaded foe was no more, fully equalled the sorrow and fear which the news of Gustavus' death spread through every Protestant country. In him the Swedes lost the noblest and greatest of their kings, and the world at large one of the bravest and most unselfish rulers that has ever filled a throne. In person, Gustavus Adolphus recalled the type of man that the Northmen associated with the image of the bravest and strongest of their early national heroes. He was tall and well made; of fresh ruddy hue, fair skin, and clear blue eyes, and with light yellow hair, ample beard and bushy moustaches, which gained for him among foreigners the name of "the goldking of the north." He had a longish face, with a grave, earnest expression, and there was a natural grace and dignity in his bearing and in all his movements, which increased the charm and attractiveness of his person and manner.

PART III.

THE SWEDISH GENERALS.

Christina's minority.—Although many great plans which Gustavus had formed for the benefit of his co-religionists perished with him, the fame of Sweden was well maintained for some time after his death by his generals and by his devoted friend and minister, Oxenstjerna, who induced the Protestant princes of South Germany to enter into an alliance with Sweden in 1633, and secured the continued good-will of France. At the same time he, in concert with four other great officers of State, conducted the regency during the minority of Gustavus' only child, Christina, following in all respects the directions laid down by the king himself before he left Sweden. The government, in accordance with these directions, was conducted in five national courts or colleges of state; a new court of law, known as *Göta Hofrätt*, was established at Jönköping; the kingdom was divided into Län or districts, each presided over by a bailiff or mayor; and every town by a chief magistrate, the president of whom was the Overstäthallar or head stadsholder of Stockholm. The army and navy were much augmented, and at the close of the German war more than 100,000 men stood under Swedish colours; but fully half of that number were Germans, intermingled with some Scotch troops.

The death of Gustavus soon, however, changed the fortune of the Swedish arms in Germany, and when, in 1634, the brave but over-hasty Gustaf Horn, in consequence of jealousy on the part of Duke Bernhard of Saxe Weimar, nearly brought an inglorious defeat upon the Swedes at Nordlingen, where he was made captive, the North German princes began to withdraw from their alliance with Sweden, and before another year the majority had followed the example set by the Elector of Saxony, and made a humiliating peace with the emperor.

They even seemed to aim at driving the Swedes quite out of Germany; and although Richelieu sent an army over the frontier to co-operate with the Swedish forces, he was an untrustworthy ally, and after inducing Duke Bernhard to enter the service of France, he on the death of that officer, who died suddenly in 1639, not without suspicion of having been poisoned, incorporated his troops in the French army, and employed them to conquer Alsace for France. Gustavus had, however, left other able commanders, who gloriously maintained his reputation; and the disaster at Nordlingen was soon effaced by a gallant Swedish victory, gained by Johan Banér at Wittstock in Brandenburg. Not content with this signal success, Banér pushed his way through the very heart of Germany, threatened Vienna, and surprised Ratisbon, where he would have captured the emperor and the members of the diet holding its sittings, if a sudden thaw had not come on, which prevented his crossing the Danube. At that period the Swedes were the only troops who ventured upon a winter campaign, and Banér's German auxiliaries, unaccustomed to the hardships imposed upon them, soon deserted him, while his ally, the Duke of Weimar, left him almost enclosed by enemies. Under these desperate circumstances he nevertheless succeeded in safely accomplishing a retreat, which is regarded as one of the most masterly ever effected in any war. After almost incessant fighting with the Imperialists, whose cavalry pursued him for eleven days, Banér, in a dying state and carried on a litter, led his troops safely from Ratisbon to Halberstadt, where he died shortly afterwards in his fifty-fourth year, worn out with disease and hard service. His remains were carried by his men into battle with them, when they soon afterwards encountered the enemy at Wolfenbüttel, and until the chief command was taken by another of Gustav's generals, Lennart Torstensson, the Swedish soldiers may be said to have been without a leader. The appointment of Torstensson to the command quickly, however, restored order and confidence, and although at the time he joined the army he was so lamed with gout as to be unable to use hand or foot, and had to be carried on a litter into battle, his brilliant talents at once gave a new turn to the war. The skilful and rapid manœuvres of this great commander gave him the name of "*Swedish Lightning,*" and gained for him the reputation of being fully equal as a commander to his master, King Gustavus. In the campaign of 1642, the Swedes, under Torstensson, advanced upon Vienna, defied the armies of the emperor in his own states, and ended by gaining a brilliant victory at Breitenfeld over the Archduke Leopold and the great General Piccolomini, and taking Leipzig from the Imperialists. While completing arrangements for penetrating still further into Southern Germany, he was, however, recalled to Sweden by secret orders from the Council of State.

War with Denmark.—The cause of this sudden recall was the anxiety felt by the Swedish regents at the turn which affairs were taking in Denmark, where it was evident that King Christian IV. was preparing to make war on Sweden. To frustrate his designs, Torstensson, in obedience to his orders, left Moravia, and in an incredibly short time crossed the frontier and threw his troops into the Holstein lands, on pretence of requiring food and quarters for them. At the same time Gustaf Horn led an army into Skaania, and thus forestalled at all points, the Danes were forced to meet the Swedes as successful invaders, instead of carrying the war into Sweden as they had intended. We have seen in a former chapter how completely success remained with Sweden in this war, which ended with the peace, signed at Brömsebro in Bleking in 1645, by which the power of Denmark was severely shaken and her national spirit deeply humbled. After the Danish war, Torstensson made a fourth and successful campaign into the hereditary lands of the German emperor, and inflicted upon the Imperialists at Jaukowitz the worst defeat they had sustained during the war. This battle, which raged with great fury during the whole of an intensely cold and stormy day in February 1645, cost the emperor the lives of 4,000 of his best troops, and left in the hands of the victorious Swedes 4,000 wounded, including the chief commander, Field-Marshal Hatzfeld, and five generals, with twenty-six field pieces and seventy-seven standards. The victory of Jaukowitz placed the imperial throne in pressing danger, for Torstensson again penetrated into Austria and brought his troops within sight of the walls of Vienna. At that moment, when everything seemed to favour the great Swedish commander, he was forced to retreat, for France had failed to send the reinforcements which alone could have enabled the Swedes to hold their own in the midst of the enemy's land, and the few troops brought to their aid by the Prince of Transylvania were so undisciplined that their presence was a hindrance rather than a help. Torstensson was, therefore, forced to fall back upon Bohemia, where in consequence of increased feebleness and suffering, he resigned the command, which was at once entrusted to Karl Gustaf Wrangel, another Swedish hero of great military renown.

The manner in which the Swedes had again and again carried their arms to the very gates of his palace made the emperor anxious for peace, and at length, after a delay of some time, the treaty of Westphalia put a final end, in 1648, to the fatal but glorious war between Sweden and Germany. The Swedes went out of this struggle, rich in glory and military renown, but poor in other respects, for the possession of Western Pomerania, with Rygen and Stettin, Weimar and Bremen, and the promise of five million rix dollars—which, moreover, were never all paid—were but poor returns for the eighteen years' sacrifice of life, peace, and money which these wars had cost the mother-country.

CHAPTER XXI.

SWEDEN FROM 1644 TO 1697.

Christina, successor of her father Gustavus Adolphus—Her bringing up—Her classical learning—Her character—Her resemblance to her mother—Her favourites and her extravagant gifts to them—Disturbances in the country—The question of her marriage and the succession—Her choice of a successor—Her coronation—Her reckless squandering of lands and money—Her foreign favourites—Bad habits of nobles—Disguised Jesuits—No money to supply her kitchen—Her abdication—Her conduct and manner of giving up the Crown—Succession of her cousin Charles of the Palatinate—Her departure—Her joy at crossing the frontier—The tales reported of her later life—Her change of religion—Her return to Sweden on the death of Charles X.—Retires to Rome—Her pursuits there—Her death—Oxenstjerna's death—The Queen's mother—Her character—Conduct and fate—Charles X. a soldier and conqueror—His wars and conquests—His wars with Denmark—His assault of Copenhagen—Slight success of Danes—Charles's mortification—His sudden death—The new dynasty begun in the person of Charles X.—His character and education—His efforts to benefit his people—Regency for Charles XI.—The neglect of Regents—Indifference to young king—His want of careful training—His mother—His character and conduct when he began to reign—His early love of amusement—His first experience of war—The defeat of Swedes in Germany—The bad condition of the army and fleet—The war with Denmark—Charles joins in General Peace of Europe—His attention to government—The *Reduction* of the old Crown Lands—The recovery of money from the late Regents—Use the money is put to—The conduct of Charles XI. to the nobility—His assumption of absolute power—His efforts to benefit the lower orders—The effects of a general famine—His death—Succeeded by his renowned son, Charles XII.

PART I.

THE ONLY SWEDISH QUEEN-REGNANT.

Christina, 1644-1654.—CHRISTINA, the only child and successor of Gustavus Adolphus, had been brought up by her aunt, Katerina, the Princess Palatine, until the death of the latter in 1639, and in the year 1644, when she reached the age of eighteen, the regency was absolved, and she began to rule in her own name. She had inherited much of her father's talent, and was perhaps the most learned and accomplished woman of her times. She had received the education of a man, and under the tuition of the learned Professor Matthiæ, she became an elegant scholar, and when she came to the throne she had read Thucydides and Polybius in the original, could write and speak Latin, French, German, and several other languages, and was familiar with the theology and philosophy taught in the universities of that age. She had great taste for the fine arts and for the pursuits of science, but while she encouraged scientific men at her court, she also spent money too recklessly in rewarding artistic merit of all kinds. From an early age she showed great penetration and insight into the characters and motives of other persons, and had a fascination of manner which won the confidence and devotion of those about her person. But as a dangerous drawback to her many splendid qualities, she had all the waywardness, caprice, restlessness of mind, fickleness and love of display for which her beautiful mother, Maria Eleanora of Brandenburg, had been noted. She lavished crown lands and the money of the state upon favourites, amongst whom the young and handsome Magnus Gabriel de la Gardie was the most noted. This nobleman, a son of the great general, De la Gardie, was sent on a costly embassy to Paris, and when the aged Chancellor, Oxenstjerna, and other experienced councillors remonstrated against his extravagance, the young queen declared that she would be held responsible for all his actions, besides which she gave him lands, which brought him an annual income of 80,000 rix dollars.

In the meanwhile the national Estates had been split up into parties, the aristocrats being led by Axel Oxenstjerna, and the democrats, with whom the queen sided, by Johan Skytte. The clergy struggled to maintain their independence under the oppressive patronage of the nobles, and the peasants agitated to recover some of the power which the great Gustavus Vasa had granted them, but which his successors had by degrees taken from them. The kingdom was in a ferment, and a civil war seemed to be unavoidable. The council urged upon the queen to marry, and her cousin, Karl Gustaf of the Palatinate, entreated her to fulfil the promise which she had given him in earlier years of choosing him for her husband. At length, after showing great reluctance to consider the question of her marriage and the succession to the throne, she proposed him for her successor; and when pressed by the council and by the prince himself to give him her hand, she would only pledge herself so far as to declare that she would not make any other man her husband. After much opposition, Karl Gustaf was declared successor to the throne in the event of the queen having no children of her own, and when she had carried this point, she made magnificent preparations for her own coronation, and was crowned with more state than had as yet been seen in Sweden.

Christina's extravagance.—The few years of Christina's reign after her solemn coronation were disquieted by continued dissensions in the diet, attempts at revolts, and by a general distress, which was greatly increased by her profuse wastefulness and her reckless squandering of the property of the crown. As early as the year 1648 she had conceived the idea of abdicating, but being hindered by her old friends and councillors, she deferred carrying out her wishes till 1654. During that interval her conduct was such as to leave her people but little cause to regret the step she had resolved to take. Lands and titles and patents of nobility were scattered abroad among all classes, so that during her reign the Riddarhus was augmented by 32 new counts and barons and by the admission of the representatives of 428 freshly ennobled families, including the court tailor, Jan Holm, who assumed the proud name of Leijonkrona. The same baronies were so often disposed of by sale, that the matter was taken up by the council in 1651, when the clerk of a chancery secretary was publicly beheaded for having sold forty-two false patents.

Under the influence of the new favourites, Don Antonio Pimentelli, Spanish ambassador at her court, and her French physician, Bourdelot, Christina became more and more absorbed in frivolous pursuits; and finding the cares of government more and more irksome, she gave up all her time to amusement. Singers, actors, dancers, and jugglers were invited to Stockholm, and soon the queen herself took part in the plays and ballets performed at the palace. Cromwell's representative, Whitelocke, has left us a report in his journal of the habits and pursuits of the young Swedish nobles when he went to Upsala, in 1654, to obtain the queen's signature to a treaty concluded between Sweden and England, and he expresses his surprise and reprobation at the sight of young nobles going along the streets on a Sunday, singing aloud, and at last kneeling down in the market-place and drinking the queen's health with loud huzzahs. Among the numerous foreigners who flocked into Sweden were Jesuits in disguise, who came in the hope of converting Queen Christina, perhaps invited by herself; for although she continued while in Sweden and for a year after her abdication publicly to profess Lutheran doctrines, she had long expressed great interest in the history of Catholicism, and in 1655 she made a formal declaration of her adhesion to the faith of the Romish Church. Her extravagance exhausted all sources of income, and twice the royal kitchen had to be closed for want of money, and the queen's servants were forced to beg a dinner for her and themselves.

Her Abdication.—Early in the year 1654 Christina informed her council of her fixed resolution to give up the throne, and at a diet held in May at Upsala the terms of abdication were settled, and after much discussion it was agreed that she was to hold Oeland, Gotland, Oesel, and other districts, with a revenue of 240,000 rix dollars. On the morning of June 6th the final ceremony was accomplished. The queen came forth from her room, with the crown on her head, wearing her coronation robes over a simple white dress, and bearing in her hands the globe and sceptre, and then, taking her stand before the throne in the great hall of the palace at Upsala, she made farewell speeches to her council and the crown prince; and at the close of her address she walked down the steps of the daïs with a firm tread, and laid aside the regalia one by one. All present were moved at the spectacle, and even men were seen to shed tears as they watched the young queen giving up all the signs of royalty; for at that moment the old companions of her father, who had watched faithfully over her in her childhood, forgot all causes of anger against her in their grief at the step she was taking. In the afternoon of the same day the crown prince was proclaimed, and crowned in the presence of the diet at the cathedral, and on the following day Christina left Upsala. Twelve ships of war were lying ready off Calmar to convey her and her suite from Sweden, but instead of embarking from there, she passed through Halmstad and crossed the Sound to Denmark, and proceeded on her travels through Germany and the Low Countries. She took only four Swedes with her, having dismissed all the rest of her suite, and when she reached a little brook which then formed part of the boundary-line between Sweden and the Danish territories of Skaania, she got out of her carriage, and springing lightly over the stream, exclaimed, " At last I am free ! and out of Sweden, to which I hope I may never return."

And thus Queen Christina passed like a meteor from amongst her people. Her change of religion, and the strange tales which were from time to time brought to Sweden of her conduct and mode of life, estranged her more and more from her former subjects. She was at first received with the greatest respect and enthusiasm in the Catholic countries that she visited ; but her eccentric conduct, her contempt for all feminine pursuits, her constant want of money, and her disregard of the laws of the lands in which she took up her abode, made her in time an unwelcome and troublesome guest, and one prince after the other forced her to leave his dominions. At the death of her cousin and successor, Karl X. Gustaf, as he was called by the Swedes, and who is known to us as Charles X., she returned to Sweden and claimed the crown for herself, but neither then, nor in 1667, when she renewed her pretensions, would the council encourage her hopes, and after a final attempt to gain the vacant throne of Poland in 1668, she gave up all schemes of ever reigning again, and retired to Rome, where she died in 1689 at the age of sixty-three. Her latter years were spent in the midst of learned men, and in the indulgence of her taste for collecting scarce books and costly works of art ; and while she lived, her talents, strange history, and eccentric conduct, made her an object of wonder and interest to every country in Europe. Her father's friend, Oxenstjerna, whose counsels had offended her, did not long survive his dismissal from her service, and his death in 1654 saved him from the pain of knowing how thoroughly she had turned aside from all the principles which Gustavus Adolphus had made the guides of his actions, and for the maintainance of which he had sacrificed his life.

Christina's mother, Maria Eleanore of Brandenburg, a fickle, frivolous woman, incapable of taking part in business, had been kept as much away from the young queen as was practicable, since her caprice and incapacity were well known to Oxenstjerna and the old friends of Gustavus. Dissatisfied with the little influence allowed her by the regency, she had fled from Sweden in disguise in 1640, accompanied only by a few attendants, and embarking in a Danish man-of-war, she had gone to Denmark and remained away for many years. To the end of a long life this queen maintained a querulous discontent towards all who refused compliance with her demands, and died unregretted.

PART II.

SWEDISH CONQUESTS.

Charles X., 1656-1660.—The short reign of Charles X. from 1655 to 1660 was a time of great disorder and unquiet in Sweden. To obtain money to carry on the government, Charles was forced to exact from the nobles the restitution of one-fourth of the crown lands which had been granted to them under former rulers. And to keep down the restless discontent which had sprung up under the late queen, he resolved to engage the people in active war; but it was not without difficulty that he obtained the consent of the diet to make the necessary preparations, and for a time the question remained undetermined whether the arms of Sweden should be turned against Denmark or Poland. The Danish traitor, Korfitz Ulfeld, strongly urged the advisability of attacking Denmark, whose unprotected condition was well known to him, but the ill-timed demand of the Polish king, Johan Kasimir, to be proclaimed the true heir to Christina's throne, drew the first attack upon Poland.

Charles X. was born to be a soldier and a conqueror, and the success and rapidity with which he overran all Poland and crushed the Polish army in a three days' engagement at Warsaw in 1656, showed that he was a worthy pupil and successor of his uncle, the great Gustavus Adolphus. But it was easier for him to make conquests than to keep them, and when the Russians in their jealousy of the increasing power of Sweden took part in the war, and began to attack Livonia and Esthonia, while an imperial army advanced into Poland to assist the Poles, who, infuriated at the excesses of the Swedish soldiers, had risen *en masse* against them, Charles saw the expediency of retreating; and leaving only a few detachments of troops to watch his enemies, he turned upon Denmark. This war, which was closed by the peace signed at Roeskilde in 1658, enriched Sweden at the expense of Denmark, and gave to the former the old provinces of Skaania, Halland, and Bleking, by which the Swedish monarchy obtained natural and well-defined boundaries. The success of this first Danish war, in which Denmark for a time lay crushed under the power of the Swedish king, emboldened him to renew his attacks, and between 1658 and 1660 Charles X. made war five times on the Danish monarch; more than once laid siege to Copenhagen; and, under his able captain, Wrangel, nearly destroyed the Danish fleet. At the close of 1659, when it seemed as if Denmark must be wholly subjugated by Sweden, the English and Dutch, alarmed at the ambition of the Swedish king, sent an allied fleet into the Cattegat to operate with the Danes, whose courage and confidence rising with every slight success, repulsed vigorously the attacks of the Swedes on the island of Fyen. Charles, unaccustomed to defeat, and annoyed at the failure of his plans, determined to turn the war directly against Norway, and for this purpose called together the diet at Göteborg, and demanded new troops and fresh subsidies. While the Estates were sitting, Charles X. was seized with severe illness, and died suddenly in the winter of 1660, aged thirty-eight.

With Charles X. a new dynasty—that of the Palatinate—

began in Sweden; but although he was the son of the Count Palatine, Johan Kasimir, he can scarcely be reckoned as a foreign prince, for he had been brought up in Sweden, and was thoroughly Swedish in speech, habits, and modes of thinking. His mother, Katerina, the only sister of Gustavus Adolphus, had been careful to educate him in a manner that might fit him for ruling over Sweden, as she had from his childhood entertained the hope that he would marry his young cousin, Queen Christina. He was a man of sound sense and strong will, and possessed great capacity for ruling; but his insatiable thirst for war so thoroughly absorbed his time and thoughts that he was not able to effect much for the good of his people during his short reign. The few reforms which he brought about in the government showed however an anxious endeavour to extend the resources of the working-classes by introducing and encouraging manufactures, while he helped to augment the national credit by bringing better order into the finances.

Regency under Charles XI., 1660-1675.—By the early death of Charles X., Sweden was again brought under the rule of a regency, for his son and successor, Charles XI., was only four years old when he became king. By the will of his father, the queen-mother, Hedvig Eleanore of Holstein-Gottorp, and his uncle, Duke Johan, were appointed members of the council of regency, which also included Magnus de la Gardie, his uncle by marriage. But the chief officers of state, objecting to the presence of so many members of the royal family, tried to set aside the will of the late king, on the ground that a woman could not sit at the council board, and that Duke Johan, as a German-born prince, was also excluded. These difficulties threatened at the very outset to disturb the peace of the kingdom, but as the diet confirmed all the provisions made by the late king, the regency was carried on in the form which he had prescribed, but with such a spirit of dissatisfaction and mutual ill-will among the members that they appeared always more eager to gratify their own prejudices and thwart one another than to attend to the welfare of the monarchy. Every department of the government was left to suffer from mismanagement, the army and navy were neglected, the defences

of the frontiers fell into decay, and the public servants were
unable to procure their pay. To relieve the great want of
money, the regency accepted subsidies, or payments of
money from foreign states to maintain peace towards them,
and hired out troops to serve in other countries.

In this state of things the young king grew up without
receiving any very careful education, for the queen-mother was a
woman of narrow mind, who neither cared for nor knew anything
of intellectual pursuits, and thought more of his health than of
his learning, while the rest of the council gave themselves no
trouble about the manner in which he was being trained.
Charles was declared of age in his eighteenth year, when the
regency was dissolved, and he was left to rule in his own
name. At that time he was noted for self-will and obstinacy,
great distaste for business, and mistrust towards the council
and the higher nobility; but although he seemed to find his
greatest delight in riding, hunting, and fencing, and spent
most of his time among companions of his own age, he never
showed any vicious tastes, and was noted from his earliest
youth for his attention to his religious duties and for his
blameless mode of conduct. But he was not left long in the
enjoyment of mere exercises of amusement, for in 1674
Louis XIV. of France, in conformity with the treaty which
the regents had concluded with him, called upon the young
Swedish king to help him in the war which he was carrying
on against the German princes. Charles sent an army into
Germany, which advanced without opposition into the heart
of Brandenburg, but before these forces could form a junc-
tion with the French troops then encamped in the Rhine-lands,
the Elector came upon them unawares at Fehrbellin and defeated them. The losses of the Swedes on this occasion were
not great, but the result of their defeat was to give encouragement to the old rivals of Sweden; and early in 1675 both
Holland and Denmark declared war against the Swedish king,
who, finding that he had been left by the regency almost without army, navy, or money, resolved for the future to take the
management of public affairs entirely into his own hands.

Long Peace under Charles XI.—There had been peace in
Sweden since the beginning of this king's reign, for the regents,

feeling the necessity of bringing the various wars in which Charles X. had plunged the kingdom to an end, had shown great promptness in agreeing to the terms proposed by the enemy. Johan Casimir of Poland on his part had smoothed the way for peace by formally renouncing all claims on the Swedish throne, and in the treaty which he concluded with Sweden in 1660 he had been joined by the Emperor and Elector of Brandenburg. Denmark and Russia had been equally ready to make peace at the same time, and thus the regency had carried on the government without having any war to provide for. Instead, however, of peace having restored the prosperity of the kingdom, it had only served to make the regents indifferent to the condition of the materials of war; and when the young king, in the hope that his fleet would prove more than a match for the Danes, began the war by a sea engagement with the enemy off Oeland, he found that his ships of war had suffered as much as the land-defences from the long-continued neglect of his regents. The Danes, under their great admiral, Niels Juel, and supported by a Dutch squadron, beat the Swedish fleet, many of whose ships were burnt or sunk. This defeat was atoned for by a victory on land, gained by Charles himself in 1676, over the Danes on the snow-covered hills around the town of Lund. Success was not won without heavy cost, for after a most sanguinary fight, continued from daybreak till night, King Charles, although master of the field, found that more than half his men had been killed. The Danes, who had suffered fully as much, were forced to retreat, leaving Lund in the hands of the Swedes; and although they several times repeated the attempt, they failed in recovering the province of Skaania, which was the great object of their ambition.

In Germany the fortune of war did not favour the Swedes, although they fought gallantly under their general, Otto Königsmark; and Charles XI. was glad to enter into negotiations for taking part in the general peace which France was urging upon all the leading powers of Europe, and which was signed at the palace of St. Germains, in 1679, by the representatives of the respective princes. Sweden recovered the whole of Pomerania, which had been occupied during the war by Austria and Brandenburg, and all Swedish and Danish conquests were mutually renounced, while as a further proof of the good-will established between the Swedes and Danes, Charles XI. married the Danish princess Ulrika Eleanora, whose gentle influence and constant endeavour to maintain friendly relations between the two northern kingdoms made her subjects regard her as a second "*Fred-kulla.*"

PART III.

THE KING BECOMES ABSOLUTE.

Charles regains the Crown Lands.—At the close of this war Charles XI. began in good earnest to put his kingdom in order. In the stern policy which he pursued towards the higher nobility, he was mainly influenced by the counsels of his devoted friend, the able Johan Gillenstjerna, who, together with his chief supporters, Klas Fleming and Erik Lindsköld, made a thorough investigation of every department of the State. Their inquiries brought to light the seemingly hopeless financial condition of the monarch. There was absolutely no money at his disposal, while nearly all the crown lands had been given away under Queen Christina and other rulers. In this state of things Charles made a direct appeal to the National Estates, and with their consent the former regents and councillors were called upon in 1680 to refund five million silver dollars, which, according to the charges made against them, had been squandered, or otherwise wrongfully appropriated by them. They further granted to him the right of "Reduction," as it was called, by which was meant the power to draw back some of the crown lands which had been wantonly alienated by former rulers. This measure, which circumstances justified, and which at first was restricted to estates acquired within the previous thirty years, and then only to a fourth part of the lands in question, led in the course of time to great injustice, and by the severity with which it was enforced reduced the wealthiest nobles to a condition of poverty. Thus even Count Marcus de la Gardie, who was the husband of Charles' aunt, the princess Maria Euphrosine, was deprived of all he owned, and forced to dismiss all his servants. But the king, who was a stern man, and had suffered heavily from the former arrogance of his nobility, showed no pity to the sufferers, and never rested till he had thoroughly crushed their power and reduced the National Estates to the condition of a mere royal chamber, summoned only to approve and confirm his acts, until at length they of their own accord proclaimed him, in a diet held in 1693, to be an absolute sovereign king, " who had the power and right to rule his kingdom as he pleased."

Charles XI. an Absolute King.—Like his father-in-law in Denmark, King Charles XI. of Sweden became an absolute sovereign by a most important, yet bloodless revolution, which confirmed all the ancient rights of the crown, and increased the authority of the sovereign at the expense of the hitherto all-powerful nobles. The Swedish king used his power for the good of his people at large. He spent the money which the regents had been forced to refund in paying off some of the national debt, and in carrying out many important measures. He put the army and fleet on a good footing, granted land to his soldiers, who in time of peace were thus converted into useful citizens ; and he took stringent measures to give a Swedish character to the old Danish provinces of Skaania and Bleking, while he so thoroughly crushed the power of the independent nobles of Livonia and the Baltic provinces of Sweden, that many of these old families preferred exile to the restrictions imposed upon them by the Swedish king.

The Swedish Church was brought under a new code of laws in this reign, and although King Charles was himself deficient in cultivation, he showed himself anxious to encourage learning, and he enjoined upon the bishops and clergy generally to see that all persons in the parishes under their control were taught to read, and were instructed in the most important doctrines of the Christian faith. Charles XI., with all his harshness, was a popular king, at least among the lower orders ; for during the journeys which he made through all parts of his dominions to see and judge for himself of the real condition of his people, he entered freely into their amusements, and listened patiently to the numerous petitions and complaints laid before him. The last years of his reign were troubled by an almost total failure of the crops and a murrain among the cattle, which were said to have led to the loss of nearly 100,000 persons, who perished from hunger, notwithstanding the measures which the king caused to be taken for their relief. After a long and painful illness, Charles XI. died in 1697 at the age of forty-two, having survived his queen only a few months, and leaving three children, the eldest of whom succeeded him, and, under the title of Charles XII. of Sweden, gained for himself a greater and more widely spread renown than any attained by his predecessors on the Swedish throne.

CHAPTER XXII.

DENMARK FROM 1648 TO 1730.

Differences between Denmark and Sweden—Hard terms enforced by nobles on Frederick III. of Denmark—Queen Sofia Amalia's jealousy of the Ulfelds—Conduct and success of Korfitz Ulfeld—War against Sweden—Assault of Copenhagen by Charles X.—Peace—Denmark's mortification—Insults of Swedes—Defence of Copenhageners—Success of Swedes—Character of Frederick III.—Help from the Dutch—Treaty and Peace of Copenhagen—The different orders rise against the nobles—Conduct of Bishop Svane, and of Nansen, chief magistrate of Copenhagen—They force the nobles to give the king absolute power—Monarchy changed without bloodshed—The power remaining to the nobles—Colleges of State appointed—The Minister Griffenfeld—His acts—His character and fate—Cruelty to the Ulfelds—Their fate—Christian V. first hereditary monarch—The titles of Counts and Barons first used in Denmark—Extravagance of Court—War with Sweden—Bad fortune of Danes—Troops hired out for pay—Olaus Römer—His many useful inventions—Bigotry of king and Court—Cruelty to the peasant classes—Christian V. is succeeded by his son Frederick IV., who had been neglected by his father and not trained to rule—Frederick has to make peace with his enemies—Has to contend with William of Orange—Holstein-Gottorp—The type quarrel—Subjugation of Duchy by Denmark—War in the North—Frederick's merits as a ruler—His queen's extravagance in building—Public calamities—Efforts to convert heathens—Colonies in Greenland—Troops hired out—State of the peasantry—Number of schools—Great preponderance of educated people in Denmark.

PART I.

DENMARK HUMBLED.

Frederick III., 1648-1670.—IN the present chapter we have to consider the course of events in Denmark during the latter half of the seventeenth and the earlier part of the eighteenth century, while the immediate successors of the great Gustavus Adolphus of Sweden were continuing by their conquests and personal achievements to draw the attention of all Europe to that kingdom. In Denmark the same period of time, although marked by great and most important internal changes, presented little or nothing to excite the wonder or admiration of foreign nations. Sweden had absorbed the interest of Europe, and made the great powers value her alliance in proportion as Denmark continued to fall away from her former reputation ; and when her able king, Christian IV., died in 1648, baffled by the nobles in all his efforts to benefit his kingdom, and crushed under the weight of their tyranny, it seemed as if Denmark must inevitably sink into the condition of an oligarchy, and that independent sovereignty would cease to have even a nominal existence.

Some months elapsed after the death of Christian IV. before the Council would elect his son Frederick to the throne, but towards the close of the year 1648 the nobles offered to proclaim him king of Denmark if he would sign the charter which they submitted to him. The conditions which they imposed upon the prince were harder than any ever before enforced in Denmark, but Frederick, seeing no present way of escape, agreed to them, and thus found himself almost a slave in the hands of his own council, without whose consent he could not leave the country, make peace or war, or exercise any of the powers of a king. While Frederick and his ambitious queen, Sofia Amalia, were thus little more than puppets in the State, the Ulfelds by their wealth and power, were able to maintain a brilliant position, and to eclipse the court in respect to the magnificence of their entertainments and the number of their attendants. These circumstances helped to increase the jealousy which the queen had long felt for the beauty, wit, and accomplishments of Eleanore Kristine Ulfeld, and having awakened the king's distrust of his sister, she never rested till she had destroyed the happiness of this unfortunate couple. Ulfeld's conduct in negotiating the peace with Holland, by which the Dutch were allowed to evade the Sound dues on the payment of a sum of money, and his administration of the finances under the late king, were made grounds of accusation against him ; and feeling how little chance of justice he had, he escaped from Copenhagen by night with all his family, and, after many wanderings in Holland and elsewhere, went to Sweden, where

he was received with every mark of respect. The confidence
placed in him by Queen Christina and her successor led him
to turn traitor to his own country, and even to take an active
share in the war against Denmark.

Fatal War with Sweden.—This war, which broke out in
1657, was the most fatal in its results that the Danes had ever
known, for after enduring the disgrace of seeing one Danish
province and island after the other overrun by the Swedish
troops under their king, Charles X., and even Copenhagen itself
threatened by the enemy, Frederick III. had to sign an unfavourable treaty of peace, drawn up by his foe, Korfitz Ulfeld, by which he gave up to Sweden Trondhjem and Aggerhus
in Norway, the old Danish provinces of Skaania, Halland,
and Bleking, besides the islands Lessö, Anholt, Femern,
and Bornholm, and the lands of the Ditmarshes. He was
also obliged to resign to Sweden half of the Sound dues,
twelve ships of war, and a large sum of money in return for
the damage done by the Danes to the fortresses in the territories of the Swedish king's brother-in-law, Duke Frederick III.
of Holstein-Gottorp. In addition to these very severe terms,
Charles X. had insisted on the restitution to Korfitz Ulfeld of
all his forfeited lands in Denmark, and the liberation of Duke
Frederick of Holstein-Gottorp from all future obligations of
dependence on the crown of Denmark. Frederick III. had
no alternative but to submit, and so crushed were the Danish
armies, that when, in 1658, the Swedish king broke faith with
the Danes, and appeared before the walls of Copenhagen with
a large fleet, the troops would scarcely exert themselves to
defend the capital. The burgher and working-classes showed,
however, much more spirit, and determined at the cost of their
lives to repel the invaders, who had roused their fury to the
highest pitch by declaring that " the Swedes intended to seize
upon the kingdom first, and give their reasons afterwards, for
as it was evident Denmark's end had come, it could matter little
whether the king's name was Frederick or Charles."

The success of the Swedes was at first not so great as they
had anticipated, but their superior numbers enabled them to
seize upon the castle of Cronborg and other points of defence
commanding the passage of the Sound; and the unhappy city

would have had to surrender for want of provisions had not the Dutch admirals, Opdam and De Witte, forced their way through the opposing Swedish fleet, and brought food and help to the starving citizens. When Charles of Sweden found his schemes thus thwarted, he determined to take the city by assault, and on the night of the 10th and 11th February, 1659, his generals, Stenbock and Sparre, led a storming party against the fortifications of Copenhagen. The citizens, who had received warning of the intended assault, were, however, well prepared to defend themselves, and, after a desperate conflict, in which many women took part by throwing burning brands and boiling tar on the heads of the assailants, the Swedes had to fall back, leaving 2,000 dead and wounded in the hands of the Danes. Relinquishing his attack on Copenhagen for the moment, the Swedish king turned upon the small islands of Laaland, Falster, Moen, and Langeland, which were made to expiate the offence of having supplied the city with provisions, and were overrun and subjected to all the horrors of invasion by troops to whom every excess and license were allowed. King Frederick showed great fortitude and sagacity in the fearful position in which he found himself placed, and while he gave his subjects an example of personal valour and great powers of endurance, he succeeded by his earnest representations to foreign powers in securing the attention and intervention of France, England, and Holland. A conference was held at the Hague, in accordance with whose decisions a Dutch fleet, under Admiral de Ruyter, was sent to the aid of the oppressed Danes.

By the help of the Dutch admiral De Ruyter the Danish king was enabled to send an army, composed of Danes and allied troops, to the relief of Fyen, where they obtained decided advantages over the Swedes, whose commanders, the Count Palatine of Sulzbach and Count Stenbock, were barely able to make their escape, and with a remnant of their forces to join King Charles at Korsör. After an unsuccessful invasion of Norway by the Swedish king, his sudden death in February 1660 brought this disastrous war to a close, and King Frederick of Denmark joyfully concluded a peace with the widowed queen, regent of Sweden, which was signed at Copenhagen on the 27th May,

X

1660. The terms of this treaty were hard upon Denmark, which only recovered Trondhjem in Norway and the island of Bornholm, and had to submit to the unconditional surrender in perpetuity of Skaane, Halland, Bleking, and Bahus, but the kingdom had sunk so low that peace had to be bought at any price.

PART II.

ABSOLUTE POWER ESTABLISHED.

Frederick's sudden change of power.—It would be impossible to conceive a more hopeless position than the one in which King Frederick III. of Denmark found himself in the very year when his cousin, Charles Stuart of England, was restored to the throne of his forefathers.[1] The kingdom was laid waste, the treasury was empty, and the monarchy seemed in the last stage of its existence, when King Frederick, in his great need, called together a meeting of the States in Copenhagen, and laid before them a true account of his necessities. The nobles as usual tried to throw off all responsibilities from themselves to the other orders of the State, and appealed to their special privileges of exemption from taxes. This unworthy conduct roused the anger of the burgher classes, who were conscious that it was owing to them alone that the kingdom had not been thoroughly subjugated by the Swedish king in the late war; and when the nobles refused to give anything to defray the expenses of the siege, the town council of Copenhagen, headed by their burgomaster, Hans Nansen, made an appeal to the king for the curtailment of the privileges of the nobles. The clergy, under the guidance of the learned and ambitious court-preacher, Bishop Svane, seconded their proposals, and joined with them in a demand for an inquiry into the terms on which the crown fiefs were held, with the further view of having these valuable tenures given to the highest bidder, without respect to rank. While these motions were being made within the hall of assembly, the gates of the city were closed by order

[1] Anne, wife of James I. of England and VI. of Scotland, and grandmother of King Charles II., was the aunt of the Danish king, Frederick III.

of Hans Nansen, and a strong civic guard drawn around the doors of the building. The nobles taken by surprise, and finding that several influential members of their own body had gone over to the side of the burghers, gave up their resistance against the payment of the taxes demanded of them; but when Nansen and Svane next proposed to make the crown hereditary in the descendants of the king, whether male or female, they opposed the motion with strong and bitter expressions of dissent. This important measure was, however, passed by the burghers and clergy at another meeting of the diet, held on the 8th of October, and when the nobles refused their assent, they were informed that every door of exit was held by troops, and that the whole of the city guard was ready to rush to arms on the first sound of the alarm-bell. Under these circumstances the nobles found themselves forced to submit, and on the 18th of October, 1660, Frederick III. received the homage of the several orders of the state as hereditary king of Denmark. Thus by a bloodless and sudden revolution of the existing principles of the government, one of the most strictly bound elective monarchies in the world was converted by the determination of a few men into the most absolute hereditary state in Christendom. Frederick III. was a silent, cautious man, who knew how to keep his own counsel, and while he appeared to be wholly ignorant of, and indifferent to, all that was being done by his partisans, Svane and Nansen, he had in fact co-operated with them from the first through his secretary, Gabel; and when he once found himself master of his kingdom, he resented the slightest attempt to circumscribe his powers. Gabel had had the address to propose that the question of the form of government which the king ought to pursue under the changed condition of the monarchy should be left for discussion till the next meeting of the diet, and when this proposal had been agreed to, Frederick took care to prevent all further opposition by bribery or force. Amongst other means he adopted that of commanding the University representative, Professor Villum Lange, to absent himself from the assembly, as he had been known to express the opinion that Denmark, like all other civilized monarchies, ought to have a written constitution of its own. At the same time the queen and court party laboured assiduously to put down all opposition, and the result of their combined efforts was to secure a large number of signatures among the nobles, clergy, and burghers of the different provinces, to a charter which proclaimed the *absolute independence* of the hereditary sovereignty settled upon the king and his heirs. The peasants were not consulted in regard to these important matters, and the frequent appeals which they made to the king for a mitigation of the heavy burdens and forced service by which they were oppressed, met with no consideration whatever from Frederick III. The power of the nobles over this class had not been interfered with when they lost many of their long-established prerogatives, and so completely were they in the power of their masters that, in accordance with the Danish game-laws, the lord of the manor might still put out the eyes of the peasant who shot a deer on his lands, or might hang him under certain conditions. In Norway the peasantry never fell into so low a condition as in Denmark, although after the final union of the two kingdoms in 1537, when Danish nobles began to obtain fiefs and secure a footing in the country, the subjects of this ancient monarchy lost many of their rights under the careless rule of their Danish kings.

New offices of government.—With Frederick III.'s acquisition of independent power a new system of government was introduced into Denmark, and the Council of State gave place to six " colleges " or offices for the transaction of home and foreign affairs. These changes and all the improvements made in the administration of the universities and of military and naval affairs, finance, &c., were mainly due to the able counsels of the king's secretary, Peder Schumacher (Count Griffenfeld), a man of low origin, who by his talents raised himself to the place of the most powerful minister of the crown, both under Frederick and his son, Christian V. After being created a count of the empire, and receiving every mark of confidence and distinction in the power of the king to bestow upon him, the jealousy of his many enemies at court brought about his ruin. Being accused of treason, he was condemned to death, but the sentence was commuted at the scaffold to close imprisonment for life; and for eighteen years Count

Griffenfeld was kept in confinement, and only liberated the year before his death, in 1699; yet Denmark never had a greater minister, or one who met with a more unworthy return for all the good he did his country.

Frederick may be said to have used the extraordinary powers of which he had so unexpectedly become possessed with moderation. The few acts of cruelty which can be laid to his charge seem moreover to have been due to the evil influence of his hard-hearted, vindictive queen, Sophia Amalia of Hesse Cassel. It was through her jealousy and hatred that Frederick's half-sister, Eleanore Kristine Ulfeld, was brought to trial on various false and absurd charges, and shut up in the Blaataarn in Copenhagen, where she was kept for twenty-two years a close prisoner, and left to endure every form of privation and indignity that the queen could heap upon her. From this cruel fate she was only liberated on the death of her enemy in 1685, when she was permitted by her nephew, Christian V., to end her days in peace on her own estates in Lolland. This unhappy lady had been betrayed and given up, in the year 1663, to the Danish queen by Charles II. while she was living in England, whither she had come to demand payment from Charles of a large sum of money which her husband, Korfitz Ulfeld, when Danish envoy at the Hague, had lent him during his exile. The year after she had been thus shamefully betrayed by her father's great-nephew, the ungenerous king of England, Ulfeld met his death by the upsetting of a boat in which he was attempting to cross the Rhine while wandering with his sons as a fugitive from place to place in Germany. He was buried under a tree at the spot where his body was recovered at Neuenburg in Baden, and from that time forth his outlawed sons and descendants were no more heard of in the two Scandinavian lands, where Korfitz Ulfeld had earned for himself—whether rightly or wrongly it is not possible now to determine—the title of a double traitor to both countries.

PART III.

THE ORIGIN OF TITLES.

Christian V., 1670–1699.—Christian V., who succeeded his father, Frederick III., in 1670, was the first Danish king who had ever mounted the throne without having to agree to some compact or other, or having to accept terms from those who had elected him. Christian had no one to thank for his crown, which came to him by heritage, and his first thought after his accession seemed to be to create a brilliant court after the fashion of that of *le Grand Monarque*, Louis XIV. of France. Many of the heads of the noblest families in Denmark had withdrawn themselves from the capital, where they no longer exercised the influence which they had enjoyed in former times, and they endeavoured to show their indifference to the court by remaining on their own lands. The young king therefore resolved to create a new order of nobility, more brilliant and distinguished than the old. Previous to this time hereditary titles were unknown among the Danish nobility, but Christian V., who was thoroughly German in all his feelings, now by one absolute decree established all the titles and grades of rank recognized among the higher classes of Germany. And soon his court was filled with counts and barons, who, on the payment of certain fees, had obtained with the newly adopted rank many seignorial rights which had never been exercised by the older nobles of Denmark. The latter now saw themselves supplanted at court and in the service of the state by a band of German adventurers, who had procured their dignity by money and not birth. All the ceremonials and rigid etiquette of Versailles were adopted by the Danish king, who, to complete his new system of courtly favour, established two orders of knighthood, known as the Dannebrog and the Elephant, in the former of which a white riband, and in the latter a blue one was used.

The expenses of the court rose in this reign far above any hitherto known in Denmark, and it was the difficulty of finding money to gratify his love of display, and the unpalatable advice which Griffenfeld gave Christian in regard to the ne-

cessity for retrenchment, that first brought that minister into
disfavour with his sovereign. His counsel that Christian
should remain neutral in the war which had broken out in
1672, between France and Holland, still more irritated the
young king, who, thirsting for distinction, rushed into the
conflict and took up arms with the Emperor and Elector of
Brandenburg against Louis XIV. By this alliance Denmark
was brought into hostilities with Sweden, which was the staunch
ally of France, and soon the province of Skaania became the
scene of war. The two young northern kings, Christian of
Denmark and Charles XI. of Sweden, commanded in person
when their armies met in a fierce engagement at Lund in 1676,
and both gave repeated proofs of personal valour; but
although Christian kept his 15,000 Danes in the field against
the 25,000 Swedes of his rival's army, he was unable to secure
a footing in the country. Success had indeed generally attended
the Danish fleet under their renowned admiral, Niels-Juel; but
as Griffenfeld had foreseen, Denmark could effect nothing
against the allies of France; and in 1679, when Louis XIV.
had concluded secret treaties with the emperor and with Holland and Brandenburg, there was no alternative for Christian
but to accede to the peace proposed by the French king, and
by which all that had been taken by Denmark from Sweden
had to be restored to the latter power.

Denmark gained nothing by this costly war but good training
for her fleet and her army, both of which had been brought
into a flourishing condition under Christian. As soon as peace
was concluded with France, the finance minister, Sigfrid von
Pless, hired some of the troops to the English king to be used
against the Irish, and others to the emperor for his wars against
the Turks. But this short-sighted policy, while it drained the
country of some of her best men—for only a small number
returned to their homes—brought meagre supplies to the exhausted finances; and on the death of the king in 1699, the
State was found to be hampered with a debt of more than one
million rix dollars, notwithstanding the flourishing condition of
trade. During this reign the eminent Danish astronomer, Ole
(Olaus) Römer, did good service to his country by the improvements which he was the means of bringing about in reforming

the coinage, regulating the weights and measures, repairing the public roads, and setting up mile-posts and sign-posts. While holding the place of chief of the police department of Copenhagen, he also organised a good system of lighting the streets, established an efficient night-watch and a fire-brigade, and gave plans for the construction of better fire-engines than any that had yet been in use. He was at a later period named Chancellor of the Exchequer and an assessor of the Supreme Court of Justice, and was engaged for seven years in compiling a great land-book, in which all land was taxed in accordance with a certain mode of measurement known by the name of the Hartkorn Standard. This land-book was made the basis for the code of laws and the mode of assessing taxes established by Christian V. in 1684.

The bigotry of the king and of the court clergy was the means of depriving Denmark of the labours of many thousands of Huguenots, who, after the revocation of the edict of Nantes in 1685, petitioned for leave to settle in the country. This was sternly refused, and hence these industrious men carried their skill to other lands, where no obstacles existed to the profession of the doctrines of Calvin. The condition of the peasants had been made so much worse by the creation of numerous countships and baronies, which gave the holders full power over the serfs upon their lands, that many of the younger men left the country. At length a law was passed decreeing that all Bonder who did not marry and remain settled on the estate to which they belonged should be taken as soldiers, while any peasant who left his master's service without leave might be sent to the hulks to work in irons for a year. The consequence of these cruel measures was that the poor fell into a state of dependence, scarcely better than slavery, while the land was only half-cultivated and the owners became in time impoverished.

PART IV.

"THE TYPE-QUARREL."

Frederick IV., 1699-1730.—On the death of Christian V. in 1699, after a reign of nearly thirty years, his eldest son was proclaimed king under the title of Frederick IV. This prince, who in the latter part of his life showed great capacity for ruling, and considerable practical knowledge of all the details of government, had been so neglected by his father in his childhood and youth, that he had not even been taught to spell or to express himself correctly, and had never been permitted to take any part in public affairs until within a few days of Christian's death, when the old king, either because he was too feeble to resist, or because he repented of his unworthy conduct to his son, summoned him for the first time to take his place at the council-board. Frederick was then more than twenty-eight years of age, and his first measure after his coronation was to plunge the kingdom into an unnecessary war with Sweden by seizing upon the territories of Duke Frederick IV. of Gottorp, the near kinsman and close ally of the young Swedish king, Charles XII. The Danish king had probably trusted to the youth and inexperience of his cousin, Charles XII., but in this expectation he was soon undeceived, for although the young Swedish king was scarcely eighteen at the time, and had previously seemed to be wholly taken up with bear-hunting and other daring pursuits in which he took special delight, he, on the first news of Frederick's invasion of Gottorp, collected troops and ships, made a rapid descent on Sjœlland, and in person advanced to the assault of Copenhagen. These prompt and unexpected measures had the effect of inducing King Frederick to make a hasty peace with his namesake in Holstein-Gottorp, to whom he assured the independent sovereignty of his duchy and the payment of a large sum of money for the expenses of the war. In this short and inglorious war, the Danish king had had to contend with a far more powerful foe than his still untried cousin. This was William of Orange, who, as king of England and Stadtholder of Holland, exerted an overwhelming weight on the politics of Europe at this time, and who had sent a large fleet of English and Dutch ships into the Baltic to co-operate with his ally, the Swedish king. King William's threats of bombarding Copenhagen, unless Frederick IV. at once concluded a peace with Charles XII., had therefore had a great share in bringing hostilities to a sudden close.

Holstein-Gottorp.—The death of Duke Frederick IV. of Gottorp, in 1702, was the means of exciting new causes of difference between the Danish crown and the duchy. This was mainly due to the ambition and craft of Count Görtz, one of the members of the council of regency, who, together with the widowed duchess, Hedvig Sofia, sister of Charles XII., ruled the state during the minority of the young Duke Carl Frederick. This man, whose aim was to separate the province entirely from Denmark, and who afterwards, as prime minister to Charles XII. of Sweden, did all in his power to bring about the ruin of the Danish monarchy, had roused the anger of Frederick by causing certain public notices, which referred to the joint government of the king and duke, to be issued in the name of the latter only. He had still more offended the king by having the duke's name printed in the same type as his own, instead of letting the royal signature, as was usual in such cases, be struck off in larger letters. This frivolous cause of strife, known as the "*type-quarrel*," gave rise to many other differences, and led in the course of time to open war between the parties, which ended, after the peace between Sweden and Denmark in 1721, in the entire subjugation of the duchy of Holstein-Gottorp, which, in accordance with a royal decree of that year, was again re-united to the Danish crown-lands, after having been separated from them since the year 1386, when it was given by the regent, Queen Margaret, to Count Gerhard VI. of Holstein as an hereditary fief.

Internal state of Denmark.—The war in which Denmark was embroiled in common with the other northern powers between 1709 and 1720 belongs so much more to the history of Charles XII. of Sweden, who was the most prominent character in all the scenes of that stirring period, than to that of any other prince who took part in it, that it will be unnecessary here to enter into any details in regard to it. We will therefore turn at once to the events which belong to the internal rule of Frederick IV. of Denmark, whose economy, industry, common sense, and moral rectitude formed a striking contrast to the characteristics by which his father had been distinguished. By his careful reduction of all unnecessary expenses in his court and in the various departments of the government, Frederick IV. succeeded in reducing to a very small sum the national debt left to him by Christian V., notwithstanding the cost of the long war and the outlay required for the erection of the palaces of Fredericksberg and Fredensborg and other public buildings, which the foolishly extravagant tastes of his queen, Louisa of Mecklenburg, had led him to incur. The reign of Frederick was visited by several public calamities, which called for the prompt and liberal aid of the state. In 1710 a frightful pestilence cut off 25,000 people in Copenhagen alone, and in 1728, a destructive fire laid waste two-thirds of the city, which cost the lives of many of the citizens and reduced to ashes many of the principal buildings, amongst others the magnificent University Library, with most of its rich stores of oriental manuscripts and other valuable works, while in 1717 an inundation had destroyed large tracts of the rich pasture lands of the Ditmarshers. In all these national misfortunes Frederick evinced the greatest liberality and sympathy towards the sufferers, and took means to relieve their distress to the utmost of his power. This king was the first sovereign who endeavoured to extend a knowledge of the Gospel to his heathen colonial subjects by organizing missions for their conversion and instruction. In 1705 the missionary Ziegenbalg was sent by him to the Danish trading station at Tranquebar in India to teach the Hindoos, and in 1721, as we have seen in Chapter VI., Hans Egede with his wife went to Greenland to preach to the natives, who, since the Black Death in 1350, had been apparently forgotten by the mother-country. Frederick caused the town of Godthaab to be founded in 1721, and a Greenland trading company to be incorporated in 1723; and thus this long-neglected colony was reopened to the rest of the world.

This king's attention to his fleet was well repaid by the able body of seamen which the Danish navy possessed at the close of his reign; while the gallant deeds of his brave admiral, Peder Vessel, better known as " Tordenskjold (Thundershield), recall by their daring, success, and extraordinary character, the memory of those northern sea-kings of old, whose name like his own was a shield to their friends and a thunderbolt to their foes. In accordance with the unwise policy of the poorer rulers of those times, Frederick let out his armies to other princes who needed and could afford to pay for foreign auxiliaries. Thus 12,000 Danes were lent to England for ten years to fight in the Spanish War of Succession, while 8,000 swelled the ranks of the Imperialists at the same time, and the money which they too often purchased with their lives was used by the king to pay off the arrears of an old debt due to Holland.

Frederick IV. tried to improve the condition of the peasantry by abolishing serfdom, but his measures in their favour lost much of the benefit they might otherwise have afforded by the organization of a country militia, which the great landowners were called upon to maintain at their own expense, and which they filled up by sending into the ranks any of their peasants whom they wished to get rid of or punish for insubordination. His measures for the education of the poorer classes were more immediately successful, and at Frederick's death, in 1730, free schools had been so generally opened in all parts of his kingdom, that no sovereign of those times numbered so large a proportion of educated persons amongst his subjects as the Danish king.

CHAPTER XXIII.

DENMARK FROM 1730 TO 1839.

Frederick IV. succeeded by Christian VI., who encourages Germans—The Queen despises everything Danish—Her mania for building and pulling down—Crown Prince discouraged in learning Danish—Bigotry of Court—Tyranny in Religion—Reproofs and penalties and stocks awarded to those who neglected services of the Church—Orders sent to Iceland to regulate domestic life—Hypocrisy—Frederick V. and English Queen undo all that his father had done—Great reaction—French manners followed—King's weakness—Good ministers—Their services—The Gottorp princes—Russian emperor—His hatred to Denmark—His threats—Danger of invasion—His murder averts the peril—Peace with Russia—Christian VII. and his Queen Caroline Matilda of England—King's weakness—His acts—His favourites—Struensee and Brandt—Their power, influence, acts—Their fate—Queen's disgrace—Removal from Copenhagen—Her early death—The execution of the ministers—The power of Queen Dowager and her son—The Guldberg Ministry—Prince Frederick acts as Regent—Guldberg's party dismissed—Bernstorf's influence and acts—Slave trade abolished—Armed neutrality—Difficulties with England—Nelson's appearance—Battle—His admiration of Danish valour—Danish heroes—Peace with England—Some years of quiet—Denmark trading agent for other countries—English squadron under Gambier seizes on Danish fleet—Danes nearly crushed—Gustavus IV. of Sweden attacks Norway—Frederick VI. reigns alone from 1808 on the death of his father—Critical position—Forced into alliance with Napoleon—French army under Bernadotte sent to Jutland—The mutinies of troops—Bernadotte withdraws without striking a blow—Paper money issued—Merchants ruined—Frederick's fickle policy—Norway given to Sweden—England takes Heligoland—King disappointed in not securing Swedish throne, which is obtained by Bernadotte—Gradual improvement of country—Legislative Chambers opened—King anxious to draw back from further political concessions—Laws against the press—Great turmoil—His death.

PART I.

A PERIOD OF RESTRAINT.

Christian VI., 1730-1746.—THE reign of Christian VI. of Denmark, who succeeded his father, Frederick IV., in 1730, is only remarkable for its peculiarly un-Danish and strong German character. The queen, Sophia Magdalena of Kulmbach-Bayreuth, exerted her great influence over the king in filling all offices of trust with Germans, and in banishing from the court the language and usages of the country; and in her dislike for everything Danish, she even tried to prevent the crown prince being taught to understand his native tongue. She had a fatal mania for building, which led her to pull down one palace only to erect another on some site that pleased her better. Thus she demolished the noble castle of Axelhus in Copenhagen, which Frederick IV. had restored and enlarged at great expense, and substituted for it the enormous building known as Christiansborg, which cost near 3,000,000 rix dollars and was seven years in building. To gratify a whim of hers, a beautiful hunting palace was erected at Hirschholm on a piece of swampy land, where the foundations soon gave way, and the house had to be pulled down. While the queen was thus indulging her expensive hobby, the king was introducing a system of bigotry and pietism into the country to which Denmark had hitherto been an entire stranger, and which soon brought about the most deplorable state of hypocrisy and intolerance. A General Church Inspection College was established in 1737, which may be regarded as a Protestant form of the Court of Inquisition, for the duties of its directors consisted in taking cognizance of the doctrines and lives of all preachers and teachers in the kingdom, watching over the proper performance of church services, and inspecting all works that passed through the Danish press. Heavy penalties were inflicted, and severe reproofs were publicly given from the pulpits in accordance with the decisions of this inquisitorial court, which moreover punished neglect of attendance at church by money fines, and in default of payment with the long disused penalty of standing in the stocks, which were for that purpose erected before every church door. All public amusements were forbidden, together with recreations that had hitherto been thought harmless, as riding or driving on a Sunday; and all the old national games and festivities were put down as "things offensive to God and injurious to the working man." A royal decree was drawn up for the maintenance of household piety and domestic virtue in Iceland, in which the islanders were warned to abstain from reading idle stories, and so-called Sagas, which were not "seemly for a Christian soul's entertainment, and were a cause of offence to the Holy Ghost." The result of these coercive measures was to create great dissensions in churches and families, and to form a party who, in spite of all restrictions, showed utter indifference to religion, and tried by ridicule to bring the pietists into discredit.

Frederick V., 1746-1766. *French manners.*—When, by the death of Christian VI. in 1746, his eldest son, Frederick V., ascended the throne, all the ordinances of the former reign were annulled, and brilliancy and liberty were restored to the court under the direction of the good-humoured sociable king, and his lovely young queen, Louisa, daughter of George II. of England. The royal couple, by their youth, beauty and affability, won the hearts of the people, and the nation at large rejoiced publicly at their release from the religious thraldom in which the late king had bound them. At first the reaction seemed harmless and even beneficial, and as long as Queen Louisa lived, the amusements of the court were kept within the bounds of moderation, but after her death in 1751, and when another queen, Juliana Maria of Brunswick, had taken her place, greater luxury began to prevail, and in the attempt to imitate the sumptuous habits of the French, the Danish royal family were led to incur expenses for which the ordinary resources of the crown were quite inadequate. Frederick himself towards the close of his life fell into habits of drinking, which, coupled with his naturally easy good nature, often made him a tool in the hands of unworthy favourites. But although he was not himself an active or efficient ruler, he had the good fortune to secure able ministers, amongst whom the most distinguished were Counts Schimmelmann and Bernstorf. To the latter Denmark owes a large debt of gratitude, for to him are mainly due all the great improvements in manufactures, trade, and agriculture which distinguish this reign. He encouraged learning, established societies for the promotion of science, invited learned teachers, as Mallet and Schlegel, into the country; was the means of sending Niebuhr to Arabia to make archæological researches; co-operated with the Norwegian Holberg, the greatest dramatic writer of his time, in the reorganization of the noble academy of Sorö near Copenhagen; founded hospitals in the chief towns of the kingdom, and in many other ways used his great influence in promoting the general education and improved cultivation of the people.

This reign was peaceful, although more than once war seemed imminent, owing to the new influence acquired by Denmark's old enemies, the Gottorp princes, through the accession of Charles Peter Ulrik, the head of their house, to the throne of Russia, on the death of his mother's sister, the Empress Elizabeth. This prince, who assumed the title of Peter III., bore strong feelings of hatred to Denmark on account of the losses inflicted upon his family by the incorporation of the Slesvig territories with the Danish crown lands, and in 1762 he sent an army into Mecklenburg, with orders to advance on the duchies, and openly announced his intention of driving the Danish royal family out of Europe, and forcing them to take refuge in their East Indian settlement at Tranquebar. The danger was threatening, and the Danes were in daily expectation of hearing that the fleet, which had been equipped in haste to defend the coasts, would come into conflict with the Russian squadron lying in wait for it in the Baltic, when their fears of coming war were suddenly set at rest by the news of the murder of the emperor, Peter III., on the 14th of July, 1762. The empress, Catherine II., who succeeded her husband, the murdered prince, and was known to have been averse to the war, at once concluded a peace with Denmark, by which she renounced, in the name of her son, all claims to the Gottorp lands in Holstein in exchange for Oldenburg and Delmenhorst. This treaty, which was brought about by the able diplomacy of Count Bernstorf, relieved Denmark of a very great cause of danger, and although only conditional at the time it was first drawn up, owing to the minority of the Czarevitz, Paul, it was duly confirmed by him when he reached his majority in 1773.

PART II.

STRUENSEE'S RULE.

Christian VII., 1766-1808.—Christian VII. was only seventeen years of age when he succeeded his father, Frederick V., in 1766, and in the same year he married his cousin, Caroline Matilda, the beautiful sister of George III. of England. This prince was both obstinate and morose, and was weak in body and mind. His distrust of his stepmother, the dowager queen Juliana Maria, induced him to dismiss from his service all who had enjoyed favour during the former reign, and to fill their places with new favourites. Thus within the first few years of his reign, Count Bernstorf, Admiral Danneskjold-Samsoe, to whom the Danish navy owed much of its efficiency, and several other able ministers of the crown, had been driven out of the country, and all the power of the state thrown into the hands, first of Count Holk, a young man of vicious habits, who did much to injure the king in health and character, and afterwards into those of Brandt and Struensee. These two men, whose names are intimately associated with the extraordinary events which in the course of a few years brought about their own and the young queen's ruin, and threw the king into the power of his enemies, were by no means of equal ability or like responsibility. Johan Frederick Struensee, the originator and guiding spirit in all the despotic measures in which both were engaged, was a man of great natural ability and extensive knowledge. At the time he was appointed private physician to Christian VII. during the tour which that king made in 1768 through the principal countries of Europe, he had already acquired considerable reputation both in his profession and by his literary productions, and when the University of Oxford in the course of the same year conferred the degree of D.C.L. on King Christian, they gave that of M.D. to Struensee " in recognition of his great merits in science and literature." By his address this able man soon supplanted the favourite, Count Holk, and succeeded in persuading the king to recall from banishmen his former chamberlain, Enevold von Brandt, and Count Rantzau-Ascheberg, a dismissed minister, whose acquaintance

Struensee had made in Paris, and on whose gratitude he thought he might rely. The new favourite soon appeared to enjoy the confidence of the young queen as thoroughly as that of her half-witted husband, and after rapidly rising from one degree of power to another, Struensee was nominated in the summer of 1771 to the rank of Prime Minister of the Privy Council, a dignity hitherto unknown in Denmark. From that moment his word was supreme, for instead of acting in concert with the various ministerial colleges, as had been customary in the case of other Danish ministers of the crown, Struensee governed by means of " *Cabinet orders*," signed only by himself, which were to have the same weight as if they had been royal decrees bearing the sovereign's signature.

The downfall of Struensee and the Queen.—Struensee's extraordinary talents, liberal ideas, and great capacity for business, joined to his rapid and unhesitating mode of forming a judgment, led him to introduce new and better systems of government into many of the departments of the public service. He improved the routine of the law courts, organized police and sanitary reforms, established freedom of the press, and made much-needed retrenchments in the expenses of the court and of all the public offices. On the other hand, his insolent conduct, his contempt for all the observances and doctrines of religion, his ignorance of the language and habits of the country over which he ruled, his headstrong haste in effecting changes, and the suspicion that he was making himself and his friends rich at the expense of the working classes, who were heavily oppressed with taxes, all concurred in raising a host of enemies against him in every class of the community. The queen dowager and her son, the so-called "Hereditary Prince" Frederick, watched the minister's rapid rise with fear and indignation, and when on the occasion of some disturbances amongst the sailors in the docks, Struensee had given evidence of want of personal courage and presence of mind, they thought the moment favourable to join with Count Rantzau-Ascheberg and others, who had been estranged from him by his own arrogance. A plot was soon formed, and on the night of April 20th, 1772, the conspirators forced their way into the king's bedroom, and by their representations of the queen's conduct and of her intimacy with Struensee, they obtained Christian's signature to an order for her arrest and that of the minister and his devoted friend, Brandt. The unhappy Caroline Matilda, who only three hours before had closed a court ball in a dance with Prince Frederick, was awakened out of her sleep by the presence of an armed guard, who commanded her to rise and dress herself in all haste for a journey. The same night she was conveyed in a closed carriage to the castle of Cronborg, near Elsinore, without being allowed to see her two children, the elder of whom, the Crown Prince Frederick, was only three years old, and the younger, a daughter, still an infant in arms. After a formal deed of separation had been passed between the king and herself, she was removed from Cronborg through the influence of her brother, King George III. of England, and conveyed in an English man-of-war to Zelle in Hanover, where she died in 1775, at the early age of twenty-four, from an attack of chicken-pox, which she had caught while visiting the poor and sick.

Struensee and Brandt had in the meantime been condemned to death for treason, and sentenced to lose their right hand before they were beheaded, and this sentence was publicly executed outside the gates of Copenhagen on the 28th of April, 1772; but beyond these two victims this eventful revolution was free from bloodshed. The king's constantly-increasing feebleness of mind and body left him a mere tool in the hands of the queen-dowager and her son, who in fact, although not in name, ruled the kingdom till the year 1784, when the Crown Prince Frederick attained the legal majority of sixteen, and at once claimed the right of acting as regent or joint ruler with his father. During the period of his minority the affairs of the state had been for the most part in the hands of the Hereditary Prince's friend, Count Ove Högh Guldberg, who had been a chief agent in bringing about the downfall of Struensee, and whose policy was in every respect the opposite of that of the minister whom he had ruined. Under Guldberg all the laws, whether good or bad, that had been passed under Struensee's ministry were set aside; and the chief merit of this minister was that he showed a patriotic love of his own country; encouraged the use of the Danish language, and tried to check the influence of Germans in the country by appointing only native-born or naturalized subjects of Denmark to places of trust in the public service. But his reckless system of issuing paper money threw the finances into great disorder, and thus helped to bring about many of the troubles which disturbed the credit and peace of the country in later years.

PART III.

ENGLAND HUMBLES DENMARK.

Prince Frederick rules for his father.—The first act of the young prince was to dismiss Count Guldberg and his party, and recall Count Andreas Peter Bernstorf, the former minister of foreign affairs, who had some years before retired from the public service in consequence of differences with the rest of the council. By Bernstorf's cautious policy, Denmark was kept at peace while almost every other state in Europe found itself forced to take part in the revolutionary wars of the times. The Danes during this period enjoyed a remarkable degree of prosperity, owing to the condition of armed neutrality which Denmark was allowed to maintain, and which now enabled her to carry her trade to all the principal mercantile ports of the Baltic and German Ocean. While the trading part of the community were thus gaining wealth rapidly, the government, under the direction of the crown prince and Count Bernstorf, were bringing about many great and useful changes in the state. Their first care had been to inquire into the condition of the peasants, and in 1788 a law was passed giving this long oppressed class complete freedom from all the bonds by which they had hitherto been kept in subjection to the lords on whose lands they were born. In order to prevent any undue license on the part of the younger peasants, the measure was not to come into full force, till 1800, for those who were under thirty-six years of age at the time of its first enactment. The slave trade was also declared illegal at this period in all the Danish West Indian islands, and the example thus set by Denmark in 1792 was soon followed by England and other European powers.

As long as Count Bernstorf lived, causes of strife had been kept down between Denmark and England, but not without difficulty, for the English often made complaints against the Danes for carrying food and forage into French and German ports, which they declared was contrary to the laws of neutrality; and when, after his death in 1799, Danish men-of-war were sent to sea to protect the merchant vessels, there was a new source of trouble raised up which soon led to open hostilities. The first quarrels were smoothed over; but when, in the summer of 1800, Russia, Sweden, and Prussia formed a treaty for an "*armed neutrality*," which they invited Denmark to join, England took alarm, and, to prevent this compact, sent a fleet under Admirals Parker and Nelson to the Cattegat in the spring of the following year. The Danes were wholly unprepared for such a step, and did their best to prevent the English from passing the Sound. But Parker's fleet of fifty-one ships, including twenty line-of-battle ships, by keeping close in to the Swedish coast, got clear of the heavy cannons of the fortress of Cronborg, near Elsinore, at the mouth of the narrow strait between Sweden and Denmark, and cast anchor in the harbour of Copenhagen on 1st of April, 1801. The next morning, Shrove Tuesday, Nelson attacked the Danish defences, and then followed a fierce and bloody engagement, which lasted between four and five hours, and ended by Nelson sending an English officer on shore under a flag of truce as a bearer of a letter, in which he declared that unless the Danes ceased firing he would burn the Danish ships in his hands without being able to save their crews. The crown prince, against the wishes and advice of his commanders, consented to give orders for stopping all further firing on the part of the Danes, and agreed to discuss terms of peace. And thus ended a battle of which Nelson said, that it was the best contested and the fiercest of the hundred and five engagements in which he had taken part. The Danish seamen, under their brave and able commander, Olfert Fischer, fought with the daring for which their nation had in former ages been noted. Three times the aged Fischer left one burning ship to hoist his flag on another, while several of the younger captains, amongst whom the Danes dwell with special pride on the names of Lassen, Risbrich, and Villemoes, defended their ships against larger vessels as long as the shattered hulks kept above water.

Denmark the carrier of Europe.—The death of the Emperor Paul, and the new alliance made by his son and successor, Alexander, with England, put an end to the compact of armed neutrality which had given rise to this unfortunate war. Denmark now enjoyed a few years of peace, and her trade both in the new and the old world rose to a degree of activity which it had never before reached. At this period the Danes were, in fact, the great trading agents for all the other countries in Europe, which during those early years of the present century were more or less engaged in war with France. This prosperous condition of things was, however, rudely disturbed in 1807, when the English government, having or believing that they had good grounds for thinking that Denmark had entered into a treaty with Napoleon and the Emperor Alexander of Russia against England, sent fifty-four ships of war under Admiral Gambier to demand the immediate delivery of the Danish fleet in order to prevent its use in the cause of the French emperor.

The moment was an unfavourable one for the Danes, as the royal family and nearly all the Danish army were in Holstein, where the crown prince had reason to fear that an attack might be made from the German frontier, and Copenhagen was thus left in a specially unprotected state. When the commandant of the city, General Peymann, refused to comply with the demands of the English admiral, 33,000 men were landed under General Cathcart, and the town formally attacked by land and sea. A fierce bombardment of three days laid a large portion of the city in ashes, and forced General Peymann to admit the English troops into the citadel of Frederikshavn. The result of this attack, which the Danes looked upon as a wanton act of piracy, unworthy of a great naval power like England, was that the English carried off 18 ships of the line, 21 frigates, 6 brigs, and 25 gun-boats, besides an immense amount of naval stores of every kind.

The Danes were nearly crushed by the blow, and a genera-

tion passed away before this fatal wrong was forgiven by the
nation, amongst whom the memory of the deed stills recalls a
bitter sense of injury. The troubles of Denmark increased
when, the year after, Gustavus IV. of Sweden, trusting to the
support of England, made an attempt to seize upon Norway,
and in that dark hour of his country's history, poor King
Christian VII. ended his useless life on the 13th of March,
1808.

Frederick VI., 1808-1839. — When Frederick VI., on the
death of his father in 1808, exchanged his title of regent for
that of King of Denmark, the country was sinking into a state
of abject misery. The harsh policy of the British government
had at one blow crushed its commerce as well as its fleet, for
Danish trading ships were nowhere safe from the attack of
English men-of-war, and before the restoration of peace it was
computed that upwards of 1,200 of these vessels had been
seized with their cargoes, valued at more than thirty million of
rix dollars. The position of Denmark at the outbreak of the
war between France and the northern powers had been most
critical and difficult. The bombardment of Copenhagen in
1807, and the seizure of the well-appointed fleet, to which the
nation trusted as a means of certain defence against foreign
invasion, had created so bitter a feeling of resentment amongst
the people against England, that whatever might be the real
feelings of King Frederick, he had no alternative but to
follow the general wishes of his subjects, and unite himself
with Napoleon against Great Britain, although he and his
government seem from the first to have been fully aware that
the emperor in his policy would consult only his own interests.
This alliance soon brought on the most unhappy results, for, on
pretence of supporting Denmark against an invasion by the
Swedes, and aiding her in recovering her old Swedish provinces,
Napoleon sent an army of 30,000 men under General Bernadotte (Prince of Ponte Corvo) into Slesvig-Holstein, where
they remained over a year on one pretence or another without
affording any help to Denmark. The cost and disturbances
to which the presence of such a large body of foreign troops
necessarily gave rise were rendered still more burdensome by
the want of discipline and the discontent of the men, amongst

whom there were 14,000 Spaniards, under the command of the Marquis de la Romana, who during the whole of their stay in the Danish peninsula were engaged in intrigues to escape from the service of the French emperor and unite with the English. When the news reached them that Napoleon had deposed the King of Spain and placed his brother Joseph on the Spanish throne, their long-brooding discontent broke out into open rebellion, and the country was disturbed by a civil war amongst its self-appointed defenders. A squadron of English ships, which had been sent to co-operate with the Spanish detachment in the Danish provinces, succeeded in taking large numbers on board from Jutland and the island of Langeland, while the few regiments which were unable to escape were disarmed by the Danes and kept as prisoners of war. In 1809, Bernadotte, without striking a blow in defence of Denmark, withdrew with his well-recruited troops, and immediately afterwards the English seized upon Anholt, which they retained as a favourable station to control the passage between Denmark and Norway. At this time the government of Frederick VI. took the desperate resolution of meeting the heavy debts which they had incurred in this unfortunate war by issuing 142 millions of paper notes, and when it was seen that their nominal value could not be obtained even in the Danish provinces, they were suddenly reduced to one-sixth of their assumed worth. This measure saved the government from the bankruptcy that seemed inevitable, but it ruined nearly all the chief trading and banking houses in Denmark, and created great distress in almost every class of the population.

Denmark loses Norway.—The Danish king's policy was throughout this period weak and changeable, and after a series of mortifications and disappointments, he found himself compelled in 1814 to agree to the peace of Kiel. In accordance with the terms of this treaty, Denmark was forced to give Norway to Sweden, after the Danish and Norwegian crowns had been united for 400 years, and to accept in exchange Swedish Pomerania and Rügen, which, however, were at once ceded to Prussia in return for Lauenburg and the payment of two million of rix dollars. England required for herself the cession of Heligoland, to secure the command of the Elbe; and, thus bereft of all her best points of defence, Denmark was forced to join the allies, and at the Congress of Vienna, in 1814, her king had to content himself with being admitted into the German confederation as Duke of Holstein and Lauenburg. These terms were peculiarly mortifying to Frederick VI., because he had more than once thought himself secure of the crown of Sweden in addition to those which he bore as king of Denmark and Norway. When the Swedes resolved in 1809 to elect a successor to their childless king, Charles XIII., Prince Christian August of Augustenborg, Danish viceroy of Norway, led King Frederick to believe that the Swedish nation were anxious to be re-united with Denmark, but that monarch soon learnt how little faith could be placed in such assurances when he found that the prince himself had been elected to succeed King Charles. The sudden death of Prince Christian in 1810 re-opened the question of the succession, and King Frederick again allowed himself to be deluded by false hopes, which were destroyed by the choice of one of Napoleon's marshals, General Bernadotte, who was proclaimed Crown Prince of Sweden in the same year, and succeeded to the joint throne of Sweden and Norway on the death of Charles XIII. in 1818.

Frederick VI. released the Norwegians from their oaths of allegiance to him in accordance with the treaty of Kiel, and in all outward respects he apparently complied with the engagements which he had entered into towards the allied powers. But it does not seem that he was entirely ignorant of the measures which were being taken at the very time by his cousin, Prince Christian of Denmark, to separate Norway from Sweden and declare it an independent state. For a few months the prince gained ground in his efforts to rouse the national dislike of the Norwegians for their Swedish neighbours; and in May 1814 he was proclaimed King of Norway at a diet held at Ejdsvold, where he gave the people a new code of laws, based upon that of the French Revolution of 1791. Before the close of the same year, the Swedish crown prince, Bernadotte, put down this movement, forced Prince Christian to leave the country, and in the name of the king, Charles XIII., received the homage of the Norwegians, and confirmed all their national privileges.

The Danes rally from their troubles.—Many years passed after the peace of 1814 before the Danes began to recover from the depression and calamities of the earlier part of the century. The establishment, in 1818, of a national bank, which was wholly independent of the state, was the first step towards a better condition of the monetary system. By degrees, trade and confidence in the resources of the country revived, and a proper and fair proportion of silver money was made to replace the former worthless paper notes of the government. The more prosperous condition of the people soon led them to interest themselves in the course and management of public affairs, and this newly awakened feeling had assumed so decided a character after the revolution of 1830 in France, that King Frederick, to avert any dangerous results of the popular desire for self-government, and entirely in opposition to his own conservative principles, proclaimed the establishment of legislative chambers in the spring of 1831. The nation seized with eagerness upon this opportunity of asserting their rights, and poured forth their gratitude to the king in the most enthusiastic manner. In 1831, when the scheme for the new assemblies was fully arranged, different chambers were opened for the Islands at Roeskilde, for Jutland at Viborg, for Slesvig in the town of Slesvig, and for Holstein at Itzehoe. To these chambers were to be submitted for consideration and approval all laws affecting the personal condition of the citizens of the respective provinces, and all projects of taxation. The finances of the kingdom became the first object of consideration for the new chambers, which, not satisfied with the amount of information accorded to them on the subject of the disposal of the revenue, petitioned the king for leave to form a committee of inquiry into the working of the financial departments of the government. This was not granted to the satisfaction of the chambers, and during the remainder of Frederick VI.'s reign little progress was made in this direction. In the meanwhile the question of the freedom of the press had begun to excite the minds of men of all classes. The king and his chief friends taking speedy alarm at the free discussion of public matters which now for the first time filled the papers, and unable to rescind the rights of free speech granted to the members of the different chambers, although they would gladly have put them down, determined to impose restrictions on the press. The first decisive step taken by the government was to interdict the further publication of *Fædrelandet*, a weekly paper, conducted by the learned C. N. David, professor of political economy in the University of Copenhagen. Dr. David was brought before the law courts on the charge of seditious writing, but acquitted, to the universal joy of all the liberal party and to the extreme annoyance of the government, which deprived him in the following year (1836) of his chair.

In the midst of a turmoil of strong political feeling Frederick VI. died after a rule of fifty-five years, leaving the character of a well-meaning but feeble ruler, whose thoroughly patriotic love of his country and his people made him personally dear to all classes of his subjects, in spite of the many blunders and shortcomings of his administration.

CHAPTER XXIV.

SWEDEN FROM 1697 TO 1771.

Charles XII. better known than other Swedish kings to foreigners—The Regency appointed by Charles XI.—The Estates set it aside and allow Charles XII., at the age of fifteen, to rule—His absolute power—His character—His bringing up—Dangerous pursuits—His enemies plot against him—He leaves his sports and turns in earnest to work—Carries the war into Denmark—Attacks Copenhagen—Shows wonderful military skill—Danish king forced to make peace—Charles relieves Riga—Defeats the Russians—Takes more prisoners than he can keep—New victories in Poland—Charles regulates Polish affairs, humbles King Augustus, opens a court in Saxony—Czar Peter begins to build his capital on Swedish ground—Marvellous advance of Swedes—Their daring, their sufferings—Mazeppa—Czar advances—Charles wounded—Defeat and capture of the Swedish army—Flight of Charles to Turkey—Troubles at home during his absence—No generals but Stenbock to defend Sweden—His "wooden shoes"—Charles in Turkey—Troubles of Czar—Catherine saves the Russian army—Charles plots, and feigns illness—At last escapes and returns to his dominions—Defends Stralsund—Remains at Lund—Görtz—His measures—Denmark saved by thaw—Charles attacks Norway—Is killed—The suspicion of murder—Love of people for him—His merits—His place of burial—Question of succession—How settled—His sister Ulrika proclaimed—Her submission to nobles—Resigns supreme power to her husband—Frederick I. His weak rule—His little power—Factions—"Hats and Caps"—Swedes go to war with Russia—Their defeat—Adolph Frederick of Slesvig-Gottorp succeeds—A mere puppet—Humiliation—Sarcastic remark of king's brother-in-law, Frederick II. of Prussia—Wishes to abdicate—Dies in the midst of party troubles.

PART I.

THE SWEDISH CONQUEROR.

Charles XII., 1697-1718.—CHARLES XII. of Sweden is better known to the people of foreign countries than almost any other Swedish monarch, because the wonderful exploits of his life have been made the subject of many special works by writers in almost every European tongue. His father, Charles XI., left at his death full directions for the appointment of a regency to rule the kingdom until the young king reached the age of eighteen; but the National Estates of Sweden did not like the idea of again placing the supreme power in the hands of regents, and in the diet which met soon afterwards they declared Charles XII. to be no longer a minor. The young king, who was at the time only fifteen, at once called upon the different orders of the state to do him homage, and went through a simple form of coronation, in which he with his own hands placed the crown on his head, without, however, having tendered the oath of fidelity to his people which was usual in these cases. A mere lad thus became the absolute and sole master of the fate of his people and kingdom, and before long he gave evidence of a self-willed obstinacy and independence of character which did not promise well for the quiet and comfort of his subjects. Without consulting the opinions or wishes of the Council of State, he managed the affairs of the government as he thought best, and would listen to no one but his own special favourite, Karl Piper.

Charles XII. was not wanting in good sense and upright feelings, and by his mother, Ulrika Eleanora, the "*Fred Kulla*" of Denmark, he had been trained to observe all the practices of religion and to show deference towards the opinions of his elders, but after her death very little was done for him beyond giving him masters in various branches of learning. Thus at the time he became king, although well-informed for his age, he was wholly unsuited from want of proper training to perform the duties entrusted to him. He had soon squandered all the money collected by his father, plunging with childish eagerness into every kind of daring amusement that he could devise, and risking his life in break-neck rides, mock fights, bear-hunts, and other dangerous sports. Neighbouring princes who heard of these pursuits, and thought that there could be nothing to fear from a king whose time and strength were wasted on such occupations, began to scheme against him, and soon a secret plot was formed between his cousin, Frederick IV. of Denmark, the Czar Peter the Great, and Augustus King of Poland, to recover some of the lands conquered by Charles's predecessors. Early in the year 1700 the Polish king invaded Livonia, while the Danes attacked the lands of Charles's brother-in-law, the Duke of Holstein-Gottorp, and after taking Gottorp laid siege to Tonningen.

Charles begins life in earnest.—The Swedish king, who was only eighteen at the time, showed no surprise or alarm at finding himself thus made the object of attack by his supposed friends and allies. Leaving the sports in which he had seemed to take so much delight, but which he never again resumed, he turned to meet the danger which beset him, and sending an army of Swedes and Luneburgers to relieve Tonningen, he applied for ships to William of Orange, King of England, and with a united fleet of Swedish, Dutch, and English vessels, proceeded to bombard Copenhagen. Seeing that little progress was made in this undertaking, he determined to attack the city by land as well as by sea, and taking the command himself, he effected a landing at the little village of Humlebek, where he made all the necessary arrangements for encamping his troops with as much order and quickness as if he had been long experienced in the art of warfare. By the strict discipline which he maintained in his army, he won the good-will of the Sjæland peasants, who in those times were not accustomed to great men willing to pay for what they had the power of taking from them by force. Wonderful tales of the coolness and daring of the young Swedish hero were long current amongst the country people ; and it was related of him, that when he was bringing his troops to Humlebek, in his impatience to land he sprang from the boat, and waded through the water which came nearly up to his waist, till he reached the shore, when, springing first to land, he waved his sword over his head, and cried out joyously as he heard the enemy's balls whistling through the air, "This is the very best music I have ever heard, and I shall never care for any other as long as I live!"

When King Frederick learnt that his Swedish cousin in person was attacking his capital on land, and that a fleet was threatening it from without, he at once made peace with the Holstein-Gottorp prince, and agreed to the terms proposed by Charles. As soon as this matter was settled, the Swedish king crossed the Baltic to the relief of Riga, which was being in-

vested by a combined army of Poles, Russians, and Saxons;
and having driven off the assailants and relieved the garrison,
which, under the command of the Swedish general, Dahlberg,
had made a gallant and nearly desperate defence, he advanced
towards Narva in Ingermanland. This place, which belonged
to Sweden, was being besieged by 60,000 Russians, under the
command of the Duc de Croy. With perfect indifference to
the numbers of the enemy, Charles advanced against them
with only 8,000 men, whom he led to the attack by seemingly
impassable tracks and through well-defended passes, and,
storming their entrenchments, he thoroughly routed the Russians, 18,000 of whom were drowned in the Narva, and so
many made prisoners that the Swedes were forced, after disarming them, to let them disperse in whichever direction they
liked. This victory, which was unparalleled of its kind in
history, spread the fame of the young king over all Europe;
but it may be said to have been attended by evil rather than
good to himself; for while his vanity and self-will increased
with the adulation everywhere paid to his military skill, he
was led on to pursue a course of wild and aimless invasion of
neighbouring lands which led to his own later misfortunes and
nearly ruined his kingdom.

Charles keeps Court in Saxony.—In the following year
Charles advanced into Poland, took Warsaw by storm, and
in the battles of Klissov and Pultusk so completely humbled
Augustus, the Saxon king of the Poles, that he had to give up
the Polish crown and retire into his own dominions of Saxony.
At the diet of Warsaw in 1704 the young Vojvod of Posen,
Stanislaus Leczinsky, was, through Charles's influence, proclaimed king; and, after several brilliant victories in Silesia and
Saxony, Augustus was forced to sue for peace and to accept
the terms offered him by the young Swedish monarch, which
included the surrender of the Livonian noble, Baron Patkul.
This man, who had been outlawed by Charles XI. on account
of his numerous attempts to free his country from the power
of Sweden, had never slackened his efforts to injure that
kingdom during the years in which he had found a safe retreat
at the court of Augustus; and by the command of Charles XII.
he was now made to expiate these offences by a cruel death.

The Swedish king, after humbling Augustus and taking vengeance on his father's old foe, spent a year in visiting and entertaining the crowd of foreign princes who thronged to his little court in Saxony and sought his friendship and alliance ; and so great was Charles's influence that the German emperor, Joseph I., at his request granted liberty of conscience to all the Protestants in his Silesian territories. During the six years that Charles remained in Poland the Russians, under their Czar, Peter the Great, had been busy in securing their footing in Ingermanland and Livonia, the control of which was essential to the success of the schemes which that prince had in view for carrying the Russian boundaries to the shores of the Baltic. To prevent the possibility of his people ever giving up these lands, Peter took the extraordinary resolution of building his new capital on the banks of the Neva, which was still included in the old Swedish province of Ingermanland. Thousands of Russian peasants and Swedish prisoners of war fell victims to the severity of the labours they were forced to undergo in draining the swampy ground on which the future St. Petersburg was raised. The few Swedish commanders who had been left to defend the frontiers could effect very little against the overwhelming numbers of the Russians ; but Charles XII., instead of coming to their aid after he had secured peace with Poland and Saxony, attempted to change the course of the war by plunging into the heart of his enemy's country and attacking their capital, Moscow. This policy, which was not regulated by any proper plan, did not prove as successful as in the case of Denmark ; and, finding that the Czar seemed in no way affected by his movements, he determined to throw himself into the Ukraine, because a Hetman, or chief of the Ukranian Cossacks, called Ivan Mazeppa, had offered to help him with 30,000 men against Peter.

PART II.

CHARLES IN TURKEY.

Troubles and defeat of Charles.—The Swedes drove the Russians before them wherever they appeared, and let nothing stop their march. When they came to any piece of water or stream that could be forded, they waded across, holding their weapons high above their heads to keep them dry; and in this way they went onwards till they reached Holovin on the Dnieper, where they gave the Russians battle and routed them. This victory increased Charles's confidence, and without waiting for his general, Levenhaupt, who was to have joined him with reinforcements from Courland, he pushed on, and only stopped in his insane march when the excessive cold forced him to go into winter quarters. The season was more than commonly severe even for that climate, and the Swedes suffered greatly from hunger and cold. Charles shared cheerfully in all their privations, eating the same coarse food as his men, and often having to content himself like them with mouldy bread, while he had no means of keeping the frost out of his tent except by having heated cannon balls rolled along the floor. In the meanwhile the czar, who was not so incautious or inexpert as Charles wished to believe, caused the country to be laid waste through which the Swedes would have to make their retreat, fortified all the passes, and used his influence over the Cossack chiefs so well that they all fell away from Mazeppa, who had to flee from his own revolted soldiers and take refuge in the Swedish camp. To complete the misfortunes of the king, his friend Levenhaupt was met and overpowered by an immense army of Russians while on his way to join him; and although he kept up a desperate defence for two days, and escaped with a remnant of 6,000 men, he lost all his baggage and stores, with more than half his men, and reached the Swedish lines in a battered and worn condition. Hunger and disease reduced the army to 18,000 men, and with this small number Charles laid siege to Pultava, where he hoped to find food and clothing, of which he stood in sore need. The czar and his minister, Menkikoff, were, however, advancing with 55,000 men to the relief of the place, and soon the two armies lay encamped within sight of each other. The Swedes awaited the attack, but finding that the czar would not venture upon making the first move, Charles resolved to try to take the Russian entrenchments by assault. Having been badly wounded in the foot during a previous skirmish, he had

z

to be carried in a litter, and, giving the chief command to his general, Rehnsköld, he reduced Levenhaupt to the rank of second in authority. This act created much jealousy and ill-will between the generals, and dispirited the soldiers, who, missing their king's authority, lost much of their usual daring and steadiness. Their old spirit and long-used habits of assault made them bear the Russians down before them on their first attack, but in consequence of the contradictory orders of their commanders the men got confused and began to waver, when the overwhelming numbers of the enemy soon crushed them. Rehnsköld was taken captive with a great number of his division, and after a few days Levenhaupt was forced to surrender with the remnant of the army, few of whom survived through their long and severe captivity to revisit their own country. Charles himself only escaped falling into the power of the Russians by a most adventurous and hazardous flight over the Steppes to Bender, in the Turkish dominions, where he was hospitably received by the Seraskir, or commandant. He had at first determined to remain with his men and share their unhappy fate, but his personal attendants insisted so strongly on his flight that, yielding to their remonstrances, he let himself be placed on a litter, and in this helpless state, only attended by a few hundred men, the Swedish king was borne along over the Russian frontier into Turkey.

Defeat creates new troubles.—The defeat at Pultava, which took place on the 27th of June, 1709, was a signal to all the enemies of Charles to take up arms against his humbled kingdom. A new league was formed between Frederick of Denmark and Augustus of Saxony, who soon found themselves backed by the power of Prussia and Russia; and before the close of 1709 Sweden was attacked by their armies on all her frontiers. The only man who at that moment showed both the wish and the skill to defend his country was General Magnus Stenbock, who had gone to the Ukraine with the king, but in consequence of ill-health had returned to Sweden, where he held the post of Governor of Skaania. By his indefatigable activity and energy he contrived to gather together and drill 15,000 young peasant lads, who, although badly armed and wearing only tattered sheepskin coats or coarse woollen jackets, proved themselves, under his training, to be more than equal to the well-equipped and experienced regiments which Frederick IV. threw into Skaania. After a few encounters with the Danish army, these peasant lads, who were nicknamed the "Wooden Shoes," learnt the art of war so well that they were able to rout the enemy, only half of whose troops escaped in a pitiable condition to their ships; and since that beating by the "Wooden Shoes" the Danes have never invaded Sweden. On the Russian frontier the fortune of the Swedes was not equally good, for, besides losing Livonia and Esthonia, they had to give up to Russia a large tract of land in the ancient Swedish duchy of Finland.

Charles plots and makes his escape.—While these events were going on in his own dominions, Charles XII. was plotting at Bender to bring on a war between Turkey and Russia, and at length by the help of his crafty agent, Poniatovsky, who had gained great personal influence over the sultan, Achmed III., differences were excited between these powers, and a Turkish army was sent against the czar. Peter in his encounters with the Grand Vizier, Baldatdschi Mehemed, more than once narrowly escaped the fate that had befallen Charles, for like him he had allowed himself to be drawn on by promises of help from traitors, who failed him at the last moment; and on the banks of the river Pruth he was so completely shut in by the enemy's superior numbers that all attempts at breaking through their ranks proved useless. The czar had given himself up to despair, and saw no possible means of escape, when he was saved by the clever device of his brave wife, Katherine, who, trusting to the avarice of the Grand Vizier, sent him as a gift all her jewels and all the gold and silver she could collect in the Russian camp, promising at the same time in a flattering letter to present him with still more costly gifts on her and her husband's return to St. Petersburg. The effect of this timely offering was to make the Vizier willing to conclude a peace, by which, on the surrender of the little fortress of Azov, Peter was allowed to withdraw his army without further opposition. When Charles remonstrated angrily with the Vizier for letting his foe escape at the moment he had him in his power, the

Turk coolly replied, that "all princes were not able to be away from their own states."

The position of the Swedish king now became extremely unpleasant. The sultan wished to be rid of him, and gave him large sums of money to pay his debts and make the necessary preparations to leave, but Charles spent the money in other ways, and asked for more. Then the sultan ordered his arrest; but when the Turkish officers attempted to take him he locked the doors of his house at Varnitz, and, shutting himself in with a few hundred men, he defended himself against a whole army. Many Turks were shot down in the affray, but after his house had been set on fire he was seized while escaping from the flames, and after a desperate struggle, when he fell owing to his spurs having become entangled, he was overpowered and carried by main force to a village near Adrianople, called Demotika. Here he remained for a long time in sullen inactivity, closely guarded by the Turkish Janizaries, who called him, from his obstinacy, "*Demürbasch*"— the Iron Head. For ten months he remained shut up, and generally in bed on pretence that he was dangerously ill, but when he found that he would obtain no further help from Turkey he resolved upon making his escape. Accompanied only by two persons, he succeeded in the incredibly short time of fourteen days in riding from Adrianople through Hungary, Austria, and Germany to the Swedish port of Stralsund in Pomerania, before whose gates he presented himself on the 7th of November, under the name of Captain Peder Frisch. The guard did not at first recognize the king, for he looked haggard and worn in face and shabby and dirty in person, never having changed his clothes, and scarcely having left the saddle night or day since he made his escape, excepting to exchange one wearied horse for another and fresher animal.

Charles at home.—While Charles had been shut up in a Turkish prison engaged in frivolous disputes with his guards, his enemies in the North had been dismembering his kingdom : Russia striving to secure the whole of Swedish Pomerania, while George I. of England was master of the townships of Bremen and Verden, which the Danes had sold to him as soon as they had seized those districts by force of arms from Sweden.

A Danish fleet under the brave Tordenskjold was at the same time harassing the Swedish coasts, while an allied army of Russians, Saxons, and Danes was investing Stralsund. Charles on his return refused to confirm the surrender of Bremen and Verden, and, taking the command of the garrison at Stralsund, he defended the place till the walls were blown up and the outworks reduced to ashes; then, going on board a small yacht, he crossed the Baltic, and landed safely in Skaania, although Tordenskjold was scouring the seas to prevent his passage.

The king now took up his abode at Lund, either because he wished to be near the scene of war, or because he did not like to return to his capital till he had retrieved his bad fortune. His presence in his own country forced the nobles to refrain from further attempts to secure peace, and gave new courage to the lower classes, who, in their love and devotion to their idol king, were ready to risk their all and follow him into new wars. But men fit for service were scarce in the land, and there was no money left; and in this dilemma Charles had to take lads of fifteen into the ranks, while his minister, Görtz, who was hated by the nobles for his indifference to their interests, contrived to raise funds by coining copper pieces, and selling to foreigners all the silver taken from the royal mines. During the severe winter of 1716, when the Sound was frozen over, Charles determined to carry an army over the ice into Sjælland and to invade the Danish islands; but at the moment when everything was ready for this hazardous adventure a thaw set in, and thus Denmark escaped the threatened invasion. He then directed his attacks against Norway, and advanced on Christiania; but meeting with more opposition than he had expected, he fell back and laid siege to the fortress of Frederiksten near Frederikshald. No better success awaited him there, for the citizens, under the guidance of the brothers Peder and Hans Kolbjörnsson, set fire to their own town, and thus drove the Swedes out of their quarters, and at length forced them to give up the assault. Strangely enough, it was owing to the warning given of the approach of the Swedes by Anna Kolbjörnsdatter, a member of the same family as the rescuers of Frederikshald, that Charles's plans of surprising Christiania had been defeated in the first instance; for this woman, the wife of the pastor of Norderhoug, went by night through difficult forest paths to warn the nearest Norwegian guard of the danger threatening them.

A shot strikes Charles down.—At this moment it seemed as if a thoroughly new character was about to be given to the war; for Peter the Great, being discontented with his allies and the share of the Baltic lands which he had gained for himself, showed great willingness to treat with Sweden. Charles, however, left everything in the hands of his favourite, Görtz, who had succeeded in forming an alliance with the all-powerful Alberoni, minister of Spain; and while he was preparing to lay siege to Frederikshald with an army of 30,000 young soldiers, the czar and Görtz were planning in Aaland the terms of a treaty between Sweden and Russia against the other northern powers. Although nothing certain was known abroad in regard to these plans, the meeting in Aaland was exciting much uneasiness in the North, when the sudden death of King Charles changed the current of events, and created at once a new epoch in the history of Sweden.

All that is known of the manner in which Charles XII. met his death is, that on the morning of December 11, 1718, while he was leaning over the side of a breastwork and giving orders to the men in the trenches before the fortress of Frederikshald, he was struck by a ball, which, entering one side of his head, passed out through the opposite temple. The few officers who were near him reported afterwards that they had noticed him stagger, and had seen his head sink on his breast, but that before they could raise him up he had breathed his last without uttering a sound.[1] Thus suddenly the bravest and most renowned of the Vasa line was cut down in the midst of his own people at the early age of thirty-six; and with him perished the military glory and greatness of Sweden, as well as the absolute and personal influence of the Swedish kings. His memory is cherished among the Swedes to the present day

---

[1] The common people, who idolised their king "Karl," did not believe this report, and it was soon whispered abroad that he had been struck down by treachery, and owed his death indirectly to his brother-in-law, Prince Frederick of Hesse, husband of the heiress to the throne, the Princess Ulrika.

as that of the best loved of their rulers, and his reign is looked back to with pride as "*Karolinska tiden*"—Karl's time. The love of the people for this king was not won so much by his valour and military renown as by the fortitude, cheerfulness, and sobriety with which he went through the dangers and excitements of war, and shared in all the experiences of his soldiers. The moderation with which he exercised his absolute power, his simple habits, his respect for religion, his love for national customs, the many useful changes which he effected in the public administration of the laws and in the government offices, and the moral purity of his life in an age of great corruption, all combined to win the respect and admiration of his people. Charles's remains were buried in the Riddarholmkirka, where his mortuary chapel, with its mouldering trophies, stands immediately opposite the grave of his great predecessor and model in war, Gustavus Adolphus.

PART III.

SWEDEN UNDER A GERMAN PRINCE.

Sweden after Charles's death.—Charles XII. left no will, and had made no settlement in regard to the succession, and hence at his death it became a question whether the crown should devolve upon his sister, Ulrika, or his nephew, Charles Frederick of Holstein-Gottorp, the son of his elder sister, Hedvig Sofia, who, in the absence of direct heirs, were the nearest in the line of succession. The claims of both were open to doubt, but the Princess Ulrika secured her own election by inducing the Council of State to do homage to her immediately on the death of her brother, on her promising to renounce absolute authority and to rule by the will of the diet. The nobles, glad of the opportunity to recover their lost influence, drew up a strict compact, which left little or no power to the crown, and secured the majority of the votes in the diet to their own order in the state. The queen, although a proud woman of impatient and self-willed disposition, agreed to all the terms proposed for her acceptance; and as soon as she could, she drove her nephew, Charles Frederick of Holstein, out of Sweden, and forced him to seek safety at the court of the czar, Peter, who, however, received him well, and gave him his daughter the Grand Duchess Anna in marriage.

In the meanwhile Ulrika's husband, Prince Frederick of Hesse, had taken the chief command of the army on the death of the king, and, having withdrawn all the troops from Norway, he prepared to negotiate terms of peace with the allies. His next step was to arrest Görtz, who was equally hateful to him and to the nobles. The fallen minister was seized while returning from Aaland and carried to Stockholm, where he was brought before a military commission, composed of his enemies, and, contrary to the provisions of the laws, was condemned to death on the sole authority of the queen, without being allowed to defend himself from the charges of treason advanced against him.

Frederick I., 1720-1750.—Queen Ulrika, with the consent of the diet of 1720, resigned the supreme power into the hands of her husband, who thenceforth, till his death in 1750, ruled Sweden under the title of Frederick I. His long reign was a period of humiliation, during which Sweden had to make peace on the most disadvantageous terms with her enemies, and to give up all the great conquests which she had won at the price of so much blood. By the peace of Nystad in 1721, Russia obtained Ingermanland, Esthonia, Livonia, and East Karelia for two million rix dollars, which the czar paid to the Swedish crown, and which proved a very poor return for the lives and money sacrificed in the conquest and defence of these lands during so many ages. Finland was reduced to a desert, and Sweden had now sunk so low that, from being the leading power in the north, she was unable to protect her own shores.

The death of Charles XII. proved an important turning-point in the history of Sweden. Old times were gone, and little more than the memory of past conquests and of glorious victories was now left to the Swedes; while in the new era that was opening before them there was nothing in the national history of the monarchy to rouse the energies or awaken the sympathies of the people. The internal arrangements, form, and spirit of the government were completely re-modelled at the diet of 1720, when the nobles obtained from King Frederick, as the price of their allegiance, a *konunga forsäkran*, or royal assurance, by which he agreed to the withdrawal of absolute power from the crown. By the new form of government settled in 1720 all power passed from the hands of the king to that of the nobles, who shut out the lower orders from any share in the administration of public affairs. Parties were soon formed amongst the nobles, whose struggles to supplant one another in the diets of the Estates kept the country in a state of constant disquiet. Some good was, however, done in this reign, for trade was encouraged, skilful workmen were brought to the country, and many plants, hitherto unknown to the Swedes, amongst which the most important was the potato, were introduced. Under Horn, the code of laws which had been begun in the time of Charles XI. was completed, and formally approved in the diet of 1734.

The Hats and Caps.[1]—In 1738 the Hats of Horn had to give way to the Caps of Count Gyllenborg, who, renouncing the more cautious policy of the former minister, entered into an alliance with France against Russia. The French government, which wanted to secure the aid of Sweden, had helped to foment the national hatred of the people against the Russians, which had been strongly excited by the murder of Major Malcolm Sinclair while on his way from a mission to Turkey, entrusted to him by the king of Sweden, and who was believed to have been killed by orders of the czar. Without considering the unprotected state of the kingdom, and influenced only by national hatred, the Swedes rushed hastily into a war with Russia in 1741. The loss of Finland, a great defeat at Vilmanstrand, and the capitulation of the Swedish army to the Russians at Helsingsfors, only made the nation more fierce against their powerful foes; and nothing but the condemnation and execution of the two chief commanders,

---

[1] These parties were known in Swedish as *Hattar* "the hats," and *Nattmössor* "the nightcaps."

Generals Levenhaupt and Buddenbrock, could satisfy the rage of the Swedish people. But in spite of the national wish for vengeance, Sweden was forced to sue for peace, and by the treaty of Abo in 1743 she had to resign eastern Finland to Russia, and even to submit to the degradation of begging for help from the czar against Denmark, and to receive 10,000 Russians as protectors within her frontiers. While these disastrous events were passing, King Frederick gave himself up to his amusements, and showed no concern for the humiliating position in which he and his kingdom were placed. As he was childless, the question of the succession had to be considered. The party of the Hats favoured the claims of the young Karl Peter Ulrich, son of the Holstein-Gottorp prince, Karl Frederick; but when they found that he had been chosen to succeed his mother's sister, the Empress Elizabeth, on the throne of Russia, they by her wish gave their votes in favour of another Holstein-Gottorp prince, Adolf Frederick. The diet of 1743 confirmed the election of Adolf Frederick, and on the death, in 1750, of the easy-tempered, pleasure-loving king Frederick I., he ascended the throne of Sweden.

Humiliation of King and Queen.—The twenty years during which Adolf Frederick reigned over the Swedish people, from 1751 to 1771, were marked by the increasing decline of the kingdom. The king was a mere puppet in the hands of the council and the nobles, and the regal power existed only in name. An attempt by Counts Horn and Brahe in 1756 to give more weight to the authority of the crown brought the leaders to the scaffold, and exposed the king and his queen, Louisa Ulrika of Prussia, to still further humiliations. The council drew Sweden into the Seven Years' War which was being carried on against Frederick II. of Prussia, but so feeble had been the efforts of the Swedish armies, that the Prussian king had some grounds for his sarcastic observation when peace was concluded at Hamburg in 1762, "that he was not aware he had been at war with Sweden." The Hats, who were in office at the time of this inglorious war and mortifying peace, became so unpopular in Sweden that they had to give up their power in favour of the Caps, but the change of ministers brought no amendment to the state of public affairs, although by the intro-

duction of freedom of the press the discontented party had a
better opportunity of making their complaints heard. The
weak but well-meaning king, after making an attempt to lay
down the crown, which the nobles would not allow, died in
1771, at the moment when party differences were the strongest,
and the country seemed on the eve of a revolution.

CHAPTER XXV.

SWEDEN FROM 1771 TO 1872.

Gustavus III. first of the native-born line of Holstein-Gottorp—His education—His character—Qualities and failings—His success in recovering nearly absolute power for the crown—His early efforts for his country—His vanity—Love of French manners—Expensive travels—Folly in going to war with Russia—The result—Mutiny of Anjala—The king's success in securing his own authority—Result of war—Lack of money—Discontent of the nation—Conspiracy—Gustavus assassinated at a masquerade—Ankerström—His escape—The king's sufferings and death—His fortitude—The Regency—Duke Charles—His policy—His favourites—The young king's betrothal interrupted—His marriage—His rule without Regency—His character—His religious fancies—Aversion to Napoleon, "the Great Beast"—Gustavus IV. joins coalition against France—French generals in Pomerania—The Great Powers make peace with Napoleon—War in Finland—War with Denmark feebly maintained—English auxiliaries leave without helping the Swedes—Napoleon's contingent equally inactive in Denmark—Conspiracy to force Gustavus IV. to abdicate—Driven out of Sweden—His death—Diet deliberates—Gives the crown to Duke Charles—A successor chosen, who dies—Napoleon consulted as to a second successor to childless Charles XIII.—Bernadotte, General and Marshal of France, at length allowed to accept title of heir apparent—Goes to Sweden—Takes the command of affairs—Depressed condition of Sweden—Previous loss of Finland and Aaland—Bernadotte joins Russia against France—Rewarded by annexation of Norway—Pays off national debt—Bernadotte succeeds as Charles XIV.—His reign—His merits and demerits—The result of his rule—Condition of prosperity in Sweden—Oscar I.—His character—Early measures—Policy—Helps the Danes—Encourages Scandinavian unity—State of Norway—Charles XV. continues the same policy—Settlement of government for joint kingdoms—Death—Succession of present king, Oscar II.

PART I.

THE SWEDISH LINE OF KINGS.

Gustavus (Gustaf) III., 1771-1792.—With Gustavus III., son of the late king Adolphus Frederick of Holstein-Gottorp, a native born royal dynasty was established in Sweden. This young king, who had been carefully brought up under the guidance of his tutor, Tessin, was handsome in person and graceful in his movements; accomplished, eloquent, possessed of great imaginative powers, impressed with exaggerated ideas of the importance of his rank, and moved by a strong desire to emulate the renown of his predecessors and restore Sweden to its former place in European history. Gustavus was in Paris when the tidings of his father's death reached him, and, hastening back to Stockholm, he was crowned king with much display. At that time he was twenty-five years of age, and his first thought was how to free himself from the thraldom in which he was held by the nobles. He found that a large party in the state were willing to help him in this design; in furtherance of which one of his chief adherents, Captain Hellichius, proposed to get up a mock revolt to give him the opportunity of collecting a large body of troops. The scheme succeeded, and by help of the guard, who had been gained over to his side, Gustavus arrested the council, called together the troops, and laid before the diet a *new form of administration*, which the members were forced to sign, as the burghers of Stockholm had declared in his favour, and they were at the mercy of the soldiers. By these bold steps Gustavus effected, without bloodshed, a complete revolution in the state, and secured for himself the administrative power, while he left to the diet the right of approving or rejecting declarations of war, with the control of the taxes, and of the modes of administering the laws. The king used his powers at first with moderation, while he liberally rewarded all his supporters, more especially Hellichius, who was made a count under the title of Gustavskjold.

Gustavus laboured diligently during the first ten years of his reign to improve the army and navy, and he made himself generally popular by the ease of his manners, and the readiness he showed to receive and listen to the personal appeals of his poorest subjects. He, moreover, effected some useful changes in the government, but his vanity and love of amusement marred all his good qualities, while his aping of French manners and fashions, and the favour he showed to foreign actors, singers, and dancers, had a bad effect on public morals, and threatened to destroy the national simplicity of the Swedes. French became in this reign the language of the court and of society, theatres and an opera-house were opened at Stockholm, where only French pieces were given; and in all the concerns of life Gustavus tried to make himself conspicuous by the adoption of Parisian manners and by his elegance and polished taste. But his costly foreign travels, during which he squandered large sums of money on objects of art, while his subjects at home were suffering from famine, murrain, and distress of all kinds, and his extravagance in raising showy regiments of horse guards merely for his own gratification, excited much ill-will amongst his subjects.

Gustavus's folly in declaring war against Russia in 1788 ended in extreme mortification to himself, for although at the outset the absence of the Russian army, which was engaged in war with Turkey, enabled the Swedish king, as he had anticipated, to advance on St. Petersburg without being intercepted in his march, the empress, Katherine II., had the address to thwart all his plans. She succeeded in winning over a number of disaffected Swedish officers, who, while encamped at Anjala, a little town on the Swedish frontier of Finland, formed a plot to oppose the king's orders for their advance upon Russia, declaring that they considered the war illegal, since it had been undertaken without the consent of the Estates. At the same time, the empress induced Denmark to form an alliance with Russia, and to send an army into southern Sweden, while Gustavus was in the north of his kingdom with all the troops he could muster. When he received the declaration of war from Denmark, he exclaimed, "I am betrayed;" and, leaving Finland, he hastened into Dalekarlia and appealed in person to the loyalty of the Dalesmen, who rose in a body and followed him to Göteborg, which was being besieged by a Danish army. The intervention of the Prussian and English envoys forced the Danes, however, to withdraw from the Swedish territories, and Gustavus was relieved from a threatening danger.

Gustavus gains absolute power.—The mutiny of the officers in Finland had excited great indignation in the country against the nobles, to which class they all belonged; and the king availed himself of the general sympathy shown him to appeal to the diet; and by means of his personal eloquence and the efforts of his friends, he obtained so great an increase of power allowed him by an act known as the *Safety measure*, that he became almost absolute. The conspirators were mildly dealt with, and only their leader, Colonel Hestesko, suffered death for his treason. In the meanwhile the empress had been busied in fitting out a powerful fleet and armies to carry on the war against Sweden; and although King Gustavus could boast of one great victory at sea, in which the enemy lost 55 ships and 12,000 men, he had himself in a previous engagement lost many of his best men-of-war and 7,000 men; and seeing how impossible it would be to carry on the war against such a power as Russia, he was glad to make peace in 1790, and resume the position which he had occupied before the war.

Gustavus assassinated.—Gustavus next turned his thoughts to the useless project of trying to restore the Bourbon family to the throne of France, and wished to send a fleet to attack the French coast, while he even conceived the flattering notion that he might act as commander-in-chief of the Prussian and Austrian armies, which were to attempt to crush the revolutionary government of the French people. To carry out these grand schemes money was needed, but when he called a diet to consult with the Estates in regard to the manner in which the necessary supplies were to be obtained, they refused even to consider the question. His incessant demands for money, and his wastefulness while the country was nearly crushed with debt raised much dissatisfaction, and a conspiracy was formed against him amongst the highest nobles of the kingdom. The leaders in the plot were the Counts Ribbing, Horn, Pechlin, and Bjelke; but the person selected to carry out their design of assassinating the king was a man of inferior rank, called Ankerström, possessed of a daring and vindictive temper, who had formerly served in the army, and who hated Gustavus for private reasons. On the night of March 16, 1792, at a masquerade held in the Opera House, Ankerström approached the king and discharged a pistol into his side, and then disappeared in the crowd, while the remainder of the conspirators, disguised in black masks and cloaks, rushed in a body towards the doors of the hall. Gustavus called out as the shot struck him, "I am wounded; seize the traitor;" but when his attendants on recognizing his voice pressed around him, he declared that he did not think he had been hurt. The result proved, however, that he had been fatally wounded, and after suffering extreme agony for thirteen days in consequence of the jagged and rough surfaces of the broken bits of lead with which the pistol had been charged, he died on 29th of March, 1792, at the age of forty-six.

Gustavus showed great fortitude in his sufferings, and devoted his last hours to the settlement of the affairs of his kingdom. He appointed a regency for his only son, then scarcely fourteen years old; and named his brother, Duke Charles, to be president or chief director of the administration. The duke was an able, upright man, but he had visionary ideas on many subjects, and had no confidence in his own judgment, which led him to intrust all important matters of state to his favourite. Baron Reuterholm, who by his haughty, overbearing temper soon drew upon himself the dislike of the old friends of the former king. The regent showed great indulgence to most of the conspirators concerned in his brother's murder, but Ankerström was made to expiate his crime by a barbarous and cruel mode of death, and bore the infliction of his sentence with a fortitude worthy of a better cause. In nearly all respects the regent followed a policy directly opposite to that of his brother, and he entered into an alliance with the leaders of the French republic, assuring them of his good-will; while he joined the Danish king in forming a compact of armed neutrality for the defence of the shipping of their respective kingdoms. By these measures, Sweden gave offence to Russia, and a war between the two countries was only averted for the time by a proposal made by Baron Reuterholm to the empress, that the young king should marry her granddaughter, the Grand Duchess Alexandra. Gustavus went to St. Petersburg with his uncle, and everything seemed settled for the betrothal of the young couple, which was to be publicly announced at a court ball. But when the evening appointed for the ceremony arrived, and the empress, surrounded by her court, was ready to receive the young king, he did not appear, and after waiting for him for several hours, the company dispersed. The duke then had to explain to the imperial family that his nephew had refused to sign the marriage contract, because it secured to the future queen the free exercise of her own religion, and allowed her to have a chapel fitted up in accordance with the rules of the Greek Church, to which she belonged. The empress refused after that to hold any further communications with the young king, who therefore had to return to Sweden without celebrating his betrothal. He soon afterwards chose a wife for himself, and in 1796 was married with much state to the Princess Frederika of Baden, who was only sixteen at the time. This princess, who was celebrated for her great beauty and her sprightly disposition, was a Lutheran like himself, and therefore Gustavus was not called upon in marrying her to make any concessions of which his conscience disapproved.

PART II.

TROUBLES IN SWEDEN.

Gustavus IV., 1792–1809.—The first act of Gustavus after he began to reign independently of the regency was to dismiss all who were known to be supporters of the duke, and to recall his father's former friends and companions. At first his people had great hopes of having better times under him, for he was simple in his habits, very averse to show or extravagance, and upright in his conduct; but they soon found that his pride and obstinacy led him to take steps which proved most calamitous to his kingdom. The main cause of his troubles was the strong aversion which he felt towards Napoleon, and his resolution to devote all his energies to the ruin of the emperor. Gustavus had taken up some strange ideas in regard to the meaning of prophecy, and he looked upon Buonaparte as the Great Beast spoken of in Revelation. At first the Swedish king's conduct excited only ridicule, and was looked upon as a proof of his religious insanity; but when he joined *The Triple Coalition*, formed by Austria, Russia, and England against France, Napoleon sent an army under his general,

Marshal Brun, to seize upon Swedish Pomerania and drive the Swedes out of this last of their German possessions. Soon afterwards Gustavus brought still greater troubles upon Sweden itself by opening his ports to English ships without heeding the conditions of a compact which Russia, Prussia, and other lesser powers had been forced to make with Napoleon at Tilsit in 1807 to keep British traders out of foreign markets. As Gustavus continued in defiance of all warning to keep up an active trade with the English, and to allow them to make Göteborg a free port for their trading ships, Russia declared war against Sweden, and the Russian emperor, Alexander, sent an army into Finland, which thenceforth became the chief theatre of the war in 1808-9. The Swedes, under Adlerkreuz, fought with desperate valour, and gained several great victories; but the overwhelming numbers of the enemy forced them to fall back, and at last to evacuate the whole of Finland. Gustavus, more interested in finding passages in Scripture that pointed, as he believed, to the French emperor, than in attending to the welfare of his people, left the army to melt away before the Russian forces; and when, by the treachery of its commandant, the fortress of Sveaborg, which was regarded as impregnable, was given up to the enemy, the fate of Finland was decided, and the whole of northern Sweden was laid open to the attacks of the Russians.

While these events were passing, war was being feebly carried on between Sweden and Denmark on the Norwegian frontiers, where the Danish stadtholder, Prince Christian of Augustenburg, drove back the Swedes under their commander Armfeldt. England sent troops to help Sweden, and Napoleon threw an army under General Bernadotte into Jutland, on pretence of supporting Denmark. The English forces, numbering 10,000 men, which were under the command of Sir Thomas Moore, returned, however, to England without striking a blow, as soon as it was found that Gustavus wanted to send them into Finland to fight against the Russians, while the French and Spaniards in Napoleon's army did nothing to help Denmark; and after a year spent by them in mutiny and in pillaging the Jutlanders, disappeared from the provinces without having done any fighting except among themselves.

Gustavus forced to abdicate.—The unhappy results of the Russian war and the senseless obstinacy of Gustavus, which nearly brought him into a quarrel with his best ally, England, excited universal anger in the minds of the Swedes against their king, and a conspiracy was formed to force him to abdicate, which consisted of a large number of officers, headed by the Generals Adlerkreuz and Adlersparre. The object of the conspirators was at first not merely to remove the king, but to unite Sweden and Norway under the rule of the Danish stadtholder, Prince Christian Augustus of Augustenburg, who is believed to have been aware of the plot, and to have given his sanction to it. At all events the prince allowed the war to be carried on in a very inactive manner against Sweden, and consented to a truce with Adlersparre, immediately after which the latter hurried to Stockholm to carry out his designs. On the evening of the 13th of March, 1809, while Adlersparre was keeping his troops under arms before the gates of Stockholm, Adlerkreuz with six attendants entered the king's apartment and announced to him that he had come in the name of the army to insist that the king should not carry out the design which he had in view of going to Skaania to superintend preparations for further hostilities, since the Swedes would not go on with these useless wars. Gustavus on hearing this drew his sword, and called aloud for "help against traitors," but Adlerkreuz's men closed in around him and disarmed him. After an hour's detention he succeeded in making his escape through a concealed door in the wainscoting, and hurried into the courtyard to rouse the watch. He was, however, pursued and carried back to his apartments, and the following day conveyed under a strong guard to the palace of Drottningholm, where he was forced to sign a deed, renouncing the Swedish throne for himself and all his descendants. No attempt was made from any quarter to help him, and in the same year he was formally banished the kingdom, and forced to leave the country. After wandering about the Continent and leading a strange, restless life, he died in obscurity in the year 1837 at St. Gall, in Switzerland, under the name of Colonel Gustafsson, which he had assumed on leaving Sweden.

PART III.

GREAT CHANGES IN SWEDEN.

Charles XIII., 1809-1818.—When this new revolution had been completed without bloodshed or disturbance of any kind, the Estates met, and in accordance with the general wishes of the nation invited Duke Charles of Sodermanland to undertake the administration until more lasting arrangements could be made for the disposition of public affairs. In a diet held in 1809, Gustavus IV. was declared to have forfeited the crown, and Duke Charles was proclaimed king, after having agreed to accept the charter drawn up by the Estates, which gave to the sovereign the administrative power, and left to the diet, which was thenceforth to consist of the four orders of nobles, clergy, burghers, and peasants, the right of legislation and the power of assessing taxes. At this diet the Danish Stadtholder of Norway, Prince Christian Augustus of Augustenburg, was elected successor to the childless king, Charles XIII., as a reward for his friendly conduct towards Sweden during the late war with Denmark. This prince had carried his goodwill so far that, in defiance of stringent orders from the Danish king, Frederick VI., to advance, he had abstained from attacking Vermland when his road lay open to that province. Peace was concluded between Sweden and Denmark at the close of 1809, when the Augustenburg prince went to Stockholm, and, under the name of Charles Augustus, was received by the people as their future king. His sudden death at a review near Helsingborg in the spring of the following year excited a very strong feeling among the citizens of Stockholm, to whom he had greatly endeared himself, and, under the idea that he had been poisoned, a great disturbance broke out on the day of his funeral. The suspicion of the populace was chiefly directed against the old, rich, and proud Count Axel Fersen, who was much disliked for the haughtiness of his manners; and in their fury they literally tore him to pieces, and could scarcely be kept from treating the prince's medical attendants with equal cruelty.

After the death of Charles Augustus, the government proposed to take his brother as successor to the throne, and sent the young Baron Mörner to Paris to inform Napoleon of their purpose. This young man, however, like many others of his rank, had a great wish to see his native country brought more closely into connection with France, and, thinking to please the emperor, he proposed that one of his French generals should be chosen king of Sweden. Napoleon appeared at first to be gratified by this proposal, but when Baron Mörner suggested Jean Bernadotte (Prince de Ponte Corvo) as the best fitted for the dignity, and, after receiving the consent of the diet, begged the emperor to sanction their choice, difficulties were thrown in the way, and some time passed before the Swedish envoy could obtain a definite reply, and when at length Napoleon gave the marshal permission, it was coupled with the ominous farewell words, "Go, then, and let us fulfil our several destinies." Marshal Jean Bernadotte, who was in the prime of life when he was thus suddenly and unexpectedly adopted as a member of the Swedish royal family and proclaimed successor to the throne, was a man of ability, judgment, and resolution, besides being one of the bravest and most successful of Napoleon's generals. On his arrival in Sweden he at once renounced Catholicism, and was admitted into the Lutheran Church; and assuming the management of affairs as the first prince of the realm, he, without delay, turned his mind to the task of raising the kingdom from the deplorable condition into which it had fallen. At the moment of Bernadotte's arrival, Sweden was utterly and helplessly at the mercy of the great Powers, and may be said to have been little better than a dependency of France. Napoleon, after forcing her to declare war on England, and being offended at the want of vigour with which hostilities were carried on, retook Swedish Pomerania, which had been restored for a time to Sweden, and made known to the British and Russian governments that he did not care to what extent Sweden was dismembered. This humiliating insult roused the spirit of Bernadotte, who exclaimed, when he learnt what the emperor had done, "Napoleon has himself thrown down the gauntlet, and I will take it up!" and he forthwith began to prepare in earnest for the struggle which he saw was coming.

Position of Sweden.—Never at any time had Sweden been in a worse condition for taking part in war. Charles XIII., after fitting out an army to defend the northern frontier, had found it impossible to continue the struggle, and in 1809—the same year in which he came to the throne—he had had to make a peace with Russia, which cost Sweden one-third of her entire area, by depriving her of Aaland and of the whole of Finland, after that province had been more than 600 years united with her, and had shared with her in all those great wars which had for a time raised the Swedish monarchy to the rank of one of the most renowned powers of Europe. An unfavourable peace with Denmark had closely followed on the loss of Finland, and when Bernadotte, or "Prince Karl Johan," as he was generally called, came to Sweden, the state had been bound hand and foot by the treaty of Paris, and Napoleon now thought that he held the Swedish king and people completely in bondage. It was reserved, however, for the emperor's old brother-in-arms to rescue the unhappy kingdom from these bonds, for the new prince, by entering into a secret treaty with Alexander of Russia, secured safety on his weakest boundaries, and by joining heart and soul in the war in Germany against Napoleon after his fatal retreat from Moscow, gained the gratitude of the allied powers, who at the close of those terrible struggles, which ended in the total defeat of the French emperor, rewarded the fidelity of Sweden at the cost of Denmark by the annexation of Norway.

The Norwegians, as we have seen in a former chapter, were not at first willing to transfer their allegiance from Denmark to Sweden, and for a time they cherished the hope of being able again to raise their country to the rank of an independent kingdom; but neither they nor the Danish prince, Christian Frederick, whom they proclaimed king, could cope with the Swedes under such a skilful commander as Bernadotte. In 1814 the Swedish army entered Southern Norway, while the Swedish fleet cruised along the coast, and the Norwegians, driven from one point to another, had to submit. The Danish prince left the country, and Charles XIII. was declared joint king of Sweden and Norway before the close of 1814. In the following year the union was completed by the so-called

Riksakt, or act of the realm, by which the respective functions of the Swedish "Riksdag," or diet, and the Norwegian "Storthing" were clearly defined, and the various obligations of the two countries settled. Sweden, by the decree of the Congress of Vienna in 1814-1815, was empowered to give up the whole of her Pomeranian territories to Prussia in exchange for 4,800,000 rix dollars, and this money Bernadotte, with the consent of the diet, used to pay off the various foreign loans which the Swedish government had incurred, and thus gave Sweden the advantage, which few other countries enjoyed, of being free from a state debt.

PART IV.

A FRENCH LINE OF KINGS.

Charles XIV., 1818-1844.—Charles XIII. was never much more than a cipher in the state, and public affairs had been so completely under the control of Bernadotte since his arrival in the country in 1810, that the death of the king in 1818 made very little real change in the administration. Bernadotte, who reigned over Sweden from 1818 till 1844 under the title of Charles XIV., by his able rule fully justified the choice that the Swedes had made, for as soon as he could secure peace he devoted his energies to the internal improvement of his kingdom, which now rapidly recovered from the exhaustion of the late wars, and learnt to develope her own great natural resources. The Swedish people never forgot what they owed "Karl Johan" for his successful efforts in raising them from the depressed condition in which he found their country to one of stability and comparative prosperity. But as time passed, and men found that the burgher-king whom they had placed upon the throne showed an obvious disinclination to extend general political freedom, while he preferred and favoured the nobles at the expense of the lower orders, the nation at large lost much of their first enthusiastic and devoted loyalty, and towards the end of his life Charles John certainly cannot be said to have been a popular king. His openly-shown dread of treason, his persecution of all liberal writers, his opposition to the adoption of reforms in the government, and his ignorance of the language of the country, all contributed to produce a feeling of discontent and impatience among the people during the latter years of this reign. The period of Charles John's rule is, however, one of immense importance in the history of Sweden, and is marked by improvements in every form of the national life of the people. Trade and commerce increased, canals, roads, and bridges opened the country in every direction, colleges and higher schools sprang up in all the towns, and parochial national schools brought education within reach of the poorest in the land ; while, amongst others, the names of Berzelius, the chemist, Gejer, the historian, Tegner, the poet, and Fogelberg, the sculptor, afford honourable testimony to the scientific, literary, and artistic progress of the Swedes during this period.

Oscar I., 1844-1859.—When Charles XIV. died in 1844, at the age of eighty, he left by his early marriage with a French lady of Marseilles, called Désirée Clary, an only son, who succeeded him under the title of Oscar I. At the first diet held by the new king in 1844-1845, he fully confirmed the expectations which the people had formed of his liberal views, by giving his consent to acts for the improvement of the mode of electing the members of the "Riksdag" and the "Storthing," for the greater freedom of the press, and for securing equal rights of heritage to brothers and sisters. So well did King Oscar and his people understand each other that the disturbances created in almost every European state by the French Revolution of 1848, scarcely affected the Swedes, who during the whole of this reign continued to enjoy peace and a greater amount of personal security and individual prosperity than their forefathers had ever known. By the formation of a network of railways, carried out at the cost and under the management of the government, the country, which was already intersected by splendid canals, and had been made easy of access by means of the steam navigation of the great lakes, was thrown open in every direction, and under this newer state of things the foreign commerce and the home trade of Sweden have increased enormously. Although, from the nature of the country and its more severe climate, Norway has not gained as much in these respects as the sister kingdom, the Norwegians have prospered since their union with the Swedes, and are as remarkable as ever for the intellectual vigour and sturdy independence which more than a thousand years ago made their forefathers masters of every land against which they turned their arms, and which since then has enabled them to hold on to fixed principles of social equality through all the changes of their political existence.

Scandinavian Unity.—The long peace had the effect of deadening old jealousies and drawing the Scandinavian nations more closely together; and this better state of feeling, which began among the students of the different countries, was powerfully aided by King Oscar, who encouraged international meetings for scientific, literary, or other objects, which he regarded as the best means of preventing future wars between the Northern peoples. In the struggle carried on by the Danish king, Frederick VII., against his Slesvig-Holstein subjects, King Oscar sent troops to help him, and gave his cordial approval to those amongst his own people who wished to serve as volunteers in the Danish ranks. At the same time, King Oscar was anxious to keep his kingdom at peace, and when the Crimean War broke out he tried to remain neutral, but after a time, finding himself forced to side with one party or the other, he entered, in 1855, into an alliance with England and France against Russia, in return for which he secured a promise of support from those powers in case his kingdom should at any time be attacked by the Russians. At the close of the Crimean War a compact was entered into between Sweden and Denmark, mainly in consequence of the personal friendship of the kings, Oscar and Frederick, who wished to establish such relations of mutual affection between their subjects as to make war thenceforth impossible among Scandinavian brothers.

In 1857, King Oscar, whose health had long been feeble, resigned the administration into the hands of the crown prince, his eldest son Charles, and, after lingering for two years, he died in 1859, deeply regretted by his people, who justly regard him as one of the most patriotic and enlightened of their kings in modern times. By his queen, Josephine of Leuchtenburg, granddaughter of the French empress Josephine, Oscar left, besides one daughter, four sons, of whom two, Charles and Oscar, have succeeded him on the throne of Sweden.

Charles XV., 1859-1872.—Charles XV. continued the policy of his father, King Oscar I., and at the diet of 1859-1860 he approved of the measures proposed for giving a more liberal form to the government, and encouraged the extension of the railway system. Differences soon sprang up between the Swedish Riksdag and the Norwegian Storthing, which for a time threatened to cause serious evils, and the Norwegian people showed great jealousy of the subordinate position which, according to their view, they held in the representation of the national chambers, but the angry excitement subsided nearly as quickly as it had sprung up, and in 1864 the two people celebrated with mutual good-will the fiftieth anniversary of the union of Sweden and Norway.

In 1866 a new form of government was finally agreed upon for the two kingdoms. In accordance with the system then adopted, and which still continues in force, the Swedish diet is to consist of two chambers and to meet annually. The first chamber is composed of members chosen for nine years by the Landsthing of each province and by the civic authorities in some of the larger towns; while the second chamber is filled by members chosen by universal suffrage to decide upon special questions. The king can dissolve the chambers when he likes, and demand a new election.

Charles XV., at his death in 1872, left only one child, the Princess Louisa, wife of the present Crown Prince of Denmark, and he was succeeded by his next brother, who reigns under the title of Oscar II. of Sweden and Norway.

CHAPTER XXVI.

DENMARK SINCE 1839.

Frederick VI., King of Denmark, succeeded by Christian VIII.—Expectations of the people—Character of the King—Disappointment of the Danes—Christian's merits—His unpopular policy in regard to Holstein and Slesvig—Disputes in regard to use of Danish in the Duchies—Lornsen's measure—The Augustenburg Princes—The King's ill-placed confidence in them—The Prince of Nöer's appointment cancelled—The question of the succession—How settled—The calm followed by outbreak of storm—The Germanizing influences at work—Dahlmann's discovery of original draft of Charter—Influence of discovery—Christian's death—Frederick VII.—Troubles—Rebellion in Duchies—False news circulated by Frederick, Prince of Nöer—Prussia interferes and keeps up strife — War in Holstein — Confederate troops outnumber Danes—Wrangel retaliates on Danes—Prussians recalled—Truce of Malmö—War breaks out again—Rye and the other Danish generals—Their conduct—Frederitz relieved—Another truce—Duchies governed by commissioners—Confederate troops—Peace with Prussia—Denmark puts down rebellion—Willisen commands Holstein troops—Is defeated by Danes at Isted, in Slesvig—Joint Commission governs Holstein—Assembly frame Constitution—Its nature—The Rigsdag—Mode of election—Great liberty of Danes—Question of succession—Choice of Prince Christian of Glücksburg—Ten years to death of the king—Troubles at home—Interference from abroad—Prussia supports the Augustenburg claims—Renunciation of family to all claims in the Duchies—Compact broken—Frederick VII. dies suddenly—Christian IX.—Troubles in Duchies—War renewed—England mediates, but does not help—Denmark fights unaided—Subdued by Prussian arms—Austria cedes rights acquired in the former war to Prussia after her defeat in 1866—Prussia evades conditions—King William of Prussia drops pretensions of the Augustenburg Princes—Is crowned Emperor—Realization of the dream of German unification—Denmark recovers herself—Her prosperity—Her complete freedom.

PART I.

THE LANGUAGE TROUBLE.

Christian VIII., 1839-1848.—As Frederick VI. left no son he was succeeded by his cousin, Christian VIII. The coming of this prince to the throne was hailed with joy by the entire Danish nation, who believed that in him they would find a ruler of liberal and advanced views. But the great expectations of the people were only partially satisfied, for although King Christian was a man of talent, aptitude for literary research, and of varied scientific information, and was known to be well versed in all the political questions of the day, he showed from the moment of his accession a reluctance to pledge himself to any liberal measure, and a resolute determination to stand by the old prerogatives of the crown, which caused universal disappointment and fear for the future. The relations between the king and the chambers became more and more unfriendly during each year of his reign, and although he effected many improvements in the government, reduced the national debt from 124 to 104 millions rix dollars, encouraged the promotion of learning and extension of schools, and impressed a new and more enlightened spirit into the public institutions of the country, the people remained unsatisfied, and the press, in defiance of restrictions and severe penalties, continued to give circulation to works of decided reactionary character. The most important cause of popular dissatisfaction against the king was his unpatriotic policy in regard to Slesvig and Holstein, where the most flagrant acts of disobedience to the orders of the crown on the part of the provincial authorities—which had not unfrequently proceeded to the length of open treason—were allowed to pass unpunished.

The questions of school-management and of the language which should be used by preachers and teachers in the duchies had become serious causes of dissension between all political parties in the kingdom as early as 1836, when a Slesvig peasant, Nils Lornsen, a member of the Assembly of the States at Slesvig, made a motion that Danish should be established by law as the language for legal and administrative purposes in every part of the duchy, where it was the predominant tongue used in the pulpits and schools. This proposition met with violent opposition from all the great landowners of the duchies, who, through the negligence and indifference of successive Danish governments, had been allowed to bring German teachers and preachers into the parishes over which they had manorial or other rights. Although Lornsen motion passed by a small majority, it made little difference in the condition of things, and soon the question of a separate independence for Slesvig and Holstein was openly brought forward by the German leaders of the anti-Danish party. The chief movers in this matter were Duke Christian of Augustenburg and his brother, Prince Frederick of Nöer, who, by their personal influence, through anonymous writings, and by other direct as well as indirect means, laboured for the complete severance of the provinces from the mother-land.

Great ill-will and suspicion were therefore excited against the king when he raised the Prince of Nöer, in 1842, to the rank of Stadtholder and commander-in-chief in Slesvig and Holstein, and made him president of the government of the duchies. As the queen, Caroline Amalia, was a sister of the Augustenburg princes, this appointment was thought to be due to her influence, and was looked upon as so injurious to the cause of the Danes in the Slesvig-Holstein provinces, that it drew forth violent and angry remonstrances in every part of the Danish islands. Some of the ministers resigned in consequence, and general discontent prevailed; but the king paid no attention to the dissatisfaction, and, declaring that he had entire confidence in the honour of the Augustenburg princes, he further displeased and surprised his Danish subjects by giving the posts of chancellor and foreign secretary for the duchies to the Counts Joseph and Heinrik Reventlow Criminil, the devoted friends of the duke and his brother, Prince Frederick. This fresh proof of the king's favour gave the greatest satisfaction and encouragement to the Augustenburg party and to all the malcontents, who at the following meeting of the Assembly at Slesvig were emboldened to propose that steps should be taken for the admission of Slesvig into the German Confederation, in anticipation of which the use of the Danish language was to be suppressed in the duchies, and the Danish flag, the *Dannebrog*, was to be replaced by a special flag for the united state of Slesvig-Holstein. These treasonable propositions called forth the strongest expressions of resentment among the patriotic Danes, and petitions against the outrage done to the language and flag of the kingdom poured in upon Christian VIII., who in his replies showed a want of interest in the concerns and wishes of his Danish subjects that filled the country with consternation. The ill-will and suspicion generated by these proceedings were somewhat allayed in 1846, when the king deprived Prince Frederick of Nöer of the important posts which had been intrusted to him in 1842. This change of policy, which restored temporary order to the duchies, had been forced upon the king by the pretensions of the Duke of Augustenburg to rights of succession in Slesvig, and by his protests against the open royal letter published in 1846, in which Christian VIII. had set forth the order of succession to the throne of Denmark in accordance with the opinion given by a commission called together to consider the question. In this document Slesvig was declared to be an indivisible and integral part of the Danish monarchy; but the title to certain portions of Holstein was admitted to be open to dispute, and was therefore left for further consideration.

The storm bursts.—The calm that had followed the dismissal of the Prince of Nöer in the duchies was only the lull before the greater storm, which burst forth a few weeks after the death of Christian VIII. in January 1848. The outbreak of open rebellion was probably hastened by the French Revolution of February 1848, which carried the waves of disturbance over almost every part of Continental Europe. In the Danish provinces everything was ripe for a final revolutionary movement against the monarchy. The higher classes, who had been indoctrinated with German ideas by the professors of the University of Kiel, which was the centre of Germanising influences, were eager for a union with what they termed their true *Fatherland*, whilst the lower orders were roused into temporary excitement against Denmark through the press of Germany, by public appeals, and by every other means at the command of the leaders of the party. Foremost amongst the learned advocates of the independence of the duchies was the great historian, Dahlmann, who, in his researches, had discovered among the archives at Preetz the original draft of the long-forgotten compact between Christian I. and the nobles of Slesvig and of Holstein, drawn up in 1460, in which that king had agreed that both provinces should remain "for ever undivided."[1] Through the instrumentality of Professor Dahlmann, this document was printed as the unchangeable charter of the liberties of Slesvig and Holstein, and by the importance attached to it in the minds of the people it became a very powerful agent in the work of separating the duchies from the mother-country.

Frederick VIII., 1848–1863. War in the Duchies.—Christian VIII. died almost suddenly in January 1848, at the height of popular disturbances in every part of his dominions; for while the Slesvig-Holsteiners were clamouring for the realization of their dream of a union with Germany, the people of the islands and Jutland were equally impatient to secure the free constitution for which they hungered. Frederick VII. had only just ascended the throne of Denmark when the outbreak of the French Revolution brought the many troubles which he had inherited with his crown to their full maturity. The Slesvig-Holsteiners, taking courage from the success of French malcontents by the Revolution at Paris of February 1848, sent a deputation to Copenhagen to demand the immediate recognition by the king of a joint state of Slesvig-Holstein previous to its admittance into the German Confederation. King Frederick's reply, in which he admitted the right of Holstein as a German confederate state to be guided by the decrees of the Frankfort diet, but declared that he had neither "the power, right, nor wish" to incorporate Slesvig in the confederation, was immediately followed, if even it had not been preceded, by an outbreak of open rebellion. On the very day in which the king wrote his reply, Prince Frederick of Nöer gained over the garrison of the Castle of Rendsburg by circulating the false news that Copenhagen was in a state of siege and Frederick VII. a prisoner, while at the same time his elder brother, the Duke of Augustenburg, had gone to Berlin to demand help from the Prussian king, William IV. At that time the insurrection had taken no hold of the mass of the people; and the Danish army, which advanced rapidly into the duchies, found no difficulty in dispersing and thoroughly breaking up the regiments under Prince Frederick, who neither

[1] See Chapter XV.

on this nor on any subsequent occasion gave proof of military skill or even of ordinary courage. The rebellion would speedily have been put down had not Prussia and the German Confederation made it a pretext for drawing away the minds of Germans from the ideas of constitutional liberty, which they were beginning to entertain ; and hence the war of the Danish duchies was used as a safety-valve for troublesome agitation.

The Danes had met the Holstein army near Flensborg, and forced it to fall back ; but before they could follow up their advantages, the insurgents received strong reinforcements of German Confederate troops, under Generals Wrangel and Halkett. On the 23rd of April, 1848, a fierce battle was fought near Slesvig between the allied armies, amounting to 28,000 men, and the Danes, who were under the command of General Hedemann. The result was unfavourable to the Danish army, which, numbering only 11,000 men and being unprovided with the better and more modern weapons carried by the German troops, was forced, after a gallant stand prolonged through the whole day, to retreat upon the little island Als, which is separated by a narrow, but deep sound from the mainland, and was at the time protected by Danish ships of the line. Here the Danes were able to recruit their strength, whilst their ships harassed the enemy's encampments on the opposite shore ; but General Wrangel, by way of retaliation, advanced inland, and, throwing himself into Jutland, demanded the payment of four million rix dollars from the Jutlanders in return for the damage inflicted on his army by the Danish shipping. Before he could enforce his demands, however, he received orders from the Prussian court to retire south of the little stream known as the Konge-aae in Slesvig ; and he was therefore forced at once to evacuate the territory of Jutland. This sudden and unexpected movement was the result of Russian intervention, which the Prussian monarch was not in a position to defy; and hence the Berlin war minister had been constrained to instruct General Wrangel that the old line of the Konge-Aae was not to be crossed by his army.

At the same time, King Oscar of Sweden sent troops into Fyen to help the Danes, but before they could strike a blow the great Powers interfered, and by their exertions a truce for seven months was agreed upon, and signed at Malmö on the 26th of August between Denmark and the German Confederation.

PART II.

SUCCESS OF THE DANES.

End of Truce.—By this treaty it was agreed that the duchies should be governed till the conclusion of the war by five Slesvig and Holstein commissioners, chosen conjointly by the kings of Prussia and Denmark. But so much dissatisfaction was caused in the provinces by this mode of government, which pleased neither party, that Frederick VII. determined to continue the war as soon as the seven months' truce had ended. The Germans were equally eager to resume hostilities, and in the spring of 1849, 80,000 insurgent and German confederate troops were brought under arms in the duchies. The Danes beat back the Hanoverians under General Wynecken at Ullerup, and inflicted a severe loss on an army of Saxons, Bavarians, and Hessians, who tried to take the Dybbel works by storm; but they were unfortunate in losing some of the best of their men-of-war; and when the fine line-of-battle-ship, *Kristian VIII.*, and the war-frigate *Gefion*, were forced to surrender from want of ammunition, a feeling of profound depression spread through the kingdom. General Rye, in conjunction with the Generals Schleppegrell and Moltke, succeeded in relieving Kolding in Jutland and driving out the insurgents; and this achievement, together with his masterly retreat before an army triple his own in numbers, by which he was enabled to bring his men in good order to the help of Frederits, somewhat restored the failing hopes of the Danes, while it excited the admiration of their enemies. Rye fell in the engagement which took place before Frederits in July 1849, when the Danes, under the chief command of General Bülow, carried by assault the Holstein lines, and, in addition to a large number of prisoners, took 31 cannons and 3,000 arms from the insurgents. With this Danish victory the campaign ended and another truce was agreed upon, during which the provinces were again placed under commissioners, among whom was included an English plenipotentiary, Colonel Hodges, the others being for Denmark Chamberlain Tillisch, and for Prussia Count Eulenburg. The southern districts were under the guard of Prussian troops, and the northern under Swedes and Norwegians. The result was much as in the former case; the Germans did all in their power to thwart the intentions of the Danish king, and the English and Danish commissioners found themselves unable to maintain order. Soon, however, a peace was concluded with Prussia, and after that Denmark for the first time since the beginning of the war found herself at liberty to deal single-handed with the insurgents, who had, however, succeeded in getting together an army of upwards of 30,000 men, which was under the command of a Prussian general, Willisen.

On July 1st, 1850, before the armistice had expired, Willisen took up a strong position at Isted, near Slesvig; after having made a public entry into the town accompanied by the Duke of Augustenburg, who assumed the title and character of sovereign of the provinces, and made constant appeals to the people as if he were a wronged prince, about to fight for his own and their independence against an oppressive tyrant. The Danish army, numbering 37,000 men, under General Krogh, attacked the insurgents July 24th, and on that and the following day, in the midst of rain and heavy mist, a decisive battle was fought at Isted, which ended in the retreat of Willisen, and in the occupation by the triumphant Danes of Slesvig and the old Danish frontier defences, the Dannevirke. An attack on Midsunde in the following September by Willisen was equally unsuccessful; and after the insurgents had been driven back with frightful loss from Fredericksstad, where one Holstein battalion lost all its officers and was nearly destroyed, the German Confederate government interfered, and sent 40,000 Austrians into the Holstein territory, after which the rebel army was disbanded, and a joint Danish, Prussian, and Austrian commission was appointed to govern Holstein till its relations to Denmark could be defined, while Slesvig was left under the control of the Danish king to be dealt with as he and his advisers might determine.

The Constitution framed.—While the Danes in the provinces had been going through this hard struggle against the superior power of the German armies, the members of the national assembly in Copenhagen had been busied in trying to form a new constitution for the country. Frederick VII. immediately after his coming to the throne had promised to resign the nearly absolute power which still belonged to the Danish crown, and to share his authority with his people. In fulfilment of his pledge he had called together an assembly to consider and plan the system of constitutional and representative government that should be adopted in Denmark both for the islands and the duchies. The charter, which was drawn up by the assembly of 1849 and signed by the king in 1850, is the basis of the very great individual and political freedom which the Danes now enjoy; although in consequence of the interference of the German Confederation, which claimed the right to settle the mode of government to be adopted for Holstein, and owing to the obstacles thrown in the way of granting free constitutional power to the people both by Austria and Prussia, the original plan of the Danish constitution received for some years numerous modifications and limitations never designed by the patriotic Frederick VII. Without referring to any of these temporary changes and interruptions to the course of Danish constitutional liberty, we may here content ourselves with giving merely the result of the movement begun under King Frederick, which is, that at present Denmark and Jutland enjoy a free constitution; in conformity with which no public measures can be adopted, no taxes can be imposed, and no law passed without the joint consent of the "Rigsdag," or diet, and of the king. The latter governs by a ministry, who are responsible for their acts, while the sovereign is considered irresponsible. The Rigsdag meets every year, and is composed of a Landsthing and a Folksthing. The right of voting and of being elected to sit in the Folksthing is universal, being only dependent upon certain requisite qualifications of age, character, education, &c., and has nothing to do with rank or station. Election to the Landsthing is restricted by certain very moderate qualifications of property and standing, while, according to the resolutions of

1866, twelve of the sixty-six members are nominated for life by the king, and the remainder are chosen for a term of eight years by deputies from Copenhagen and the other great towns of the kingdom. Freedom of religion is allowed to all persons in Denmark; the press is quite unrestrained; no one can, according to the Danish law, be kept in confinement more than twenty-four hours without being brought before the proper authorities and charged with his offence, when judgment must be given on his case within a definite period. In every particular the liberty of the subject and the power of the law are protected; and, as at present constituted, there is no form of government in any country that can boast of greater freedom and justice in regard to every class of the population than the one established in Denmark.

The Succession settled.—In the year 1850 the question of the succession to the Danish crown was settled, and in consequence of the king and his uncle and nearest heir, Prince Ferdinand, being both childless, it was determined to make choice of some prince connected with the royal family of Denmark to succeed to the throne. By the consent of the Rigsdag and with the concurrence of the great European powers, expressed in a protocol signed in London 1852, Prince Christian of Glücksburg was named successor to the throne, which after his death was to devolve on the male descendants of himself and his wife the Princess Louisa of Hesse, who, through her mother, Princess Charlotte of Denmark, was the niece of the late king Christian VIII. of Denmark. The ten years of Frederick VII.'s reign which intervened between this settlement of the succession and his death in 1863 may be said to have been one continued struggle to reconcile the jealous demands of the various portions of his kingdom for special political concessions; and to keep at a distance the officious interference of foreign powers, who in consequence of having been called upon to be parties to the treaty of London of 1852, which settled the question of succession to the Danish throne, thought themselves justified in offering advice and making remonstrances in regard to all questions of internal Danish policy. Prussia especially never ceased her efforts to prevent an amicable adjustment of the differences between Slesvig and the mother-country; and as a handle for future action in the matter of the succession to the Danish throne, the Prussian king gave secret support to the Duke of Augustenburg in the duchies, and thus advocated his claim to the crown lands of Denmark in defiance of the London treaty of succession and of the act of renunciation by which Duke Christian had pledged himself in his own name and in that of his heirs to give up all pretensions he might be supposed to have to the Slesvig-Holstein lands. At the close of the war the Duke and his brother, Prince Frederick of Nöer, being in the position of rebels bearing arms against the sovereign, were amenable to the penalties of treason. They at that time accepted the free pardon offered them on the conditions attached to it; and these were the renunciation of all pretensions to the sovereignty of any part of the Slesvig-Holstein lands, the removal of all members of the Augustenburg family from the Danish territories, and their acceptance of a large sum of money as a full and final settlement of all their claims. This compact did not prove of much avail, for, immediately after the sudden death of Frederick VII. of Denmark in 1863, the eldest son of the Duke of Augustenburg hastened into the duchies, and, with the concurrence of his father and uncle, assumed the title of Duke Frederick VIII. of the united and independent province of Slesvig-Holstein.

PART III.

THE REIGNING DYNASTY.

Christian IX., 1863.—Frederick VII. of Denmark had died very suddenly, at the age of fifty-five, at the castle of Glücksburg, in Northern Slesvig, in the autumn of 1863; and as soon as the news of his death reached Copenhagen the appointed successor to the throne, Prince Christian of Glücksburg, was proclaimed king under the title of Christian IX. The death of Frederick created universal sorrow among the Danes, by whom he was much beloved on account of his patriotic self-denial in giving up his own supreme power in order that he might gratify the wishes of his people for a constitutional form of government. The event brought the long slumbering discontent to a crisis in the duchies, where for a time the pretensions of the self-styled Duke Frederick VIII. of Slesvig-Holstein were supported by Austria and Prussia, as well as by the lesser German powers. And before the close of the year the duchies of Holstein and Slesvig were occupied by Austrian and Prussian armies under the respective commands of Generals Gablenz and Wrangel, who were sent to enforce the demand made by those powers that Slesvig should be given up to them to be held under military occupation until the question of the claims of the House of Augustenburg to the duchies should be definitely settled. These steps on the part of the great German powers left Denmark no alternative but to prepare for war. While Prussia and Austria in the name of the German Confederation were pressing one condition after the other upon the Danish government, each more galling than the last, England strove to avoid the rupture of peace at any cost, and so often volunteered to act as umpire between the different parties and to mediate in favour of Denmark, that the Danes felt convinced they might rely upon the active support of the British government. In full expectation of being backed by England, the Danish king sent an army of 40,000 men under General de Meza to defend the Dannevirke; but after several skirmishes with the Prussians, De Meza threw up his position and retreated on Dybbel, from which he carried his army across the Sound into the little island Als.

The news of this retrograde movement and the loss of the ancient national line of defences, to whose preservation the Danes attached an almost superstitious importance, created the deepest depression in the islands and was followed by the substitution of General Gerlach, as commander-in-chief in the place of General de Meza, who gave in his resignation. As time went on, and it became certain that France and England were not going to afford the aid which the Danes had expected from them, and that even Sweden, on whose friendly support the people had relied, was following the example set by those great powers of non-interference in the war, the general depression was changed into hopeless despair. The English government had so often in the course of the preceding events offered advice to the Danish king, and by their mediation with the German powers had shown so strong an interest in the maintenance of the integrity of the kingdom, that the Danes were the more dispirited when they found that they would be left singlehanded to oppose their powerful foes. This feeling was, however, not betrayed by any hesitation in meeting the invaders; and in spite of inferior numbers and imperfect appliances for warfare, the Danes made a gallant defence, and gave proofs of courage and endurance which won for them the admiration and sympathy of all who looked dispassionately at the unequal struggle in which they were engaged. But it was impossible long to maintain a contest against such fearful odds. The Prussians had seized upon one strong point after the other, and occupied the provinces from the Eyder to the northernmost extremity of Jutland. Then in order to save the monarchy from entire annihilation, Christian IX. and his government were forced to accept the terms offered them by the peace of Vienna, which was signed in October, 1864, and by which the Danish king renounced all claims on the duchies of Lauenburg, Holstein and Slesvig, and pledged himself to abide by whatever decision Austria and Prussia might take in regard to the future disposal of those provinces.

Prussia in the ascendent.—After the war between Prussia and Austria in 1866, when the former remained victor and could dictate her own terms, she secured to herself by the treaty of Prague all the rights vested in the Austrian emperor in regard to the occupation and disposal of the Slesvig-Holstein provinces, and since then Denmark has been made to feel very sharply the force of Prussian domination. Austria had stipulated that North Slesvig should be restored to Denmark unconditionally, provided the people by a *plébiscite*, or universal vote, should proclaim their wish to be reunited to the Danish monarchy. Hitherto, however, Prussia has retained her hold on the Slesvig territory without having had recourse to this test of the popular feelings and wishes. The pretensions of the House of Augustenburg have in like manner been entirely laid aside, and all idea of their future re-assertion has been destroyed by the absorption of Slesvig-Holstein in the present German empire, which is intended by its founder to realize the dream of the unification of a Fatherland, and, therefore, designed to embrace under one rule all German or Teutonic-tongued nations. The successful head of this vast conglomeration of states is William I., late king of Prussia, who, after his great war with France in 1870—71, solemnized his victories by the assumption of the crown of the German empire.

Denmark has recovered rapidly from her past calamities and troubles, and under the popular rule of her constitutional king, Christian IX., is in the enjoyment of the most complete political and social freedom, coupled with a degree of internal quiet, industrial and commercial activity, and intellectual progress, hitherto unparalleled in the history of any other equally small state.

INDEX.

INDEX.

A.

Aagard, battle of, 191

Aase Sound, battle on, 211, 215

Abel, King of Denmark, his quarrels with his brother Erik, 122; he causes him to be murdered, 123; his false oath before his accession, 124; his reign, *ib.*; he is murdered by Hans of Pelvorm, *ib.*; his sons, 125

Absalon, Bishop, gift of lands to his king, 92; more a sailor or soldier than a churchman, 105; he baptizes the heathen for two days and two nights, 106; the peasants on his estates rebel against him, 107; he defeats them, 108; his victory over the Wends, 109; his learning and labours, 111; what he did for the church, *ib.*; his death, *ib.*

Adam, canon of Bremen, 91; his *Chronicle*, *ib.*

Adela, Queen of Knud the Saint, her flight to Bruges, 96

Adolf, Count of Holstein, 111; defeated by Valdemar II., 113; his victory over the Danes, 119

Adolf, Duke of Holstein, declines the Danish crown, 192

Ælla, King of Northumbria, puts Regner Lodbrog to death, 28; he is tortured and killed, 29

Æsir, or lesser gods, 12, 76

Ætheling Ælfred, his murder, 56

Æthelstan, King of England, his foster child Hakon, 70

Agnes of Brandenburg, Queen Regent of Denmark, 130, 131

Aix-la-Chapelle pillaged by Gorm, 40

Albert of Mecklenburg, his parentage, 141; he is chosen King of Sweden, 165; his reign, *ib.*; his weakness and wars, 166; Bo Jonsson rules for him, *ib.*; new wars and troubles, 167; his defeat by Queen Margaret, 167, 178; he is taken prisoner and tortured, 178; his punishment for insulting Margaret, *ib.*; his claims to the Danish crown, 175, 177; his release from prison, 179; he dies in neglect and want, 167

Albert of Orlamunde, Duke of North-Albingia, 114; his defeat and imprisonment, 118

Albert the Younger, grandson of Valdemar III., 175, 177

Albinensis, Cardinal Nicholas, his mission to Sweden, 145

Alexander III. of Scotland, defeats the Norwegians, 171

Alexius, Greek emperor, and Magnus Barfod, 152

Alfred the Great, his history of Orosius, 7; his victories over the Vikingar, 29
Altmark, truce of, 277
Amager Island peopled by Flemish gardeners, 218
Amber, its mythical origin, 9; beads of, worn by Roman ladies, 8
America discovered by Northern explorers, 73, 84
Amlet, the story of, and Shakespeare's "Hamlet," 22
Angeln, land of the Angles, 19
Angermannus, Abraham, Lutheran primate of Sweden, 263, 264
Angles in Britain, 18, 19
Anglesea, subdued by Magnus Barfod, 152
Anglo-Saxons in Britain, 21; they retain their northern customs, *ib.*
Anna Catherine, first Queen of Christian IV., 255
Anne, Queen of James I. of England, 249, 250
Anscarius, the Apostle of the North, goes to convert the Northmen, 34; his want of success, *ib.*; his labours in Sweden, 35; he is made Archbishop of Hamburgh, *ib.*; what happens to him there, *ib.*; his death, 36
Anund, King of Sweden, 84
Arcona taken by the Danes, 105; the temple of Svanteveit is destroyed by a stratagem, *ib.*; the demon that the Danes said they saw, 106
Arnfast, Bishop of Aarhus, 127
Arnulf, King of Germany, his victory over the Danes, 43
Aryan races, 13
Asbjörn, brother of Svend, his treachery, 90
Aschloo, camp of the Northern rovers, 40, 41
Asgaard, home of the gods, 12
Autbert, monk, his mission to Slesvig, 34
Axel Hvide. See Bishop *Absalon*.

B.

Baal worshipped in the North, 5
Baglerne, or "the Croziers," 154
Baner, John, his victory at Wittstock, 286; his appearance before Vienna, *ib.*; his masterly retreat, *ib.*; his death, *ib.*
Beltanes, midsummer-night dances, 6
Benedict, brother of Knud the Saint, 95
Berangaria, second Queen of Valdemar II., 118, 120, 121
Bernhard, Duke of Saxe Weimar, enters the service of France, 286; his death, *ib.*
Berserkers, why so called, 26
Berthelsen, Ivar, his imprisonment, 247
Birch Legs, or Birke-benerne, 154
Birger, King of Sweden, Torkel Knudsson's influence for good, 160; his troubles after Torkel's death, 161; he imprisons his brothers and starves them to death, 161, 162; anger of his people, 162; he flees to Denmark, *ib.*; his son is beheaded, *ib.*; his death, 163.
Birger Brosa, Jarl of the Swedes and Goths, 149; his son chosen King of Sweden, 150; his anger at the choice, 150, 157; Ivar's retorts, 157, 158; he submits, 158; his rule in Sweden *ib.*; his laws in favour of women, *ib.*; his death, *ib.*
Birke-benerne, or the "Birch Legs," 154
Bjarne, Icelandic navigator, visits Greenland, 80
Bjelke, Gunilla, second wife of Johan III., 259; she conceals his death, 261
Biorn, Icelandic skald, 88
Bjorn, King of Sweden, sends for Christian monks to convert his

people, 34 ; his reception of Anscarius, 35
Black Death, and the desolation it caused, 85, 173; the "Partridge," 173
Black Henry. See *Henry, Duke of Schwerin.*
Blanka of Namur, Queen of Magnus Smek, 163, 173 ; her death, 139
Bleking, Swedish province of Denmark, 23, 38 ; origin of its name, 23; laid waste by King Erik of Sweden, 246
Blood-bath at Stockholm, 215, 216
Bo Jonsson, rules Sweden, 166 ; he slays Karl Nilsson before the altar, *ib.*; his death, *ib.*
Bondar race of kings in Sweden, 146, 147
Bonder, or peasants of Denmark, 104
Bornhöved, battle of, 119
Botilda, Queen of Denmark, her death, 99
Braga, or "Good-health" horn, 61
Brahe, Tycho, the great astronomer, 241 ; his observatory, *ib.* ; he is obliged to seek safety abroad, 249; he settles and dies at Prague, *ib.*
Brask, Bishop, his speech, 233, 234
Bravalla, battle of, 26, 27, 28
Breakspear, Nicholas, his mission to Sweden, 145
Breitenfeld, battle of, 279
Bremen Chronicle, 91
Britain visited by Pytheas, 3 ; invaded by the Northmen, 17 ; the Vikingar expelled, 29 ; invaded by Svend Tveskæg, 50
Brodersen, Abraham, his execution, 181
Bromsebro, treaty of, 254
Brunnbäk, battle of, 230

C.

Calmar Act of Union, 180, 217
Calmar war, 269, 273, 274

Casimir, Johan, appointed director-general of Sweden, 278
Charlemagne, Charles I. of Germany, his wars against the Saxons, 20; his tomb pillaged by the Northmen, 40
Charles. See *Karl.*
Charles the Dane, Count of Flanders. See *Karl, son of Knud.*
Charles the Fat, Emperor of Germany, his foolish conduct and cowardice, 40, 41, 43 ; his laws in favour of the Danes, 41 ; defeated at Louvaine, 43
Chersonesus Cimbrica, 19, 22
Christian I., is chosen King of Denmark, 192 ; he marries the widowed Queen Dorothea, *ib.* ; he obtains the crown of Sweden, 195 ; the Swedes rebel and defeat him, 196; he is defeated by Sten Sture, 197 ; his character, 198 ; his nickname, 199 ; he is crowned in Norway, *ib.* ; his schemes for getting money, 200 ; the union of Slesvig and Holstein, *ib.* ; anger of the Danes, 201 ; he loses the Shetlands and Orkneys, *ib.* ; his daughter Margaret's dowry, 202 ; his misuse of money, *ib.* ; his death, 203
Christian II., King of Denmark, his birth, 212 ; he is nearly killed by an ape, 213 ; how he was brought up, *ib.*; his singing in the choirs of Copenhagen, *ib.* ; his knowledge of Latin, 214 ; his father's use of the rod, *ib.* ; in Norway, *ib.* ; he invades Sweden and finally becomes king, 210, 211, 215 ; he is crowned at Stockholm, 215 ; his massacre of ninety Swedish nobles, 216 ; his cruelty, 227, 230; he is called "the Tyrant," 217 ; some of his good works, *ib.*; puts down strand rights, 218 ; favours cultivation of fruits and flowers, *ib.*;

he encourages the Reformers for a time, 219; his adviser, Mother Sigbrit, *ib.*; he puts Torbe Oxe to death, 220; the fatal glove, *ib.*; his defeat by rebels, 221; his captivity with a dwarf, and death seventeen years after, *ib.*

Christian III., King of Denmark, his feud when Count, 223; he is proclaimed king, 224; puts down the Romish Church, *ib.*; establishes the Lutheran faith, *ib.*; persecutes the Calvinists, 225; his death, *ib.*; progress of the country during his reign, *ib.*

Christian IV., King of Denmark, his minority, 249; his accomplishments, 250; his love for the sea, *ib.*; his visit to England, *ib.*; the report of King James's courtiers, *ib.*; war with Sweden and Germany, 251, 253, 254; his great merits, 252; he revises the laws, *ib.*; his gallantry, 255; his death, *ib.*; his queens, *ib.*; how the Danes revere his memory, 256; his wars with Sweden, 270, 273, 287

Christianity, its rise and progress in Scandinavia, 31, 46, 49, 51, 82, 143, 148, 155

Christina, daughter of Gustaf Adolf, her minority, 254, 278, 285

Christopher, son of Valdemar II., his father gives him Laaland and Falster, 122; he is chosen King of Denmark, 125; his disputes with his primate, 126; he is excommunicated, *ib.*; his sudden death, 127

Christopher of Bavaria, elected King of Denmark, 188; succeeds to the crowns of Norway and Sweden, 188, 189, 193; his agreement with Karl Knudsson, 189; his queen, *ib.*; his troubles with his people, 190; his easy temper, *ib.*; Jutland revolts, *ib.*; the ways he raised money, 191; his death, *ib.*

Christopher II., how he was brought up, 131; he arrests the primate, 132; he is proclaimed king, 133; the terms imposed on him by his nobles, 134; civil wars, *ib.*; he is driven out of his kingdom, *ib.*; his death, 135; his contemptible character, *ib.*; his sons, 136

Cnut. See *Knud.*

Conrad, the Magister, tutor of Prince Christian, 214

Copenhagen, its site, 92; attacked by the Hansers, 186; improved by Christian IV., 252

Copenhagen University, its opening, 202; its reputation, 225

Croziers, or Baglerne, 154

D.

Dagmar, or "Day's Maiden." See *Margrete of Bohemia.*

Dan, King of the Danes, so-called founder of Danish monarchy, 24; his body after death, *ib.*

Danebod, or Danes'-hope. See *Queen Thyra.*

Danes in early times, 17; of Jutland and the Isles, 21; their rovings in King Gorm's time, 40; the booty they got from Charles the Fat, 40, 41; they besiege Paris, 41, 42; King Arnulf defeats them at Louvaine, 43; how they were intermingled with the Swedes, 65; the way they chose their kings, 97, 104, 125

Danneberg Castle, royal captives in, 117, 118

Dannebrog, or national standard, 115

Dannevirke, or Danish outworks, 47; burnt, 49

Danzig, an impostor claims the

INDEX. 383

crown of Norway and is executed at, 175
David, Irish monk, 148
Denmark, position of, 22 ; origin of its name, 23, 24 ; names of its provinces, 23 ; in A.D. 871, 30 ; Christianity in, 31, 46, 49, 51 ; visited by Anscarius, 34 ; the first King of all Denmark, 36 ; in early times, 45 ; its first Queen, *ib.* ; Knud and his sons, 51 ; joined with Norway for five years, 56, 57 ; the Estridsens, 89 ; descent of the royal family, 93 ; its laws, 97, 120 ; the Valdemars, 103 ; civil war in A.D. 1147, 104 ; the peasants are poor and powerless, *ib.* ; prosperity of the country under the Valdemars, 109, 113 ; its history from A.D. 1202 to A.D. 1259, 113 ; first appearance of the national standard, 115 ; a century of troubles, 122 ; the burgher classes send representatives to the Danehof, 125 ; differences between Church and State, 126 ; from A.D. 1259 to A.D. 1387, 128 ; decline of the royal power, 130 ; under an interdict, 126, 133 ; the credit of the country revives, 136 ; without a king for four years, 140 ; union with Sweden and Norway, 168, 180 ; from A.D. 1412 to A.D. 1448, 183 ; and Sweden, from A.D. 1450, 198 ; crown bartered for favours, 203 ; its history from A.D. 1500, 212 ; the Swedish crown lost, 215, 231 ; the Reformers in, 219, 222, 224 ; the Count's Feud, 223 ; from A.D. 1559 to A.D. 1648, 244 ; its decline, 254 ; wars with Sweden, 239, 244, 251, 254, 287
Didrik Slaghœk, Regent of Sweden, 229
Ditmarshes, inhabitants of the, 205 ; their courage, *ib.* ; their rebellions, 119, 206, 207, 244, 245
Dönsk tunga, or Danish tongue, 59
Dorothea of Brandenburg, marries King Christopher, 189 ; re-marries King Christian, 192
Dyveke, or the Dove, her death, 220

E.

Ebbo, Archbishop of Rheims, his mission to Jutland, 32
Edmund Gammal, King of Sweden, 84, 144
Egede, Hans, his mission to Greenland, 85
Egede, Paul, Greenland missionary, 85
Egnen, battle of, 276
Ejnar, son of Jarl Rögnvald, 69
Ejsten, King of Norway, his reign, 152 ; his death, 153
Elizabeth, Countess of Holstein, seeks aid from Queen Margaret, 181
Elizabeth, Princess of Holstein-Gottorp, seized by Valdemar Atterdag, 138, 139, 164 ; Magnus Smek offers to marry her, 139
Elizabeth, Queen of England, her suitor Erik, 237
Emma, Queen, her conspiracy, 52 ; her conduct during her son's reign, 55
Englebrecht Englebrechtsson heads a rebellion against Erik, 186 ; his conduct to the bishops, *ib.* ; he is murdered, 187
Enköping, battle of, 165
Erik Blod-öxe, his harsh rule, 77 ; he is dethroned and driven out of the country, 78 ; his sons invade Norway, 79
Erik, Duke of Slesvig, defeats the Royal troops, 129
Erik Ejegod, King of Denmark, 98 ; his beauty and great skill in arts

and exercises, *ib.*; his pilgrimages, 99; he and his queen die on the way to Jerusalem, *ib.*; the grief of the Danes at his death, *ib.*

Erik Emun, revenges his brother's murder, 101; he is raised to the throne of Denmark, 103; he causes his brother with his ten sons to be murdered, 104

Erik Eriksson Læspe, last of the Bondar kings, 148, 149; his death, 150

Erik Glipping, King of Denmark, his minority, 129; he is imprisoned by Duke Erik of Slesvig, *ib.*; he pays a fine to Erlandsen, *ib.*; his evil habits, 130; he is slain in a barn, *ib.*

Erik Graafell, son of Erik Blod-öxe, 79

Erik Johansson Vasa, his execution, 216, 228

Erik Knudsson, King of Sweden, his marriage, 149; he is the first king crowned by the clergy, *ib.*; his death, *ib.*

Erik Menved, King of Denmark, his minority, 130; how he was brought up, 131; his useless wars, *ib.*; he misrules his kingdom and quarrels with the clergy, 132; the loss of his infant children, 133; his death, *ib.*

Erik of Pomerania, his adoption by Queen Margaret, 176; he is appointed her successor, 168, 174, 176; he is crowned joint King at Calmar, 179; his incapacity, 180; he executes Abraham Brodersen, 181; his war with Holstein, 181, 184, 185, 186; he rules alone, 183; his incapacity is confirmed, 184; his appeal to the Emperor Sigismund, 185; his pilgrimage, *ib.*; he is taken prisoner, *ib.*; his English queen, *ib.*; he loses his three kingdoms, 186, 187, 188; his death, 188

Erik Plov-peng, King of Denmark, his quarrels with his brothers, who refuse to do him homage, 122, 123; he makes war against the pagans, 123; why he was called "Plov-peng," *ib.*; he is murdered, *ib.*; how his body was discovered, 124

Erik Præste-hader, King of Norway, his troubled reign, 172; death of his daughter Margrete, *ib.*

Erik Raudi discovers Greenland, 84; his son brings monks to Greenland, 85; he declines to return with his son, 86

Erik Sejrsœl, King of the Svea, 82

Erik, son of Gustaf, is proclaimed King of Sweden, 237; his wooings, 237—239; his violent temper, 238; he quarrels with his brother Johan, *ib.*; the Seven Years' War, 239, 245, 246; his cruelty to the Stures, 240; his fits of insanity, 240, 241; his submission to Karren Mannsdatter, 240; he marries her, 241; his deposition, *ib.*; his miseries and death by poison, 242; his love for his wife, 243; his sons, *ib.*

Erik, son of Magnus Ladu-laas, his quarrels with King Birger, 160; he is imprisoned and starved to death, 161, 162

Erik, son of Magnus Smek, rebels against his father, 164; his sudden death, *ib.*

Erik, son of Valdemar of Sweden, 159

Erik the Lamb, King of Denmark, who spent his time with the monks, 104

Erik the Saint, is chosen King of Sweden, 146; the three things he laid to heart, *ib.*; his laws in favour of women, *ib.*; his crusade against the Finns, 147; he is

slain by the Danes, *ib.*; his remains honoured as relics, *ib.*
Erik's course, or royal progress, 157
Erlandsen, Jacob, primate of Denmark, 126; he is imprisoned by King Christopher, *ib.*; his release, 129; a fine paid to him, *ib.*
Eskil, Archbishop of Lund, 108
Esthonia, religious wars in, 114, 115, 123
Estrid, sister to Knud, 53; she marries Robert, Duke of Normandy, 54
Estridsen race of kings, 89
Europe, ancient ideas of Northern, 1, 8
Ey-Gotaland, or Insular Goths' land, 19, 22, 59
Eyrbyggja Saga, 74

F.

Falköping, battle of, 167
Farö Islands discovered by the Norwegians, 67
Femern, Island of, its inhabitants defeat King Erik, 184
Finland united to Sweden, 147; crusade in, 150; War of Clubs, 265
Floki Rafn, a Norwegian, discovers Iceland, 73
Fodevig, battle of, 101
Folkungar race of Swedish kings, 149, 156
Frälse and Ofrälse classes in Sweden, 159
France ravaged by the Northmen, 41, 42
Frederick Barbarossa, Emperor of Germany, and Knud VI., 109; he stirs up strife in Denmark, 110, 111
Frederick I., King of Denmark, his ambition when Prince, 203; his bad advice, 204; his war with the Ditmarshers, 206, 207; he is chosen king, 220; defeats King Christian, 221; his conduct and reign, 221, 222; his death, and the feud which followed, 223
Frederick II., King of Denmark, his campaign against the Ditmarshers, 244, 245; his coronation, 245; the Seven Years' War, 245, 246; his intolerance, 247; the great men of his reign, 248; his death, 249; his daughter Anne, *ib.*
Freia, Finnish goddess, 11
Frey-Yngve, King of Sweden, 60; the last of the gods, 61
Frode, King of the Danes, his golden bracelets, 24; his victories, 25

G.

Galt, Admiral Peter, allows the Swedes to escape, 255
Gardar, a Swede, discovers Iceland, 73
Gardcrike. See *Russia*.
Geert, Count of Holstein, expels King Christopher II., 134; his influence in Denmark, *ib.*; he is slain by Niels Ebbesön, 135; his son avenges him, *ib.*
Gerhard, Count of Holstein. See *Count Geert*.
Gerhard VI., Count of Holstein, his death, 181
Gods of the Scandinavians, 11. See *Odin* and *Thor*.
Godwine, Earl, murders Ætheling Ælfred, 56; gives a ship to Harthaknud, *ib.*
Göran Persson, favourite of King Erik, tortured and put to death, 240, 241
Gorm the Old, first King of all Denmark, his birth and descent, 36; how he was brought up, 37; his kingdom of Lejre, *ib.*; a chief

C C

priest of Odin, 37, 38; how he extended his rule, 38; his rovings, 40, 41; he besieges Paris, 41, 42; Queen Thyra rules in his absence, 45; nicknamed the "Church's worm," 46; his war with, and defeat by, Henry the Fowler of Germany, *ib.*; he tolerates Christianity, *ib.*; how he was told of his son's death, 47; he dies of grief, 48; his grave mound, *ib.*

Gospel first preached in the north, 32

Göta Hofrätt, Swedish court of law, 285

Göta-land, or land of the Goths, 63

Gotfred's Wall, 47

Goth's land, Chersonesus Cimbrica of the Romans, 19

Goths in Scandinavia, 10; their language, 13; their letters, 14

Gothus, Archbishop, his character, 258

Grand, Johan, Primate of Denmark, 132; he is arrested and imprisoned, *ib.*; his escape to Rome, *ib.*

Greenland discovered by Erik Raudi, 84; settled by Norwegians and Icelanders, *ib.*; monks baptize all the people, 85; sad fate of the colony, *ib.*; Hans Egede labours and dies there, *ib.*; its Danish settlements, 86

Gudleif, an Icelander, is taken prisoner in Vinland, 87; he returns with gifts, 88

Guld-Harald, how he slew Harald Graafell, 48; his murder, 49

Gule-laws of Thorleif the Wise, 77

Gustaf, son of Erik, 243

Gustaf Eriksson, known as Vasa, King of Sweden, his birth, family, and early school life, 228; how he escaped the Danes, *ib.*; the peasants ill-treat him, but afterwards repent, 228, 229; the beginning of his army, 229; his first flag, *ib.*; he defeats the Danes, 230; fate of his mother and sisters, 230, 231; his letter to the Christian princes, 231; he is proclaimed king, *ib.*; his coronation, 232; state of Stockholm, *ib.*; his want of money, *ib.*; he puts down the Romish Church and seizes its property, 232, 233, 235; he favours the Reformers, *ib.*; his threat to leave Sweden, and its effect, 234; he establishes the power of the crown, 235; his restless activity, *ib.*; his family troubles, 237; he divides his kingdom, *ib.*; his death and burial-place, *ib.*

Gustaf II., Adolf, his birth, education, learning, and early practice of government, 272, 273; he is invested with sword and shield, 273; and the Calmar war, 273, 274; he is chosen king, 274; his war with Russia, 274, 275; peace, 275; his careful government of the kingdom, and the reforms he effected, 275, 276; his war with Poland, 276; his narrow escapes, *ib.*; he helps his Protestant allies in Germany, 277, 278, 279; he takes leave of the Diet, and confides his daughter to the Council, 278; the battle of Breitenfeld, 279; the battle of Lützen, 280, 281; his death, 282, 283; victory of the Swedes, 283; his body recovered, *ib.*; and embalmed, 284; his heart enclosed in a casket and kept by his queen, *ib.*; monument, *ib.*; his appearance, *ib.*; his friends, 285

Gustaf Trolle, Archbishop, his treachery, 210, 215; he demands reparation for having lost his see, 216

Guttorm, the child-king of Norway, 155
Gyllenstjerna, Erik's envoy to Elizabeth, 238, 239

H.

Hafursfjord, sea-battle of, 68
Hakon Æthelstane-fostre, son of Harald Haarfager, 70; he is placed on the knees of King Æthelstan, *ib.* ; his good training in England, 71 ; his laws, 77, 78 ; becomes King of Norway, 78; his reign, *ib.* ; his subjects refuse to become Christians, *ib.* ; Sigurd Jarl tries to screen him, *ib.* ; his defeat and death, 79
Hakon Jarl, King of Norway, and Harald, 48; his treachery, 49, 79
Hakon III., King of Norway, his brief reign, 154; he is murdered, *ib.*
Hakon IV., King of Norway, his accession, 155; his character, 169; his wars, 170; he defeats Skule Baardsson at Oslö, *ib.* ; his fame in distant lands, *ib.* ; he subdues and annexes Iceland, *ib.* ; his invasion of Scotland, 171; he is defeated at Largs, *ib.*; his death, *ib.*
Hakon V., King of Norway, his reign, 172; his successor, 173
Hakon VI., King of Norway, marries the Princess Margaret, 139, 164; succeeds to the throne, 172, 173; his death, 142
Halfden Svarte, Small King, of Norway, 67
Hamburgh, created an archbishopric, 35; burnt by the Northmen, *ib.*
Hans, King of Denmark, 203 ; is chosen King of Norway, 203, 208; Prince Frederick's ambition, 203; the king follows his bad advice, 204; he conquers and loses Sweden, *ib.*; his queen imprisoned in Sweden, 205; and Sten Sture, 209; campaign against the Ditmarshers, 206; he is defeated, 207; his only successful war, *ib.*; his death, *ib.*; how he brought up his son, 212, 213, 214
Hans of Pelvorm, he slays King Abel, 124
Hansers secure fisheries, and forbid royal servants to fish, 132; their quarrel with Valdemar Atterdag, 137; they are insulted by him, 138; admitted to electoral rights, 140; attack Copenhagen, 186
Harald Blaatand, King of Denmark, his cruelty and craft, 48; his profession of Christianity, 49; he is defeated by Otho I. of Germany, *ib.* ; his death, 50
Harald Gille Magnusson, goes through the ordeal of a red-hot iron, and is owned by the king as his brother, 153; his joint reign, *ib.*; he blinds his fellow-king, 154; he is strangled in his bed, *ib.*
Harald Graafell, King of Norway, his death, 48
Harald Haardraade, King of Norway, harasses the Danes, 90; his wish to invade Denmark, 150; his adventures in the East, 151; his escape from prison, *ib.*; his marriage, *ib.*; his invasion of England and death at Stamford Bridge, *ib.*
Harald Haarfager, first King of all Norway, 68; his oath, *ib.*; his severity to the Norwegians, *ib.*; he condemns Rollo the Norman as an outlaw, 69; his family troubles, 70; he dies at a great age, *ib.*; his gift of a gold-beaked

ship to King Æthelstan, 71; a result of his stern rule, 72
Harald Harefoot, King of England, 55; his reign, *ib.*; his body disinterred, 56
Harald Hejn, King of Denmark, his reign, and why he was called "Hejn," 94
Harald Hildetand, King of the Danes, slain by Odin, 27
Harald Kesia, son of Erik Ejegod, 100; his murder, 104
Harald Klak, King of the Danes, his conversion, baptism, and sponsors, 33; the oath he took, *ib.*; his many presents, *ib.*; he returns to the Emperor's court, 34
Harald, son of Sweyn, King of Denmark, 51
Hardegon, or Hardeknud, King of Lejre, 36
Harthaknud, his mother conspires to get him the Danish throne, 52; his reign, 55; his liberality to the clergy, *ib.*; his hatred of his brother Harald, *ib.*; Earl Godwine gives him a ship, 56; his death, *ib.*
Hedeby. See *Slesvig*.
Heinriksson, Johan, murderer of King Erik, 242
Hejde, battle of, 245
Helge, a Danish king, 26
Hemming Gade, Bishop of Linköping, 210
Hemmingen, Nils, his persecution, 247
Henrik, first archbishop in Sweden, 147; his zeal and death, *ib.*
Henry, Count of Holstein, the "Iron Count," 135
Henry, Count Duke of Schwerin, his hatred of Valdemar II., 115; he seizes the king and his son, and imprisons them in Danneberg Castle, 116; the terms upon which he released them, 118; the Pope's message to him, 119

Henry of Neustria, attempts to relieve Paris, 42; is defeated, 43
Henry I., Emperor of Germany, surnamed the Fowler, defeats Gorm, 46
Herjar-Thing, or Icelandic assize, 75
Hinze, Canon George, tutor of Prince Christian, 213
Holmgang, or fight on an island, 74
Holstein, beginning of the Slesvig wars, 126; its Counts and Christopher II., 134, 135; wars with Denmark, 134, 135, 140; with Sweden, 181, 184—186; union with Slesvig, 200
Hother, slain by Starkodder, 25
Hyperboreans, or Outside Northwinders, 1

I.

Iceland first visited between 861 and 868, 73; reported to be a land of mountain giants, *ib.*; the Norwegians revisit it, *ib.*; its settlement by Ingolf, 74; Thorolf brings an image of Thor and takes formal possession of the country, 74, 75; he builds a temple, 75; he founds the "Herjar-Thing," *ib.*; the island is divided into districts, 76; a code of laws prepared by Ulljot, *ib.*; a republic for 300 years, 77; cruel wars for the mastery, *ib.*; is annexed to Norway, 171
Inge Baardsen, King of Norway, his troubled reign, 155
Ingeborg, daughter of Valdemar Atterdag, her marriage and death, 141
Ingeborg, Queen of Denmark, her great grief, 133
Ingjald Ill-raada, burns the six Small Kings, 61; his death with his daughter Aasa, *ib.*; his children expelled, 62

Ingolf, leaves Norway for Iceland, 74; he throws the consecrated door-posts of his house into the sea, *ib.*; he lands at and founds Reykiavik, *ib.*
Ireland, settlements made by the Northmen in, 70; invaded by Magnus Barfod, 152
Ivan Vasilievitsch II. of Russia, his war with Sweden, 246, 262
Ivar Blaa, and the election of King Valdemar, 157; his answer to Birger, 157, 158
Ivar Vidfadme, King of Svea, 64

J.

Jacob Andreæ, professor at Tübingen, 247
James I. of England, his Queen, 249; Christian IV. visits him, 250; Charles IX. sends an embassy to him, 270
Jaukuwitz, battle of, 287
Jellyfish, or Medusa, called "Lung of the Sea," 4
Johan, nephew of Charles IX., he declines the regency, 274
Johan, son of Gustaf, his marriage, 238; he and his wife are imprisoned by his brother, *ib.*; he escapes and rebels, 241; causes his brother to be poisoned, 242
Johan, son of Sverker Karlsson, 145; his death, 149
Johan III., crowned King of Sweden on deposition of his brother, 258; his suspicion of Duke Karl, *ib.*; his learning and zeal for Catholicism, *ib.*; his liturgy, 259; the Pope disapproves of his conduct, *ib.*; his second wife and consequent change of views, *ib.*; the miseries of his reign, 260; his son succeeds to the Polish crown, *ib.*; he imprisons most of his council, *ib.*; his death, 261; the Queen's conduct, *ib.*
Jomsborg, pagan republic of, 50
Jöns Bengtsson, Archbishop, rebels against Karl Knudsson, 195; he is arrested by Christian, 196; he defeats Christian, *ib.*
Jorde bog, or "Book of Lands," 120
Jutland, South. See *Slesvig.*
Jutland and the Isles, Danes of, 21; revolt against Christopher, 190
Jury, trial by, 120
Jutes, their origin, 18; they found a kingdom in Kent, 19; their language, *ib.*
Jutta, daughter of Erik Plov-peng, 158

K.

Kæmpeviser, or Danish rhyming verses, 121, 248
Karl, a peasant, story of him and King Svend, 90
Karl, Duke. See *Karl IX.*
Karl Knudsson, Erik appoints him Marshal, 187; proclaimed King of Sweden, *ib.*; he exacts terms from Christopher, 189, 193; his influence in Sweden, 193; he goes to Finland, 194; he is crowned King of Sweden, *ib.*; and of Norway, *ib.*; his enemies, 195; he leaves his kingdom, *ib.*; he is recalled, 196; his death, *ib.*
Karl Nilsson, is murdered by Bo Jonsson, 166
Karl, son of Knud the Saint, his fate, 96
Karl IX. of Sweden, deposes Erik, 258; his abilities and zeal for Protestantism, 258, 267, 268; on the death of Johan he conducts the government, 261; he summons the assembly at Upsala,

ib. ; Sigismund's return, 263 ; Karl as Regent, 265 ; he defeats Sigismund at Stängebro, *ib.* ; he subdues Finland, 266 ; is proclaimed king, *ib.* ; his learning, character and conduct, 267, 268 ; he improves the country, 268, 269 ; his foreign wars, 269 ; his death, *ib.* ; his alliances with Protestant powers, 270 ; as a poet and author, *ib.* ; his family, 271

Katerina, daughter of Charles IX., 271

Katerina Jagellonica, Queen of Johan III., 258 ; her death, 259 ; and Ivan II. of Russia, 262

Kimbri, and the Romans, 7

Kings, Pontiff, of Scandinavia, 63

Klas Fleming, governor of Finland, 263, 265

Knipperdolling, an Anabaptist, driven out of Sweden, 233

Knud Dan-Ast, son of Gorm, 46 ; his death, 47

Knud Lavard, his murder by prince Magnus, 100 ; the vengeance taken by his brother, 101

Knud the Great, his Christianity, 51, 52 ; he murders his brother-in-law, Ulf Jarl, 52 ; his remorse, 53 ; he pays his sister Estrid a blood-fine, *ib.* ; he brings up his nephew, Svend, 54 ; his death, *ib.* ; his conquests, *ib.* ; the fate of his sons, *ib.* ; his share in the defeat of Olaf the Saint, 80

Knud the Saint, King of Denmark, his character, 94 ; his severity to pirates, *ib.* ; how he favoured the clergy and oppressed the laity, 95 ; the result of his conduct, *ib.* ; his murder and the fate of his only son Karl, 96 ; his canonization, 96, 99

Knud VI., King of Denmark, defies the Emperor of Germany, 100 ; his great successes, 110 ; a rebellion in Slesvig is put down, *ib.* ; his disputes with Philip Augustus of France, 111 ; his death, *ib.*

Konúngr, northern name for King, 20

Kristina, second wife of Charles IX., 271 ; declines the regency, 274

Krumpe, Otte, Danish general, 211, 215, 246

L.

Largs, the battle of, 171

Laurentius Andreæ, Gustaf's chancellor, 232 ; the address he read to the Diet, 233

Laws of Thorleif the Wise and Ulfljot, 77 ; of Denmark, 97, 120, 252 ; of Sweden, 160

Leahy, battle of, 178

Leif, son of Erik Raudi, 84 ; he sails from Greenland, 85 ; his discoveries, 86 ; his death, 87

Lejre, or Ledra, in the Island of Sjælland, 21 ; its kings and their influence as pontiff-kings, 22, 38, 63 ; how Hardegon and Gorm ascended the throne, 37 ; its sacred character, 37, 63

Lena, battle of, 149

Lenbelfing, August von, witnesses the death of Gustaf Adolf, 282 ; his death, 283

Lochlin, the men of, 70

Louis I. of France, surnamed Le Debonnaire, his wish to convert the heathen, 32 ; stands sponsor to Harald Klak, 33 ; sends missionaries to Denmark, 33, 34

Louis IX. of France, sends an embassy to Hakon IV., 170

Louvaine, battle of, 43

Lübeck, treaty of, 254

INDEX. 391

Lübeck Traders, their defeat by the Danes, 207
Lund, capital of Skaania, 64 ; Archbishopric of, 23, 145
Lung of the Sea, its meaning, 4
Lutheran faith established in Denmark, 224 ; in Sweden, 232, 233, 235, 261
Lützen, battle of, 280
Lyö, the fatal hunt on, 116

M.

Mads, Bishop, of Strangnœs, his execution, 216
Magdeburg, siege of, 279
Magnus Barfod, King of Norway, his wars, 152 ; he marries Margrete, the "Peace Maiden," *ib.* ; he invades Ireland and is slain, *ib.*
Magnus, brother of Erik, his insanity, 241
Magnus, brother of Frederick II., 246
Magnus Henriksen, attacks the Swedes at Upsala, 147
Magnus Ladu-laas, seizes on Valdemar, 159 ; his able reign, *ib.* ; his merits as a law-giver, *ib.* ; his nickname, *ib.* ; he ranks men as free and un-free, *ib.* ; establishes the service of *russ-tjenst*, 160 ; his court, *ib.* ; he supports the church, *ib.* ; his death and burial-place, *ib.*
Magnus Laga-bœter, King of Norway and the Hebrides, 171 ; as a law-giver, 172
Magnus Smek, son of Duke Erik, offers to marry Princess Elizabeth, 139 ; is chosen King of Sweden and Norway, 163 ; his minority, *ib.* ; his vicious conduct and weakness, *ib.* ; his Queen, 163, 164 ; his son Erik killed, 164 ;
Hakon made King of Norway, *ib.* ; his friendship for Valdemar Atterdag of Denmark, *ib.* ; he gives up Skaania and other provinces, *ib.* ; he outlaws twenty-four nobles, 165 ; what they do, *ib.* ; his fate, *ib* ; the respect of the Norwegians for him, 173
Magnus, son of Birger, is treacherously beheaded, 162, 163
Magnus, son of Neils, murders Knud Lavard, 100 ; he is slain at Fodevig, 101
Magnus the Blind, King of Norway, his troubled reign, 153 ; he is killed in battle, 154
Magnus the Good, King of Denmark and Norway, his kindness to Svend, 57, 81 ; his death, *ib.*
Man, Isle of, subdued by Magnus Barfod, 152
Mannsdatter, Karren or Katherina, wife of King Erik, 240, 241 ; his love for her, 243
Margaret, daughter of Erik the Saint, 154
Margaret, Queen, her marriage, 141 ; she is Queen Regent of Norway and Denmark, 142 ; is chosen Queen of Sweden, 167, 177, 178 ; she defeats King Albert, 167, 178 ; her able rule, 167 ; her nephew Erik appointed her successor, 168, 174, 176 ; she effects the union of the three kingdoms, 168 ; is chosen Queen of Norway, 168, 174 ; and of Denmark, 168, 175 ; her popularity, 175 ; what foreigners thought of her, 176 ; she avenges the insults of King Albert, 178 ; Stockholm resists her, 179 ; she releases King Albert on payment of a ransom, *ib.* ; Erik's incapacity, 180 ; she sails to Slesvig, 181 ; her death, 182 ; her fame, *ib.* ; the tact with which she ruled, 184

Margaret of Pomerania, Queen Regent of Denmark, 129; she is imprisoned by Duke Erik of Slesvig, *ib.*

Margrete, "Maid of Norway," her death, 172

Margrete of Bohemia, Queen of Valdemar II., 121; called Dagmar, or "Day's Maiden," *ib.*; ballads in celebration of her, *ib.*

Margrete, Swedish Princess, the "Peace-Maiden," 152

Maria Eleanore, Queen of Gustaf Adolf, mourns his death, 284

Marta, Queen of Sweden, and the murder of the princes, 161, 162

Massilia, the present Marseilles, 2

Mats Ketilmundsson, and Magnus Smek, 163

Metzenheim, Hans, brings up Prince Christian, 213

Mikkelsen, Niels, his persecution, 247

Munk, Kirstine, second wife of Christian IV., 255; her banishment, 256

N.

Nadod, a Norwegian, discovers Iceland, 73

New Testament translated into Danish, 223.

Niels, King of Denmark, 99; his feeble reign, 100; his defeat in Fodevig, 101; he takes refuge in Slesvig, *ib.*; he is slain by Knud's guild-brothers, 102

Niels Ebbesön, a Jutlander, slays Count Geert, 135; he drives the Holsteiners to their own territory, *ib.*; his defeat by the Iron Count, *ib.*

Nikolaus, grandson of Valdemar II., 122

Nils Sture, proclaimed a traitor, 240; he is stabbed by King Erik, *ib.*

Nilsson, Professor, of Stockholm, 5

Nordlingen, battle of, 285

Normandy, its settlement by Rollo, 69, 70; origin of its name, 70

Norræna Mál, or Northern speech, 13, 14

Northmen. See *Scandinavians*.

Norway, joined with Denmark for five years, 56, 57; but little known in early times, 58; fabled foundation of its monarchy, 62; the first King of all Norway, 68; in early times, 72; Harald Haarfager's stern rule drives many of his subjects away, *ib.*; the discovery and settlement of Iceland, *ib.*; invaded by the Danes in A.D. 963, 79; early troubles, 150; the election of the Three Kings, 152; troubles caused by claimants to the throne, 153; the "Birch-Legs" and the "Croziers," 154; the crown declared to be a fief of St. Olaf, 155; its kings first crowned in a church, *ib.*; increased influence of the clergy, *ib.*; union of the three kingdoms, 168, 180; from A.D. 1217 to A.D. 1400, 169; under Queen Margaret, 174, 176; union with Denmark renewed, 199

Norwegians, their old faith, 63; the little regard they had for life, *ib.*; their voyages, discoveries, and settlements, 67, 69, 72, 84

O.

Oath of the Braga, 61; of the Icelanders, 75

Ocean discoveries by the Norwegians, 67

INDEX.

Odense, King Knud murdered there, 95, 96 ; his shrine, 96
Odin, his faith, 12 ; its precepts, *ib*. ; his favour to the rich, 13 ; his last appearance on earth, 27 ; sacrifices to him at Lejre, 36, 37 ; victims to, 37, 63 ; he founds the Empire of the Svea, 59 ; horse-flesh eaten by his worshippers, 145
Ofrälse and Frälse classes in Sweden, 159
Ohthere, visits Britain, 7 ; his settlements and discoveries, 67
Olaf-Hunger, how he became King of Denmark, 97 ; the famine in his reign, 98 ; his death, *ib*.
Olaf, King of Denmark, 141 ; the regency of Queen Margaret, 142 ; succeeds to the crown of Norway, 142, 175 ; his death, 142, 174, 175 ; his funeral, 175 ; his heart carried to Denmark, *ib*.
Olaf, King of Lochlin, 70
Olaf Kyrre, King of Norway, his peaceful reign, 151 ; his death, 152
Olaf, son of Magnus Barfod, 152
Olaf, Swedish chief, invades Lejre, 37 ; his sons Ehnob and Gurd, *ib*.
Olaf the Lap-King, the first Christian King of Sweden, 82 ; his people remain heathens, 83 ; his quarrels with Olaf the Saint, King of Norway, *ib*. ; bold language of the peasants to him, *ib*. ; his son Anund made joint ruler, 84
Olaf the Saint, King of Norway, 80 ; his death, *ib*. ; the miracles wrought by his corpse, 81 ; his shrine of silver, *ib*.
Olaf Trætelje, he clears Vermland, 62 ; is sacrificed to Odin, *ib*. ; his descendants found the kingdom of Norway, *ib*.

Olaf Trygvasson, King of Norway, 79 ; his deeds, wars and death, 80
Oldenburg race of kings, 188
Orgil Ragnarsen, hung for piracy, 95
Orkneys lost to Norway, 201
Oslö, battle of, 170
Osmanni, or East-men, Danish vikingar, 21
Otho I., Emperor of Germany, defeats the Danes, 49
Otto of Schaumberg, and the Holstein lands, 201
Otto, son of Christopher II., 136 ; enters the monastic order of the German Knights, *ib*.
Oxe, Peder, minister of Frederick II., 247
Oxe, Torbe, his execution, 220

P.

Palnatoke, brings up Svend, 49 ; story of his famous archery, 50
Paris, the first siege of, 40
Peter's pence first paid by the Swedes, 145
Petri, Laurentius, the Reformer, 232 ; his death, 258
Petri, Olaus, the Reformer, 232
Philip Augustus of France, his cruelty to his Queen, 111
Philippa, Queen, rules during Erik's absence, 185 ; her abilities, *ib*.
Phœnicians in the north ; their religion, 5
Pontiff-kings of Scandinavia, 63
Poppa, German monk, 49
Protestant faith established in Denmark, 224 ; in Sweden, 232, 233, 235, 261
Pytheas, his travels, 2 ; in Thule, 3 ; a scientific traveller, 5

R.

Rane Jonsen, his treachery, 130; his execution, 131

Rantzau, Daniel, Danish general, 239, 245, 246

Reformers in Denmark, 219, 222, 224; in Sweden, 232, 233, 235, 261

Regner Lodbrog, his dangers and adventures, 28; his death, *ib.*; his sons avenge it, 28, 29; they divide Ælla's kingdom, 29

Reid-Gotaland, or the Firm Goth's-land, 19, 20, 21, 22

Reinhard, Martin, preaches the Gospel to the Danes, 219

Rhode Island, "Vinland den Gode," 87

Riddarhuset, or Knight's House, of Sweden, 275

Rikissa, sister of Valdemar II., marries Erik Knudsson, 149; she returns to Denmark, *ib.*

Ringsted Abbey, royal burials in, 108, 121, 163

Rink, an Anabaptist, driven out of Sweden, 233

Robert, Duke of Normandy, his wife Estrid, 54

Röda Boken, or Red Book, 259

Rögnvald, Jarl of Mære, 69; his death, *ib.*

Rolf Krake, King of the Danes, his virtues, 25; his death avenged, 26

Rollo the Norman, his practice of "Strand-hug," 69; he is outlawed by King Harald, *ib.*; he founds Normandy, 70

Roman ladies wear amber beads, 8

Romans defeat the Northmen, 7

Rome, visited by Knud, 54; Erik's pilgrimage to, 99; pilgrimage of King Valdemar to, 158

Runes, letters used by the Northmen, 14

Rurik, subdues the Slaves and Finns, 66; visits Greece, *ib.*; settles in Russia, *ib.*

Russia, the Northmen settle in, 15; their descendants, *ib.*; pillaged by Gorm, 40; founders of the empire come from Sweden, 65; invasions by the Swedes, 269; defeated by them, 274

Russians show their power in Sweden, 262

Russ-tjenst, or service with men and horses, 160

Rybe, or the Partridge, story of, 173

Rygen, the Island of, its inhabitants subdued and baptized, 105, 106

S.

Sagas, or tales, 9; of the Danes, 23; the Ynglinga Saga, 62; the Eyrbyggja Saga, 74

St. Peter's pence first paid by the Swedes, 145

St. Petersburg on Swedish ground, 275

Saxo Grammaticus, historian of Denmark, 23, 50, 64, 111

Saxons in Britain, 18, 19; they are subdued by Charlemagne, 21

Scandinavia in early times, 1, 58; its division into small states, 20, 29; Sagas of its people, 23; end of the mythic age, 26

Scandinavians, ignorance of Southerners in regard to, 1, 8; in the South, 7, 15; their German origin, 9; their language, 13; their letters, 14; at home, 17; their invasion of Britain, 18, 19; they are driven out of Britain, 29; how the Gospel was first preached to them, 31; their early habits, 39; their rovings in King Gorm's time, 40

Scotland, settlements made by the Danes and Norwegians, 70

Shetlands lost to Norway, 201
Siegfred, a King in Jutland, 21
Siegfred, an Englishman, his labours among the Swedes, 82
Siegfred, Vikingar, his rovings, 40, 41 ; his death, 44
Siegric, King of Lejre, 37
Sigbrit, Mother, her influence over Christian II., 219 ; the death of her daughter Dyveke, or the Dove, 220
Sigismund, son of Johan III., succeeds to the Polish crown, 260 ; he returns to Sweden, 263 ; his zeal for Roman Catholicism, *ib.* ; he is crowned at Upsala, 264 ; the charter he signed, *ib.* ; he returns to Poland, *ib.* ; he is defeated by Karl, 265 ;. he reigns in Poland until his death, 266
Sigrid, daughter of Erik, 243
Sigtuna, Odin's temple at, 59, 60
Sigurd Jarl turns the anger of the people from Hakon, 78
Sigurd Jorsalafar, King of Norway, goes to Jerusalem, 152 ; gives away his ships and returns to Norway over-land, 153 ; the ordeal of a red-hot iron, *ib.* ; his death, *ib.*
Sigurd Ring, King of Sweden, defeats Harald Hildetand, 27 ; how he honoured his memory, 28
Sjælland, the Island of, 21 ; origin of its name, 23
Skaania, Swedish province of Denmark, 23, 38 ; origin of its name, 23, 64
Skalds, or poets, 9 ; their Sagas, 9, 23, 62, 74
Skrælingar, or dwarfs, of North America, 87
Skule Baardsson, rebels against Hakon IV., 170 ; his defeat and death, *ib.*
Skytte, Johan, tutor of Gustaf Adolf, 273

Slesvig, visited by the monks, 34 ; under Knud Lavard, 100 ; wars with Holstein begin, 126 ; granted to Counts of Holstein, 142 ; wars, 181, 184 ; Erik's appeal to the Emperor Sigismund, 185 ; peace, 186 ; Slesvig and Holstein united, 200
Smaa Kongar, or Small Kings, 20, 61
Snorre Sturlasson, his murder, 171
Sofia, Queen of Sweden, 158
Sophia of Mecklenburg, Queen of Denmark, 249, 250
Sorö, monastery of, 23 ; academy of, 253
Spread Eagle, torture of the, 29
Stærkodder, King of the Danes, who alone ould kill him, 25
Stängebro, battle of, 265
Sten Sture, proclaimed Marshal of Sweden, 197 ; he defeats King Christian, *ib.* : the country prosperous for a time, 197, 208 ; his unpopularity, 208 ; he submits to King Hans, 204, 209 ; he drives the Danes out of the country, 205 ; his death, 205, 209
Sten Sture the younger, the best of the Stures, 210 ; he defeats Christian II., *ib.* ; he is excommunicated, 211 ; his death, 211, 215
Stenkil, first Christian King of all Sweden, 144 ; peace during his reign, *ib.*
Stettin, peace of, 247, 260
Stiklestad, battle of, 80
Stockholm, its foundation, 158 ; Franciscan monastery at, 160 ; anger of the citizens with Birger, 162 ; they refuse to accept Queen Margaret, 179 ; the Blood-bath at, 215, 216
Stolbova, peace of, 274
Strand-hug, old northern practice,

69; forbidden by Christian II., 218

Stures rule Sweden, 208, 209; Erik's cruelty to, 240

Svante Sture, is adopted by Sten Sture, 209; chosen Marshal of Sweden; his love of war and soldiers, 209, 210; his sudden death, 210

Svanteveit, god of the Slaves, destruction of his temple at Arcona, 105, 106

Svea. See *Swedes*, and *Sweden*.

Svend Aagesen, Danish historian, 23. 111

Svend Estridsen, nephew of Knud, is brought up by him, 54; Magnus makes him Jarl of Denmark, 57; he rebels, *ib.*; Magnus forgives him and appoints him his successor to the Danish crown, *ib.*; his wars with Harald Haardraade, King of Norway, 90; his message to William the Conqueror, *ib.*; the fate of his hostile fleet, *ib.*; his character and appearance, 91; his learning, and love of learned men, *ib.*; his friendship for Adam, Canon of Bremen, *ib.*; his intimacy with William, Bishop of Roeskilde, *ib.*; his act of murder, 92; Bishop William turns him out of church, *ib.*; his penitence, *ib.*; why he was called "Estridsen," 93; the ancestor of the Royal families of Britain and Denmark, *ib.*; his sons, 94

Svend, King of Norway, 54; his body disinterred, 56

Svend, son of Knud, King of Norway, 80, 81

Svend Tveskæg, son of Harald Blaatand, his bringing up by Palnatoke, 49; he defeats his father, 50; invades England, *ib.*; his death, 51

Sverker Karlsson, King of Sweden, his reign, 145; his cruelty, 148;
he flees to Denmark, *ib.*; he returns, and is defeated at Lena, 149; he is murdered, 145, 146

Sverre, leader of the "Birch Legs," crowned King of Norway, 154; his able rule, *ib.*; his death, *ib.*

Svithjód, greater, and lesser, 59

Svold, battle of, 80

Sweden, visited by Anscarius, 34; Christianity in, 31, 82, 143; but little known in early times, 58, 65; fabled account of its foundation by Odin, 59; its Pontiff-kings, 63; quarrels between the Svea and the Göta, 82, 83; the first Christian kings, 82, 143; bold language of the peasantry to Olaf the Lap-king, 83; its history in early times, 143; troubled times, 147; the influence of the monks, 148; from A.D. 1250 to A.D. 1400, 157; the Folkungar kings, *ib.*; the Free and Un-free first distinguished, 159; half a century of troubles, 163; under foreign rule, 165; union with Denmark, 168, 180; under Queen Margaret, 177; under Danish rulers, 192; and Denmark, from A.D. 1450, 198; the crown bartered for favours, 203; the fall of the Stures, 208; between A.D. 1520 and A.D. 1568, 227; union with Denmark dissolved, 231; the Protestant faith in, 232, 233, 235, 261; wars with Denmark, 239, 244, 251, 254, 287; between A.D. 1568 and A.D. 1611, 257; females allowed to reign, 258; religious troubles in, 263; rise of the Swedish power, 267; from A.D. 1611 to A.D. 1644, 272

Swedes, their descent, 60; their old faith, 63; how they were intermingled with the Danes, 65; in Russia, 65, 66, 209

T.

Tast, Hermann, Danish Reformer, 222
Tausen, Hans, Danish Reformer, 222
Thing, or public assembly, 67, 97, 120
Thomas, the Junker, his cruelty, 231; his execution, ib.
Thor, son of Odin, 11; favourite god of the Norwegians, ib.; temple dedicated to him by Thorolf, 75; his silver ring, ib.; his mallet, 79
Thorleif the Wise, his laws, 77
Thorolf-Moskar-Skegg, sails from Norway, 74; he takes with him an image of Thor to Iceland, 75; he lands and takes formal possession at Breida-Fjord, ib.; he builds a temple to Thor, and deposits in it the sacred silver ring, ib.; he prepares for the Herjar-Thing, ib.; he divides Iceland into districts, 76
Thule, the search for, 3
Thure Thuresson, the "Peasants' Butcher," 196
Thurida, daughter of Snorre Gode, 88
Thyra, Gothic princess, defended by a serpent, 28
Thyra, first Queen of Denmark, her descent, 45; she rules in Gorm's absence, 45, 47; her memory much respected, 45; she favours the Christians, 46; how she built up ramparts, 47; the way she told Gorm of his son's death, ib.; her grave mound, 48
Tilly, Count John, defeated by the Swedes, 279; his death, ib.
Ting allra Göta, or Diet of the Goths, 35
Tithes disputed by the Danes, 95, 108

Torkel Knudsson governs for King Birger, 160
Torstensson, Lennart, Swedish commander, his talents and infirmities, 286; called the "Swedish Lightning," 287; his victories, ib.; war with Denmark, ib.; battle of Jankowitz, 287; he resigns his command, 288

U.

Ulf Jarl, murdered by Knud, 52
Ulfeld, Eleanore Kirstine, and her husband, 256
Ulfljot, studies the laws in Norway and draws up a code for Iceland, 76, 77
Unni, Archbishop of Bremen, visits Denmark, 46
Upp-Sala, or the High Halls, temple to Odin, 60
Upsala, burning of the six Small Kings, 61; a sacred place, 144; the first church is built there, 146; the death of Erik the Saint at, 147; Assembly at, in 1593, 261; University of, its foundation, 197; enriched by Gustaf Adolf, 275

V.

Væringjar, body-guards of the Emperors at Constantinople, 15
Valdemar Atterdag, King of Denmark, how he came to the throne, 136; his brother Otto's fate, ib.; his marriage, ib.; he recovers crown lands by purchase, 137; his taking of Wisby, ib.; his contempt of the Hansers, 138; wars with Germany, ib.; he seizes Princess Elizabeth of Holstein, ib.; marries his daughter Margaret

to the heir of Sweden, 139; in trouble, *ib.*; his humiliation, flight, and return to Denmark, 140; people's hatred of him, *ib.*; why called "Atterdag," 141; his death, *ib.*

Valdemar, Bishop of Slesvig, 110; his imprisonment, 111; his enmity with Valdemar II., 114

Valdemar, Duke, son of Magnus, his quarrels with King Birger, 160; he is imprisoned and starved to death, 161, 162

Valdemar, King of Sweden, how he was elected, 150, 157; his father rules through him, 158; his incapacity, and quarrels with his brothers, *ib.*; his imprisonment and death, 159; his son, *ib.*

Valdemar, son of Valdemar II., 117, 121

Valdemar of Slesvig, is crowned King of Denmark, 134; he surrenders his claim to the throne, 136

Valdemar, son of King Abel, Duke of Slesvig, 126, 129; and the murderers of Erik Glipping, 132

Valdemar I., King of Denmark, his coronation, 104; his cowardice in youth and his subsequent courage, 105; his campaigns against the pagans, 105, 106; he assists Bishop Absalon to subdue the peasants in Skaania, 107; his death, 108; his burial, *ib.*

Valdemar II., defeats the Bishop of Slesvig, 110; is chosen King of Denmark, 112; prosperity of the country under his rule, 113; he is surnamed "Sejr," *ib.*; his successes, 114; he is defeated in Sweden, *ib.*; his crusade against the pagans, *ib.*; his downfall, 115; the fatal hunt at Lyö, 116; he and his son are captured and imprisoned for three years, 116, 117; the terms on which they are released, 118; he is defeated and wounded at Bornhöved, 119; his merits in peace, *ib.*; his death and children, 120; his Queens, 120, 121; how the Danes cherish his memory, 121

Vasa, derivation of the name, 228

Vedel, Anders Sörensen, Danish historian, 248

Vermland, its forests burnt by Olaf, 62

Verona, battle at, 8

Vesteraas, battle of, 230

Victoria, (Queen, her Danish ancestry, 93

Vikingar, its meaning, 15; they harass Britain, 21; are driven out of England, 29

Vilhelm, Bishop of Roeskilde, his character, 91; he thrusts King Svend out of church, 92

Vinland den Gode, its discovery by Leif, 86; its grapes, 87; settlers all murdered by natives, *ib.*; last notice of it, *ib.*

Vitalen, or Victualling, Brotherhood, 179

Vögg, revenges the death of Rolf Krake, 25

W.

Wallenstein, Duke, tries to foment a rising in Sweden, 277; in disgrace with the Emperor, 278; battle of Lützen, 280

Walo, Abbot of Corvey in Picardy, 33

Week-days, their names, 11

Wends, or Vanen, 65, 100, 109

Westphalia, peace of, 288

Wittekind, Saxon chief, 21

William, Bishop of Roeskilde. See *Vilhelm.*

William the Conqueror, King Svend's message to him, 99

Wind blowing from the north, a good omen, 229

Wisby, taken by Valdemar Atterdag, 137

Wulfstan, visits Britain, 7; his settlements and discoveries, 67

Y.

Ynglinga Saga, 62

Ynglingar, royal race of the, 60; their descent from Odin, *ib.*; how they lost Sweden, 61

Yule, its meaning, 6

Z.

Zoe, Empress, her love for Harald Haardraade, 151

THE END.

www.ingramcontent.com/pod-product-compliance
Lightning Source LLC
Chambersburg PA
CBHW030556300426
44111CB00009B/997